Oswald Heer, James Heywood

The primaeval world of Switzerland

Oswald Heer, James Heywood

The primaeval world of Switzerland

ISBN/EAN: 9783337198084

Printed in Europe, USA, Canada, Australia, Japan

Cover: Foto ©Andreas Hilbeck / pixelio.de

More available books at **www.hansebooks.com**

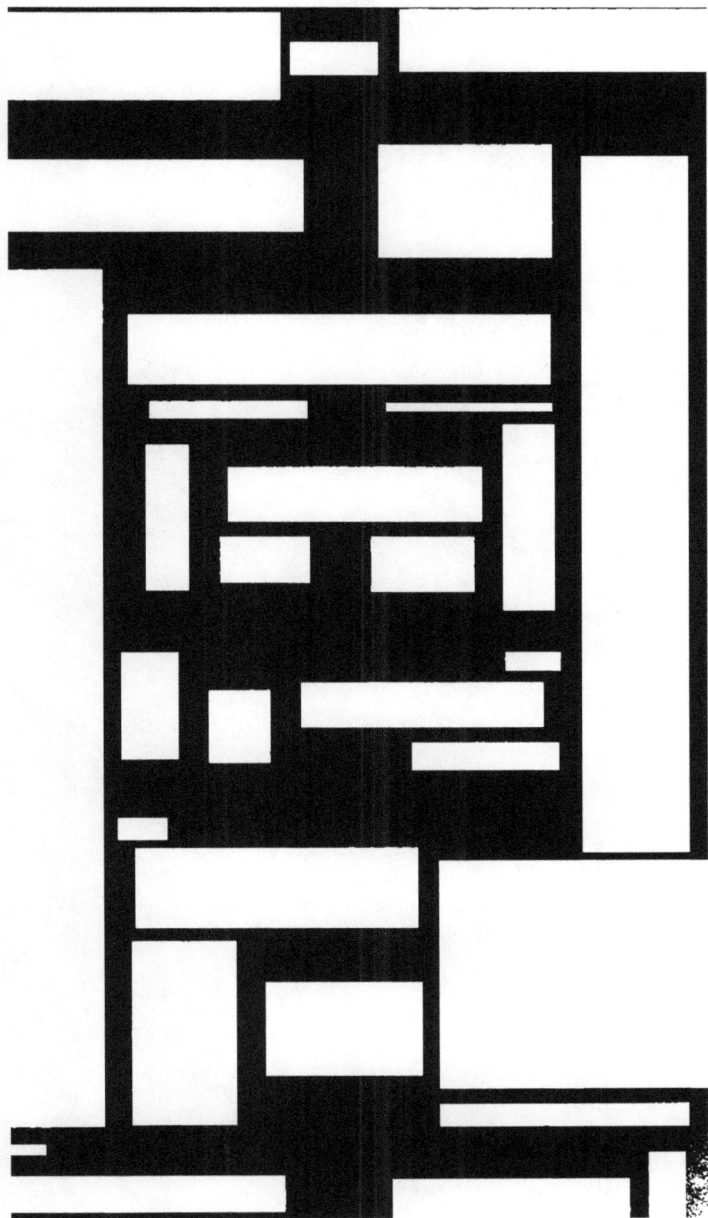

CONTENTS

OF

VOLUME II.

CHAPTER IX.

SWISS MIOCENE FAUNA.

CHAPTER X.

DESCRIPTION OF SOME SWISS MIOCENE LOCALITIES.

CHAPTER XI.

CLIMATE OF THE MIOCENE DISTRICT.

CHAPTER XII.

QUATERNARY PERIOD.

CHAPTER XIII.

GLACIAL HISTORY.

CHAPTER XIV.

RETROSPECT, WITH NOTICES OF EARLY PALÆOZOIC STRATA.

CHAPTER XV.

GENERALIZATIONS ON THE DEVELOPMENT AND TRANSFORMATIONS OF NATURE IN SWITZERLAND.

Part I. INORGANIC NATURE.

Section 1. *Upheaval and Depression of Land.*

Section 2. *Action of Water.*

Section 3. *Climates of the various Geological periods.*

Zu

Life

Lan

Dür

Pla

PRIMÆVAL WORLD

OF

SWITZERLAND.

———◆———

CHAPTER IX.

MIOCENE FAUNA OF SWITZERLAND.

I. Animals belonging to Land and Fresh water.

Fossil remains of animals are found in most of the Swiss Miocene localities which have furnished plants of that· period. Hence the Swiss Miocene fauna occupied the same area with the Miocene flora of Switzerland. No remains of either Annelida or Infusoria have been found; but vertebrated animals and insects have supplied so many species that the leading characteristics of animal life are well represented.

The principal animals of the Swiss Miocene fauna may be thus described :—

1. Mollusca.

All the univalve Mollusca which inhabited the Swiss Miocene forests, and the Bivalves which peopled the brooks and lakes, belong to living genera. The species, however, are almost entirely extinct; and their nearest allies are no longer inhabitants of Switzerland. Snails (*Helix*) formed, as at present, the most numerous genus; but none of the species attained the size of the common Swiss vineyard-snail (*Helix pomatia*, Linn.). One of the most abundant species of the Swiss Lower Miocene (*Helix Ramondi*, Br., fig. 201) is nearly related to a species (*H. Bow-*

dichiana, Fér.) the shells of which lie by millions buried in the sands of Caniçal in Madeira and in Porto Santo. On the spit of Caniçal, Prof. Heer saw a piece of ground completely covered with the shells of this species (associated with those of several others), so that numbers of them were crushed at every step. Here and there, however, they are imbedded in the sand, and thus protected. They have evidently been brought together during a long period of time into a small lake-basin, and enveloped in sand and mud; but they have perfectly preserved their form, as they were exposed to no pressure. In the same way probably have been produced the accumulations of snail-shells which we not unfrequently meet with in the Swiss Miocene marls, as at the Paudèze, at Delsberg, near Schwamendingen, at Frauenfeld, &c.; but in these places the shells are generally so crushed by the pressure of the overlying masses of rock that they can rarely be determined.

Helix inflexa, Mart., which occurs near Delsberg, like *H. Ramondi*, is nearly allied to a species inhabiting the Atlantic islands (*H. portosantana*, Sow.); while *Helix sylvestrina*, Ziet. (fig. 202), the commonest species of the Swiss Molasse, and the allied species *H. moguntina*, Desh., which is also of frequent occurrence, represent European forms (*H. sylvatica* and *splendida*, Drap.). The former is so well preserved at Vermes (in the Delsberg) that we can still recognize dark bands (three to five in number) which ornamented the shells. In *Helix rugulosa*, Mart., which is very plentiful in the valley of Delsberg, four coloured bands may still be seen on the shell. This species finds its nearest allies (*H. elevata*, Say, and *H. pennsylvanica*, Green) in the West Indies and North America. *Helix ehingensis*, Kl. (from Delsberg), and *H. osculum*, Th., most nearly approach a species from Texas (*H. Berlanderiana*, Mor.), whilst the great *Helix insignis*, Schübl., which has also been found abundantly in the valley of Delsberg, must be characterized as a West-African form (allied to *H. rosacea*, Müll.).

The *Helices* are frequent in the Swiss Miocene, appearing almost in all places where plants occur. Eleven species are found in the marine Molasse; these have been carried by running water into the sea, and have thus mingled with its inhabitants. The *Pupæ* and *Clausiliæ* are much less common; but these elegant little mollusks, which feed on the mosses clothing the Swiss trees and rocks, and live chiefly in sunny dry localities, are now very abundant. Two species of *Pupa* (*P. acuminata*, Kl., and P. *Buchwalderi*, Grep., fig. 200) occur at Vermes

Fig. 197.   Fig. 198. Fig. 200.   Fig. 203.   Fig. 204.

Fig. 199.   Fig. 201.   Fig. 202.

Fig. 197. *Melania Escheri*, Brogn.   *a*, from the Michelsberg near Ulm; *b*, from the lignitic marls of Käpfnach.

Fig. 198. *Limnæus pachygaster*, Th., from Veltheim.

Fig. 199. *Cyclas Escheri*, K. May., from Schrotzburg.

Fig. 200. *Pupa Buchwalderi*, Grep., enlarged three times, from Delsberg.

Fig. 201. *Helix Ramondi*, Br.

Fig. 202. *Helix sylvestrina*, Ziet., from Delsberg.

Fig. 203. *Planorbis solidus*, Th.

Fig. 204. *Clausilia maxima*, Grat., from between Ferrach and Rüti.

and Tramelan; and a very large *Clausilia* (*C. maxima*, Grat., fig. 204) has been obtained at various places, as in the marl of Bäretschweil, between Ferrach and Rüti, and near Unterdevelier, where a second large species (*C. antiqua*, Schübl.) also occurs. The latter resembles a Javan, and the *Clausilia maxima* is like a Chinese species (*C. shanginensis*, Pfr.).

Freshwater mussels and pond-, mud-, and marsh-snails (*Anodonta, Unio, Cyclas, Planorbis, Limnæus, Paludina*, and *Neritina*) were very generally distributed in the rivulets and lakes of the Swiss Miocene country. Two of the species (*Neritina fluvi-*

atilis, Linn., and *Paludina tentaculata*, Linn.) still exist in the Swiss fresh waters; but the other species are extinct.

Among the bivalves the largest and most abundant species is the *Unio undatus*, Humb., which ranges from the Aquitanian stage up to the Œningian stage, and is most nearly allied to an American species (*Unio rugosus*, Lea). Of the numerous localities in which this shell occurs we mention the following particularly, because they belong to various stages of the Swiss Miocene:—Brullée above Lutry, Rüdholz near Soleure, Küttigen near Aarau, Dettinghofen near Eglisau, Sitterwald in the Canton of St. Gall, Stein, Berlingen, Steckborn, and Wangen near Œningen. The freshwater mussels (*Unionidæ*) have hitherto been found only in the Upper Miocene. One species (*Anodonta Lavateri*, Münst., sp.) occurs in great quantities in one of the beds at Œningen. It has also been found in the marls of the Schrotzburg, where a smaller, broader, and more obtusely rounded species (*A. Heerii*, May.) is met with. The latter has been observed near Spreitenbach. In the same locality of the Schrotzburg Prof. Heer has found an elegant new *Cyclas* (*C. Escheri*, May., fig. 199), which is nearly allied to a living species (*C. lacustris*).

Of the univalve Mollusca the pond-snails and mud-snails are most abundant. They are sometimes accumulated in enormous masses, but are generally crushed quite flat. Of the turreted mud-snails (*Limnæus*) the most frequent species is *L. pachygaster*, Thom. (fig. 198), which occurs in the Lower Miocene, near Rufi in the Helvetian stage, and in the Œningian stage near Zürich, Veltheim, Steckborn, and Œningen. It is most nearly allied to a species living in the Ganges (*Limnæus amygdalum*, Trosch.).

Of the flat pond-snails about half a dozen species occur, of which the large *Planorbis solidus*, Thom. (fig. 203), is the most generally distributed; it is found in the vicinity of Zürich (near Schwamendingen, at the Faletschen, and in the Stöckentobel), near Käpfnach, in the Turbenthal, near Steckborn, &c. The nearest ally of this species is the West-Indian and Mexican *Planorbis tumidus*, Linn. Another species, from Delsberg and Locle (*P. declivis*, A. Br.), most nearly resembles a South-American shell (the *Planorbis kermatoides*, D'Orb.).

Besides the *Neritina fluviatilis*, four species of *Neritina* now extinct lived in the fresh waters of Switzerland. These are *N. picta*, Fér., *N. Grateloupana*, Fér., *N. Linthæ*, May., and *N. Heerii*, May. One little species of *Valvata* (*V. multiformis*) occurs in the third stage, and a *Paludina* (*P. acuta*, Drap.) in the fourth and fifth stages; the latter occurs in some places by thousands. Of *Melanopsis* there are three species in the Swiss collections, one of which (*M. Kleinii*, Kurr.) sometimes occurs in great quantities; it is nearly allied to a species of the Mediterranean zone (*M. prærosa*, Linn.).

To these genera, which belong to the European fauna, the Swiss have to add *Melania* as a striking exotic form. One species (*M. Escheri*, Br., fig. 197) was discovered many years ago at Käpfnach by Escher de la Linth; and it has now been discovered in almost all the Miocene formations of Europe. It appears even as early as the Upper Eocene (in the Bartonian stage of the Rälligstock), and may be traced thence up to the Œningian stage. It seems to have had its centre of origin in Switzerland, and to have first spread towards Eastern Europe during the Upper Miocene period. Its nearest living allies (*Melania varicosa*, Trosch., and *M. pulchra*, Busch) inhabit the rivers of tropical Asia.

2. ARTICULATA.

a. *Crustacea*.

The Crustacea are chiefly inhabitants of the sea; but a few representatives of most of the families which live in fresh water or on land occur in the Swiss Miocene.

Of the Isopods there is at Œningen a species of woodlouse (*Armadillo*), one of those which, when in danger, draw in their legs and roll themselves up like a hedgehog. The Œningian species (*Armadillo molassicus*, Heer) retained this spherical form even in death, as shown by the animal represented in fig. 210, which closely resembles the common *Armadillo*.

Of the little Ostracodes the carapaces are very common, of which we find great masses of a species which was very widely distributed in Miocene times (*Cypris faba*, Desm., fig. 205) in

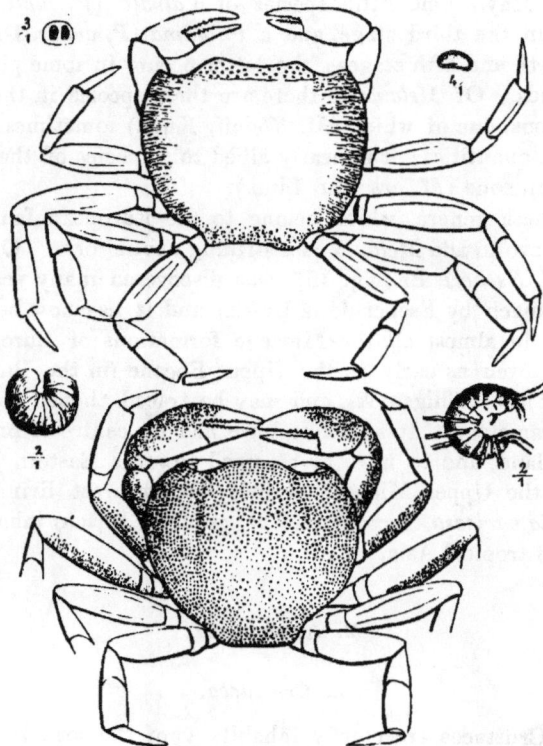

Fig. 206.   Fig. 207.   Fig. 205.

Fig. 210.   Fig. 208.   Fig. 209.

Fig. 205. *Cypris faba*, enlarged four times, from Locle.
Fig. 206. Eggs of a *Daphnia*, enlarged three times, from Œningen.
Fig. 207. *Telphusa speciosa*, Myr., sp., from Œningen.
Fig. 208. *Gecarcinus punctatus*, Heer, from Œningen.   (Figs. 207 & 208 restored from several specimens.)
Fig. 209. *Gammarus œningensis*, Heer, enlarged.
Fig. 210. *Armadillo molassicus*, Heer, enlarged, from Œningen.

the freshwater limestone of Œningen and Locle. These are small animals with bivalved kidney-shaped shells, very like species which still live in the Swiss fresh waters, where they swim about by the action of their antennæ, which are fringed with long hairs, and of their fore legs, which project beyond the shells. They serve as the food of a great number of aquatic insects.

The Gammaridæ are represented at Œningen by a species (*Gammarus œningensis*, Heer, fig. 209) very like the common *Gammarus pulex*, Deg., sp., of the Swiss lakes and rivers. The existence of water-fleas (*Daphniæ*) is shown at least by their eggs, which have been found at Œningen (fig. 206). The *Daphniæ* have two kinds of eggs—summer eggs, which have no peculiar envelope, and winter eggs, a pair of which are placed in a small shallow receptacle called the ephippium (saddle). The ephippia found at Œningen form small oval scales, in which the two eggs may be clearly recognized. They are consequently winter eggs, like those which may be met with in the Swiss waters from autumn to spring.

The largest and most important animals of this class are the Decapods, fragments of which are found here and there in the freshwater Miocene. In most places (as at Schwamendingen), however, they are so imperfect that we cannot determine them. Œningen, again, gives us some definite information about them. The three species occurring there belong, curiously enough, to the Prawns and Crabs, which, with very few exceptions, are inhabitants of the sea, whilst the Lake of Œningen undoubtedly contained fresh water, as is proved by the numerous freshwater animals of other kinds which have been found in its deposits. The Œningian prawns constitute a peculiar and extinct genus (*Homelys*, Myr.), the sole species of which (*H. major*, Myr.) is distinguished by its extremely delicate long antennæ and its smooth pectoral spine. It is a little smaller than the common prawn (*Palæmon squilla*, Linn.), and is very like the freshwater prawn (*P. fluviatilis*, Mart.), nearly allied to the common prawn, and living in the Lago di Garda as well as in the fresh waters of Parma. *Homelys major* occurs only in the insect-bed of the lower quarry at Œningen. The Crabs are found almost exclusively in the "Kesselstein" of the upper quarry. There are two species of crabs, belonging to two genera. One of them is probably to be referred to *Telphusa*, the other to *Gecarcinus*. In the former (fig. 207) the carapace is but slightly rounded at the sides, and its back is covered with small tubercles arranged in rows; whilst in the latter (fig. 208) the carapace is heart-shaped and very much narrowed behind. Its upper surface is closely punctate. In both the Œningian species the two chelæ are of equal strength, and the legs are furnished with a knife-like pointed terminal joint; the third pair of legs are somewhat longer than the rest. The Œningian river-crab (*Telphusa speciosa*, Myr.)* resembles the southern European species, the only crab which inhabits rivers and lakes in Europe, and which appears to be distributed in all Mediterranean countries. It is captured in great numbers in the Lake of Albano, and eaten in Rome during Lent by all classes of people. Even in ancient times it must have been of importance, since it appears on old coins of Agrigentum in Sicily. There is nothing remarkable therefore in the occurrence of this genus at Œningen, as it is one of those Mediterranean types which were at that time numerously represented in Switzerland, and lived in fresh water.

The Land-Crabs (*Gecarcinus*) are quite foreign to the European fauna. They occur at present only in tropical America, especially in the West Indies, where they are known under the name of "Tulurlu." They live in the forests in the interior of the country, and form burrows in the ground, which they quit only at night in order to seek for prey. Once in the year they unite

---

* M. de Meyer described this species as *Grapsus speciosus* (Palæontographica, x. p. 168, 1863); and it certainly belongs to the group of the "Brachyures quadrilatérales" of Latreille, which includes the *Grapsi* and the Land- and River-Crabs. But of these it seems to Professor Heer that *Telphusa* is the genus in which it must be ranged. The form of the carapace, which is more narrowed behind and not toothed at the margin, and the comparative lengths and form of the legs, seem to contradict its reference to *Grapsus*. In that genus the second pair of legs (the first from the chelæ) are much shorter than all the rest, which also have broader and stronger femora. In all these characters the Œningian crab agrees with *Telphusa*, as well as in the form of the outer maxillipeds. That the chelæ are unarmed, and the legs not set with stiff bristles, are important specific characters. Fig. 207 represents a small specimen; the species occurs twice of this size. The tail in the female is much broader than in the male.

in great bodies, and make their way by the shortest course to the sea in order to deposit their eggs in its waters. When this object is accomplished, they return in a weakened condition to their burrows. Whether the Œningian species had similar habits it is hard to say. At the Œningian epoch the sea had disappeared from these regions; but perhaps salt marshes and small basins of salt water may have remained here and there, which these crabs may have taken advantage of for the deposition of their eggs. The Swiss land-crab (*Gecarcinus punctatus*, Heer) is rare at Œningen; the river-crab is more common. Of the latter Prof. Heer has obtained twenty-eight, and of the former only eleven specimens.

b. *Arachnida.*

Œningen alone furnishes information with respect to the Spiders of the Swiss Miocene, these soft animals being preserved only in the fine calcareous marl of the lower Œningian quarry. From the upper quarry only two much-mutilated specimens have been received.

The Spiders hitherto found at Œningen belong to twenty-eight species; but their generic determination is very difficult, as the principal characters, which depend upon the position of the eyes, are not recognizable. Prof. Heer has endeavoured to determine them by the general form of the body and the comparative length of the legs; and in accordance with these characters they may be referred to ten genera. Figs. 211–221 represent the principal forms of the Œningian spiders. We observe among them a cross-spider (*Epeïra molassica*, Heer, fig. 221) of the size of the Swiss common species; several crab spiders (*Thomisus œningensis**, *T. lividus*, and *T. Sulzeri*, figs. 215–217), which run sideways like crabs, and are distinguished by the shortness of the two hinder pair of legs; some weaving spiders (*Theridion annulipes*, fig. 212, and *T. globulus*, fig. 220),

---

* Thorell refers this *Thomisus* to *Xysticus* and *Theridion maculipes* to *Asagena*. But, according to Koch, *Xysticus* must not be separated from *Thomisus*; and, according to Walckenaer, *Asagena* is to be united with *Theridion*. Considering the bad state of preservation of the fossil Arachnida, they can only be referred to the most important genera.

in which the legs of the third pair are smaller than the rest and the abdomen is nearly globular; three small elegant *Macariæ* (*M. tenella,* fig. 218), with the cephalothorax and abdomen long and narrow and the legs short; a hairy lurking spider (*Clubiona Eseri,* fig. 213); and a long-legged water-spider (*Argyronecta?*

Fig. 215.　　Fig. 214.　　Fig. 213.　　Fig. 211.

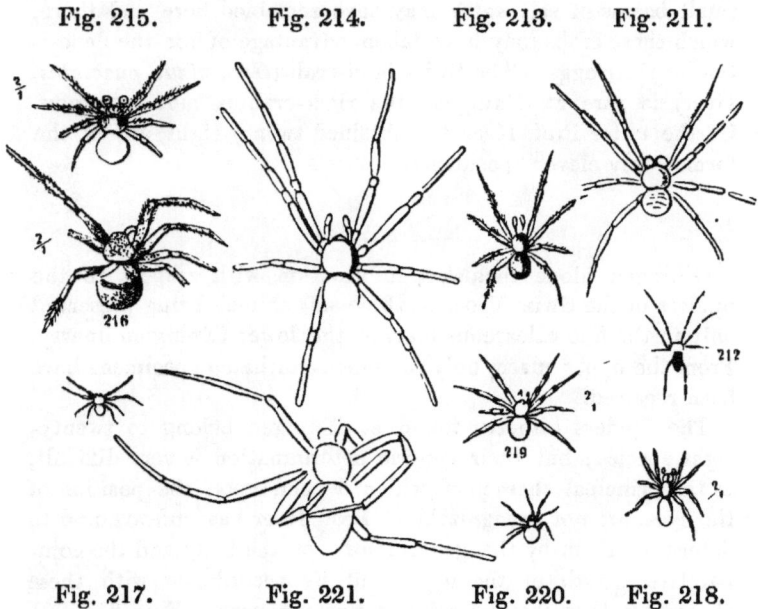

Fig. 217.　　　Fig. 221.　　　Fig. 220.　　Fig. 218.

Fig. 211. *Schellenbergia rotundata,* Heer.
Fig. 212. *Theridion annulipes,* Heer.
Fig. 213. *Clubiona Eseri,* Heer.
Fig. 214. *Argyronecta longipes.*
Fig. 215. *Thomisus œningensis.*
Fig. 216. *Thomisus lividus,* Heer, twice nat. size.
Fig. 217. *Thomisus Sulzeri,* Heer.
Fig. 218. *Macaria tenella,* Heer.
Fig. 219. *Theridion maculipes,* Heer.
Fig. 220. *Theridion globulus,* Heer.
Fig. 221. *Epeïra molassica,* Heer.

longipes, fig. 214). The other species are, for the most part, small delicate creatures, probably belonging chiefly to the group of the weaving spiders. One of them, however, is very remarkable, and seems to Prof. Heer to represent an extinct genus (*Schellenbergia rotundata*, fig. 211), characterized by short palpi with a large globular apical joint, a short nearly globular abdomen, closely adpressed to the cephalothorax and marked with transverse impressions. The legs of the third pair are the shortest; and the rest are nearly of equal length. The femora are traversed by a longitudinal rib. This is the only spider found at Œningen which differs considerably from living genera; the others have little that is remarkable about them, and belong chiefly to genera which have at present a very wide distribution. Most of them probably lived on the banks of the Lake of Œningen, the cross-spider spreading its net between the reeds and rushes, the crab spiders attaching their flat sacks to the marsh-plants, on the flowers of which they sunned themselves and lay in wait for insects, the weavers stretching their horizontal nets on plants and trees, after the fashion of their living relatives, and the lurking spiders and *Macariæ* dwelling under the bark of trees and under stones. All these spiders consequently lived on land, and got accidentally into the water, where they were enveloped by its mud; but one species (*Argyronecta? longipes*) probably* lived in the water, and represents the remarkable water-spider *A. aquatica*, Deg., which also occurs in Switzerland (as in the Katzensee). This spider builds in the water a sack-like nest of silk with the opening downwards. This it fills with air by the following process:—the spider comes to the surface and raises its hairy abdomen above the water, and then, suddenly diving down, carries with it the adherent air-bubbles, which it sweeps off with its legs after reaching the interior of its nest. Although its respiratory apparatus does not differ from that of other spiders, the air surrounding its abdomen enables it to carry on its operations under water.

* Unfortunately the two specimens which Prof. Heer received are not sufficiently well preserved for certain determination. The comparative lengths of the legs, the thin filiform palpi, and the rounded form of the sides of the cephalothorax are in favour of its being referred to *Argyronecta*; but the cephalothorax is less prominent in front than in the existing species. A similar form of cephalothorax and legs also occurs in *Tegenaria*. According to Thorell this species does not belong to *Argyronecta*, but seems to form a distinct genus; this is also the case with the *Clubiona*.

If the Œningian spiders are compared with those which have been discovered in amber, no exactly accordant species are found ; but there are some nearly allied species*. Most of the amber-spiders may be referred to existing genera ; but some of them are of extinct types, one of which (*Archæa*) forms a distinct and very remarkable family. Amber encloses a great number of species of spiders, the resin flowing from the amber-bearing trees having enveloped the animals dwelling under the bark, or sitting on its surface, and embalmed them for ever.

Of the great section of the Mites (Acarina) a single species has been found at Œningen. It is a little oval animal, 1 millimetre (·039 inch) in length and ½ millimetre in breadth, with eight delicate legs of nearly equal length.

c. *Insects.*

Notwithstanding their small size and their delicate fragile structure, so many species of insects have been preserved that the class of insects must have included the great mass of species of animals. Only 33 species of insects have remained in the Swiss Miocene; but from Œningen we have 844, only one of which occurs in the Swiss Miocene, so that at present we know 876 species belonging to the Swiss environs. Of these, 543 species are Beetles, 20 Orthoptera, 29 Neuroptera, 81 Hymenoptera, 3 Lepidoptera, 64 two-winged flies, and 136 Hemiptera or Rhynchota. The beetles are consequently the most numerous; and they are followed in order by the Rhynchota, the flies, and the Neuroptera. The Lepidoptera (butterflies and moths) are most feebly represented both in species and individuals; for Prof. Heer has hitherto seen only 5 specimens of Lepidoptera (perfect insects and larvæ) from Œningen, whilst he has examined 2456 specimens of beetles, 882 Neuroptera, 699 Hymenoptera, 310 flies, 598 Rhynchota, and 131 Orthoptera. Of the Neuroptera only about 80 specimens are in the adult state, all the rest being larvæ of dragonflies, which lie in a particular bed at Œningen, and were probably killed by some sudden catastrophe, so that a great part of the insects contained in the pit have been preserved. Hence

---

* *Clubiona Eseri* is very like *C. lanata*; and *Macaria tenella* resembles *Macaria procera*, B. & K.

the order Neuroptera, as regards the number of individuals, is much more predominant at Œningen than in the existing fauna of any part of Europe. The most abundant insects, as regards the number of both species and individuals, are the beetles; and we may say that, on the average, out of two specimens found at Œningen one belongs to this order. Among the Hymenoptera the ants occur most abundantly, and among the Diptera the gnats and midges.

Of land-insects, only those have remained which were carried down into the lake by running water and driven from the shore over the lake, and which there perished. The winged insects were more exposed to this danger than the wingless ones; the latter, consequently, occur but rarely. Thus, of the ants we find the winged males and females, but seldom the wingless workers. Of the beetles we find many lying with outspread wings, exactly in the position which they assume when they have fallen into the water and are endeavouring to save themselves by extending their wings (fig. 255). Nevertheless the wingless land-insects are not entirely deficient. Prof. Heer has obtained from Œningen a caterpillar, larvæ of grasshoppers, and two or three worker ants; and indeed the spiders and the woodlouse, already referred to, prove that the Œningian collection of annulose animals is by no means limited to winged insects accidentally carried by the wind over the lake. The wingless forms probably fell from the bank into the water, perhaps from trees which overshadowed the lake; but they were also swept into the lake by the brooks. Of the insects which fell into the water, only those have been preserved which were quickly covered by the mud and thus saved from destruction. Aquatic insects belonging to the Lake of Œningen are very numerous, and are found in all stages as larvæ, pupæ, and adult animals. Most of the aquatic insects have no doubt been destroyed without leaving any traces; but many were so rapidly enveloped by the fine calcareous deposit that they have not merely produced an impression in it, but even the organic substance has been preserved. By this rapid covering, the softest midges are so admirably preserved that, under the microscope, the hairs on their legs and wings can be recognized, and the colours of the land-bugs can still be ascertained.

In some parts of the Lake of Œningen exhalations of poisonous gases probably took place, such as may still be observed in various places (as near Tarasp in the Engadine). By these the insects would be killed when they fell into the water. This notion is confirmed by the circumstance that the males and females of several species of insects (*Cydnus œningensis, Pseudophana amatoria,* and *Ponera veneraria,* Heer (fig. 288), are found united in the stone.

The Œningian collection of insects embraces many centuries, and extends over all seasons of the year; so that it probably lays before us the majority of the forms that we require for the representation of the insect-fauna of that stage of the Miocene period.

A great number of wood-eating insects are found at Œningen. In the existing Swiss fauna the wood-beetles are to the rest of the Coleoptera as 1 : 8·56, but at Œningen they are as 1 : 3·3; the Œningian forests were therefore much richer in insects than the existing forests of Switzerland; and they afforded a shelter on the whole to larger species. Stag-beetles were wanting; but the gold-beetles (Buprestidæ) were represented by a great number of species, which are among the largest and most abundant beetles of the Miocene period. With them were associated numerous Longicorn Beetles and Trogositidæ. The larvæ of these Beetles doubtless lived under the bark and in the wood of trees; the numerous Bibionidæ which are found at Œningen passed their early life in mould and rotten wood; and the little dipterous mushroom-eaters (Mycetophagidæ) were in the Agarics which spread over the humid soil of the forest. The Termites and the majority of the ants also certainly had their nests in the forests; and many species (such as *Termes Hartungi* and *Buchii, Formica procera, lignitum,* and *obesa*) set up their dwellings, after the fashion of their existing relations, in old trunks of trees. Their business was to destroy dead plants, and to nourish themselves from dead animal substances, thus aiding in the perpetual change of matter.

Some insects climbed to the summits of trees, in order to obtain honey-dew from the colonies of Aphides settled there; Chrysomelinous and Rhynchophorous beetles also dwelt on the trees; and great *Cicadæ* hid themselves in the dense canopy of leaves and filled the air with their monotonous chirping. Thus the insects which fell by mere chance into the lake reveal to us a rich and multifarious forest life at Œningen.

If we could visit the former meadow-ground, we should find upon its herbs and flowers exactly the same kinds of insects that we now meet with in Swiss forest-pastures. We should see numerous Chrysomelina and Rhynchophora, spotted and golden Lamellicorns (*Trichius*), metallic shield-bugs, flies of various colours (*Syrphus*), bees and humble-bees sucking the honey of the flowers; but there were also predaceous beetles near (especially the species of *Telephorus* and *Malachius*), watching the peaceful nectar-drinkers and seeking to overpower them.

Passing to the Lake of Œningen we should find among its reeds and rushes the same forms of insects which we now observe on the banks of the Swiss lakes—golden Chrysomelas (*C. calami*) sunning themselves on the leaves of the reeds, green *Donaciæ* sitting in the flowers of the rushes, active species of *Lixus* climbing about on the aquatic Umbelliferæ, and numerous dragonflies, often adorned with varied colours, hovering over the vegetation. The water-beetles, especially the *Dytisci* and *Hydrophili*, are exceedingly numerous, and they are also remarkable for their large size. The thirty species from Œningen with which Prof. Heer is acquainted no doubt committed great devastation among the spawn of fishes. The Dytiscidæ especially are very voracious creatures; and of these there are found two large species (*Dytiscus Lavateri* and *Cybister Agassizi*, Heer). If we add to these the shining whirligig-beetles (*Dineutus*), which, no doubt, like their living relatives, collected in joyous companies and performed circular evolutions on the surface of the water), the numerous larvæ of dragonflies and midges, the water-scorpions, and gigantic water-bugs, we must admit that in the Lake of Œningen life was exhibited under multifarious forms.

Most of the aquatic insects were predaceous animals feeding on young fishes, Mollusca, and other Annulosa. The land-fauna comprises many species which lived by preying upon other insects; but in general the carnivorous species were less numerously represented than the herbivorous forms, the proportion among the existing beetles being as 1 : 3·62. Among the whole number of the Coleoptera of Œningen the carnivorous species are to the herbivorous as 1 : 4·62. In the existing Swiss fauna the proportion is as 1 : 3, in Europe generally as 1 : 3·87, in North America as 1 : 4, and in South America as 1 : 9·59. Towards the warmer zones the vegetable-eaters (Phytophaga) increase in number much more rapidly than the flesh-eaters (Creophaga), and predominate in warm climates far more than in the temperate zones. The preponderance of the Phytophaga in the beetle-fauna of the Tertiary strata of Switzerland is by no means so great as in the fauna of beetles in tropical countries; but in Miocene times, vegetable-eaters were in a larger proportion among beetles than in the existing fauna of Switzerland and Europe.

Of the vegetable-eaters many have no special choice of nourishment, whilst others are exclusively confined to certain species or genera of plants, and on these derive their food from particular organs. We have already noticed (vol. i. p. 309) that many insects that we possess from Œningen reveal to us the existence of plants which have not yet been discovered. On the other hand we can indicate the food-plants of a considerable number of insects. The poplar-beetles (*Lina populeti*) most probably lived on the poplars and willows, the Cantharides and Cicadæ on the ashes, *Ancylochira tincta*, *Ampedus Seyfriedii*, *Hylecœtus cylindricus*, *Acanthoderus sepultus* and *lepidus*, and *Syromastes affinis* on the pines and firs, the beautiful *Chalcophora lævigata* on the almond-trees, *Rhynchites silenus* on the vines, *Chrysomela Calami* and *Donacia Palæmonis* on the reeds and rushes, and *Lygæus tinctus* on *Acerates veterana*, all plants known to Prof. Heer from Œningen.

Delicate aquatic plants served as food to the minute but exceedingly numerous *Cyprides*, which in their turn afforded nourishment to the larvæ of midges; and these again were pursued by the predaceous beetles, larvæ of dragonflies, and fishes. The larvæ of the ladybirds (*Coccinellæ*) and wasp-flies (*Syrphus*) settle down among Aphides at the present day, so as to devour them at their ease; and from Œningen Prof. Heer knows of nineteen species of *Coccinella* and two species of *Syrphus*—and also two species of Aphides, among which the ladybirds and wasp-flics may have taken up their abode. Aphides furnished honey-dew for ants, which no doubt obtained it from them in the same way as their relatives of the present time. The large species 'of *Cercopis* found at Œningen probably also supplied saccharine juices for ants like their existing representatives in warm climates.

One gadfly has been found of the family of Tabanidæ. Prof. Heer has obtained from Œningen thirty-three species of dung-beetles, of which nineteen belong to the Lamellicorns, which live not only in but upon the excrements of Mammalia, and fourteen to families (Histeridæ, Oxytelidæ, and Staphylinidæ) similar species of which dwell in excrements and carrion, for the purpose of chasing and feeding on the larvæ of the true coprophagous insects. From the analogy of existing species we may indicate even the genera of mammalia, the existence of which is betrayed by these insects. Most of the species of the genera *Copris, Onthophagus,* and *Gymnopleurus* that we know from Œningen represent living species which live chiefly or exclusively in the fresh excrements of horned cattle, and therefore presuppose the existence of such animals, although the remains of cattle have not yet been discovered. The genera *Oniticellus* and *Geotrupes* (allied to the *Scarabæus*) lead to the supposition that animals of the horse race lived in the forests of Œningen. A quadruped of this kind (*Hipparion gracile*) is known in Switzerland.

If we compare the Œningian insect-fauna with that now existing we find in it numerous peculiar types. Prof. Heer is acquainted with 44 peculiar genera, 21 of them belonging to the Coleoptera, 6 to the Neuroptera, 6 to the Diptera, 11 to the Rhynchota, and 1 to the Orthoptera. They include 140 species, many of which were among the most abundant and widely distributed of the insects. But by far the greater part of the fauna must be ranged under existing genera; and many of the species are so nearly allied to living forms that they are probably to be regarded as the ancestors of the latter. Prof. Heer calls them *homologous species.* Most of these species belong to genera at present distributed over both the Old and the New World. There are in the Œningian fauna 180 of such genera, of which 114 belong to the Coleoptera. Of the latter, two

(*Dineutus* and *Caryoborus*) are now wanting in Europe, but all the rest are represented both in Europe and America. As the whole number of genera of beetles from Œningen now known to Prof. Heer is 156, those common both to Europe and America constitute two thirds of that number, the proportion in the present beetle-fauna of Europe (according to Lacordaire) being only one third. Hence the genera spread over both hemispheres were more numerous in Tertiary times than at present. Of exclusively European genera we find only 5; but there are 18 which now occur in Europe and Asia or Africa, but not in America. These are chiefly genera belonging to the fauna of the Mediterranean region (such as *Pentodon, Glaphyrus, Capnodis, Brachycerus, Zonitis, Ælia*), which reinforce the Œningian fauna with Mediterranean forms; and the genera common to both hemispheres are in part represented by species most nearly allied to those of the Mediterranean region. There are two exclusively African types (*Lepitrix* and *Gymnochila*), and also two which are now confined to America (*Anoplites* and *Naupactus*). But there are several genera now absent from Europe which are chiefly American, although not exclusively so (as they occur also in Asia or in Africa): such are *Belostoma, Hypselonotus, Diplonychus, Evagoras, Stenopoda, Plecia, Caryoborus,* and *Dineutus.* In all, Œningen furnishes 29 species which have their nearest living allies in America, and 102 which most closely approach European forms. Of the latter, the majority belong to the south of Europe.

On the whole the insect-fauna of Œningen has more of a Mediterranean character, and less of a more southern and American stamp, than the flora. This applies particularly to the insects with a complete metamorphosis, and less to those in which the metamorphosis is incomplete, especially the Rhynchota. By the great prominence of the Reduviidæ, Scutata, and Corcodea, by the large Cicadidæ, the fine species of Cercopidæ, and the gigantic Water-bugs, the Rhynchota furnish evidence of a warmer climate, and especially a milder winter, than are now known in Central Europe. The cause of this may probably be as follows:—The insects with an incomplete metamorphosis (the Rhynchota, Orthoptera, and a part of the Neuroptera) have no quiescent pupa state, and the majority of them live as larvæ

not in the earth but upon plants, and are therefore much less
protected from the inclemencies of the weather during their
development than the insects with a complete metamorphosis.
The chief habitation of these insects is therefore between the
tropics, in the lands which know no winter, where their development can go on uninterruptedly. This applies particularly
to the Reduviidæ, Scutata, and Corcodea, which are found in
astonishing abundance and variety in warm countries. Only
a comparatively small number of these insects can .exist in
countries where their development is interrupted by a long cold
winter.

Insects with a complete metamorphosis, on the other hand,
pass the winter in the egg, larva, or pupa state, dormant in the
interior of plants or deep down in the earth, and are thus almost
entirely out of reach of the action of cold. Thus the cold of
winter has little influence upon them; but the summer temperature has a great effect. A country with a cold winter and a
hot summer has therefore more southern insects with a complete metamorphosis than a region of similar mean annual
temperature more uniformly distributed, because in the case of
insects with a complete metamorphosis, as in that of annual
plants, the summer temperature is really the sole consideration of importance; while for perennial and especially woody
plants, and for many insects with an incomplete metamorphosis,
the winter temperature is also of great consequence. This
explains why, in America, tropical forms of insects and cultivated annual plants (such as maize), but not tropical forms
of trees, advance further towards the north than in Europe,
because under the same latitudes (at least on the east side of
the American continent) the summer is hotter and the winter
much colder than in Europe. And inversely, from the circumstance that in Œningen the insects with incomplete metamorphosis exhibit more tropical forms than those in which the
metamorphosis is complete, we may infer that in Œningian
times the winters must have been very mild, the temperature of
the winter rather than of the summer having been higher in
the Swiss Miocene country than that now prevailing in Central
Europe.

Insects in general, being of a small size, do not attract much attention; and it will therefore be sufficient here to give merely a short survey of the principal forms* met with in the Swiss Miocene country.

A. *Orthoptera.*

Cockroaches, to which we have already referred in the description of Liassic insects (vol.i.p.83) reappear at Œningen (fig. 229), and prove, by two species of *Blatta,* that this most ancient type of insects existed in the Tertiary period. But the most abundant Orthoptera at Œningen are the Grasshoppers, Locusts, Crickets, and Mantidæ, which four groups include thirteen species.

Of the Locustina, one species (*Decticus speciosus,* Heer, fig. 222) is distinguished by its beautifully white-spotted fore wings; it is very nearly allied to a Southern European species (*D. albifrons,* Fab.). This was the most abundant grasshopper of Œningen. No perfect specimens of it have yet been found, but plenty of wings and hind legs.

The Acridiina are represented, as in the existing Swiss fauna, by three genera (*Œdipoda, Gomphocerus,* and *Tetrix*), and are met with beautifully preserved both in the adult state and as wingless larvæ. One species (*Œdipoda Germari,* Heer) is of the size and form of the migratory locust (*Œdipoda migratoria*), and its fore wings have dark spots: the specimen is much crushed; and Prof. Heer has therefore figured instead of it a nearly allied species from Radoboj (*Œdipoda Haidingeri,* Heer, fig. 223), which is the best-preserved of ancient grasshoppers. *Œdipoda Fischeri* (fig. 224), from Œningen, is a much smaller species.

Among the Crickets (Gryllina) are seen a long narrow mole

---

* Prof. Heer has described and figured the insects of Œningen in his works "On the Insect-fauna of the Tertiary formations of Œningen and of Radoboj in Croatia" (Denkschr. der schweiz. naturf. Gesellsch. for 1847, 1850, and 1853), "Contributions to the Insect-fauna of Œningen" (Harlem, 1862), and "Hyménoptères fossiles" (Denkschr. &c. 1867). The figures which the Professor has selected for the present work mostly represent new species not described in his earlier works. In all cases where no locality is given the insects are from Œningen.

cricket (*Gryllotalpa stricta*, Heer) and a remarkably small cricket (*Gryllus troglodytes*, Heer, fig. 225), such as are now no longer met with in Europe.

The Œningian earwigs (Forficulina) are nearly related to those now living in Switzerland, and which are very widely distributed. One species (*Forficula recta*, Heer, fig. 226) seems to

Fig. 225.   Fig. 233.   Fig. 226.   Fig. 224.

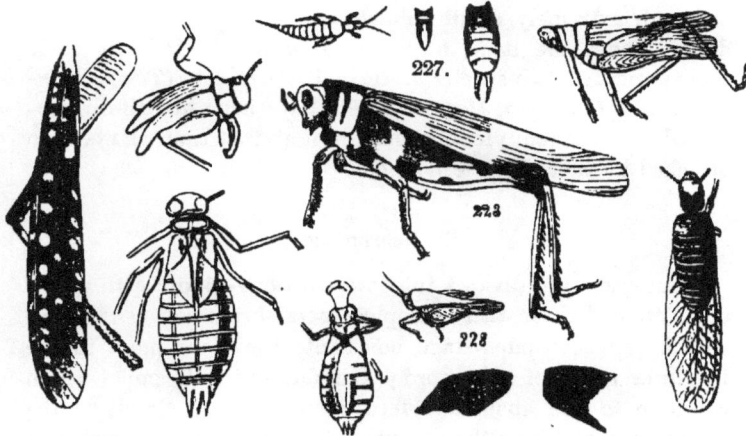

Fig. 222.   Fig. 232.   Fig. 231.   Fig. 229.   Fig. 230.

Fig. 222. *Decticus speciosus*, Heer.
Fig. 223. *Œdipoda Haidingeri*, Heer, from Radoboj.
Fig. 224. *Œdipoda Fischeri*, Heer.
Fig. 225. *Gryllus troglodytes*, Heer, twice nat. size.
Fig. 226. *Forficula recta*, Heer.
Fig. 227. *Forficella primigenia*, Heer.
Fig. 228. *Tetrix gracilis*, Heer.
Fig. 229. *Blatta colorata*, Heer.
Fig. 230. *Termes Hartungi*, Heer.
Fig. 231. *Libellula Doris*, Heer.
Fig. 232. *Libellula Calypso*, Heer.
Fig. 233. *Thrips annosa*, Heer, magnified 3 times.

represent *F. annulipes*, Luc.; a second species (*F. primigenia*, Heer, fig. 227), of which, however, only the caudal appendages are preserved, resembles the common earwig (*F. auricularia,* Linn.), which is as abundant in Madeira as in Switzerland; and a third (*F. minuta,* Heer) comes nearest to the little earwig (*F. minor,* Linn.) which in summer evenings is often seen flying in the air.

Some of the Physopoda live in great numbers in flowers, and assist in their fertilization by transferring the pollen to the stigma; whilst others collect in millions upon the leaves of plants, and by sucking their juices destroy them. The latter, although extremely small animals, are greatly dreaded by gardeners under the name of the "red spider." Delicate as is their structure, two species of these little insects (*Thrips œningensis* and *T. annosa,* Heer, fig. 233) have been beautifully preserved at Œningen, proving that even at that time plants were attacked by these little Physopoda.

B. *Neuroptera.*

Neuroptera are divided into two sections—those with an incomplete and those with a complete metamorphosis. The latter, with a quiescent pupa-stage, constitute the Neuroptera in the narrower sense of the word; the former, with pupæ which continue to run about and feed, approach very closely to the Orthoptera, and form the transition to that order. They include the greater part of the fossil Neuroptera. The twenty-five known species belonging to the Swiss Miocene fauna are subdivided among the families of the Termitidæ, Libellulidæ, and Ephemeridæ.

Of the four white ants (*Termites*) two species (*Termes spectabilis* and *T. insignis,* Heer) represent peculiar extinct species, exceeding in size even the white ant (*T. fatalis,* Linn.), so much dreaded in the torrid zone. Two others (*Termes Hartungi,* Heer, fig. 230, and *T. Buchii,* Heer) represent a species (*T. lucifugus,* Lat.) inhabiting the subtropical zone (as in Madeira), but which has also taken up its abode in the seaport towns of Southern Europe. In Madeira Prof. Heer found large numbers of this species in old fir-stumps, which the insects perforated in all directions and thus made dwelling-places for themselves. From these chambers run covered galleries, through which the larvæ pass to seek for food. Their soft bodies are so ill-defended that they cannot escape the numerous predacious insects if they venture outside their covered passages*. The winged males and females issue at certain seasons in enormous swarms into the open air; and these for the most part become the prey of their numerous enemies. In the neighbourhood of rivers and lakes many of them get drowned; and that this was the case in Œningian times is proved by the winged *Termites* which the rocks at Œningen enclose. No doubt their mode of life was similar to that of their existing relatives. The two small species probably established their dwellings in the trunks of the Conifers which were so abundant in the Œningian forest; whilst the two larger ones no doubt built conical edifices, like those inhabited by the tropical species.

The dragonflies (Libellulina) of Œningen consist of three genera and twenty species. Their larvæ no doubt lived in the water, and the adult animals in the air. Of all the three genera both larvæ and perfect insects remain; of the genus *Agrion* only one species has come down to us in the young state, and of this merely a single specimen, whilst the adults are found of six species. Only three species of *Libellula* are known from winged specimens, whilst eight are found as larvæ. The largest species (*Libellula Calypso*, Heer) is represented in fig. 232; but two other species (*L. Doris*, Heer, fig. 231, and *L. Eurynome*, Heer) are much more plentiful, and are the commonest insects at Œningen. They so closely resemble the larvæ of an existing species (*L. depressa*, Linn.) that the adult must also correspond to this, and therefore might easily be referred to the larva in case of its being found at Œningen. Its absence is the more remarkable as the female must have come upon the water for the purpose of depositing her eggs, and must consequently have been in danger of drowning. It must, however, be taken into consideration that the larvæ of *Agrion* live chiefly in running

---

* In Madeira Prof. Heer shut up a great number of larvæ and soldiers in a tin box, in order to observe their development and mode of life. But the little house-ants speedily smelt them out, made their way through the narrow crevice round the lid into the box, and attacked the *Termites*. Although the latter were much the larger, they were easily overcome and devoured by the house-ants.

water, in small brooks and springs, and that the perfect insects flutter about lazily over lakes, rivers, and ponds, so that they may easily be caught and drowned in the water; but the *Libellulæ* have a much more powerful flight, and are fond of frequenting woods and coppices, whilst their larvæ live in stagnant muddy water.

The two common *Libellulæ* of Œningen are met with in whole families together in the dragonfly-bed of the upper quarry, where small specimens are found, as well as half-grown and full-grown dragonflies and pupæ with wing-sheaths. Some of them have the labium pressed close to the lower surface of the head; others have it extended as if in the act of seizing a prey (fig. 231). This labium (lower lip) in the larvæ of the dragonflies is of very peculiar construction, and can be extended and drawn back like a hand. Gently the creatures glide towards their victim and seize it by the sudden extension of the labium, which is furnished with a pair of strong jaws at its anterior margin. The state of preservation of the larvæ renders it probable that they were killed by some sudden catastrophe. Perhaps the water was heated to boiling by volcanic eruptions, or was impregnated with gases: either supposition would account for the congregation of masses of larvæ of all ages lying together. The rock enclosing these insects is distinguished by its remarkable hardness and brittleness.

Libellula depressa, Linn., to which the two commonest Miocene dragonflies of Œningen are most nearly allied, is now distributed all over Europe. Two species of *Æschna* also resemble a European form (*Æ. mixta*, Lat.), and one species of *Agrion* (*A. Aglaope*, like *A. elegans*, Lind.); whilst two other *Agriones* (*A. Parthenope* and *Leucosia*) represent South-African types (*A. fasciatum* and *longicaudum*). These are large species. *A. Parthenope* has a dark transverse band on the wing, which was probably black or metallic during life.

The Ephemeridæ (May-flies or day-flies), which are easily recognizable by their long caudal bristles, rise in spring and early summer from the Swiss lakes in immense numbers, and not unfrequently make their way into the houses in the evening. They appear to have been rare in Tertiary times; at least hitherto

Prof. Heer has only obtained one small species (*Ephemera œningensis*, Heer) from Œningen.

Of the Phryganidæ (caddice-flies), which appear in great quantities about the rivers and lakes of Switzerland, and which are mentioned by Conrad Gessner as "Baden flies," Prof. Heer only knows two species from Œningen, and one from Locle. Their larvæ, like those now existing, constructed their dwellings of small stones and fragments of plants; one of these dwellings has been found at Œningen.

C. *Beetles (Coleoptera).*

Of the Coleoptera all the higher groups and most of the families are represented at Œningen, from which locality Prof. Heer is acquainted with 518 species. From the rest of the Swiss Miocene 26 species have been obtained. The average number of species to each family is 10, and to each genus 3 species; in the existing beetle-fauna of Switzerland there are 45 species to the family and 5 to the genus; in Europe generally the genus possesses 7·9 species, it has 4·4 species in North America, and 6·7 species in South America.

Most of the species at Œningen are comprised in the tribe of the Rhynchophora (weevils &c.) with 107 species; then follow the Sternoxi (66 species), Clavicornes (55), Carabidæ (52), Chrysomelina (50), Lamellicornes (50), Longicornes (28), and Palpicornes (21). In the present Swiss fauna the order of the tribes according to number of species is as follows—Rhynchophora, Brachelytra, Carabidæ, Clavicornes, Chrysomelina, Sternoxi, Lamellicornes, and Longicornes; and the same order is found with respect to the general fauna of Europe.

Thus not only in the fauna of the Tertiary district of Switzerland, but in that of Europe at the present day, the Rhynchophora take the first place; but while in the latter the Brachelytra hold the second or third place, in the Miocene fauna, as in that of South America or Asia, these insects fall into the background, and do not appear among the dominant tribes. On the other hand, the Sternoxi (gold-beetles and skipjacks) come up into the second rank, and even the Palpicornes take their place

among the more important groups. The remarkable predominance of the Sternoxi is chiefly produced by the Buprestidæ
(gold-beetles), a family which attained a far more important
development in the Tertiary fauna than it does at present, and
which is now most numerous in warmer zones. Many species
of Buprestidæ are found in the Lias, including the great majority
of the wood-beetles of that early period (see vol. i. p. 87). The
predominance of the Buprestidæ, the abundance of Palpicornes,
and the rare occurrence of Brachelytra are the most characteristic features of the Tertiary beetle-fauna.

Ladybirds (Coccinellidæ) are everywhere well-known insects,
characterized by the convex form of their body, and generally by
their elegantly spotted elytra. From Œningen nineteen species
have been received; and of most of these the original colouring
is still to be recognized. It was as lively and varied as in living
species. In one species (*Coccinella colorata*, fig. 234) four black
spots may be observed on the thorax, and ten upon each elytron.
One species (*C. Andromeda*, Heer) resembles the common Swiss
seven-spotted ladybird; another (*C. Hesione*, Heer) represents
the two-spotted species (*C. dispar*, Ill.); and a third (*C. ama-
bilis*, Heer) is like *C. ocellata*, Linn.; whilst a fourth, large species (*C. spectabilis*, Heer, fig. 235) agrees in size and form with
the Brazilian *C. marginata*.

Of the Chrysomelinæ (Phytophaga) fifty species are known
from Œningen; and to these must be added three more from the
Swiss Miocene. The most numerously represented families are
the Chrysomelidæ (with fifteen species), the Gallerucidæ (with
nine), and the Cassididæ (with eight species). Among the
Chrysomelidæ one species (*Lina populeti*, Heer, fig. 237) is very
like the Swiss common poplar-beetle (*Lina populi*, Linn., sp.),
and probably had also blood-red elytra; another (*Gonioctena
Clymene*, Heer) resembles *G. pallida*, Fab., which lives on the
black alder and hazel; and a third (*Chrysomela calami*, Heer,
fig. 238) is allied to *Chrysomela graminis*, Linn., which is met
with on reeds.

Among the Gallerucidæ three species had the head and thorax
light-coloured (probably red or yellow during life), and the antennæ and elytra black (probably metallic during life). The
largest of these (*Galleruca Buchi*, Heer, fig. 236) is most nearly

related to *G. halensis*, Linn., which lives in Central Europe upon the goose-grass (*Galium*), while the two others resemble Brazilian species, as does also another species, in which the elytra are adorned with large round spots.

The Cassididæ (shield- or tortoise beetles) are easily recognized, even in the fossil state, by their broad flat elytra. The two most abundant species (*Cassida Hermione*, Heer, and *C. Blancheti*, Heer, fig. 239) resemble those which live on thistles (*C.*

Fig. 235.   Fig. 236.   Fig. 237.   Fig. 239.   Fig. 241.

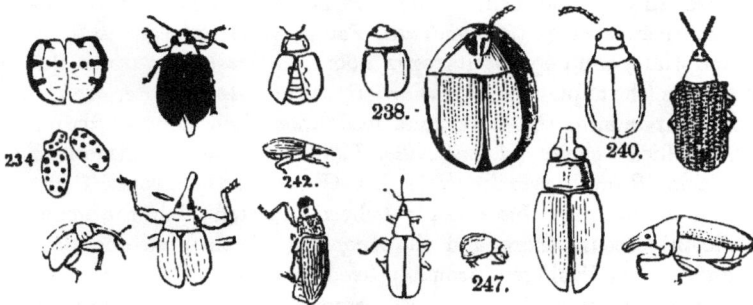

Fig. 243. Fig. 244. Fig. 245. Fig. 246.   Fig. 248.   Fig. 249.

Fig. 234. *Coccinella colorata*, Heer.
Fig. 235. *Coccinella spectabilis*, Heer.
Fig. 236. *Galleruca Buchi*, Heer, twice nat. size.
Fig. 237. *Lina populeti*, Heer.
Fig. 238. *Chrysomela calami*, Heer.
Fig. 239. *Cassida Blancheti*, Heer, three times nat. size.
Fig. 240. *Lema vetusta*, Heer, twice nat. size.
Fig. 241. *Anoplites Bremii*, Heer, three times nat. size.
Fig. 242. *Apion antiquum*, Heer, three times nat. size.
Fig. 243. *Rhynchites Dionysus*, Heer.
Fig. 244. *Attelabus durus*, Heer.
Fig. 245. *Naupactus crassirostris*, Heer.
Fig. 246. *Antliarhinites gracilis*, Heer, three times nat. size.
Fig. 247. *Brachycerus nanus*, Heer.
Fig. 248. *Sitona atavina*, Heer, four times nat. size.
Fig. 249. *Cleonus speciosus*, Heer.

Murræa, Fab., and *C. thoracica*, Kug.), and therefore afford evidence of thistles at Œningen.

Of the Crioceridæ only one species (*Lema vetusta*, Heer, fig. 240) appears; but this is of great interest, as it is allied to the red lily-beetle (*L. merdigera*, Linn.), and its existence gives a probability to the Œningian flora having been adorned with liliaceous plants.

Four species of Hispidæ occur at Œningen, whilst Switzerland now possesses only one. The fossil species differ entirely from the modern species, and belong to an American genus (*Anoplites*). One of them (*Anoplites Bremii*, Heer, fig. 241) is very abundant at Œningen, more than 100 specimens of that beetle having been already obtained. It is very nearly related to a North-American species (*A. quadrata*, Fab.), which appears in May and June, and deposits its eggs upon the leaves of various Pomaceæ (the apple-tree, *Pyrus arbutifolia* and *Amelanchier ovalis*). The larvæ mine the leaves, and feed upon their cellular tissue. An allied species (*A. suturalis*, Fab.) lives on the American acacia (*Robinia pseudacacia*). At Œningen the genera *Pyrus* and *Amelanchier* have not yet been detected; but the genus *Robinia* occurs there, and the *Anoplites*, which is so abundant an insect at Œningen, probably lived upon it.

The Donacidæ are much less common; only a few specimens of two species have been found. This is very remarkable, as at present these insects are met with in great quantities on marsh- and water-plants, and they occur by hundreds in the lignites of Utznach and Dürnten.

Rhynchophora, which are characterized by having the head prolonged into a beak, constitute the most numerous tribe both in the Œningian and in the present European fauna. One hundred and eight species are already known from Œningen, 24 of which belong to the Attelabidæ (with straight antennæ), and 84 to the Curculionidæ (with geniculated antennæ). There are therefore between one fourth and one fifth of Attelabidæ in the whole number, whilst they are about one third in the existing Swiss fauna. The Attelabidæ at the present day are relatively less numerous in the warm and torrid zones than in temperate regions.

The Rhynchophora live exclusively upon vegetable food; and indeed many of them confine themselves either to particular species or genera of plants, and feed upon special vegetable organs—some upon the leaves, others upon the flowers, fruits, or seeds, and others again upon the wood or bark. The study of the natural history of these animals and the determination of the homologous fossil species will afford many interesting hints as to the relations of the animal and vegetable worlds at this early period.

The most numerous group in the family Attelabidæ is that of the Attelabinæ, represented at Œningen by thirteen species belonging to the genera *Attelabus, Rhynchites*, and *Apion*. Figs. 242–244 show the representatives of these genera from Œningen. The little *Apion* has exactly the appearance of the living species. These are all minute elegant creatures, which live chiefly upon the seeds of the trefoils (*Robiniæ*) and other papilionaceous plants. The *Rhynchites* attack the buds and young leaves of the vine; and some of them also feed on the young fruits of pomaceous and stone-fruited trees. This insect has sometimes the names of "the spade" ("la Bêche") and of "Lisette." The species represented in fig. 243 resembles the common vine-beetle (Lisette); and probably, with a second allied species (*R. silenus*, Heer), it lived upon the vines of Œningen. These are European forms; but the *Attelabus durus*, Heer (fig. 244), reminds Prof. Heer of an American type.

Six species of the Anthribidæ probably lived in the forest, upon fungi and rotten wood. The Bruchidæ, with their three species, fed on seeds. One of them (*Bruchus striolatus*, Heer) most resembles in size and form the species living in the palm-nuts of tropical America. In the Bruchidæ the rostrum is short and broad, while in the Antliarhinidæ it is extraordinarily long and thin. To this subfamily, which is now met with only on the cycads of the Cape of Good Hope, Prof. Heer refers a very small insect from Œningen (*Antliarhinus gracilis*, Heer, fig. 246), characterized by its long rostrum of a hair-like fineness, at the base of which the antennæ are inserted.

Of the family Curculionidæ nine subfamilies are represented at Œningen; among these the Cleonidæ, Molytidæ, Erirhinidæ, and Cryptorhynchidæ include the largest number of species. The genus *Cleonus* is found in great numbers, and comprises fourteen species. The corresponding existing species are found in fissures and under stones in the moist ground of the waterside, where they obtain their nourishment from herbaceous plants. The fossil species no doubt had a similar mode of life; and most of them are analogous to European forms: thus *Cleonus speciosus*, Heer (fig. 249), resembles a Siberian species (*C. pruinosus*, Schönh.), and probably found its habitation in the mud and sedges of the Lake of Œningen. The numerous species of *Phytonomus* found at Œningen probably lived on the *Polygona* and *Rumices* of the marshes, attaching their cocoons to the lower surface of the leaves in the same way as their relatives of the present day. The species of *Lixus* presuppose the existence of marsh Umbelliferæ; *L. rugicollis*, Heer, is very nearly allied to a species (*L. gemellatus*, Schönh.) living on the water-hemlock (*Cicuta virosa*), the stems of which are perforated by larvæ, whilst the perfect insect suns itself on the flowers, but sometimes descends into the water, where it can exist for a considerable time. A second species (*Lixus œningensis*, Heer) visited the thistles, at least if it adopted the diet of the nearest allied living species (the widely distributed *L. angustatus*, Fab.).

The Brachyceri (fig. 247) very probably lived on the shore of the lake; and their existence betokens the blooming of liliaceous plants. The three species of *Cionus* remind Prof. Heer of the small globular weevils which occur on the mulleins (*Verbascum*) and figworts (*Scrophularia*), and the *Larinus* of the yellow-scaled species of the Swiss thistles and centauries. The genera *Cryptorhinus* and *Balaninus* must be ascribed to the alders and hazels, and the five *Sitonæ* to the conifers. One of the latter (*Sitona atavina*, Heer, fig. 248) is a very common insect at Œningen, and is very nearly allied to a species the larvæ of which take up their abode in fir-cones. The genus *Naupactus* is quite foreign to Switzerland, being represented in tropical America by species of numerous and beautiful colours; a species of considerable size (*N. crassirostris*, Heer, fig. 245) has been discovered at Œningen.

Longicornes, recognizable by their long antennæ, with thirty species, take the seventh place among the eight most numerous tribes of beetles in the Miocene fauna; in the present fauna of Switzerland and of Europe they occupy the eighth rank, in North America the fifth, in tropical America the third, and in the Indian archipelago the fourth place. They are consequently

more abundant in America than in Europe, and much more
numerous in the torrid than in the temperate and cold zones.
In the Swiss Tertiary country they are on the whole rare. It
is remarkable that the Lepturidæ, which belong to the temperate
zone, are absent, and that all the species are to be referred to
the genera of Cerambycidæ, Lamiariæ, and Prionidæ; they undoubtedly all inhabited the forest, and lived upon wood in their
larval state.

The genus *Prionus* includes types of large size. All the
Œningian forms are distinguished by having the margins of the
thorax destitute of teeth or serrations; they form a peculiar
and apparently extinct group. In size and general aspect the
largest species (*P. Polyphemus*, Heer, fig. 250) is very like
Prionus faber, Linn., the larvæ of which live in firs; a second
species (*Prionus spectabilis*, Heer, fig. 251) attains nearly the
size of *P. coriarius*, Linn.

Cerambycidæ are represented by the genera *Clytus* and *Callidium*, including nine species. The variegated colours which
distinguish the former may still be recognized in four Œningian
species; and the specimen figured (fig. 252) shows distinctly that
the elytra were traversed by three transverse light-coloured
bands, which were probably of a sulphur-yellow during life.
These insects differ considerably from the European species, but
two of the *Callidia* (*C. Escheri*, Heer, fig. 253, and *C. procerum*,
Heer) are nearly allied to *C. strepens*, Fab., a species which is
very widely distributed in the Mediterranean region, and also
occurs in Madeira and North Africa, and even in Georgia and
Brazil.

Of the Lamiariæ, a *Saperda* (*S. Nephele*, Heer) probably lived
on the poplars of Œningen; an *Acanthoderus* (*A. sepultus*,
Heer) and a *Mesosa* (*M. Jasonis*, Heer) upon the wood of conifers. The elytron of a small *Saperda* (fig. 254) has also been
found in the Miocene of Rovercaz.

Of the tribe Stenelytra five families are represented at Œningen; the Cistelidæ and Helopidæ include the greatest number
(fifteen) of species. The former probably frequented flowers,
while the Helopidæ lived on forest-trees; but their larvæ in all
likelihood resided in old stumps of oaks and firs. Two species

of *Helops* have also been obtained from the Miocene of Lausanne and Paudèze.

Among the Trachelidæ the family of the blister-beetles (Cantharidæ) has furnished four species, one of which (*Lytta Æsculapii*, Heer, fig. 255) was rather plentiful. Five specimens of

Fig. 251.   Fig. 250.   Fig. 257.

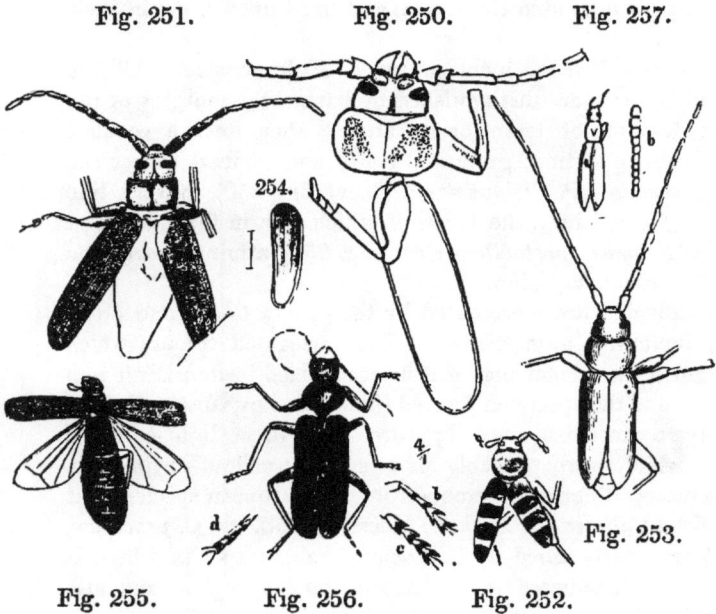

Fig. 255.   Fig. 256.   Fig. 252.

Fig. 250. *Prionus Polyphemus*, Heer.
Fig. 251. *Prionus spectabilis*, Heer.
Fig. 252. *Clytus pulcher*, Heer.
Fig. 253. *Callidium Escheri*, Heer.
Fig. 254. *Saperda valdensis*, Heer, from Rovereaz, enlarged.
Fig. 255. *Lytta Æsculapi*, Heer.
Fig. 256. *Telephorus macilentus*, Heer, four times nat. size. *b*, anterior, *c*, middle, and *d*, hind foot, much enlarged.
Fig. 257. *Tagenopsis brevicornis*, Heer. *b*, antennæ, enlarged.

this species have been preserved. It is very nearly allied to the common blister-beetle (the so-called Spanish fly, *Lytta vesicatoria*, Linn.), and probably lived in great swarms upon the ash

trees of Œningen. A species of *Zonites* (*Z. vetusta*, Heer) is
of the same size and colouring as the *Z. præusta* of Southern
Europe, and like that species probably inhabited the nests of
bees.

The Melanosomata are very uncommon in the Miocene beetle-
fauna, whilst at the present day Mediterranean countries possess
a great abundance of insects belonging to this tribe.

In the Miocene fauna a few species of *Upis* are found, resembling South-American forms, and there is a species of an extinct
genus (*Tagenopsis brevicornis*, Heer, fig. 257) which agrees in
general habit with the existing genus *Tagenia,* but is distinguished
by having the last three joints of the antennæ thickened. The
species of *Tagenia* live under the bark of trees.

The Teredyles also are very sparingly represented. A *Clerus*
(*C. Adonis,* Heer) is intermediate between *Clerus mutillarius* and
formicarius, Linn., beautifully coloured carnivorous beetles,
which pursue the larvæ of the wood-eating insects, seeking them
in their galleries. *Hylecœtus cylindricus*, Heer, resembles *H.
dermestoides,* Linn., which lives in the wood of coniferous and
leafy trees.

The Malacodermata are much more abundant. A glow-worm
(*Lampyris orciluca,* Heer) exactly resembles the common Swiss
glow-worm, and no doubt displayed its mild light in the summer
nights of Miocene times, just as its relative does at present;
the species of *Telephorus* and *Malachius* present numerous and
very elegant forms, which, notwithstanding their soft texture,
have been beautifully preserved, actually as if painted on the
stone. This is shown in fig. 256: the whole of the delicate
creature has been preserved; and in the legs we can still recognize the light colour of the tibiæ and the form and articulation
of the tarsi (fig. 256, *b, c, d*). These insects doubtless frequented
flowers, and there, like the analogous living forms, pursued
still smaller insects.

Of the 67 species of Sternoxi from Œningen, 40 belong to the
Buprestidæ, and 27 to the Elateridæ; and to these must be added
5 more species from the Swiss Miocene. They are divided into
13 genera, two of which (*Fusslinia* and *Protogenia*) are extinct.
The genera *Capnodis, Chalcophora,* and *Ancylochira* are abundantly represented. Two species of *Capnodis* (*C. antiqua,* Heer,

fig. 260, and *C. spectabilis*, Heer, fig. 261) resemble *C. cariosa*, Pall., not only in form and size, but even in the shape and coloration of the elytra, which are well preserved. The two round

Fig. 259.   Fig. 260.   Fig. 261.   Fig. 262.   Fig. 263.

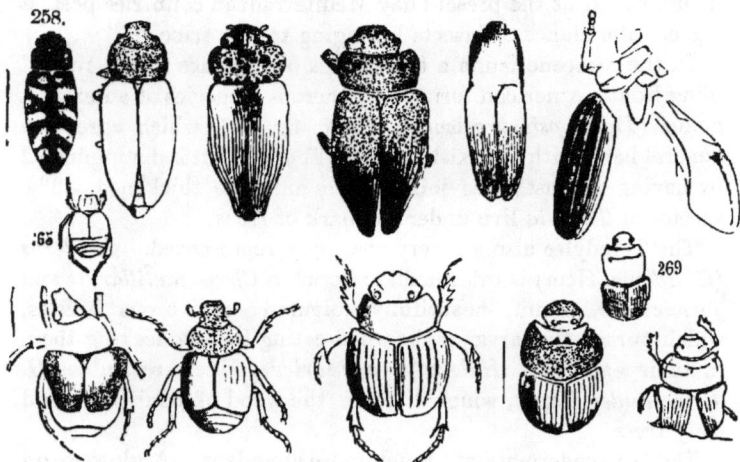

Fig. 264.   Fig. 266.   Fig. 267.   Fig. 268.   Fig. 270.

Fig. 258. *Ancylochira tincta*, Heer, twice nat. size.
Fig. 259. *Chalcophora lævigata*, Heer.
Fig. 260. *Capnodis antiqua*, Heer.
Fig. 261. *Capnodis spectabilis*, Heer.
Fig. 262. *Elater (Alaus) spectabilis*, Heer.
Fig. 263. *Melolontha Greithiana*, Heer, from Greith, on the Hohe-Rhonen.
Fig. 264. *Lepitrix germanica*, Heer, enlarged.
Fig. 265. *Valgus œningensis*, Heer.
Fig. 266. *Trichius ædilis*, Heer, restored.
Fig. 267. *Copris Druidum*, Heer, restored.
Fig. 268. *Onthophagus prodromus*, Heer, twice nat. size.
Fig. 269. *Oniticellus amplicollis*, Heer, twice nat. size.
Fig. 270. *Gymnopleurus rotundatus*, Heer.

black spots on the thorax, and the lighter colour of the base of the elytra, can be seen quite distinctly. The living species is an inhabitant of Southern Europe, Egypt, and the East, and is found upon the flowers of the sumach, whilst its larvæ live in the trunk of the mastic tree (*Lentiscus*). The most abundant *Chalcophora* (*C. lævigata*, Heer, fig. 259) is represented by an Italian species (*C. Fabricii*, Rossi), which lives on peach- and pear-trees.

Seven species of *Ancylochira* have been detected at Œningen; and, from the analogy of existing species, three of them lived upon Conifers. One of these (*A. tincta*, Heer, fig. 258) still beautifully shows its varied colours, agreeing in this respect with *A. octoguttata*, Fab. The species of the genera *Perotis, Eurythyrea, Dicerca, Agrilus, Anthaxia,* and *Sphenoptera* were probably adorned with metallic colours.

The great family of the Elateridæ includes smaller insects. The species from Œningen exhibit no remarkable forms; among them are *Ampedi,* the pale elytra of which were probably during life of a bright red colour as in the living species, which feed on the wood of Conifers and other leafy trees. There are also several species of *Corymbitis,* very like the metallic *C. æneus,* Linn., and numerous species of *Elater,* some with the elytra of a uniform dark colour, others with those organs spotted and edged with a pale border. The largest and most striking species of *Elater* is represented in fig. 262. It is a very peculiar form, most nearly resembling West-Indian species.

The Lamellicornia are numerously represented in the torrid zone. As regards the number of species, they occupy the fourth place in tropical America, the third in the Indian archipelago, and the second in Asia. In Switzerland they rank only in the seventh place. Moreover, in the tropics the species are much larger; they are the giants of the insect world. In the Swiss Tertiary land they take the sixth place, with forty-three species, most of which are represented by European species, although among them are a few exotic forms. Of the eight families from Œningen, three (the Geotrupidæ, Copridæ, and Aphodiidæ) include dung-beetles; two (the Dynastidæ and Melittophilidæ) are formed by beetles which live, in the larval state, in rotten wood, and, when adult, upon flowers; and one (the Melolonthidæ) comprises insects of which the larvæ feed on the roots of plants, while the perfect insects devour the leaves of trees.

Of the dung-beetles (Coprophaga) the Geotrupidæ and Aphodiidæ are rare, and represented by but few species; of the
Copridæ, on the contrary, we have thirteen species, belonging to
four genera. The genus *Onthophagus*, with its grotesquely
horned forms, called among the people " little bull" and "little
ox,": includes seven species, five of which are exactly represented
by those now found in the droppings of cattle: that is to say,
Onthophagus Urus, Heer, is represented by *O. nuchicornis*,
Linn.; *O. prodromus*, Heer (fig. 268), and *O. crassus*, Heer,
by *O. vacca*, Linn.; *O. bisontinus*, Heer, by *O. affinis*, St.; and
O. ovatulus, Heer, by *O. ovatus*, Linn. The genus *Copris* also
includes one species (*C. subterranea*, Heer), which is represented
by one living Swiss species (*C. lunaris*), found in cattle-manure;
another (*C. Druidum*, Heer, fig. 267) is most nearly allied to a
Brazilian species (*C. ciliata*). The genus *Gymnopleurus*, besides
a species of Indian type (*G. rotundatus*, Heer, fig. 270), presents
two or three peculiar forms; whilst an *Oniticellus* (*O. amplicollis*,
fig. 269) finds its nearest ally in the Swiss *O. flavipes*, Fab.,
which lives in horse-manure. Among the Geotrupidæ there
is a species (*Geotrupes Germari*, Heer) which, like the Swiss
Scarabæus and *Geotrupes*, lived on horse-manure; another
(*Coprologus gracilis*, Heer) constitutes a peculiar and extinct
genus.

The Dynastidæ are represented by the genus *Pentodon* (*P.
Proserpinæ*, Heer), which is now confined to the Mediterranean
region, and passes its larval stage in rotten wood.

The Melittophilidæ are known to every one by the rose-
beetles (*Cetoniæ*), so frequent on the spring flowers in the Swiss
gardens. No fossil *Cetoniæ* are known; but we find the nearly
allied genus *Trichius*, the species of which frequent flowers,
whilst their larvæ dwell in old trunks of trees. One species (*T.
ædilis*, Heer, fig. 266) is probably the ancestor of the golden
Trichius nobilis, Linn., which particularly lives on the flowers
of the elder, but deposits its eggs in old plum-trees; another
species (*T. lugubris*, Heer) was the ancestor of the *Trichius
variabilis*, Linn., a black beetle spotted with white, which passes
its young state in deciduous trees; and a third (*T. amœnus*,
Heer) may be the progenitor of *T. fasciatus*, Fab., with which
it agrees in the black bands on its elytra. *Valgus œningensis*,

Heer (fig. 265), is the precursor of *V. hemipterus*, Linn., the larvæ of which live in the wood of deciduous trees.

The family Glaphyridæ presents us with an exotic type (*Glaphyrus antiquus*, Heer), now found in the East living on the flowers of thistles.

Of the Melolonthidæ (cockchafers) ten species are found at Œningen; but none of them seems to have been there as numerous as are the living species. In the older Miocene one species must have been abundant. Of the five specimens of insects which have as yet been found at Hohe-Rhonen, two belong to *Melolontha Greithiana*, Heer (fig. 263); and these have been met with there in different parts of the Carbonaceous deposits. This species was as large as the common Swiss cockchafer, but it had much narrower elytra, and probably belonged to the same group (*Catalasis*, Dej.) as the *Melolontha australis*, Schönh., of the south of France.

At Œningen all the Melolonthidæ are rare. One species (*Rhizotrogus longimanus*, Heer) has its nearest ally in Southern Europe (*R. paganus*, Ol.); another (*Anomala fugax*, Heer) is most closely related to the common July chafer (*A. Julii*, Fab.), which ranges all over Europe; and a third (*Serica minutula*, Heer) resembles the little *Serica strigosa*, Dej. But the most interesting insect of this family is *Lepitrix germanica*, Heer (fig. 264), as it belongs to a genus which is now confined to the Cape of Good Hope, where a very similar species (*L. lineata*, Fab.) is found.

The Lamellicorns are represented in the water by the Palpicorns, twenty-two species of which, belonging to the family Hydrophilidæ, inhabited the waters of Œningen. To these must be added four more species found at Locle and Monod in the Canton of Vaud. Of the eight genera to which these species are referred, two (namely *Escheria* and *Hydrophilopsis*, Heer) are extinct, but five are still found in Switzerland. While only three species of the genera *Hydrophilus* and *Hydrous*, which include the largest species, now inhabit Switzerland, Œningen possessed ten species, several of which must have been abundant. *Hydrophilus spectabilis*, Heer, is the nearest relative of the great pitchy water-beetle (*H. piceus*, Linn.), which is distributed through all the fresh waters of Europe, whilst several others

agree with American forms in their longer and narrower elytra.
Two of them (e.g. *Hydrophilus giganteus,* Heer, fig. 271) are actual

Fig. 272.   Fig. 275.   Fig. 271.   Fig. 273. Fig. 274.

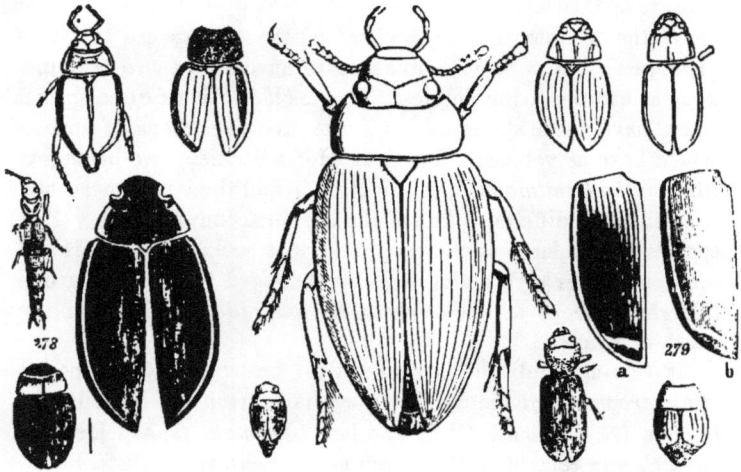

Fig. 282. Fig. 280. Fig. 281.   Fig. 277.   Fig. 276.

Fig. 271. *Hydrophilus giganteus,* Heer (restored).
Fig. 272. *Hydrous Escheri,* Heer.
Fig. 273. *Escheria bella,* Heer.
Fig. 274. *Hydrophilopsis elongata,* Heer.
Fig. 275. *Silpha tricostata,* Heer.
Fig. 276. *Hister Mastodontis,* Heer.
Fig. 277. *Trogosita sculpturata,* Heer.
Fig. 278. *Bledius speciosus,* Heer.
Fig. 279. *Dytiscus Lavateri,* Heer. *a,* elytron of the female; *b,*
     elytron of the male.
Fig. 280. *Cybister Agassizi,* Heer.
Fig. 281. *Dineutus longiventris,* Heer.
Fig. 282. *Hydroporus antiquus,* Heer, three times nat. size.

giants among insects; and in size even the tropics do not now
possess any insect species equal to them. As two large *Hydrophili* (*H. Gaudini* and *H. Ruminianus,* Heer) have been discovered
at Monod, these animals must have occupied a prominent place
in the fresh waters of the Swiss Miocene country. The existing

species spin a soft nest out of a gummy material which they secrete, and in this nest they deposit their eggs; their Miocene progenitors probably protected their offspring in a similar fashion. The larvæ of recent species live upon small aquatic Mollusca, whilst the adults prefer a vegetable diet.

The Clavicornia form a very numerous tribe. At Œningen they possess fifty-five species, and occupy the third place. In the present fauna of Switzerland Clavicornia take the third place, the sixth in that of Europe, and the eighth in that of Tropical America. Eight families of them are found at Œningen; and of these the Nitidulidæ, Peltidæ, and Histeridæ include the greatest number of species. Of the last family, twelve species lived in manure, and also partly in carrion, feeding on the larvæ of other insects which frequent those substances. One species (*Hister Mastodontis*, Heer, fig. 276) closely resembles a Southern-European species (*H. major*, Linn.), whilst several others (such as *H. antiquus*, Heer, *H. æmulus*, Heer, and *H. maculigerus*, Heer) represent forms distributed throughout Europe. Their elytra were either entirely black or presented light-coloured spots, which were probably red during life.

Of the numerous Nitidulidæ (nineteen species) several have their nearest allies in America, others in Europe. These insects live sometimes upon the juices flowing from the stems of trees, and sometimes upon flowers, but also occasionally on carrion. The true carrion-beetles (Silphidæ) are rare, and only one species of this family (*Silpha tricostata*, Heer, fig. 275) has been found. This is nearly related to *Silpha carinata*, Heer, and no doubt obtained its nourishment from the bodies of the Mammals which died in the forest of Œningen.

Of Peltidæ ten species are found at Œningen, affording a proof of the abundance of wood at that period. Whilst the genus *Trogosita* is now represented in Switzerland only by two rare species, Œningen possessed eight species, which no doubt lived under the bark of trees. They are chiefly peculiar forms (such as *Trogosita sculpturata*, Heer, fig. 277), which may be best compared with those of southern countries; but one of them (*T. assimilis*, Heer) is nearly allied to a species now spread over nearly all parts of the world (*T. mauritanica*, Linn.). A very remarkable species clothed with rounded scales (*Gymnochila obesa*, Heer) belongs to a South-African genus.

The Cryptophagidæ are very minute beetles, five species of which dwelt in fungi and under the bark of trees. The Scaphididæ, of which two species have been preserved at Œningen, are also minute fungus-eating beetles; while the pill-beetles (Byrrhidæ), five species of which occur, no doubt fed upon the soft mossy cushions of the forests, in the same way as their living congeners.

Of the numerous tribe of Brachelytra, the members of which are so easily recognized by their elongated abdomen, only ten species, belonging to four families, have been preserved at Œningen; and even these are rarely met with. The extremely numerous and difficult family of the Aleocharidæ is represented only by two exceedingly minute *Homalotæ*; that of the Oxytelidæ by an *Oxytelus* (*O. proœvus*, Heer), which probably lived in manure, and a *Bledius* (*B. speciosus*, Heer, fig. 278), which is much larger than any existing species, and differs remarkably from them in form. The Staphylinidæ furnish a *Staphylinus*, a *Lathrobium*, and two *Oxypori*.

Some of the Gyrinidæ (whirligigs) inhabited Switzerland as early as the Liassic epoch (see vol. i. p. 90). Of these water-beetles two Œningian species (fig. 281) are very different from those of the Lias. They belong to a genus (*Dineutus*) which no longer occurs in Europe, but is represented in America by similar forms.

The Dytiscidæ are the most voracious insects of prey of the Miocene fresh waters. Twelve species have been preserved at Œningen; and these differ but little from existing species. One of them, *Dytiscus Lavateri*, Heer (fig. 279), very closely resembles the bordered water-beetle (*D. marginalis*, Linn.), the commonest species of the Swiss waters. The males of the latter have smooth elytra, and the females deeply furrowed elytra, which difference also occurred in Tertiary times (fig. 279, *a*, *b*); and even the yellow border which occupies the margins of the elytra is still retained. The species of *Cybister* differ from those now inhabiting Europe; one of them (*C. Agassizi*, Heer, fig. 280) has its nearest allies in Indian and Mexican species (*C. limbatus*, Fab., and *foveatus*); a second (*C. Nicoleti*, Heer), which has been discovered at Locle and Œningen, is most closely related to a South-African form (*C. costalis*, Oliv.), and a third (*C. atavus*, Heer) to a species which is distributed from Sicily to the Cape of Good Hope (*C. africanus*, Lap.). The genera *Hydaticus*, *Acilius*, *Colymbetes*, and *Hydroporus* (fig. 282) include smaller insects, chiefly representing European forms.

The Carabidæ (Geodephaga) are carnivorous beetles, and are very active predaceous creatures, living in constant warfare with other insects, as well as with Mollusca and worms. At Œningen they occupy the fourth place with fifty-four species, in the existing Swiss fauna the third place, in Europe generally the second, and in North America even the first place, whilst in South America and in India they only come fifth in order. Of the true *Carabi* none have been found fossil; but these insects are now very abundant in the cold and temperate zones, and are among the commonest predaceous beetles of Switzerland. Their representatives in the warm and torrid zones are the nearly allied *Calosomata*. At Œningen five species of *Calosoma* have been found, and two have been obtained from Locle, making in all seven Miocene species.

The *Calosomata* probably took the place of the *Carabi* in Miocene times, as their relatives now do in southern countries. They often live together in troops, and pursue caterpillars on trees, whence they have received the name of caterpillar-hunters. The most abundant species (*Calosoma Nauckianum*, Heer, fig. 283), which also occurs in the lignites of Bonn, is very nearly related to a species distributed over Southern Europe and the Atlantic islands (*C. Maderæ*, Fab.) : this is the case also with a second species, whilst two others (*C. catenulatum*, Heer, and *C. caraboides*, Heer) have as their nearest allies North-American species (*C. Sayi* and *longipenne*, Dej.), and two others, again, are related to South-American forms, and only one (*C. Jaccardi*, Heer, from Locle) can be assimilated to a species of the existing Swiss fauna (*C. inquisitor*, Fab.). Thus during the Miocene epoch Switzerland possessed a number of *Calosomata*, the descendants of which are now scattered over both hemispheres. The genus was already developed into its extreme forms, as one species (*C. Jaccardi*) with its broad and short elytra constitutes a transition towards the Asiatic *Callisthenes*, whilst another (*C.*

caraboides) presents the long narrow elytra of an American species (*C. longipenne*, Dej.), which makes the transition to the
Carabi.

The *Calosomata* no doubt frequented the forests; but two
species of *Nebria*, a small *Brachinus*, an elegant *Cymindis*,
several delicately formed species of *Badister* and *Stenolophus*,
and a minute *Bembidium* most probably lived near the shores
of the lake of Œningen, and concealed themselves under stones
and dead plants. Œningen has furnished seven species of
Amara and fourteen species of *Harpalus*, for the most part
nearly approaching European species, as is shown by the insects
represented in figs. 284 and 285. One species of this group,

Fig. 283.   Fig. 285.   Fig. 284.   Fig. 286.

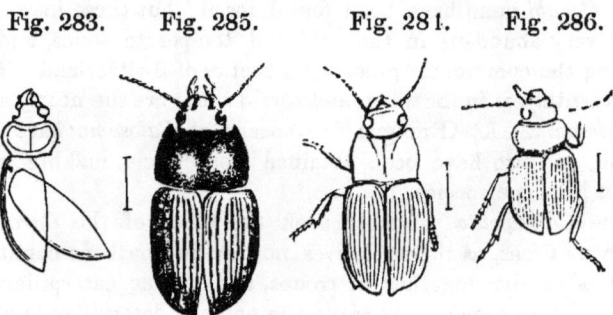

Fig. 283. *Calosoma Nauckianum*, Heer.
Fig. 284. *Harpalus tardigradus*, Heer, four times nat. size.
Fig. 285. *Amara princeps*, Heer, four times nat. size.
Fig. 286. *Sinis brevicollis*, Heer, four times nat. size.

however, constitutes a peculiar extinct genus (*Sinis brevicollis*,
Heer, fig. 286); and another form (*Dichirotrichus*) occurs now
only upon salt marshes.

D. *Hymenoptera.*

The Hymenoptera, from their including the wasps, bees, and
ants, are among the best-known of insects. The care with
which they provide for their young, the marvellous dwellings
which they construct, and the various ways in which they procure their nourishment have always attracted attention.

Many Hymenoptera live upon plants. Of these some saw holes in the leaves and deposit their eggs in them; the eggs produce larvæ resembling caterpillars, which feed upon the leaves; and the insects are consequently called " leaf-wasps " and " saw-flies." Others, called " wood-wasps " and " tailed wasps," bore into trees and provide for their tender offspring in the interior of the stems ; whilst others, with proverbial industry, collect the nectar and pollen of flowers, and with these substances nourish their young, often living together in great societies in most ingeniously constructed dwellings.

But all are not contented thus to seek their food. Many of them live by rapine and murder. Sand-wasps (Sphegidæ) dig holes in the earth, and into these drag their victims to serve as food for their young ; others, such as the Ichneumonidæ, too lazy to make such a provision for their progeny, attack other insects, especially caterpillars and larvæ, pierce them and deposit eggs in their bodies ; and the larvæ developed from these eggs devour their victim whilst still living. The last may be called Entomophaga. All these conditions were realized in Miocene times ; for among the eighty species of Hymenoptera found at Œuingen we may recognize Tenthredinidæ, Entomophaga, Sand-wasps, Ants, and Bees, all of which doubtless followed the same modes of life as their existing descendants.

The Bees furnish fourteen species. A wood-bee (*Xylocopa senilis,* fig. 295) is found which was probably of a fine blue colour, and constructed perpendicular canals in old trunks of trees, in which to provide for its young. Three *Osmiæ,* three species of humble-bees, and five Anthopharites probably made their nests on sunny banks, where they fed their young with honey and pollen. A large humble-bee (*Bombus Jurinei,* Heer) is represented in fig. 296. A honey-bee (*Apis adamitica,* Heer, fig. 287) also, even at that early period, hummed about the flowers, and no doubt lived in large societies, built waxen combs, and collected honey ; for it is so like the living species (*Apis mellifica,* Linn.) that it must probably be regarded as the ancestor of that species.

Of the Wasp family (Vesparia) one species (*Polistes primitiva,* Heer) belongs to a genus the species of which only construct small nests suspended from plants or attached to rocks and stones, without any external covering to conceal the cells. The wings of a true wasp (*Vespa atavina*, Heer, fig. 289), with dark

Fig. 287. Fig. 288. Fig. 289. Fig. 291.

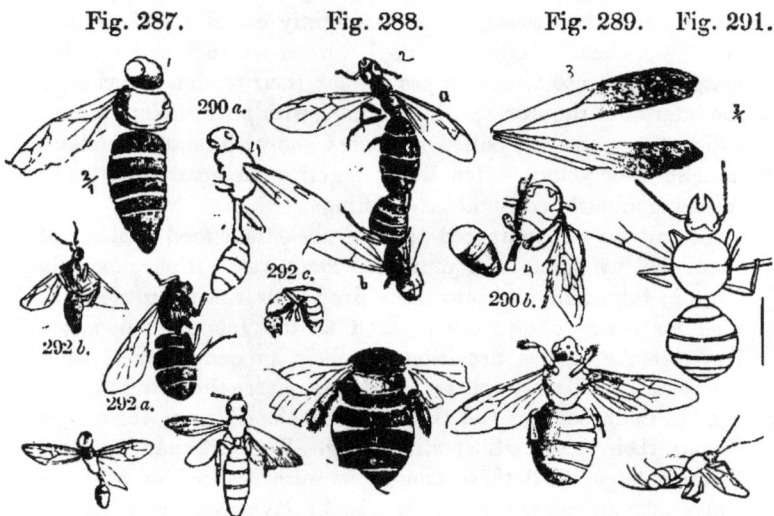

Fig. 293. Fig. 297. Fig. 296. Fig. 295. Fig. 294.

Fig. 287. *Apis adamitica*, Heer, twice nat. size.

Fig. 288. *Ponera veneraria*, Heer, twice nat. size. *a*, female ; *b*, male.

Fig. 289. *Vespa atavina*, Heer, three times nat. size, from Moudon.

Fig. 290, *a*, *b*. *Ammophila inferna*, Heer.

Fig. 291. *Imhoffia pallida*, Heer, enlarged.

Fig. 292. *Formica lignitum*, Germ. *a*, female; *b*, male (*F. heraclea*, Heer, ol.) ; *c*, worker.

Fig. 293. *Myrmica tertiaria*, Heer.

Fig. 294. *Ichneumon infernalis*, Heer.

Fig. 295. *Xylocopa senilis*, Heer.

Fig. 296. *Bombus Jurinei*, Heer.

Fig. 297. *Scolia Saussureana*, Heer.

tips, have been received from the Miocene of Moudon ; so that this type reaches back into Tertiary times.

Of the sand-wasps (Sphegidæ), which display great agility in running and flying about over the sand, and carry off spiders and caterpillars to bury them in their burrows, four species have been found. One of these (*Ammophila annosa*, Heer) resembles the common sand-wasp (*A. sabulosa*, Linn.), which supplies its young with caterpillars; another (*A. inferna*, Heer, fig. 290, *a* & *b*) is much larger, and reminds us of tropical forms. An elegant species of the Scoliidæ (fig. 297) has been preserved at Œningen : these insects now belong to southern regions.

Ants constitute by far the most numerous family of the Hymenoptera at Œningen, where forty-four species have already been discovered. That they lived there, as now, in great societies is shown by the fact that the males and females of certain species are found lying together in great quantities, especially at Radoboj. Evidently the winged insects issued from their nests in great crowds and swarmed into the air, where, being carried over the water, they got drowned, and then became buried in great masses in the mud. Similar swarms of ants may be observed almost every year towards the end of summer; but they are particularly numerous in Switzerland in dry warm seasons; and not unfrequently they fall into a lake in such masses as to cover a great extent of its surface. This sufficiently explains why, both at Œningen and Radoboj, we find almost exclusively winged ants, and that the wingless workers are so extremely rare. Of the species found at Œningen, twenty-one belong to *Formica*, ten to *Ponera*, nine to *Myrmica*, and four to the extinct genus *Imhoffia*. Some of the *Formicæ* are very large insects, considerably larger than the Swiss wood-ant (*Formica herculeana*, Linn.), which lives in old trunks of pines and firs, and in other respects closely resembles a very widely distributed fossil species (*F. lignitum*, Germ., fig. 292). Of this insect the female (fig. 292, *a*) is frequently found; but males (fig. 292, *b*) and workers (fig. 292, *c*), most probably belonging to this species, have also been detected at Œningen. Most of the other ants are small insects, which differ considerably from European forms; and this is still more strikingly the case with the *Poneræ*, which are much larger than the two or three minute European species, but yet cannot be compared with the tropical forms. They probably constitute a peculiar extinct genus. Three species (*Ponera fuliginosa, affinis*, and *elongatula*, Heer) are common to Œningen and Radoboj; so that they must have had a wide area of distribution. A beautifully preserved pair of an elegant species (*Ponera veneraria*, Heer) is represented in fig. 288.

The genus *Myrmica* is represented partly by small species, all of which differ from those now living in Switzerland, and partly by larger forms, resembling those which occur in the south of France and in North Africa. They are characterized by their large wrinkled heads (fig. 293).

The *Imhoffiæ* differ from the other ants in the large size of the thorax and in the structure of the antennæ; in habit they most resemble the *Myrmicæ* and *Attæ*. They constitute a peculiar extinct genus which lived at Œningen (fig. 291) and Radoboj.

Most of these numerous species of ants probably resided in the forests, and constructed their nests in the earth or in the decaying but dry wood of old trunks of trees. They join with the Termites and the numerous wood-eating insects to testify to the existence, at this epoch, of a luxuriant vegetation and abundance of trees, producing an immense quantity of organic material, the transformation of which was their business.

Bees form one tribe of the Hymenoptera; the Wasps, Sand-wasps, Scoliidæ, and Ants a second, that of the Prædonia; and the Entomophaga, which pierce caterpillars and larvæ, constitute a third. To this last tribe twelve species from Œningen are to be referred, among which there is an *Anomalon*, which probably attacked the larvæ of the nocturnal Lepidoptera, a *Cryptus*, and several true Ichneumons (fig. 294), which most likely laid their eggs in caterpillars.

Of the family Chalcididæ, represented in the present day by an immense multitude of minute species, some of which pass their young existence in the eggs of butterflies, one species (*Pteromalinites œningensis*, Heer) is known from Œningen.

The tribe Phytophaga, to which the saw-flies (Tenthredinidæ) belong, is poorly represented, the extant remains of its three species being very incomplete and scarce.

E. *The Rhynchota* (*Hemiptera*).

Next to the Beetles this order is the richest in species in the Miocene of Switzerland. From Œningen 132 species have been procured. The late M. Bremi during many years collected the living insects about Dübendorf (a village of the Canton of Zurich) and obtained 389 species of Rhynchota, while in the whole of Europe about 1100 species are known; consequently Œningen possesses one third of the number of species of Dübendorf, and about one eighth of those of the whole of Europe, although the insects at Œningen have been congregated together in a fortuitous manner. Except the lice and cochineal-insects, all the tribes of the recent Rhynchota are represented among the fossils. No doubt lice were not wanting; for the calling-hares, civets, deer, and elephants which lived about the Lake of Œningen cannot have been free from such parasites. Nevertheless they have not yet been detected, and probably will hardly be found in a fossil state.

Of the plant-lice there are three species. Two of these most likely lived upon leaves, as they are true *Aphides*, whilst the third (*Pemphigus bursifex*, Heer) produced round galls on the petioles of the poplars. The animal itself has not yet been obtained; but a dozen leaves have been found with galls exactly like those produced by the poplar-aphis (*Pemphigus bursarius*, Linn.) on the petioles of the Swiss poplars.

The great majority of the fossil Rhynchota are land-bugs (Geocores), as is the case also at the present day. They are, in general, very well preserved; and it is remarkable that in many specimens the colours may still be recognized. In numerous species the segments of the abdomen are adorned with elegant black spots and other markings; and similar ornaments are retained in some cases even on the elytra.

Of the eight families into which the Geocores are divided, six are represented at Œningen: the Scutati have 45 species, the Coreodes 18, the Lygæodes 23, the Membranacei 2, the Reduviini 17, the Capsini 2, and the Hydrodromici 1 species. Any one acquainted with the Hemiptera will perceive that in these numerical proportions the Hemipterous fauna of Œningen differs greatly from that now existing in Switzerland, and approaches rather that of subtropical countries. At the present day the Capsini (with 131 species) constitute by far the most numerous family both in Switzerland and in Europe gene-

rally; and even in America they occur in a great variety of forms
as far south as the southern United States, beyond which, however, they entirely disappear towards the tropics. The Riparii
belong exclusively to the temperate and cold zones, and it is
noteworthy that at Œningen they are entirely deficient; and of
the Capsini only two rare species (*Phytocoris*?) have been discovered. On the other hand, the nocturnal Reduviini are represented by numerous species between the tropics, whilst they become rare even in the temperate zones. Bremi collected eight
species at Dübendorf; and the whole of Switzerland only furnishes fourteen species, whereas seventeen species have been
obtained from Œningen.

Œningen possesses more species of Scutati than can now be
shown by any single locality in Switzerland (Dübendorf has only
twenty-three). The Coreodes are also very rich in species. All
these are families the species of which abound in warm countries,
and they give the Swiss Miocene fauna a southern or subtropical
character.

Among the Scutati there are four handsome species of *Pachycoris* (fig. 298), which have the thorax and the large scutellum
marked with light-coloured spots (probably red during life).
These are nearly allied to West-Indian species, which are adorned
with brilliant green, blue, and red colours.

The group Pentatomidæ includes a number of European forms.
Two species of *Eusarcoris* can be recognized, resembling a species which occurs under stones and on low bushes, especially
about the borders of woods; also several small species of *Eury-
dema* are found, like the beautifully spotted forms (*E. picta* and
festiva) which are often met with on flowers (especially of Umbelliferæ) in Central and Southern Europe. A *Cydnus* has been
discovered which comes very near the widely distributed black
C. tristis; and an *Acanthosoma* allied to that remarkable tree-
bug which leads its young about as a hen does her chickens.
Of the genus *Pentatomus* there are thirteen species found at
Œningen, some of them of considerable size (fig. 309); and they
differ greatly from the European species. Two species also occur
at Locle. The genus *Halys* (fig. 299) exhibits American forms;
and the genus *Cydnopsis* is an extinct type, represented at
Œningen by eleven species, three of which have been detected at

Radoboj in Croatia. The species (*Cydnopsis tertiaria*, Heer, fig. 300) is one of the most abundant of the Miocene Hemiptera.

Fig. 298. Fig. 299.   Fig. 303.   Fig. 304.

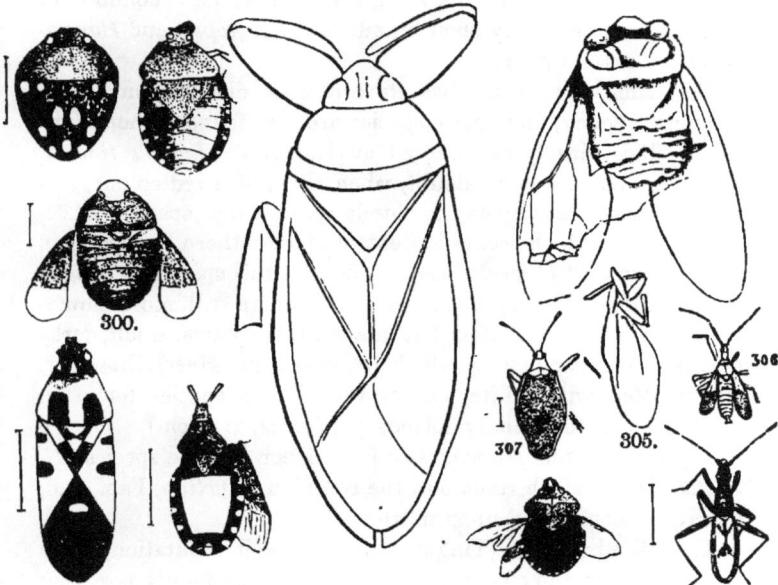

Fig. 301.   Fig. 302.   Fig. 309.   Fig. 308.

Fig. 298. *Pachycoris Burmeisteri*, Heer, twice nat. size.
Fig. 299. *Halys spectabilis*, Heer.
Fig. 300. *Cydnopsis tertiaria*, Heer, thrice nat. size.
Fig. 301. *Lygæus tinctus*, Heer, thrice nat. size.
Fig. 302. *Syromastes coloratus*, Heer, twice nat. size.
Fig. 303. *Belostoma speciosum*, Heer.
Fig. 304. *Cicada Emathion*, Heer.
Fig. 305. *Cercopis Germari*, Heer.
Fig. 306. *Harpactor maculipes*, Heer.
Fig. 307. *Tingis Wollastoni*, Heer.
Fig. 308. *Nabis gracillima*, Heer, twice nat. size.
Fig. 309. *Pentatoma pictum*, Heer.

To the family Coreodes belong several beautiful species. The genera *Hypselonotus* and *Alydus* include South-American types, and one species of *Syromastes* (*S. Seyfriedi*, Heer) represents an exotic form, while the others correspond to European species. *Syromastes coloratus*, Heer (fig. 302), is not uncommon at Œningen, and all specimens of it show the black-spotted abdomen, like that of *S. scapha*, Fab., a species which is common in thickets, and especially upon brambles. *Berytopsis* and *Harmostites* are extinct genera.

The family Lygæodes has its centre of distribution in the temperate zones; but many species are also found in hot countries. It is largely represented at Œningen. *Lygæus tinctus*, Heer (fig. 301), was, no doubt, when alive, of a red colour, and adorned with black spots; it closely resembles a species (*L. venustus*, Bœb.) which occurs in Central and Southern Europe upon the swallowwort (*Vincetoxicum*). Besides this species, Œningen possessed four *Lygæi*; but the *Pachymeri* are still more numerous. Of these, Prof. Heer has met with six species, small, dark-coloured insects, one of which (*P. cruciatus*, Heer), however, was spotted with white, and is very like a species found in Madeira and the Canary Islands (*P. luscus*, H.-Sch.). Of the nearly allied genus *Heterogaster* Prof. Heer has one species (*H. tristis*, Heer), which resembles the common *H. urticæ*, Fab., and, like it, probably lived upon nettles.

The Membranaciæ (Tingidæ) have an evil reputation, from their including the common bed-bug; but the family possesses many elegant little insects, two species of which occur at Œningen. One of them (*Monanthia Wollastoni*, Heer, fig. 307) is beautifully preserved; even the colour of the antennæ and the fine network of the wings are recognizable. Its nearest living relative is a species (*M. convergens*, Klug) which lives on the forget-me-not.

The Reduviini constitute a remarkable family. They are long-legged and exceedingly active predaceous insects, which chase other insects at night, and pierce them with their sharp beaks. Œningen has furnished more species than are now known in the whole of Switzerland; and among the fossil forms Prof. Heer has found the exotic genera *Evagoras* and *Stenopoda*. The richest genus is *Harpactor*, which includes seven species, some of them with very finely annulated tibiæ (fig. 306). The species of *Pirates* and *Prostemma* are elegant insects, which cannot be compared with any belonging to the existing fauna. The genus *Nabis*, however, presents an indigenous form (fig. 308), several species of which were distributed over the Miocene land.

The Hydrometræ (Hydrodromici) form a small family of thin-legged insects, which live on the banks of ponds and lakes in the reeds and sedges, and run with great agility upon the surface of the water. From Œningen Prof. Heer has a species (*Limnobates prodromus*, Heer) which may be regarded as the precursor of *L. stagnorum*, Linn., a species which is often seen in Switzerland.

The tribe Hydrocoræ (water-bugs) is represented at Œningen by the families of the Nepinæ (water-scorpions) and Notonectæ (boat-flies). The former includes five, and the latter a single species. The latter is a *Corisa* resembling an American species. Of the Nepinæ there are forms of *Nepa* and *Naucoris* such as occur in the Swiss fresh waters; but side by side with these are found the tropical and subtropical genera *Belostoma* and *Diplonychus*. The latter is represented only by one species (*Diplonychus rotundatus*, Heer), which has its nearest relative in India; the former by a truly gigantic insect (*Belostoma speciosum*, Heer, fig. 303), rivalling in size the largest of the tropical Rhynchota, the great *Belostoma* of Brazil, and so closely approaching it even in appearance that the Miocene species may be regarded as probably the ancestor of the Brazilian insect. A similar species has also been discovered in the lignite of Bonn, so that the type now found in America was formerly in all probability diffused over the whole of Europe. The *Belostomæ* are rapacious animals, the females of which carry their eggs about with them. Œningen has become remarkable for producing gigantic forms, not only among the water-beetles, but also among the water-bugs.

The Cicadinæ have quite a different appearance both from the land and the aquatic bugs; they are harmless and generally small insects, which are distributed in great numbers over all countries, and live exclusively upon the juices of plants. They are divided into four families, all of which existed in Tertiary times. Of the singing *Cicadæ* a large species (*Cicada Emathion*, Heer, fig. 304) occurs at Œningen. It closely resembles the *Cicada* of the ash (*Cicada Orni*, Linn.), which is common all over the south of Europe, occurring even in the Valteline, on the lake of Como, in Ticino, and in the Valais, and found upon the trees, where it fills the air with its monotonous chirping. Regarded from ancient times as the heralds of summer, and as symbols of the peacefulness of nature, the *Cicadæ* are among the best-known insects of southern countries. In Tertiary times the *Cicadæ* enlivened Swiss forests with their joyous choral chants; afterwards they departed for a warmer region.

Of the Fulgorinæ (lantern-flies and allied forms) one species (*Pseudophana amatoria,* Heer) dwelt in the forests of Œningen, and lived most probably upon oak trees; at least, its nearest living relative (*P. europæa,* Fab.) is met with upon oaks. Of the Membracinæ only one species is known at Œningen.

Cicadellinæ form the most numerous family, thirteen species of which occur at Œningen. Some of them are very small insects, resembling the green, yellow, and brown froghoppers which are so abundant in the grass, and which, as larvæ, produce what is called " cuckoo-spit " on herbaceous plants and shrubs. Others are larger party-coloured creatures, the representatives of which live sometimes in warm countries (as in the case of *Cercopis Germari,* Heer, fig. 305), and are also found in Switzerland (as *Cerc. Herrichi* and *Hageni,* Heer). An extinct genus (*Ledophora*) most resembles a *Ledra* from Madagascar.

F. *Diptera.*

As regards number of species, the Diptera are now the fourth order of insects; and they occupy the same position in the Miocene fauna. They are divided into two great suborders—the *Nemocera,* or those with antennæ composed of numerous joints, and the *Brachycera,* which have very short antennæ, containing from one to three joints. At the present day the Nemocera constitute about one seventh, and the Brachycera six sevenths, of the whole; but formerly the proportion was very different. The Nemocera, or midge-like flies, first made their appearance; and the Brachycera followed them. In Œningen the latter, with twelve species, form about one fifth, and the *Nemocera,* with fifty-one species, form about four fifths of the species; and the proportions are similar in other countries where fossil dipterous insects have been found. Of these two suborders of insects the Brachycera live principally upon flowers, especially

those of herbaceous plants, and whole swarms of them may be
seen sunning themselves upon the flowers of Umbelliferous and
Composite plants; whilst the Nemocera frequent woods and
copses, and particularly favour damp watery regions. Their
larvæ live sometimes in water, sometimes in the humid soil of
woods and forests, or in rotten wood; and a great number of
them live in fleshy fungi. Widely spread damp forest-land,
traversed by small streams and interspersed with morasses,
furnishes the chief conditions for the luxuriant development of
the Nemocera; and these favourable conditions existed in abundance during the Miocene epoch. Of the species obtained from
Œningen, from the analogy of allied living insects, the larvæ of
five lived in water, of fifteen in fungi, and of thirty in moist
ground and rotten wood.

The feather-midges (Chironomi) appear in spring in countless
swarms on the shores of the Swiss lakes, and are distinguished
by their elegantly feathered antennæ; they lay their eggs in
the water, in which they pass the whole of their young states.
Of these insects there are preserved at Œningen both the aquatic
pupæ and the active aerial forms. Of one species (Chironomus
Gaudini, Heer, fig. 316) the pupæ are abundant, and several of
them are generally found near each other. These pupæ occur
on two slabs from Œningen, side by side with the winter eggs
of the Daphniæ.

The Mycetophilidæ (fungus-midges) are very delicate little
creatures, the white maggots of which are often met with in
great numbers in fleshy fungi. At Œningen there are two
genera, Mycetophila (with nine species) and Sciara (with six
species); and the specimens (small and extremely tender) are, for
the most part, beautifully preserved, as may be seen from figs.
317, 318, and 319.

Of the little gall-midges (Cecidomyidæ), which cause gall-like
swellings on leaves, no perfect insects have come to the knowledge of Prof. Heer. On poplar-leaves from Œningen there is
a formation of galls (fig. 322) exactly agreeing with that produced by the Cecidomyia salicis of the willow, and thus leaving
no doubt that in Miocene times such flies were already in existence.

Of the long-legged crane-flies (Tipulidæ) there are two species from Œningen and one from Locle (fig. 320).

Fig. 311.　　　　　　Fig. 310.　　　　　　Fig. 312.

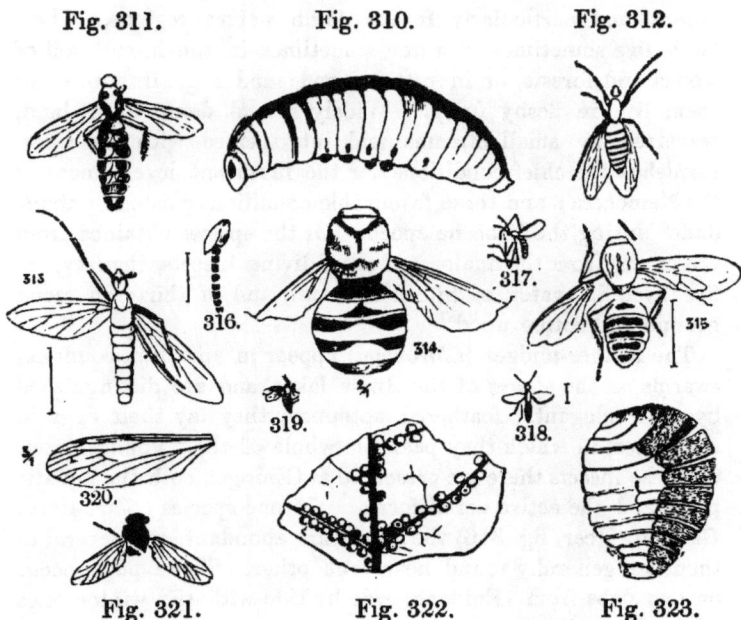

Fig. 321.　　　　　　Fig. 322.　　　　　　Fig. 323.

Fig. 310. *Bombycites Buchii,* Heer.
Fig. 311. *Bibio elongatus,* Heer.
Fig. 312. *Protomyia speciosa,* Heer.
Fig. 313. *Plecia hilaris,* Heer, twice nat. size.
Fig. 314. *Syrphus Bremii,* Heer, twice nat. size.
Fig. 315. *Syrphus Schellenbergi,* Heer, twice nat. size.
Fig. 316. *Chironomus Gaudini,* Heer, twice nat. size.
Fig. 317. *Mycetophila Orci,* Heer.
Fig. 318. *Mycetophaga pusillima,* Heer, twice nat. size.
Fig. 319. *Sciara deleta,* Heer.
Fig. 320. *Limnobia Jaccardi,* Heer, three times nat. size.
Fig. 321. *Hexatoma* (?) *œningensis,* Heer.
Fig. 322. *Cecidomyia Bremii,* galls on a poplar-leaf.
Fig. 323. *Dipterites obovatus,* Heer.

The Bibionidæ constitute one of the most numerous and important families, including the greater part of the Tertiary

Dipterous fauna. The twenty-eight species from Œningen belong to five genera, three of which (*Bibiopsis, Protomyia,* and *Myidium*) are extinct. *Protomyia speciosa,* Heer, represented in fig. 312, is one of the largest species of the genus, which is represented in Œningen by nine species. Three of them have been collected in Croatia, indicating the wide distribution of the genus in Tertiary times. Still more abundant were the true *Bibiones,* sixteen species of which occur at Œningen, some of them being black, others of a light colour with dark spots. Their larvæ probably lived in rotten wood and in the rich vegetable mould of the forests. They are flies of considerable size, distinguished by their generally broad wings, their short antennæ (which consist of from eight to twelve joints), and their thickened fore legs. Some species resemble European and North-American forms (thus *B. mœstus,* Heer, is like *B. pomonæ,* Linn.), whilst others represent peculiar and apparently extinct types (such as *B. elongatus,* Heer, fig. 311). Whilst the genus *Bibio* is at present widely distributed, having eighteen species in Europe and eleven in America, *Plecia* is confined to South America and the Cape of Good Hope. Œningen possesses a very fine species of this genus (*Plecia hilaris,* Heer, fig. 313) with a light-brown body.

Brachycera are very scantily represented in the Miocene fossil fauna. Nevertheless they form four tribes and five families, but in each case have only a few species. The Xylophagidæ furnish two uncertain species. Of the Asilidæ there are three species. Two of these belong to the genus *Asilus,* flies which lie in wait for other insects, spring upon them after the manner of a cat, and, embracing them with their hairy legs, pierce them with their proboscis. The Tabanidæ (breeze-flies) are represented by a single species (*Hexatoma œningensis,* Heer, fig. 321), and the Syrphidæ (drone-flies) by two, which, like the living forms, are distinguished by their elegantly banded abdomen (figs. 314 and 315).

The true flies furnish an *Echinomyia* (*E. antiqua,* Heer), the larvæ of which probably lived (like those of *E. echinata,* Meig.) as parasites upon caterpillars. There are also a small *Anthomyia,* and two flies with spotted wings allied to *Psila.*

The larva represented in fig. 323 probably belonged to some

remarkably large fly. It is destitute of feet, and has a very
small head, three distinct thoracic, and nine abdominal segments,
on the dorsal surface of which are fine undulating striæ.

G. *Lepidoptera*.

The Lepidoptera are seldom met with at Œningen; and as all
the other localities for fossil insects have furnished very few
species, the Lepidopterous order of insects must have been very
scarce in the primæval world. It is probably the youngest order
of insects; but in the present fauna it has been so largely developed that it has become one of the richest in species. From
Œningen there are traces of only three species, belonging to the
Nocturna. Of one species (*Psyche pineella*, Heer) the larva-sac
has been found, which was made of the leaves of pines; of a
second (*Bombycites œningensis*, Heer) only fragments of the
wings and body have remained to the present time; and of the
third (*Bombycites Buchii*, Heer, fig. 310) there is a pretty well-
preserved caterpillar*.

3. VERTEBRATA.

a. *Fishes*.

Important information may be derived from the distribution
of fossil fishes with reference to the communications of ancient
basins of water, as the investigation of the fish-fauna of the different river-regions of the present day shows that each course
of water possesses a number of peculiar species. Thus the
salmon and the eel are found in all rivers which are connected
with the North Sea, the Baltic, the Atlantic, and the Mediterranean, whilst they do not occur in the rivers and lakes which
flow into the Black Sea. The salmon-trout, the shad, the

* As yet, only one specimen has been found. It is preserved in the collection at Zurich, and the counterpart in that at Winterthur. It is much
crushed, and the boundaries of the segments are difficult to distinguish. The
head is small; the thorax enlarges rapidly; the thoracic feet are not preserved; the abdominal feet are in part indicated as black tubercles. Of the
stigmata four may be recognized. Similar caterpillars occur among the
Bombycidæ and Pseudo-Bombyces (Arctiidæ).

houting (*Coregonus oxyrhynchus,* Linn.), belonging to the Sal-
monidæ, and the sea-lamprey exist in the vine-region of the
Rhine, but are wanting in that of the Danube; while the latter
possesses here and there the zingel (*Aspro zingel*), the streber
(*Aspro vulgaris*), and several species of sturgeon, which are
wanting in the Rhine.

It is not possible, at present, to ascertain the Miocene river-
regions of Switzerland. In many places a few remains (chiefly
scales and ribs) have been found; but Œningen alone has furnished numerous specimens capable of determination. These
are frequently still furnished with their scaly covering, and are
sometimes wonderfully well preserved. They occur both in the
upper and the lower quarry of Œningen, but are restricted to
particular beds. Up to the present time thirty-two species have
been described[*], belonging to fifteen genera. Of these genera
only one, allied to the Carps, but distinguished by its rounded
caudal fin (*Cyclurus*), is extinct; all the others are still met with
living in fresh waters. The fish-fauna of Œningen therefore
differs entirely from that of Matt. Not only are the fishes of
Matt of marine origin, whilst those of Œningen belong to fresh
water, but the Œningen fishes approximate more closely to those
now living. While only half of the Eocene fishes of Matt belong to genera of the present, $\frac{31}{32}$ of the Œningian species can
be referred to existing genera.

Of the fifteen genera at Œningen, twelve (with twenty-five
species) are still to be found in the fresh waters of Switzerland.
In the Miocene age a great pike was the king of freshwater
fishes, large-scaled roaches (*Leucisci*), like *L. argenteus* and *L.
nasus,* and perches sported in the tranquil Lake of Œningen;
loaches and tenches in great numbers buried themselves in the
mud, and bull-heads (*Cottus*) and eels were not wanting.
Several of these species are very nearly allied to existing Swiss
species (such as the pike, and some of the loaches, and *Leucisci*),
whilst others are related to species of distant countries. Thus
the Miocene perch (*Perca lepidota,* Ag.) differs considerably
from the common Swiss perch, and most nearly resembles, according to Agassiz, the species of India and New Zealand. It

---

[*] See Agassiz, 'Recherches sur les Poissons fossiles,' v. p. 78; and Winkler, 'Description des Poissons fossiles d'Œningen' (Harlem, 1861).

must be remarked, in general, that of the twelve genera which
Œningen has in common with the existing fauna, only one, the
Cottus, belongs exclusively to the temperate and cold regions,
all the rest occurring also in Mediterranean countries or even
in tropical and subtropical zones.   The genera *Perca, Acanthopsis, Cobitis, Gobio, Leuciscus,* and *Aspius* are also represented
in Indian rivers; and eels are found in Madeira and Teneriffe.
To this must be added that the fish-fauna of Œningen contains
a number of species usually belonging to genera in warmer lands.
The genus *Lebias,* represented by four small species, now inhabits Italy, the East, and America; *Pœcilia* occurs only in the
swamps of Carolina and South America; and *Cyclurus* is extinct.
Thus side by side with those genera which still occur in Switzerland, but the greater part of which extend their range into
warm and even torrid zones, other fishes are found which now
exclusively belong to hot countries.

Œningen does not possess many of the commonest Swiss
forms of fishes.   Although the fishes of Œningen have been
collected most carefully for the last hundred years, no species
have been found there which can be regarded as nearly allied to
the trout, salmon, eel, barbot, carp*, barbel, grayling, and
bream of the present day.   Some of these forms are deficient in
more southern countries, or they prefer clear fresh water, like
the trout, grayling, and barbot (*Lota*).   The Lake of Œningen
probably had turbid water and a muddy bottom.   This is proved
by the occurrence of tenches and loaches, and of species of
Pœcilia and *Lebias,* the relatives of which now live in muddy
waters.

A large-headed loach (*Cobitis cephalotes,* Ag.) is very like
Cobitis fossilis, Linn., which often buries itself deeply in the
mud; and tenches, of which Œningen possessed three species,
have a similar habit; the species of *Lebias* live in shoals in the

---

* In the older collections, fishes from Œningen have been often labelled
as "carp" or "trout;" but these are all artificially constructed animals to
which the form of those fishes has been given.   The monks of the old Con-
vent at Œningen appear to have been very clever in the fabrication of such
fishes, and they have since had their imitators.   The plants and insects of
the older collections are also frequently fabricated, and consequently worth-
less.   They are usually coated with a brown colour prepared from unripe
walnut-shells.

waters of swamps, in which the *Pœciliæ* also dwell. It is said that the latter, when food is scarce, throw themselves out of the water and leap along the grass to reach another marshy locality. As all the specimens of the Œningian *Pœcilia* (*P. œningensis,* Wklr.) have the head strongly bent back, in the manner of fishes when about to spring, Dr. Winkler believes that we may ascribe to them the same propensity to leaping. They may therefore probably have made a final effort to leap out of the marsh as it was drying up, when they were overtaken by death and enveloped in the mud.

The muddy nature of the Lake of Œningen is proved by its large frogs and salamanders, as well as by the numerous aquatic insects and the pondweeds. On the other hand, the gudgeons (*Gobio*) and minnows (*Rhodeus*), which spawn in clear river-water, show that Œningen must have had a clear stream. Their spawn may have been deposited either in the river which flowed into the lake, or in that which carried off its waters towards the sea. Eels and salmon are not uncommon in Switzerland; but they do not occur in the lake of Constance, as these fishes mount from the sea up the inland waters, and cannot ascend beyond the falls of the Rhine. In Œningian times there cannot have been any such obstacle between the Lake of Œningen and the sea, as two species of eels have been found at Œningen.

The fishes of Œningen belong to six families. The richest in species is that of the carps (Cyprinoidei), which includes twenty-one species. Five of these belong to the genus *Leuciscus,* which is composed of middle-sized fishes with a spindle-shaped body clothed with large scales and terminating in a forked caudal fin. Three of the species (*Leuciscus œningensis,* Ag., *L. helveticus,* Winkl., and *L. latiusculus,* Ag.) are the commonest fishes at Œningen, but they are confined to the upper quarry. This genus was already widely diffused in Miocene times, and it is at present to be met with in the rivers and lakes of all parts of the world.

The Loaches (*Cobitis*) are small cylindrical fishes, of which Œningen possessed four species; the stone-loaches (*Acanthopsis*) are very similar to them, being remarkably long and narrow fishes with small fins (*A. angustus,* Ag.). Of the minnows only one species (*Rhodeus amarus*) occurs in Central Europe, whilst Œningen had four species. They are small fishes with large heads and short broad caudal fins.

Next to the pikes, the tenches are the largest fishes of Œningen. They are characterized by their stout form of body, small scales, and short broad fins. Only one living species is known, and this belongs exclusively to Europe; Œningen, however, possessed three species, one of which (*Tinca magna*, Winkl.) attained a length of more than a foot.

The family of the Cyprinodontes is not represented on the northern side of the Alps. It consists of small fishes belonging to the warm and torrid zones, five species of which inhabited the Lake of Œningen. The principal genus is *Lebias*, the four species of which are, next to the *Leucisci*, most frequently met with at Œningen. They occur, however, only in the insect-bed in the lower quarry, where several specimens often lie close together; these fishes therefore, like their congeners, probably lived together in shoals. The little *Pœciliæ*, distinguished by having a rounded caudal fin and the dorsal and ventral fins placed very far back, are much less common.

The two species of pike found at Œningen are very like the common pike, which is distributed all over Europe, Asia, and North America; but they have much larger scales. The most abundant species (*Esox lepidotus*, Ag.) has a somewhat broader body and longer head, but it attained the same size. Specimens of all sizes, from 6 inches to 3 feet long, have been found. The second species (*E. robustus*, Winkl.) is shorter and thicker, and had smaller fins; it would therefore be a more clumsy fish. That these pikes followed the same predaceous mode of life as the existing species, is proved by some of the specimens, in the abdominal region of which there lie the skeletons of smaller fishes which they had swallowed. In the case of an eel (*Anguilla elegans*, Winkl.), which had swallowed a small *Leuciscus* (*L. œningensis*), the skeleton remained within the eel. The heads of these swallowed fishes are always directed backward, proving that they were seized in front. Eels were common in the Tertiary period; six species are known from Monte Bolca, one from Aix, and two from Œningen, all of which differ considerably from the single European species.

Œningen possessed one species of bull-head (*Cottus brevis,* Ag.), which possessed a still smaller and thinner body than the species now common in the brooks and lakes of Europe.

The perch of Œningen (*Perca lepidota,* Ag.) differs essentially from the common Swiss perch in having only nine instead of twelve to fifteen spines in its dorsal fin. This species has been found in the Miocene of the Gurnigel, which is the only example of an Œningian species of fish being found in any other locality in Switzerland.

b. *Reptiles*.*

The Reptilian fauna of the Swiss Miocene differs greatly from that of the present day. It was certainly much richer in species; and the species were otherwise distributed in various families, as the following Table will show :—

Types.	In the existing Swiss Fauna.	In the Swiss Miocene.	At Œningen.
Salamanders'............	6	3	3
Frogs and Toads	8	4	4
Lizards	5	1	—
Crocodiles........	—	3	—
Serpents	7	3	3
Tortoises	1	18	3
	27	32	13

Forms corresponding to the small salamanders and to the Swiss frogs are wanting; but toads are met with which it is

---

* The species from Œningen have been studied by H. von Meyer in his 'Fossile Säugethiere, Vögel und Reptilien von Œningen' (Frankfort, 1845), and by Winkler, 'Tortues fossiles' (Harlem, 1869). The tortoises of Switzerland have been described by Pictet and Humbert in their 'Monographie des Chéloniens de la Mollasse Suisse' (Geneva, 1858), and those of Winterthur by Dr. Biedermann in his 'Petrefacten der Umgegend von Winterthur,' Heft 1 (Winterthur, 1862).

difficult to distinguish from the Swiss bombinators and natter-
jacks, and snakes are found which are very nearly allied to
the Swiss species. Prof. Heer also finds an enormous salamander, a gigantic frog, several crocodiles, and a surprising
abundance of tortoises, which give the fauna a very hetero-
geneous character.

The gigantic salamander* (*Andrias Scheuchzeri*, Holl., sp.) is
one of the most celebrated fossils of the Miocene region. It
was first discovered in Œningen 138 years ago, and regarded by
Scheuchzer as "a skeleton of a man drowned in the Deluge," an
error for which we must not be too hard upon him, considering
the bad preservation of the specimen which he possessed and the
very imperfect knowledge which prevailed in his time of the
anatomical structure of man and animals. Numerous specimens,
much better preserved, have since been discovered. A very perfect specimen is represented, little more than one fourth of the
natural size, in Pl. XI. fig. 1†. This is one of the smallest and
probably youngest salamandroid animals which has hitherto been
found at Œningen; and only a few bones are deficient in its skeleton. Its total length is 0·63 metre (about 2 English feet);
the head is 0·077 metre (or 3 inches) in length, by 0·086 metre
(or 3¼ inches) in breadth; the vertebral column is 0·310 metre
(or 1 foot) long, and the tail 0·241 metre (or about 9 inches)
in length. A glance at the figure shows that the animal had a
short broad head, very obtusely rounded in front, with the jaws

---

* Scheuchzer described the species as "a man witness of the Deluge."
Gessner, however, had previously recognized that this fossil was not that of
a man; but he referred it to a fish (*Silurus*). P. Camper (1700) referred it to
its proper place among the Reptilia; and Cuvier was the first to prove scientifically its position and its relationship to the salamanders, describing the
species as a gigantic salamander. Dr. J. Tschudi raised it to the rank of a
distinct genus (*Andrias*), which was accepted by Hermann von Meyer in his
admirable work on the Vertebrata of Œningen, and the species was cited as
Andrias Scheuchzeri, Tschudi. Van der Hoeven has shown that this species
is to be united in the same genus with the Japanese form. The American
species upon which Harlan founded the genus *Menopoma* (*Cryptobranchus*,
Leuck.) are also scarcely separable from it. The latter are distinguished by
a persistent branchial aperture behind the head, whilst in the Japanese species this disappears. Their skeletons cannot be distinguished.

† This recently discovered specimen is one of the ornaments of the collection of the Polytechnicum at Zurich.

armed with one row of small teeth. The orbits are large, and extend far forwards. The vertebral column is composed of biconcave vertebræ, each of which possesses a lateral process. The ribs, which are separated from the vertebræ, are short, and become thinner towards the extremities. Near the fifth vertebra are the fore limbs, in which are recognized the hatchet-shaped shoulder-blade, the rather stout humerus, 0·032 metre (or 1¼ inch) in length, the two parallel bones of the forearm, somewhat unequal in length, and the expanded hand, consisting of four digits which are rather longer than the forearm. Three of these digits are two-jointed (deducting the carpal bones) ; but one has three joints, which, however, are not equally well preserved in both limbs. The hind limbs are probably attached to the twenty-first vertebra; but this cannot be ascertained with certainty, as the pelvic bones are, for the most part, destroyed. These members show the same structure as the fore limbs ; but the toes have been displaced. From other specimens it is known that the hind feet had five toes, three of which were two-jointed, and two three-jointed. The tail is remarkable for its length and strength ; nineteen vertebræ may be counted in it; and to these must be added a partially destroyed vertebra which was close to the pelvis, and two small bones at the extremity of the tail, so that the whole number is probably twenty-two, or nearly as many as in the living species, which is said to have twenty-four. The first caudal vertebræ are remarkably stout ; and all are furnished with lateral processes.

A second very fine specimen, in the collection at Zurich, is twice as large in all its parts. The head is 0·175 metre (or nearly 7 inches) broad at the base, the first vertebra is 0·018 metre (or 0·701 inch) long, the fourth to the sixth 0·022 metre (or 0·866 inch) long, and the seventh to the twelfth 0·027 metre (or 1·063 inch) in length. The vertebræ are attenuated in the middle, and have a rather sharp median ridge. This animal must have been 1·260 metre in length (or 4 feet 1·607 inch). The Museum at Winterthur has received a still larger specimen; and the Cabinet of Natural History at Carlsruhe possesses one 4 feet long. These are the largest salamandroid animals which ever inhabited the earth. The nearest living species occur in Japan and in North America. The Japanese species (*Andrias japonicus*, Temm., sp., Pl. XI. fig. 2) agrees almost completely in the structure of the skeleton with that from Œningen, and must therefore be regarded as its homologous species. The only characters by which the Œningian species can be distinguished are that the head of the fossil is comparatively rather shorter and broader, whilst in the living species the head is a little longer than broad, and the toes of the Miocene reptile are comparatively somewhat longer. The American species are also very nearly allied to the Œningian reptile, and they agree with it in the broader and shorter form of the head; but, according to Hermann von Meyer, the fossil agrees better in size, and in the different parts of the skull, with the Japanese species. The latter attains a length of 3 feet, and lives in the brooks and lakes of Southern Japan (between 34° and 36° N. lat.), at an elevation of from 4000 to 5000 feet above the sea-level. It is an ugly creature, with small eyes and a blackish brown folded and warty skin. In the Zoological Gardens of London and of Amsterdam, where Prof. Heer has seen this animal, it lies almost immovable throughout the day; but during the night it is said sometimes to quit the water and to go in search of its food, which consists of small fishes, frogs, and worms. Of the two American species, one (*Menopoma giganteum*, Bart., sp.), which attains a length of 2 feet, is principally an inhabitant of the northern United States, whilst the other (*M. fuscum*, Holb., sp.) is found in South Carolina.

This type of animals is now altogether wanting in Europe; but in Miocene times it was represented by two species, one of which has just been described; and the other (*Andrias Tschudii*, Von Meyer) is nearly allied to the Œningian animal, but smaller, being only about 1½ foot in length; it was discovered in the lignite deposits of Bonn. By its longer, narrower head and rather shorter limbs, this species approaches more closely than the Œningian to the Japanese form; and its skeleton is scarcely distinguishable *.

* According to H. von Meyer (Palæontographica, vii. p. 53) the hind limbs are appended to the 22nd vertebra, whilst in the Japanese species they are attached to the 21st; but this is not of much importance. In the specimen examined by Dr. Schmidt, Goddart, and J. van der Hoeven the pelvic bones are united on the right side to the 21st, and on the left side to the 22nd vertebra (see ' Natuurkundige Verhandelingen, Harlem,' 1862, p. 59).

These animals are more nearly related to the Proteiform Batrachia than to the little salamanders of the present day. This applies also to two footless animals from Œningen, which H. von Meyer has described under the name of *Orthophyia*. These, however, are perhaps the larvæ (tadpoles) of the *Andrias*, in which, probably, the feet were wanting.

A worthy counterpart of the gigantic salamander of Œningen is the gigantic frog (*Latonia Seyfriedi*, Meyer). It is so nearly allied to the horned frog (*Ceratophrys cornuta*) of Brazil that its establishment as a distinct genus is probably erroneous. It is, however, distinguished from the Brazilian species by its smaller head, longer and narrower pelvis, shorter anterior and longer posterior limbs. In size it is fully equal to the Brazilian animal, which is the giant of living frogs. Probably, like its existing relative, it passed the day in the muddy water, and took to the land in search of food in the cool of the evening and during the night.

Of the three Œningian species of toads, one (*Bufo Gessneri*, Tsch., sp.) is remarkably like the green toad (*B. viridis*, Dum.), and is of the same size, but had rather longer hind limbs; while a second (*Bombinator œningensis*, Ag.) agrees, as far as it has been preserved, in all essential points with the common *Bombinator igneus*, Merr., except that its limb-bones are rather shorter and broader.

The three Miocene snakes show but few peculiarities, and appear to be nearly related to the common Swiss snake. One species (*Coluber Oweni*, Meyer) reached a length of about 3 feet; another (*C. Kargii*, Meyer) was a little more than a foot long. The Zurich Museum possesses a fine specimen with the mouth wide open.

Lizards are at present represented only by a small animal discovered in the lignites of Rochette. Dr. P. de la Harpe possesses from this locality a jaw ·005 metre (or ·197 inch) in length, armed with twenty-four teeth.

That crocodiles inhabited Swiss rivers and lakes at the time of the formation of the freshwater Miocene, is proved by a fine skull discovered on the Lindenberg near Butikon (in the Canton of Argovia) by M. Rupplin, and presented by him to the Zurich Museum. It is stretched out, and possesses a rather narrow snout, obtusely rounded at the end; and its jaws are armed with sharp teeth. The total length of the animal when perfect was about 3 feet, at least if the head and body were in the same proportion as in the living crocodile of the Nile. It was therefore much smaller than the Egyptian reptile, and so far resembled rather the alligators of America, in which the broad upper jaw projects beyond the teeth of the lower jaw, and the lower canine teeth can penetrate into hollow pits of the upper jaw, whilst in the crocodiles the canine teeth of the lower jaw are applied against the outside of the upper jaw. This appears to have been the case also in the Swiss species from Butikon (*Crocodilus buticonensis*, Meyer); so that that specimen approaches nearest to the true crocodiles.

A crocodile's tooth found in the Miocene of Stein, on the Rhine, is about seven times as large as those of the preceding species, and probably belonged to an animal of the size of the Nilotic crocodile. The same size was attained by a crocodile of which numerous remains have been discovered in the lignites of the Paudèze (at Rochette). Dr. P. de la Harpe found a lower jaw ·40 metre (or 1 foot 3·7 inches) in length, and a thigh-bone ·16 metre (or 6·299 inches) long. Smaller species also occur at the same place, but they have not yet been accurately determined. A crocodile has also been recently discovered in the lignites of Käpfnach.

The most numerously represented family of reptiles is that of the tortoises, which must have contributed not a little to the animation of the Miocene rivers and lakes. Eleven species have been discovered in the Lower Miocene, and six in the Upper (freshwater) Miocene; and to these must be added about a dozen doubtful species, which cannot yet be satisfactorily characterized.

The Swiss species belong to six genera, namely *Testudo, Emys, Chelydra, Cistudo, Trachyaspis,* and *Trionyx*. One of these (*Chelydra*) now pertains exclusively to America, whilst the others live both in the Old and New Worlds, but here keep almost entirely to the warm and torrid zones. The genus *Cistudo* alone is represented on this side of the Alps, by a small species (*C. europæa,* Linn.). The Miocene of Lausanne possesses two species (*C. Razoumowskyi,* Pict., and *C. Marloti,* Pict.)

which are allied to this *Cistudo*; and similar forms occur also in Carolina and Tennessee.

The most abundant tortoise of the Swiss Miocene is the *Testudo Escheri*, Pict., which was spread all over Switzerland at the period of the upper freshwater Miocene formation. It has been found at Locle, Veltheim, Elgg, and the Steinerberg, and is most nearly related to the Greek tortoise (*T. græca*, Linn.), which occurs in the Mediterranean countries, and is often carried about for exhibition by Savoyard boys. From this it differs in the form and size of the bones of the plastron; its length is ·22 metre (or 8·661 inches), and its breadth ·16 metre (or 6·3 inches). With it, at Veltheim near Winterthur, two other species of much larger size have been discovered; in one of these (*T. vitodurana*, Biederm.) the carapace is nearly 1 metre (or 3 feet 3·371 inches) in length and ·76 metre (or 2 feet 5·92 inches) broad; in the other (*T. Picteti*, Biedem.) it is ·78 metre (or 2 feet 6·709 inches) long, and ·52 metre (or 1 foot 8·472 inches) broad. These species, therefore, rival in size the gigantic Indian tortoises.

The alligator-tortoise of Œningen (*Chelydra Murchisoni*, Bell), of which beautiful specimens have been found, was also of considerable size. The length of the carapace is ·43 metre (or 1 foot 4·929 inches), with a breadth of ·38 metre (or 1 foot 2·961 inches) and the whole length from the tip of the snout to the end of the tail was nearly a metre (or 3 feet 3·371 inches). It has precisely the same oval carapace, with its two extremities obtusely rounded, the small cuneiform plastron, the five-clawed fore feet, and the long tail which characterize the American species. As no similar tortoises occur in the Old World, this is one of the most striking American forms of the Swiss Miocene land; it is probably to be regarded as the ancestor of the American species, and no doubt had the same mode of life as the latter, which is described as a rapacious and voracious animal, living upon fishes, amphibia, and young birds. It darts, with its long neck erected, upon its prey, which it seizes with its powerful jaws and large claws. It inhabits rivers and lakes of the United States, from New York to Florida, and especially belongs to warm and southern regions.

The river-tortoises (*Emys*) of the Miocene of Switzerland are smaller animals. They have a broad immovable plastron, and a

rather strongly convex carapace. At the present day they inhabit North America and India, and no species occurs in Europe,
whilst in Miocene times eight species inhabited the Swiss rivers
and lakes. Of two large species (*Emys Laharpii*, Pict., and *E.
Charpentieri*, Pict.) numerous fragments have been obtained from
the lignite-pits of the Paudèze; a third species (*E. Gaudini*,
Pict.), distinguished by the narrow and nearly parallel-sided
plates of the carapace, has been furnished by the sandstone of
the Solitude (near Lausanne) ; a fourth (*E. Nicoleti*, Pict.) by
the freshwater limestone of La Chaux-de-Fonds; and a fifth
(*E. Wyttenbachi*, Bourd.) by the freshwater limestone of the
Rappenfluh near Aarberg. To these must be added two species
discovered in the Aargau, and three near Rochette, besides a
small species from Œningen (*E. scutella*, Meyer). None of
these river-tortoises have yet been found so perfectly preserved
as to enable Professor Heer to ascertain the analogous living
species.

In all the above-mentioned tortoises are found a hard solid
carapace, with the plates closely fitted together; but in the soft
tortoises (*Trionyx*) the flattened body is covered with a smooth
leathery skin. The head, which is borne upon a long neck, is
produced into a short beak ; the tail is very short, and the feet
have only three toes. These animals, which differ very much
in appearance from the other tortoises, inhabit the Nile and the
rivers of Mesopotamia and India ; one species, also, is found in
the southern United States. Formerly three species lived in
the Swiss region; one (*Trionyx Teyleri*, Winkl.) was discovered
at Œningen, a second at Yverdon, and a third large species,
measuring 0·30–0·35 metre (or 11·8–13·7 inches) in diameter,
on the Paudèze. Their remains, however, are imperfect, sufficient only to characterize the genus, but furnishing no satisfactory information as to their analogies with living species.

Trachyaspis is a peculiar extinct genus, one species of which
(*T. Lardyi*, Meyer) has been discovered in the Miocene of the
Tour de la Molière. It is, however, too imperfectly preserved
to allow its relationships to be ascertained. In the markings on
the rib-plates it resembles the soft tortoises ; but it was clothed
with scales.

c. *Birds.*

Birds are the rarest of fossil vertebrates. But that this class of animals lived in the Swiss forests in Miocene times is proved by several undoubted remains of birds which have been discovered at Œningen. According to H. von Meyer they belong to six species; but in only one case are they sufficiently well preserved to enable Prof. Heer to determine their genus. Of this species the sternum, scapula, and bones of the wings have been obtained. They indicate an aquatic bird of the family Anatidæ, a little smaller than the wild goose (*Anas segetum*); H. von Meyer has named it *Anas œningensis* (fig. 323 B, *b*). Prof. Heer

Fig. 323 B.

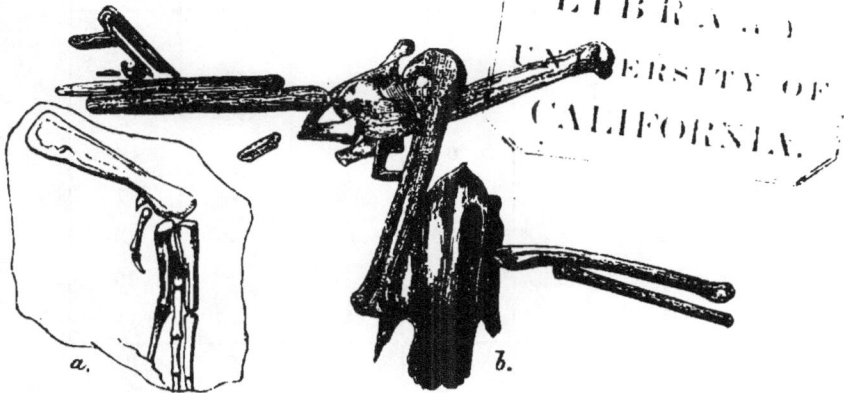

Fig. 323 B. *b, Anas œningensis*, H. von Meyer, from Œningen. Sternum with the humerus and bones of the forearm, the scapula, and the clavicle, natural size. *a*, foot of a bird from Œningen, from a photograph one fourth natural size.

possesses a fine feather from Œningen, the vane of which must have been about an inch wide (Pl. XI. fig. 3), and others only a few lines in breadth.

d. *Mammalia.*

The remains of Mammalia which have been preserved, partly in the lignites and partly in the sandstones and marls, are of much greater importance.　Where only single bones occur they are difficult to determine; but, fortunately, the teeth of many species have come down to the present time; and these permit of the exact determination of the animals, as the dentition furnishes the most important characters for their identification. The great abundance of species formerly existing in the Swiss Miocene fauna may be seen from the following Table:—

Orders of Mammalia.	In the existing Swiss Fauna*.	In the whole of the Miocene.	In the lower Freshwater Miocene.	In the Marine Miocene.	In the upper Freshwater Miocene.
Marsupialia ..	—	1	—	—	1
Chhiroptera ..	15	—	—	—	—
Insectivora ..	9	1	—	—	1
Carnivora	13	6	2	—	4
Rodentia	21	12	5	—	7
Pachydermata .	1	25	15	7	13
Ruminantia ..	3	13	5	2	10
Quadrumana..	—	1	—	—	1
	62	59	27	9	37

This summary shows that the Miocene mammalian fauna must have had a very different appearance from that now existing.　In the present Mammalia, bats, insectivorous shrews, and rodents (through the house- and field-mice) constitute the

* The numbers given here (as at p. 61) for the existing Swiss Vertebrata are derived from a Catalogue prepared by M. Victor Fatio of Geneva, and kindly communicated to Prof. Heer by him.　Schinz's previously published Catalogue has been greatly enlarged.

majority of the species. The Pachydermata are represented only by the wild boar, and the Ruminants by the stag, the roe, and the chamois. At the same time it must be remembered that several species which formerly dwelt in Switzerland have been exterminated by the hand of man. The bones from the pile-dwellings of Swiss lakes inform us that in their times two large species of oxen (the urus and the bison) lived in Swiss forests, and that, besides the common stag, the great elk and the fallow deer were to be met with. From much later days we have accounts of the wild horse, the wild goat, and the beaver, which have ceased for a century to form part of the Swiss fauna. But even if we add these animals which have been removed by man's agency, we obtain only eight species of ruminants and two pachyderms; so that undoubtedly, at the time of the formation of the Miocene, Switzerland possessed a much greater number of such animals. To these we must add Marsupials and Quadrumana (monkeys), which are now entirely wanting in Europe.

Of the thirty-eight genera to which the Swiss Miocene Mammalia belong, twenty-nine are extinct; and of the nine which are still remaining, only three (*Cervus*, *Sus*, and *Sciurus*) still occur in Switzerland. Of the others, one (*Lagomys*) inhabits the temperate zone in Asia and North America, while five are denizens of the warm and torrid zones—the gibbons in India, the opossums (*Didelphys*) in South America, the rhinoceros and musk-deer in India and Africa, and the tapirs in India and South America.

The Miocene mammalian fauna of Switzerland approaches more closely to the Eocene fauna than to that of the present day. If compared with the Eocene fauna of the Jura, six genera are found in common, although none of the species perfectly agree. The *Palæotheria* (or tapir-like animals), which were so abundant in the Eocene period, are still represented by one species; the horse-like *Anchitherium* and the *Amphicyon* (which was related to the dogs and the river-hog (*Hyopotamus*) are also continued into the Miocene period; and the squirrels extend down to the existing fauna. The opossums (*Didelphys*) also have been found elsewhere in Eocene deposits. Other Eocene genera approach the Miocene ones very closely; thus the *Hyracotheria* represent

the *Anthracotheria*. The proportions of the families are therefore very similar. In the Swiss Eocene, and likewise in the
Miocene fauna, the Pachyderms form nearly one half of the
Mammalia; the Ruminants in the Eocene constitute one fourth,
and in the Miocene between one fifth and one sixth. The herbivorous animals consequently form by far the most important
part of the fauna, and the Carnivora are much fewer than at the
present day; they constitute, in the Miocene period, only one
ninth or one tenth, whilst they are about one fifth of the existing
fauna.

The Mammalia are primarily divided into two great sub-
classes—the *Didelphya*, which place their very imperfectly developed young in a ventral pouch, and carry them about with
them; and the *Monodelphya*, which are destitute of this apparatus. The former are further distinguished by important anatomical characters, which show that they occupy the lowest
grade in the history of the development of the Mammalia. At
present they are, with the exception of a few species, confined
to the southern hemisphere, and, by means of the kangaroos
and opossums, they give a peculiar character to its fauna. An
opossum (*Didelphys Blainvillei*, Gerv.) has been discovered in
the Swiss Miocene near Vermes in the valley of Delsberg. The
opossums are small rat-like animals, with long, scaly, prehensile
tails, and pointed heads with wider mouths. They live on insects, birds, and reptiles. The young of many species, when
they have quitted the ventral pouch, creep on to the back of
their mother and hold fast by twisting their tails round hers.
The species of the genus, which are numerous, occur in Peru and
Brazil, and one or two of them in the south of the United States.

All the other Mammalia of the Swiss Miocene belong to the
Monodelphya, the most important Miocene family of which is
that of the Pachydermata. It includes not only the greatest
number of species, but also the largest ones, equalling in size
the largest of the land mammals of the present day. The Swiss
fauna possessed fifteen genera, and at the same time a variety of
forms such as no part of the earth of such small dimensions can
now present. The group of the tapirs is represented by the
genera *Palæotherium* and *Tapirus*. Of *Palæotherium* (*P.
Schinzii*, Meyer) a fine lower jaw with teeth has been found in

the sandstone of Bolligen. A species of *Tapirus* (*T. helveticus*, Meyer) lived at Hohe-Rhonen; and this animal has also been met with at Aarwangen and Käpfnach; so that it is distributed through all the stages of the Swiss Miocene. To these must be added the genus *Listriodon* (*L. splendens*, Meyer, from La Chaux-de-Fonds), which closely approaches the tapirs; but its head was probably not furnished with a trunk.

The largest animals of the Swiss Miocene are the Mastodons and the *Dinotheria*. Of the former whole skeletons have been dug out of the ground in some countries; so that a complete knowledge has been obtained of the structure of these colossal animals. They were the precursors of the elephants, and very nearly allied to them; they were of the same size, had the same formation of skull and great projecting tusks; but they differ in the dentition, as follows:—The young animals were provided with tusk-like incisors in the lower as well as in the upper jaw; and the grinding-surface of the molar teeth had numerous strongly projecting conical tubercles (*mamillæ*) arranged in rows, whence, indeed, is derived the name Mastodon ("mamillated tooth"). These teeth were thus fitted for crushing the hard and woody parts of plants. Switzerland possessed two species of this genus, which is now extinct. In one of them (*Mastodon tapiroides*, Cuv., *M. turicensis*, Schinz) the tubercles of the molar teeth stand in regular transverse rows, and form very prominent transverse ridges separated by deep furrows in which there are no tubercles; in the other (*M. angustidens*, Cuv., Falc.) the conical tubercles are narrower, and there are tubercles in the transverse furrows. The latter is the most abundant species. It begins to appear as early as the third stage of the Miocene, having been found, according to J. Schill, in the marine "Calcaire grossier" of the Lindenbühl on the Randen. In the Miocene of the Helvetian stage it has been observed at many places (on the Buchberg and the Tour de la Molière); but it appears more frequently in the most recent Miocene deposits of Switzerland. The finest specimens have been collected in these beds, as well as in the lignites of Käpfnach and the sandstone of Veltheim. Besides five molar teeth, the Zurich Museum has received from Käpfnach the tusks of this species; they are $1\frac{2}{10}$ foot in length, and but slightly curved

at the extremity.   At Veltheim two splendid skulls have been
discovered; these constitute real ornaments of the collection at
Winterthur.   One of them belonged to a young male animal;
and this has furnished important information as to the change
of teeth in the mastodons.   Elgg is the chief locality for the
first-mentioned species (*M. tapiroides*, Cuv.); but it has also
been discovered at Käpfnach and Œningen *.

The *Dinotheria* were larger than the mastodons, and they had
similar molar teeth or grinders; the lower jaw was armed with
two strong tusks bent downwards, which must have given these
animals a remarkable appearance.   The very prominent nasal
bone leads one to suppose that the *Dinotherium* had a long
proboscis, which, considering the remarkable conformation of
the teeth in the lower jaw, was requisite to enable it to take
its food.   The skull, being flat above, formerly led to the
belief that this enormous animal belonged to the family of the
sea-cows (*Sirenia*), and that it lived in the water; but a skeleton discovered about fifteen years ago near Abtsdorf in Bohemia
proved it to belong to the Pachydermata, and to be most nearly
allied to the mastodons, in accordance with the views of Cuvier
and Owen.   *Dinotherium giganteum*, Kaup, the largest species
of the genus, was distributed all over Europe in the Upper Miocene times; and that it then inhabited Switzerland is proved by
the fine teeth which have been discovered at Delsberg and La
Chaux-de-Fonds.

The richest genus of Pachyderms in the Swiss Miocene is the
Rhinoceros, five species of which have been found.   The most
abundant are *Rhinoceros incisivus* and *R. minutus*, Cuv., which
have been discovered in several localities from the lower lignite
formation (Hohe-Rhonen and Rufi) to the upper freshwater
Miocene (Elgg and La Chaux-de-Fonds).   The first-named species was of the size of the Indian rhinoceros, but is distinguished
by its large incisor teeth, its small narrow nasal bone without
any horn, and its contracted orbits.   The small rhinoceros (*R.
minutus*) also probably possessed no horn; but it was much less

---

* From a figure communicated to him, Kaup referred the molars found here
to *M. angustidens* (see his 'Beiträge zur Kenntniss der urweltlichen Säugethiere,' iii. p. 11); but Prof. Suess, who has lately examined them at Harlem,
where they are preserved, declares them to be *M. tapiroides*, Cuv.(=*turicensis*,
Sch.).

in size; whilst Goldfuss's rhinoceros (*R. Goldfussi*, Kaup), which is to be numbered among the hornless species, was larger than the Indian rhinoceros. Of this species the teeth have been found in the lignites of Hohe-Rhonen, and a fine lower jaw has been discovered on the footpath between the Röthel and the Weid (near Wipkingen). The skulls of two other large species (*R. gannatensis*, Duv., and *R. sansaniensis*, Lart.) are preserved in the Museum at Berne. They were found in the sandstone of the Engehalde near Berne, and, curiously enough, were lying close together in the same block.

The genus *Anchitherium*, which is met with in the Eocene fauna (see vol. i. p. 276), constitutes a sort of transition towards the horse of more recent times. One species (*A. aurelianense*, Cuv., sp.) occurs in the Swiss Miocene, but it has only been seen in the uppermost stages (at Elgg and Vermes). With it is associated a second genus (*Hipparion*), which very closely approaches the horse of the present day, but is more slender and more elegantly formed, and is distinguished by the more finely undulated folds of enamel in the teeth, as well as by the possession of two rudimentary lateral toes. Besides the great middle toe, which forms the hoof, the foot had on each side a small toe which did not touch the ground in walking. Our species (*Hipparion gracile*, Kaup, sp.) is intermediate in size between the horse and the ass; it has been found in the marine Miocene of the Tour de la Molière, of Schnottwyl (Canton of Soleure), and near Sainte-Croix and La Chaux-de-Fonds. In Upper Miocene times these animals were spread over Central Europe, and probably lived in large herds, as in various places the bones have been met with together in large quantities.

An abundance of swine-like animals at the same time inhabited Switzerland. No fewer than eleven species, belonging to six different genera, have been discovered in that country. They prove that the forests and marshes must have produced a great quantity of nutritive material to cause the development of so rich a fauna. Two species are referred to the existing genus *Sus*. Of one of these (*Sus wylensis*, Meyer) a fine specimen of the jaws and teeth was discovered in the lignite of Niederutzweil in the Toggenburg; the second species (*Sus abnormis*, Kaup) is furnished by the lignites of Elgg. The other species belong to extinct genera, some of which, however, are nearly allied to those now living: thus *Hyopotamus*, one species of which (*H. borbonicus*, Gerv.) has been discovered in the sandstone of Aarwangen, is very like the common pig; the head is produced into a long and slender snout, and has a long toothless space in the upper jaw; *Palæochœrus* (*P. typus*, Pom., from Aarwangen) is comparable to the American peccary (*Dicotyles*), and the *Hyotherium* to the East-Indian *Babirussa*, which is remarkable for its very long canine teeth, strongly curved backwards. One species (*Hyotherium Sömmeringi*, Meyer), about the size of the Swiss wild boar, has been found in the Upper Miocene at Elgg and La Chaux-de-Fonds; a second, more abundant, species (*H. Meissneri*, Meyer) appears in the lower freshwater Miocene (at Aarwangen and Aarberg), and it still lived in the country at the time of the formation of the Upper Miocene (Käpfnach); whilst the third (*H. medium*, Meyer) is known only in the upper Miocene (Käpfnach and Niederutzweil). But the most important genus of this group is *Anthracotherium*, so called because its remains were formerly found only in the lignites. It includes the largest animals of this group. One species (*A. magnum*, Cuv.) was as large as an ox, and it had also the appearance of a pig; it had an elongated head, attenuated in front, and produced into a sort of trunk, with large incisors, which are directed forwards as in the pig; strong canine teeth, standing upon large roots, recurved and projecting, as in the wild boar, like powerful tusks; and in each jaw seven tubercular molars separated only by a short space from the canines. The chief locality for this remarkable animal in Switzerland is in the lignites of Rochette and of the Conversion above Paudèze, where Dr. P. Delaharpe and Dr. C. Gaudin have discovered the remains of about ten individuals. In this place a nearly complete skeleton was found. The *Anthracotherium* must therefore have been abundant in the marshes of the Paudèze. It is not, however, restricted to this stage of the Miocene, as its teeth have been found in the Miocene of Schangnau in the Canton of Berne, which belongs to the third Miocene stage. A second species (*A. hippoideum*, Rütim.) has been obtained by Prof. Morlot in the sandstone of Aarwangen. It is rather smaller than the preceding, and is distinguished by the sharper and more trenchant ridges and points of its molar teeth, and its incisors, which resemble the teeth of a horse. A considerably smaller species (*A. minimum*, Cuv.) has hitherto been found only in the lignites of Rochette and of the Paudèze.

These *Anthracotheria* show an approximation to the Carnivora in the structure of their anterior molars, which are pointed in the same way as in the carnivorous animals, whilst the posterior molars have the character of those of herb-eating Mammalia. The animals therefore probably lived in part upon animal and in part upon vegetable food; they were Omnivora, like pigs.

The order Ruminantia was only announced by a few species in the Eocene period; and their full development occurs in Miocene times. The group of the *Anoplotheria*, which constitutes the transition to the Pachydermata, is continued, but under different forms. In place of the *Anoplotherium* the great *Chalicotherium* (*C. antiquum*, Kaup) is found, an animal which possessed the same dentition, except that it had only six molars in each upper jaw. It was as large as the Indian Rhinoceros, and lived in the morasses of the Lower Miocene period; its remains are preserved in the lignites of the Hohe-Rhonen. The elegant Dichobunes of Eocene times (vol. i. p. 279) are also extinct; but their place is taken by the *Microtheria*, small animals, less than the rabbit, with the head round at the back and extended in front into a short pointed snout, and possessing teeth similar in their conformation to those of the musk-deer: these little animals resemble the Pachydermata in the number of their teeth and in the bones of the feet. Two species have been observed in Switzerland (*M. Renggeri*, Meyer, at Aarau, and *M. Cartieri*, Meyer, at Aarwangen).

Two species of the Cervidæ, in Miocene times, inhabited Switzerland. Among them was a musk-deer (*Moschus aurelianensis*, Lart.) which has been found near La Chaux-de-Fonds, and is most nearly related to an African species (*M. aquaticus*, Ow.). The genus *Dorcatherium* agrees with it in the long projecting canine teeth of the upper jaw; but it has seven molars in the lower jaw, whilst the *Moschus* has only six in each jaw. *Dorcatherium Naui* was as large as a roe-deer, but was more slenderly formed, and had the appearance of the musk-deer. Its teeth have been found on the Bucheggberg and near Elgg.

The principal genus of the Cervidæ is that of the true Deer

(*Cervus*). This makes its appearance with one species (*C. medius*, Meyer, sp.) in the lignite formation at the Hohe-Rhonen; but it only arrives at its full development in the youngest Miocene, which furnishes seven species. The most abundant species is *Cervus Scheuchzeri**, Meyer, sp., which has been brought to light at numerous points in the three upper stages of the Swiss Miocene, and was distributed all over Europe at that period. It occurs in Germany, France, and Spain; so that it occupied the place of the red deer of the present day. It was smaller, however, and probably scarcely exceeded the roe in size. A second species (*C. eminens*, Meyer, sp.), discovered in the lower quarry at Œningen, if we may judge from the molars which have alone been found, was as large as the red deer; and a third species (*C. Nicoleti*, Meyer, sp.), from La Chaux-de-Fonds, was still larger. Of the other three species (*C. medius*, Meyer, sp., *minor*, Meyer, sp., and *lunatus*, Meyer) only separate teeth have hitherto occurred, so that their relations to the living deer cannot be ascertained†. This applies also to some teeth from Käpfnach which are very like those of deer, and are distinguished by their elegant structure, and have therefore been referred to a distinct genus (*Orygotherium Escheri*, Meyer).

The family of hollow-horned Ruminants, to which belong the gazelles, antelopes, goats, sheep, and oxen, has not yet been met with in the Swiss Miocene; and in the rest of Europe only antelopes are known in Tertiary deposits. But that such animals then inhabited Switzerland is rendered probable by the numerous beetles living on the excrements of horned cattle already referred to in the present volume (p. 17).

The Rodentia, which principally feed upon vegetable food, are for the most part small, have incisor teeth without roots, no

---

* It has been quite recently carefully described and figured by Prof. Oscar Fraas (Fauna von Steinheim, p. 34). Prof. Fraas has shown that this deer bore short branched antlers, whence the name of *Cervus furcatus*.

† H. von Meyer has separated from *Cervus* all the species cited, with the exception of *C. lunatus*, and united them in a distinct genus, *Palæomeryx*, because the posterior molars are furnished with a peculiar process which is wanting in *Cervus*. Whether or not they possessed antlers has not yet been ascertained with certainty; and hence their relation to the deer and musk-deer remains doubtful.

canine teeth, and only a few molars, separated from the incisors
by a wide space. The species of the Swiss Tertiary land are
distinguished neither in size nor by possessing a form different
from that of the present day. Species representing Swiss mice
and rats have not been found; and the family of the true mice
(*Muridæ*), which is now distributed over the whole world, is
wanting in the Swiss Miocene fauna.

The families of the squirrels, hares, chinchillas, and beavers
are found in Miocene strata. A squirrel (*Sciurus Bredai*,
Meyer) which has been preserved at Œningen seems to have
resembled the species now living in Swiss woods. The genus
Brachymys, one species of which (*B. ornatus*, Meyer) has been
discovered near Vermes, appears also to belong to this family.

The hare-like rodents (*Leporidæ*) are represented by the call-
ing hares (*Lagomys*), which differ from the true hares by their
shorter ears and the want of a tail. At present these animals
live in Southern Siberia, in Mongolia, and in North America,
and, like rabbits, construct their dwellings in the earth. They
collect great stores of dried plants, which they preserve in their
habitations. The Miocene species differ from the living ones in
some essential points, and form a peculiar group (*Myolagus*,
Hens.) which approaches the true hares. Two species are not
uncommon in the uppermost stage of the Miocene. One of
them (*L. œningensis*, Meyer), which was a little smaller than a
rabbit, is found not only at Œningen, but also at Elgg, where it
was the most abundant mammal. The second species (*L. Meyeri*,
Tsch.) was only half as large as a rabbit, and possessed more
delicately formed feet and slenderer claw-joints than the former,
with which it agreed in other respects. It is found at Œningen
and Vermes.

The family of the chinchillas (*Lagostomidæ*) is at present confined to South America. They are animals of considerable size,
with large ears, small fore feet, powerful hind feet, and tails
furnished with long hairs. Their fur is very soft and silky. It is
remarkable that Switzerland possessed about four species of these
animals. Two of them (*Archæomys chinchilloides* and *A. Lau-
rillardi*, Gerv., from Aarwangen) are so nearly allied to the
Peruvian chinchilla (*Lagotis chinchilla*), which furnishes a highly
prized fur, that it is probably not correct to form a distinct

genus for them. The fossil family of chinchillas includes the genus *Issiodoromys*, of which one species (*I. pseudonœma*, Croiz.) has been discovered at Aarwangen, and the genus *Theridomys*, one species of which (*T. Blainvillei*, Gerv.) comes from the same locality and a second from Rochette. The *Theridomys* have smooth incisors, and the molars of the lower jaw have a fold on each side which divides them into two lobes.

The beaver-like rodents (Castoridæ) are represented in Switzerland by two species of *Chalicomys*, a genus which is distinguished from the *Castor* by the form of the roots of the teeth and the folding of their enamel. The larger species (*C. Jægeri*, Kaup) must have been very like the common beaver. It was, however, a little smaller (about $\frac{1}{10}$ to $\frac{1}{4}$), and had narrower molars. This is the commonest mammal of Käpfnach near Horgen; so that numerous families of it must have lived in the Miocene peat-mosses of that district. The second species (*C. minutus*, Meyer), which is scarcely distinct from *C. Eseri*, Meyer, is only about half the size of the living beaver. It is much less common than the preceding species, but is not confined to the Upper Miocene, making its appearance in the lignites of the Hohe-Rhonen and Rochette. As it also occurs in the lignites of Elgg, it probably inhabited Switzerland during the whole period of the Miocene.

Only six species of carnivorous Mammals have been found in the Swiss Miocene, among which there are some which represent the hyænas, otters, and civets. The largest and most remarkable animal of this order (*Hyænœlurus Sulzeri*, Bied.) was discovered by Dr. Biedermann in the Miocene of Veltheim. Judging from the size of the jaw and teeth, it was considerably larger than the Bengal tiger, and was characterized especially by the wide gap between the great canine tooth and the first molar. In the dentition of the lower jaw it agrees with the tiger, but in that of the upper jaw rather with the hyæna*.

---

* In the Carnivora one molar tooth is furnished with a sharp cutting-edge, and is usually larger than the rest; it is known as the "flesh-tooth." The teeth in front of this are the premolars or false molars, whilst the posterior teeth are called tubercular molars. *Hyænœlurus* has, in the upper jaw, five molars, like the hyænas, and in the lower jaw only three, like the tiger (the hyænas having four).

The genus *Hyænodon* also combines the characters of the Hyænas and the Cats, and besides approximates in some degree to the Marsupials. The sandstones of Aarwangen contain the remains of one species. An animal related to the dog (*Amphicyon intermedius*, Meyer) has been found in the lignites of the Hohe-Rhonen; and an aquatic animal, nearly agreeing with the otter in size and form (*Potamotherium Valetoni*, Geoffr.), has been found at Elgg. The Swiss weasel is represented by *Trochictis carbonaria*, Meyer, from Käpfnach and Elgg, which, however, in many respects approaches the badger. The genus *Galecynus* forms a similar bond of union between two existing genera, namely, the dog and the civet. A nearly complete skeleton of one species (*Galecynus palustris*, Meyer, sp.) was discovered at Œningen. The animal was as large as a fox. It agrees with the dog in its dentition, but had the thick tail, the feet and toes, and the tubercular molars of the civet.

The order Quadrumana, which has been already met with among the animals of the Pea-ore formation in the Eocene period, was not wanting in the Swiss Miocene series. A very fine upper jaw of an ape (*Hylobates antiquus*), furnished with the teeth, has been found in the lignites of Elgg, and is now in the Museum at Winterthur. It is represented in Plate XI. fig. 4, from a drawing prepared by Prof. Rütimeyer and kindly communicated to Prof. Heer. In it the four incisors (*a*) are seen, of which the two middle ones (*a*^{1}) are rather larger than the two lateral ones (*a*^{2}). The canines (*b*) project only a little beyond the others; their outer surface is of a rounded conical form, gently bent inwards towards the apex; the inner surface is slightly hollowed, so as to produce a posterior sharp longitudinal edge. Of the five three-rooted molars which the animal probably possessed, only three are preserved on one side, and three and a half on the other. The first two (the premolars, or false molars, *c*^{1}, *c*^{2}) are furnished at the apex with two tubercles, and the third (*c*^{3}) has four tubercles, the middle part being depressed. This dentition leaves no doubt that the jaw belonged to an ape of the Catarrhine or narrow-nosed family. According to a recent examination by Prof. Rütimeyer, it agrees so well with a lower jaw discovered by Lartet at Sansan near Auch (Department of Gers), that it may be referred without hesitation to the same

species *. For this Gervais has proposed to found a distinct
extinct genus (*Pliopithecus*), whilst Rütimeyer adheres to the
opinion first expressed by Lartet, that it cannot be separated
from the Indian gibbons (*Hylobates*). At any rate, these tail-
less, long-armed apes are the animals most nearly allied to it.
With the orang-outan, the chimpanzee, and the gorilla they
constitute the most highly developed of the Quadrumana. Half
a dozen species are known; and these inhabit the Sunda Islands,
Siam, and Hindostan : they attain a height of from 1 to 3½ feet.
According to Rütimeyer, the Swiss fossil gibbon (*Hylobates antiquus*, Lart., sp.) is most nearly related to the siamang (*H.
syndactylus*, Raffl., sp.) of Sumatra †, an ape which, according
to Lartet and Vrolik, approaches in its osteology more closely
to man than either the chimpanzee or the orang. It will therefore be of interest to learn something as to its mode of life and
peculiarities; for it is very probable that in these respects its
ancient relative (which, so far as Prof. Heer knows, was the
most highly organized animal of its time) resembled it.

Fig. 324 represents this black-haired animal, which is 3½ feet
in height when full-grown, and therefore about one fifth larger
than the extinct species. Duvaucel relates ‡ "that the siamang
is very common in the forests of Sumatra." "Usually," he
observes, " we find the siamangs collected into numerous troops,
guided, it is said, by a chief, whom the Malays regard as invul-
nerable, no doubt because he is stronger, more active, and more
difficult to get at than the others. Thus united, they salute the
sun at its rising and setting with dreadful cries, which may be
heard at a distance of several miles, and which nearly stun a
person even when they do not cause fear. It is the morning-

---

* Dr. Biedermann has separated it (under the name of *Pliopithecus platyodon*)
from the French species, because the molar teeth are a little broader; but the
specimen obtained by Lartet is a lower jaw, and that from Elgg is an upper
jaw; and it is found that, in the existing gibbons, the molars of the upper
jaw are broader than those of the lower.

† The fossil species is distinguished, according to Rütimeyer, by more
massive and closer square teeth, by having comparatively larger middle
incisors in the upper jaw, and consequently larger lateral incisors in the lower
jaw, and by its smaller general size.

‡ See F. Cuvier, 'Histoire Naturelle des Mammifères,' by Geoffroy and F.
Cuvier.

Fig. 324.

Siamang (*Hylobates syndactylus*, Raffl., sp.), one eighth nat. size. From a
Sumatran specimen belonging to the Museum at Zurich.

call of the Malay mountaineers, and is an unbearable nuisance
to the townspeople who visit the hills.

"To make up for this, the siamangs maintain a profound
silence during the day—that is to say, if their repose or sleep is
not interrupted. These animals are slow and heavy; they are
not bold when they climb, and not dexterous when they leap,
so that they may always be caught when they can be surprised.
But nature, while depriving them of the means of promptly
escaping from danger, has endowed them with a vigilance which
is rarely at fault; and if they hear at a mile off a sound which
is unknown to them, they take fright and immediately fly.
When they can be surprised on the ground, they may be seized
without making any resistance, either being stupified by fear or

feeling their weakness and the impossibility of escape. At first they attempt to fly; and it is then that all their imperfections are visible. Their bodies, too tall and too heavy for their short and slender thighs, bend forwards, and, with their arms acting as if they were crutches, the siamangs advance by jerks, resembling a lame old man driven through fear to make a great effort.

"However numerous the troop may be, a wounded one is abandoned by the rest, at least if it is not a young individual. Its mother, who carries it or follows it closely, then falls with it, utters frightful cries, and throws herself upon the enemy with open mouth and arms extended. One easily sees that these animals are not adapted for fighting ; for they do not know how to avoid a blow, and at the same time cannot bear one. Maternal affection among them is not only manifested in the time of danger; and the care which the females take of their young is so tender and uncommon that one might be tempted to ascribe it to a rational sentiment. It is a curious spectacle, which I have sometimes, with many precautions, been able to enjoy, to see the females bring their young children to the river, wash their faces in spite of their grumblings, wipe them, dry them, and devote to their cleanliness an amount of time and care which our children might envy in many cases."

The ungko (*Hylobates agilis*) is much more lively than the siamang; it climbs about upon the trees with astonishing activity, whilst upon level ground it has an uncertain and vacillating gait, although it walks upright. According to Dr. S. Müller the gibbons, or long-armed apes, are inhabitants of the mountains, although rarely passing above the limit of fig-trees. During the day they reside in the summits of high trees, and towards evening they descend in troops into the open country; but as soon as they are conscious of the presence of men, they dash up the rocky slopes and disappear into the darker valleys. They live chiefly upon vegetable food, especially fruits, and they also devour insects and lizards.

Besides the *Hylobates antiquus,* two other European Miocene apes are known, namely *Dryopithecus Fontani,* Lart., and *Semnopithecus pentelicus,* Wagn., sp. The former has been met with at Sansan and also on the Swabian Alp, so that it may still be found in Switzerland; the second species occurs abundantly at Pikermi in Attica, where a nearly complete skeleton of it has been discovered. It belongs to the group of the long-tailed Indian monkeys, and is most nearly allied to the Hoonuman (*Semnopithecus entellus*). The *Dryopithecus*, which equalled the orang and the chimpanzee in stature, was placed by Lartet in a distinct genus; but, so far as can be judged from its imperfectly preserved remains, it appears to come very near the gibbons.

In the Miocene period herbs and grassy plants formed a luxuriant vegetation, on which the deer, the musk-deer, and the horses of those times found nourishment in the forest-meadows and in numerous coppices. Swine no doubt sought the oak-forests which were spread over the Swiss Miocene country with such a variety of species, and which were for the most part composed of evergreen trees, so that they furnished fruit throughout a great part of the year. Many other trees, such as figs, myrtles, jujubes, whitethorns, walnuts, and numerous Papilionaceæ, bore fruit which might serve as food for pigs.

The numerous larvæ of insects which lived in the moist soil of the forest, the grubs of many crawflies and *Bibiones* (vol. ii. p. 55), which constitute the principal part of the Miocene Diptera, also provided a rich nutriment for swine. The humid, marshy, forest soil which is indicated by the plants must have been particularly well fitted to enable pigs, tapirs, and rhinoceroses to thrive, for it is well known that their living representatives prefer such localities. Thus wild swine are fond of damp marshy woods of leafy trees, tapirs seek the banks of rivers and lakes and go readily into the water, and rhinoceroses prefer marshy low grounds. The fleshy rhizomes of the *Nymphææ* and *Nelumbia*, the irises, and the knotty roots of the Cyperaceæ (*Cyperus Braunii*, Heer) certainly furnished Miocene tapirs with food of the same nature as that which is afforded by corresponding living plants to their representatives of the present day.

The flora of the Swiss Miocene offered an abundant nourishment to the Rodents of that period. Squirrels found an ample provision of pine- and fir-cones, walnuts, and hazel-nuts; the calling-hares and chinchillas sought their food in the woods; while the beavers most probably established their colonies on the banks of the rivers and lakes, where willows and birches, alders and poplars offered their bark for sustenance, and their branches as building-materials.

For the apes sufficient provision was made by the figs and bread-fruit trees, walnuts, almonds, jujube-trees, and date-palms, the St.-John's-bread trees, and the palms. At this period rice and millet already clothed the ground and furnished these animals with farinaceous food.

For the otters (*Potamotherium*) the rivers and lakes offered abundant nourishment, as did the animals of the forest for the carnivorous hyænas, civets, and tigers.

We have already shown (vol. i. p. 315) that during the Miocene period important changes of the flora took place; and it would be interesting to know whether the land fauna also became modified. Unfortunately the materials for demonstrating such a modification in detail are still wanting. The insect-fauna of the Swiss Miocene is known almost solely from the uppermost stage of the Molasse; and this applies also to the Fishes. Few certain data are afforded by the Reptiles and Mollusca. The Mammalia, however, afford more information. From the lowest stage (Tongrian) there is in Switzerland only a species of manatee; but in other countries this stage also contains *Anthracotheria*, which, with the Swiss, are chiefly found in the Aquitanian, although they also extend up into the third stage. In Switzerland the following mammals belong to the second stage:—*Palæotherium Schinzii, Anthracotherium minimum, Chalicotherium antiquum*, and *Amphicyon intermedius*. The Mammalia of the third stage comprise *Rhinoceros gannatensis* and *sansaniensis, Hyopotamus borbonicus, Anthracotherium hippoideum*, the species of *Microtherium* and *Archæomys, Theridomys Blainvillei*, and *Issiodoromys pseudonœma*. Exclusively in the Œningian (fifth) stage:—*Dinotherium giganteum, Listriodon splendens, Anchitherium aurelianense, Sus wylensis, S. abnormis, Hyotherium Sömmerringii, Cervus lunatus, eminens, Bojani*, and *Nicoleti, Moschus aurelianensis*, species of *Lagomys, Brachymys ornatus, Sciurus Bredai, Didelphys Blainvillei, Hyænælurus Sulzeri, Galecynus palustris, Potamotherium Valetonii, Trochictis carbonaria*, and *Hylobates antiquus*. Consequently only 4 species have hitherto been found peculiar to the second stage, 20 to the third, and 22 to the fifth.

Six species extend from the Aquitanian to the Œningian stage, namely :—*Rhinoceros incisivus, Goldfussi,* and *minutus, Tapirus helveticus, Chalicomys minutus,* and *Cervus medius.*

Generally the species of the different stages overlap each other, especially if we take into consideration their occurrence in other parts of Europe. Moreover it must not be forgotten, that of many species only single specimens have hitherto been found; and upon these we must not lay too great a stress. The animals most generally distributed are of far more importance; and these tell us that, in the first period of the Swiss Miocene formation, great *Anthracotheria,* rhinoceroses, tapirs, and deer inhabited Switzerland, but that the *Anthracotheria* disappeared at the close of the lower freshwater Miocene; whilst the others outlived the period when the low grounds were converted into sea-bottoms, and they reappeared in the valleys during the formation of the upper freshwater Miocene. The Mastodons are first found in the third stage, as is proved by the remains floated out to sea and met with on the Lindenbühl; but they only became generally diffused in the fifth stage, during which the *Dinotheria* and the calling-hares are first met with [*].

II. Marine Animals.

In the history of the Miocene period the sea repeatedly occupied the low grounds of Switzerland, and has left behind numerous traces of its presence. Three times the sea covered certain parts of the country, and formed the marine deposits already referred to (vol. i. p. 295) : in this way three stages of marine Molasse have been deposited :—the Tongrian, confined to the Canton of Basle and the Bernese Jura; a second forming a band

* Lartet (Bull. Soc. Géol. de France, xvi. 1859) and Prof. Suess (Sitzungsber. der Akad. der Wiss. zu Wien, 1863) admit three Miocene mammalian faunas,—first, that of the *Anthracotheria*; second, that of *Mastodon angustidens* and *Mastodon tapiroïdes*; and, third, that of *Mastodon longirostris.* The last does not seem to appear in Switzerland. But when Suess refers to it *Dinotherium giganteum, Hipparion gracile,* and *Rhinoceros incisivus,* he forgets that these species occur in Switzerland, and that the rhinoceros already appeared in the second stage; so that these animals cannot be selected to characterize his third mammalian fauna of the Miocene period.

along the northern boundary of Switzerland, extending from the
Canton of Basle to the Randen ; and a third marine Miocene or
Helvetian stage. · They present many peculiarities in their fauna,
and will therefore be described separately.

1. *Marine Fauna of the Lowest Miocene or Tongrian Stage.*

The sea which, during the Tongrian epoch, covered the north-
west of Switzerland, formed a southern arm of the Alsatian
gulf, which was connected with the ocean that then spread over
northern Germany, Belgium, and the north of France.   Hence
the Swiss fauna of the Tongrian period will be found in close
agreement with the fauna of that sea.   In Switzerland, up to
the present time, there have been collected a few polypes and
Polythalamia, 62 species of Mollusca*, and several Vertebrata.
Elsewhere 47 species of Mollusca have been found in the Tongrian stage, 31 species in the Aquitanian stage, 3 in the Shell-
sandstone, and 8 in the uppermost Eocene formation.   The
greater part of the species of Mollusca are identical with those
of the Tongrian stage, and especially agree with the species of
the lowest stage of the basin of Mayence and the sands of Fon-
tainebleau ; many of these species also occur in the Aquitanian
stage in France, but very few are common to the Swiss middle
Miocene sea.   The Swiss fauna has also only a few species in
common with the Eocene sea.

All the species of Mollusca are distinct from those now existing ; but all the genera may now be met with in the modern seas.
The Cephalopoda, formerly so numerous, are wanting, and only
two species of Brachiopoda (*Terebratula opercularis*, Sow., and
Terebratulina polydichotoma, May.) are met with.   Among the
univalves, the *Cerithia* are the most numerous, as nine species
of the genus occur (such as *C. Boblayi*, Desh., *C. Lamarcki*, Br.,
C. lima, Br., *C. plicatum*, Lam., and *C. dentatum*, Desf.) ; but

---

* The Mollusca of the Swiss Tertiary sea have been investigated and described with great care by M. Carl Mayer.   Prof. Heer is indebted to this
thorough student of the Mollusca of the Tertiary period for a catalogue of
the species discovered in the different marine stages of the Swiss Miocene,
which constitutes the foundation of the numerical statements given in the
text.

there are four species of *Pleurotoma* (including *P. belgica,* Goldf., and *P. Parkinsoni,* Desh.) and three of *Natica* (*N. Nysti,* D'Orb., *N. crassatina,* Lam., and *N. hantoniensis,* Sow.). With these are associated species of *Patella, Melania* (*M. semidecussata,* Lam.), *Trochus,* and *Murex.*

Oysters are among the most abundant bivalves; three species (*Ostrea callifera,* Lam., *O. cyathula,* Lam., and *O. longirostris,* Lam.) occur in enormous masses. Near Stetten (in the environs of Basle) the great *Ostrea callifera* was established in large banks on the Jurassic oolite, which then constituted the bottom of the Tongrian sea. A similar oyster-bed is to be seen near Develier, and others on one of the sides of the Mettenberg and in the Delsberg, while another bed has been formed by the *Ostrea cyathula* near Neucul.

Of the numerous other bivalves we may mention the *Lucinæ* (*L. Heberti,* Desh., *L. squamosa,* Lam., *L. undulata,* Lam., and *L. tenuistriata,* Héb.), *Pectunculi* (*P. obovatus* and *angusticostatus,* Lam.), *Cardia* (*Cardium Raulini,* Desh., and *C. tenuisulcatum,* Nyst), *Cyrenæ* (*C. semistriata,* Desh.), *Cythereæ* (*C. lævigata,* Lam., *C. incrassata,* Sow., and *C. splendida,* Mer.); abundant forms of *Tellinæ, Pholadomyæ,* and *Lithodomi* are also discovered.

The long, cylindrical, indistinctly jointed filaments which are met with on the slabs from the Three Torrents (fig. 325, p. 103) may perhaps be referred to worms.

Of the remains of large fishes, the teeth of sharks and the bones of a cetacean are of most frequent occurrence. The teeth of a shark (*Cacharodon megalodon,* Ag.), with toothed margins, attain a length of 6 inches, and from them the length of the whole animal has been estimated at 85 feet; it was therefore more than twice as large as the shark of the present seas. This giant was then distributed in all seas, and it also occurs in the Swiss shell-sandstone. A smaller species (*Lamna cuspidata,* Ag.) is also found in Switzerland, the narrow two-edged teeth of which are provided with two long processes at the base.

The cetacean (*Halitherium Schinzii,* Kaup) belongs to the group of the Sirenia, those singular herbivorous animals which seem to constitute the transition from the whales to the Pachyderms. One species is most nearly related to the manatees (sea-cows), which at present inhabit the shores of America (from Florida to Brazil), and are found near the Senegal in Africa, particularly frequenting the mouths of rivers. The bones and teeth of the Swiss species are not uncommon; and a nearly complete skeleton (except the head) was found near Rädersdorf.

2. Marine animals of the second and third Miocene stages.

We have already seen (vol. i. p. 300) that during the Aquitanian period a lagoon with brackish water stretched along the Alps. It is true that only about ten species of animals have been found in its deposits; but these suffice to prove the fact. Two *Cyrenæ* (*C. convexa*, Br., and *C. thunensis*, Mayer), two *Cardia* (*C. Heerii*, Mayer, and *C. arcula*, May.), a *Dreissenia* (*D. Basteroti*, Des.), a *Lutraria* (*L. sanna*, Bast.), a *Nucula*, and two species of *Melanopsis* occur near Ralligen. Five of these species belong to the Aquitanian stage in France, and their existing relatives for the most part inhabit brackish water.

A band of marine Miocene belonging to the third stage appears on the northern frontier of Switzerland, and may be traced from the Canton of Basle (from Waldenburg, Tenniken, Diegten, Känerkinden, and Rüneburg) through the Frickthal and Klettgau to the Randen, where it is met with near Wiechs, Epfenhofen, Thengen, and Lindenbühl, and, according to J. Schill, up to 2700 feet above the sea near the Klausenhof; hence it spreads into southern Swabia as far as Donaueschingen and Nordlingen. According to M. Carl Mayer, the fauna of this marine deposit differs equally from those of the Aquitanian and Helvetian stages; but it exhibits a perfect agreement with that of the Faluns of Touraine in Central France. It is probable, therefore, that, at the time of the formation of the Swiss grey Miocene, an arm of the sea extended from Central France into Switzerland, stretching along the northern border of the latter country. The marine deposit of the third stage is characterized chiefly by the univalve shells, among which the *Turritellæ* (*T. turris*, Bast.), the *Cerithia* (*C. lignitarum, papaveraceum*, and *mediterraneum*), the *Murices* (*M. turonensis, plicatus*, and *erinaceus*), the *Columbellæ* (*C. curta* and *miocæna*), and *Neritæ* (*N. Plutonis*) may be particularly specified; but bivalves are by no means deficient, and some species (such as *Venus clathrata* and *Arca Okeni*) are characteristic of this stage.

3. *Marine animals of the fourth or Helvetian stage.*

During the formation of the three lower stages of the Swiss Miocene, the sea only touched the frontiers of the country, or traversed its low lands in separate narrow arms; in the Helvetian period, however, it had a wider extension, as has already been shown (vol. i. p. 293). The deposits formed at that period occur in two zones, known as the Shell-sandstone and the subalpine Molasse. It is a question whether or not the formation of these two zones took place at the same time. The Shell-sandstone which occurs along the Jura has been regarded sometimes as older, sometimes as younger, than the marine Molasse which follows the chain of the Alps. As the conditions of deposition furnish no satisfactory data for the solution of this question, the decision must only rest on the fossils. The Mollusca have been very carefully investigated for many years by M. Carl Mayer; and the list prepared by him shows, for the Shell-sandstone, 218 marine Mollusca, for the subalpine Molasse 360 marine Mollusca, and for both together 421 species; common to both deposits are 141 species, so that the Shell-sandstone shares about two thirds of its species with the subalpine Molasse. There are 77 species of the Shell-sandstone wanting in the subalpine Molasse; but of these only 18 are peculiar to the Shell-sandstone, 53 of these species being found elsewhere in the Helvetian or in more recent stages, and 6 species being common to the second or third stage. If the above-mentioned 53 species are reckoned among the common forms as having been found elsewhere in formations of the same age, nearly nine tenths of the species will be found in common; and there are only 24 which have not yet been observed in the Helvetian stage either in Switzerland or in other countries. From this agreement of the species alone, it would appear that the Shell-sandstone and the subalpine Molasse belong to the same epoch; and this is equally shown by the relations of the two faunas to the existing race of animals. Of the 218 species of the Shell-sandstone, 76

are still living, or 35 per cent.; of the 360 species of the subalpine Molasse, 125 (or a similar proportion, 35 per cent.). The
Shell-sandstone and the subalpine Molasse together possess 421
species, of which 147 (or the same proportion of 35 per cent.)
occur in the existing fauna. The two faunas consequently possess
precisely the same relation to the existing fauna, not only in
the numerical proportions, but also in the manner in which the
living species are now distributed; only the fact must be taken
into consideration, that Prof. Heer knows 152 species more from
the subalpine Molasse than from the Shell-sandstone. A *résumé*
of numbers is given in the following Table :—

Living species formerly belonging to Middle Miocene seas.	On the English coasts.	In Europe, comprising the Mediterranean.	In the Mediterranean alone.	Only in tropical Africa.	Only in tropical Asia.	Only in America.
Found in the Shell-sandstone	20	60	23	8	3	2
Found in the subalpine Molasse ..	32	104	41	12	5	2
Species common to both............	38	120	50	12	6	4 .

This summary shows that most of the species now living, both
from the Shell-sandstone and the subalpine Molasse, belong to
the Mediterranean * ; but that a number of tropical forms are
mixed with them, among which African types are more numerous than Asiatic. Thus the two faunas stand in the same
relation to the existing fauna, and they must consequently be
ranged in the same stage. The differences between them are
caused less by time than by local circumstances. The Shell-

* Almost all the species in the first column also live in the Mediterranean.
About one third of the species are now exclusively confined to the Mediter-
ranean. Nine species of the second column occur also in tropical Africa; so
that the Swiss Molassic fauna altogether possesses twenty-one tropical
African forms, nine of which, however, still inhabit the southern coast of
Europe.

sandstone has preserved to Switzerland the fauna of the shallow coast-line; and the varied mixture of the shells which lie together in all directions and are often broken and rolled, and the sharks' teeth and fragments of wood which lie among them, indicate a shore-formation; while the animals of the subalpine Molasse, which lie together often in great masses, with the valves of the bivalves not unfrequently united, probably lived in the sandy locality where they are found and where they had been covered up. This would sufficiently explain why the species in the Shell-sandstone and the subalpine Molasse are differently associated, and would afford a reason for some of the common species being more abundant in the subalpine Molasse, and for others prevailing more in the Shell-sandstone.

We therefore unite the animals of the Shell-sandstone and of the subalpine Molasse into one stage, and compare them with those of the other Miocene stages.

Of the Mollusca of the Cretaceous sea, no single species remained in the Miocene sea; and even from the Eocene deposits only five species (*Solecurtus coarctatus, Corbulomya complanata, Pholadomya arcuata, Tellina crassa,* and *Arca nivea*) are found in the Swiss Helvetian stage of the Miocene. Hence a great change of forms had taken place since the preceding epochs. With the Tongrian stage of the Miocene the Helvetian marine Molasse shares only 15 species; whilst it has 118 species in common with the Aquitanian, and 303 in common with the third stage. It has almost an equal number of species (namely 299) in common with the younger stages (the Tortonian, Placencian, and Astian of Carl Mayer) and with the existing fauna.

In about three fourths of its species the molluscan fauna of the Swiss Helvetian stage agrees with the molluscan fauna which inhabited the European seas in the third stage of the Molasse; it also agrees in about the same proportion with the molluscan fauna of the younger Upper Miocene and the Pliocene formations; and about one third of these species has descended to the present fauna. A similar proportion may also be observed in other parts of the sea which at that time covered Central Europe *.

* Prof. Hörnes has described 476 marine univalves (or 500, including land and freshwater shells) from the basin of Vienna. Of these, 99 species are certainly still living; 27 more are doubtful. Thus there are from 21 to 26·5 per

On examining the extinct species of the fauna of the Swiss Molassic sea, it is found that among the Mollusca the Mediterranean ·forms predominate, that exclusively northern forms are wanting, but that, on the other hand, numerous tropical types now absent from the Mediterranean occur; so that on the whole the Swiss Miocene marine fauna acquires a more southern character than that of the existing Mediterranean zone. We find in it genera which now pertain exclusively to tropical seas, such as the splendid Volutes, the long turriform *Terebræ*, the *Nautili*, and the genera *Oniscia, Pyrula, Ficula, Delphinula,* and *Tugonia*, with others which chiefly inhabit the tropics, and are only represented in the Mediterranean by a few species, such as the variegated Cones, the brilliant *Cypreæ*, the genera *Mitra, Cassis, Cancellaria, Pleurotoma, Turritella, Turbo,* and *Tritonium,* and among bivalves *Tellina, Psammobia, Cytherea,* and *Chama*.

On recapitulating the forms hitherto collected in Switzerland, we find among the 431 species of Mollusca, 203 marine univalves and 228 marine bivalves. The former belong to 15 families. The Cephalopoda, which were so numerous and varied in preceding periods, are represented by only a single species (*Nautilus Aturi*); and even this is extremely rare, and has only been found near Würenlos. Of the family Conidæ, which principally belongs

---

cent. of living species. In the Swiss Helvetian stage the living species constitute 25·5 per cent. of the marine univalves, in the Shell-sandstone alone 22·6 per cent., and in the subalpine Molasse 25·7 per cent. Of the bivalves there are in the Vienna basin, as in Switzerland, more living species than of the univalves, so that higher percentage numbers are obtained for the whole of the Mollusca. The Swiss Helvetian Molasse represents the middle and upper marine beds of the Vienna basin. In the lowest beds (called " Hörner " beds) the living species of marine univalves constitute only from 12 to 15 per cent. The marine beds are followed in the Vienna basin by a brackish-water formation, which coincides with the Swiss Œningian stage; it passes into a freshwater formation (the Congerian or " Inzerdorfer" beds), in which *Mastodon longirostris* has been found; whilst in the brackish-water and marine beds the *Mastodon tapiroides* and *angustidens* are met with, which consequently frequented the shores of the Viennese sea, just as they did those of the Helvetian sea. The Swiss Molasse has 138 marine univalves, or 68 per cent., in common with the Vienna basin. Of the bivalves there are no doubt a still larger number of common species.

to the torrid zone, the Swiss fauna possesses 17 species, remarkable for their brilliant shells; two of the species (*Conus betuloides* and *Aldrovandi*) are most nearly related to an Indian species (*Conus figulinus*, Linn.), another (*C. antidiluvianus*, Brug.) to a species from the Chinese seas (*C. Orbignyi*), and only one (*C. ventricosus*, Bronn) belongs to tropical and Mediterranean forms.

Of the Cypræidæ, besides the small European species (*Cypræa europæa*), there is another (*C. pyrum*, Gmel.) which now inhabits the North-African coast, the Senegal, and India, and a third (*C. sanguinolenta*, Gmel.) which now occurs only in Senegambia. The genus *Erato* is represented by a widely distributed species (*E. lævis*) which now lives both on the English coast and in the Mediterranean.

The family Columbellariæ presents exotic forms in the beautiful genus *Voluta* (*V. bernensis*, May.), which principally belongs to the southern hemisphere, and the great genus *Mitra*, of which, however, only three species (*Mitra scrobiculata*, *striatula*, and *fusiformis*) are found. There are also four species of *Columbella* in Switzerland.

The family Buccinidæ offers numerous species of the genus *Buccinum* (whelks); it played in Miocene times the same part as at present, for it spread over numerous seas and was abundantly represented. Of the sixteen known species, four are still living in the Mediterranean. Of the tropical genera *Terebra* and *Oniscia* three species, and four of *Cassis*, inhabited the Swiss Molassic sea. One species of the last-named genus (*C. saburon*) was spread over a great part of the Miocene sea, and it occurs now in the Mediterranean, in the Red Sea, and at the Senegal. It deserves especial notice that many species which are now remarkable for a very wide area of distribution, reach back into Tertiary times, and are therefore of great antiquity. This applies also to the only wing-shell of the Swiss Molasse (*Chenopus pes-pelecani*, Linn.), the present distribution of which is, however, from the Mediterranean northwards.

The numerous family Canalifera, in which the shell is produced into an elongated beak, furnishes many species of *Murex* and *Fusus* (spindle-shell). These, like most of their allies, are predaceous animals, which bore with their proboscis into other shells and eat out the soft parts. Of the former genus one of the Swiss species (*Murex trunculus*) still occurs in the Mediterranean and at the Senegal, and four others still live in the Mediterranean, which is also inhabited by one of the eleven *Fusi* of the Molasse (*Fusus rostratus*, Ol.). Of the genus *Cancellaria* eighty species are known, all being inhabitants of the tropics, except one which is found in the Mediterranean and at Senegambia. This species (*C. cancellata*) lived formerly in the Molassic sea; but with it there were nine other species, one of which (*C. piscatoria*) now occurs only in India. One of the largest genera is *Pleurotoma*, of which 369 living and 305 fossil species are known. It made its appearance as early as the Trias, and has taken part in the population of the seas in all geological ages. At present its chief seat is in the torrid zone, although many small forms occur in the Mediterranean and even in the north. These little forms are the last scanty remains of a genus numerous species of which were formerly spread through the European sea. The Swiss Molassic sea possessed twenty-two species, only one of which (*P. ramosa*, Bast.) is found still living at Senegambia. This species, like many other species of the Molasse (such as *P. gradata* and *granulato-cincta*) had the shell elegantly sculptured. Such sculpture is a still more striking characteristic of the allied genus *Cerithium*, the turriform shells of which are most beautifully adorned. *Cerithium* is a very large genus; commencing in the Trias, it attained its highest development in the Eocene period, and then diminished, although it is still represented by 140 living species. The *Cerithia* live chiefly at the mouths of rivers and in brackish water, where they sometimes occur in immense quantities. They have already been repeatedly mentioned. Eight species lived in the Molassic sea; and of these, two (*C. mediterraneum* and *scabrum*) still occur in the Mediterranean, and the latter also inhabits the North Sea. *Pyrula* and *Ficula* are smaller genera of this family, including tropical forms, which had a wide distribution in the Miocene sea (such as *Pyrula rusticola* and *Ficula clava* and *condita*). Two *Tritoniæ* also are types of the torrid zone; whilst of the two *Ranellæ* one (*R. marginata*, Mart.) inhabits West Africa, and the other (*R. scrobiculata ?*) the Mediterranean.

Of the Turbinaceæ six genera were represented in the Swiss Molassic sea. *Turbo* and *Trochus* had been already met with in the Swiss Jurassic sea (vol. i. p. 136) ; and seven species of these genera appear in the Miocene, six of them belonging to the genus *Trochus*, which is distributed through all seas, whilst *Turbo* chiefly inhabits the torrid zone. A similar remark may be made of the *Turritellæ*, thirteen species of which inhabited the Swiss Molassic sea. These are all extinct species, several of which (such as *T. turris* and *T. Archimedis*) received a screw-like appearance from the spiral twisting of the angles of their long turriform shells. The genus *Xenophora* is remarkable for the numerous shell-valves which the animal affixes to the whorls of its shell, which thus acquires a singularly ragged appearance. Switzerland has two species, one of which (*X. turicensis*, May.) is tolerably abundant in the Shell-sandstone, while the other (*X. Deshayesi*, Mich.) occurs in the subalpine Molasse. Of *Monodonta* we have a Mediterranean species (*M. Aaronis*, Desh.) ; of *Adeorbis* one, and of *Solarium* two extinct forms (*S. carocollatum* and *simplex*) occur.

The family Scalariidæ receives its name from the shells of the animals composing it being twisted in a long spiral, sometimes almost tubular, with a round aperture. The genus *Delphinula*, which lives in the seas of warm climates, possesses only one species (*D. helvetica*, May.) in the Molasse. *Scalaria*, which is distributed in all seas, has four species. The worm-shells, which are furnished with tubular shells like those of the Tubicolar Annelides, are represented by two species (*Vermetus arenarius* and *V. intortus*, Lam.) still living in the Mediterranean, and the very similar *Siliquariæ* by one species (*S. anguina*, Linn.), which is now met with both in the Mediterranean and in Indian seas.

Among the Plicaceæ, *Natica* forms a genus already known in Switzerland since the Jurassic epoch (vol. i. p. 136). It has inhabited the sea at all times, and extends from the icy sea to the South Sea, 189 species being known from all parts of the world. The species are predaceous animals, living at the bottom of the sea; they bore into other Mollusca, and bury themselves in the sea-bottom. Of the nine species of the Molasse, we find four living in existing seas; and three of these (*N. millepunctata*, Linn., *N. helvicina* and *Joséphinæ*, Risso) are confined to the Mediterranean.

The *Pyramidellæ* and *Sigareti* are less numerous. Of the latter genus one species, which is very rare in the Molasse (*S. haliotoideus*, Linn.), is still living in the Mediterranean, whilst a second species, which was then plentiful (*S. clathratus*, Rec.), is now extinct.

The species of the families Phyllidiacea and Calyptræacea are now met with everywhere on the sea-coasts, where they cling to stones and rocks. The limpets (*Patella*) occur in the oldest formations, and also inhabited the Swiss Jurassic sea (vol. i. p. 136) ; one species (*P. helvetica*, May.) is tolerably abundant in the Shell-sandstone. The very similar *Fissurellæ* (key-hole limpets) and the *Capuli* are represented in the Molasse by two species; *Calyptræa* includes four, and *Crepidula* one species. The last (*C. unguiformis*, Lam.) clings to the rocks, with its thin shell fitting all their irregularities. It is still living not only in the North Atlantic and Mediterranean, but also in Africa and India, and is even met with on the coasts of New Zealand, proving that the magnitude of the area of distribution bears a relation to the antiquity of the species.

The toothshells (Dentaliidæ) are peculiar nearly straight tubes open at both ends. The genus *Dentalium* makes its first appearance as early as the Carboniferous period, and has continued to the present day. Five species are preserved in the Molasse ; and two of these (*Dentalium incrassatum*, Sow., and *D. entalis*, Gm.) are still met with living in European seas, whilst the other three (*D. fossile*, Gm., *D. mutabile*, Död., and *D. Michelottii*, Hörn.) became extinct in Pliocene times.

In the marine bivalves the same conditions are repeated which have been seen to prevail with the univalves, only the bivalves have in general a wider distribution both in time and space. Consequently more bivalves than univalves have come down to recent times from the Tertiary sea ; and among them species are found which are at present spread over all European seas, living on the Norwegian and English coasts as well as on those of the Mediterranean. The Molasse does not possess a single purely fossil genus ; and, just as all the genera, without exception, have continued to the present day, so many of these genera may be traced back to the most remote antiquity.

The bivalves of the Molasse include species of thirty families belonging to two orders—the Brachiopoda and the Lamellibranchiata. The Brachiopoda took an important place among the Mollusca of former ages (see vol. i. pp. 75 & 136), and were reduced, in the Miocene, to three species of *Terebratula*, two of which (*T. Buchii,* Mich., and *T. miocenica,* Mich.) have been found at La Chaux-de-Fonds.

The Lamellibranchiata are divided according to the number of muscular impressions on the inner surface of the valves, into Monomyaria, with one muscle, and Dimyaria, with two muscles. To the former belong the families Ostreacea, Pectinacea, and Aviculacea, numerous species of which inhabited the Molassic sea.

Oysters are represented by twelve species. Among them is the common oyster (*Ostrea edulis,* Linn.). The shells which have been found at Münsingen and St. Gall cannot be distinguished from those furnished by the present seas; and the group of the American oysters was also represented. One species (*O. virginica,* Lam.), which now lives on the coast of Florida, inhabited the Shell-sandstone sea, and is abundant near Münsingen and in the Siggenthal; and even the commonest species of the Molasse, remarkable for its long shells weighing several pounds (*Ostrea crassissima,* Lam.), which occurs in great beds near Hütlingen on the Belpberg and near Münsingen, also belongs to this group, which had made its appearance in the Eocene. Near Hütlingen a bed 1½ metre (or 5 feet) thick consists almost exclusively of such oyster-shells.

Pectinacea constitute a very ancient type, which peopled the sea through all geological periods, and is manifested within a limited number of forms in an inexhaustible multiplicity of species. In the Molasse they are represented by the genera *Lima* and *Pecten*. The former, which were abundant in the older seas of Switzerland (see vol. i. pp. 44, 75, and 136), are certainly approaching extinction, since only four species occur in the Molasse, two of which (*Lima inflata,* Linn., sp., and *L. squamosa,* Lam.) have continued to the present day.

The scallops (*Pecten*), on the contrary, although commencing just as early, have been developed into a great variety of species in all periods down to the present time. The Molassic sea contained fourteen species, several of which (such as *P. burdiga-*

lensis, Lam., *P. cypris,* D'Orb., *P. palmatus,* Lam., *P. pusio,* Linn., sp., *P. scabrellus,* Linn., and *P. solarium,* Lam.) are abundant. Eleven species are extinct; but three are still to be met with in European seas.

The pearl-mussels (Aviculacea) and the Mytilidæ are much less numerous, the former being represented only by a few species of *Avicula, Perna,* and *Pinna,* and the latter by four species of thin-shelled *Modiolæ,* which probably lived at great depths.

The Dimyaria are far richer in species than the Monomyaria. They are divided, in accordance with the structure of their mouth, into two great groups, namely :—the

> *Integropallealia,* in which the impression of the mantle is entire ; and the
> *Sinupallealia,* with a sinus or bend in the impression.

Of the former, nine families were represented in the Molassic sea. Of the Arcacea there are four species of the nearly circular *Pectunculi,* two of which (*P. insubricus* and *pilosus*) are abundant, and nine species of *Arca,* with regular boat-shaped shells. One of these (*Arca nivea*) appears as early as the Upper Eocene, and is still found living in the Red Sea; two other species (*A. lactea,* Linn., and *A. barbata,* Linn.) have also survived to the present day. The *Carditæ,* distinguished by their thick shells traversed by strong longitudinal ribs, are also among those Mollusca which made their appearance very early in the history of the earth; and eleven species still peopled the Molassic sea, of which one (*Cardita caliculata,* Linn.) is now met with in Europe and near Senegambia, whilst another species (*C. antiquata,* Linn.) is confined to the Mediterranean, and the remaining nine became extinct during the Miocene epoch.

The family Lucinida furnishes the genera *Diplodonta* and *Lucina,* the former with two still-living species, the latter with twelve species ; the Nuculida are represented by the genera *Nucula* and *Leda,* with eight species ; the Chamacea by two extinct forms of the now tropical genus *Chama* ; and the Cardiacea by the genera *Cyprina, Isocardia,* and *Cardium,* the last-mentioned being among the most abundant bivalves in brackish-water deposits. The Molasse possesses eighteen species, generally with large convex shells traversed by strong longitudinal ribs, some of them being peculiar extinct forms, whilst others are either still living or are represented at the present day by very similar species. Thus the common cockle (*Cardium edule,* Linn.) of the Swiss Molassic seas occurs in the sandstones of St. Gall, Lucerne, and Münsingen; some Mediterranean species (*C. oblongum,* Chemn., *C. hians* and *C. tuberculatum,* Linn.) are met with in the Molasse of the Cantons of Berne and St. Gall. The Indian cockle (*C. indicum*) has been found at the Belpberg, and a Senegambian species (*C. costatum,* Linn.?) near Berne. The genus *Cardium,* which makes its first appearance in very early times, was therefore abundantly developed in the Molassic sea, where it included species the areas of distribution of which are now widely separated. The fine genus *Isocardia,* in which the heart-shaped valves are furnished with spirally twisted beaks, is much less abundant. One species (*I. cor,* Linn.), which is met with in the Mediterranean, and more rarely on the British coasts, has been discovered near Rorschach.

The Dimyaria with the impression of the sinuated mantle (*Sinupallealia*) are represented by numerous families in the Swiss Miocene sea. The Veneracea, the valves of which have large beaks projecting over an internal concave lunula, furnish twenty-seven species. No doubt they lived, like their existing representatives, on shallow sandy shores, and buried themselves in the soil. They are now distributed upon all coasts, but the greatest number of species is found between the tropics. Several of these tropical forms (such as *Venus plicata,* Gmel., *V. multilamella,* Lam., and *Dosinia Adansoni,* Poli) formerly occurred in the Swiss area; but with these were associated five more species (*Venus ovata,* Mont., *V. casina,* Linn., *V. verrucosa,* Linn., *Cytherea minima,* Mont., and *C. rudis,* Poli) which now live in the Mediterranean or on the European coasts generally. One species (*Dosinia lincta,* Pult.), which has been found at the Belpberg, the Weinhalde, and the Rothsee, and near Niederhasli and St. Gall, is still living on the coasts of England, in the Mediterranean, and near Senegambia; and another species (*D. exoleta,* Lam.), which may be obtained in the Molasse of the Rothsee and at Imi in the Canton of Berne, has at present the same distribution.

The *Psammobiæ* furnish two large extinct species (*Psammobia*

Labordii, Bart., and *uniradiata,* Br.), the nearest allies of which live in tropical seas; the *Tellinæ* also occur in the greatest abundance and variety in the torrid zone, and possess only a few insignificant species in northern regions. Of the twelve species found in the Swiss Molasse, three (*Tellina senegalensis,* Hanl., *T. lacunosa,* Chemn., and *T. crassa,* Gmel.) are West-African forms, although *Tellina crassa* occurs in the North Sea and, with six other species, in the Mediterranean. It is worthy of notice that the Eocene species are of tropical and Australian types, but that half of the Miocene species are still continued in European seas.

The Corbulacea, in *Tugonia anatina,* afford a West-African type, and in *Corbula* they show a genus which previously occurred as early as the Carboniferous epoch. Of the latter the Molassic sea was inhabited by three still-existing species, one of which (*C. carinata,* Duj.) is now found in tropical Asia, the second (*C. revoluta,* Broc.) occurs in the Mediterranean, and the third (*C. gibba,* Ol.) on almost all European coasts.

The *Pholadomyæ* were represented in the Jurassic sea (see vol. i. p. 136) by numerous forms; at the commencement of the Tertiary period they had already become rare, and at present only a single West-Indian species remains of the genus. The two species of the Molasse (*Pholadomya helvetica,* May., and *P. arcuata.,* Lam., from St. Gall and Lucerne) are extinct. On the other hand, the *Amphidesma*-group is represented by three European species (*A. Syndosmya*); and the Pandorida has also three species in Europe.

The Mactrina have been distributed over all seas from very ancient times. Twenty-five species are known from the Molasse, most of them belonging to the genera *Mactra* and *Lutraria,* forms which bore into the sandy bottom of the sea. The Miocene species no doubt had the same mode of life; and to them is probably to be ascribed the production of those remarkable spirally twisted structures which have been found in various parts of the Molasse. These are rod-like bodies, about as thick as one's finger, on the sides of which are seated spirally twisted branches of equal thickness. Probably several animals lived together; first of all they would dig a hole perpendicularly into the sand, and then, starting from this aperture, make several spiral side-passages, each of which served as a dwelling-place for one animal. The tubes were afterwards filled up, and thus these singular "screwstones" (fig. 326) were produced. In favour of

Fig. 327.

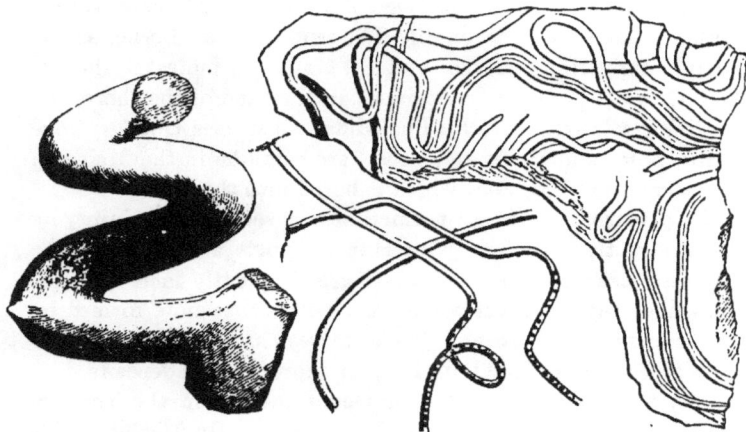

Fig. 326.   Fig. 325.

Fig. 325. *Gordiopsis valdensis*, Heer, from the shales of Troistorrents, in the Val d'Illiers.
Fig. 326. "Screwstone" from the Martinsbruck, in the Canton of St. Gall, half nat. size.
Fig. 327. *Helminthoida molassica*, Heer, from Reiden.

this explanation, the fact may be noticed that near the Martinsbruck in St. Gall, where these sandstones are particularly fine, M. Carl Mayer has found a *Lutraria* (*L. sanna*) in one of them. Near Rorbas, according to Dr. Biedermann, the screwstones are found in the uppermost layer of the lower freshwater Molasse at the boundary of the marine Molasse, which has furnished the materials for them; these animals consequently bored their holes in the hardened soil.

The Glycimerida, Solenacea, Pholadida, and Teredina, belonging to the same great division, form their dwellings, in like manner, sometimes in the sandy bottom and also in wood and rock; and in earlier periods of the earth's history they had the same habits as at present. The Molassic sea possessed representatives of all these families, and some of the species are still living. Near St. Gall *Saxicava arctica*, Linn., has formed in the rocks pear-shaped holes precisely similar to those made by its descendants, which now live on all northern coasts and also in the Mediterranean. A large *Panopæa* (*P. Menardi*, Desh.) forms great shell-beds on the Längenberg near Berne, and is found near Eriz, Lucerne, and St. Gall. It indicates shallow water, and it probably buried itself in the sand of the shore like its living relative. Of the Pholadida two species (*Pholas cylindrica*, Sow., and *P. rugosa*, Broc.) are common in the Molasse; the second lived in holes which it bored into the rock.

Ship-worms, which have sometimes caused so much injury by the destruction of wooden vessels in sea-ports, also inhabited the Molassic sea; fragments of wood are frequently met with traversed by tubes perfectly identical with those now formed by the common ship-worm (*Teredo norvegica*, Spengl.). As this species has been found in Italy in more recent deposits, it is hardly to be doubted that it has continued from the Tertiary epoch to the present day, and has constantly inhabited this region.

The Clavagellida are represented by four *Clavagellæ* and *Gastrochenæ*, which bored into various substances. The Solenacea (or razorshells), deriving their name (*solen*, a water-pipe) from the form of their long narrow shells gaping at the two ends, are still more numerous. They present several genera (*Solen, Psammosolen, Ensis,* and *Polia*), including species which are for the most part still living in Europe; these animals dig perpendicular holes in the sand to a depth of 2 or 3 feet. The Lithophagæ bored into stones; and one species (*Petricola lithophaga*, Retz.) is not unfrequently met with in rolled fragments of limestone. All these animals are characteristic of the sea-coast; and the holes bored by them into the rocks enable us to recognize the ancient shore and the level of the water upon it, even when the animals themselves have entirely disappeared.

The Mollusca constitute the principal part of the fossils of the marine Molasse. The Polythalamia, which occur elsewhere in great quantities in contemporaneous formations (for example, in the Vienna basin), have not as yet been investigated. Of corals only a few species have been found, and they did not form reefs. Among the Polyzoa are the *Celleporæ,* which constitute bark-like incrustations on the shells and stones (such as *Cellepora pumicosa,* Lam., from Corban), and round-celled *Milleporæ* (*M. truncata,* Lam.).

The sea-urchins, which were numerous in the Nummulitic sea, are much less frequently met with in the Molasse period. Only about half a dozen species are known; all of them are extinct, but they belong to living genera. Two species (*Psammechinus mirabilis,* Nic., sp., and *Spatangus ocellatus,* Desf.) have been discovered at La Chaux-de-Fonds; two others (*Brissopsis Nicoleti,* Des., and *Echinolampus scutiformis,* Dum.) have been found near Verrières in the Canton of Neuchâtel; a *Scutella* occurs near Kilwangen; and *Echinocardium Deikei,* Des., near St. Gall. The existence of starfishes in the Molassic sea is proved by slabs of sandstone covered with them which have been found near Reiden.

It is remarkable that few Crustacea remain in the marine Molassic strata. Only a small number of cirripedes (*Balani*) have been discovered, which doubtless had been attached to the rocks of the shóre. One species, identical with the common European *Balanus* (*B. tintinnabulum,* Linn.), is abundant in the marine Molasse, as in the quarry of Stockeren at the foot of the Bantigerhubel, near Berne, and near St. Gall; smaller species are found at the Belpberg, at Imi, and near Lucerne. When they are still attached to rocks they enable us to ascertain the limits of the sea and the height of its surface, as these animals always live on the border of the sea in the zone of breakers.

Scanty traces remain of worms of the Molassic sea; but here and there great quantities of the calcareous tubes of *Serpulæ* are found adhering to shells; and in some places the tortuous galleries of the Nemerteans occur, which have produced in the Molasse worm-stones of the same kind as in the Flysch. At least it seems very probable that to animals of this kind the fossil remains on the fragment of Shell-sandstone from Reiden, in the Canton of Lucerne, are to be ascribed. The specimen was communicated to Prof. Heer by M. Bachmann, and is represented in fig. 327, p. 103.

Of the remains of reptiles in the Molassic sea only a few large

crocodiles' teeth are found, which were discovered near Corban;
and there is a singular deficiency of fishes. Hitherto the principal remains discovered are those of cartilaginous fish, such as
Chimæroids, rays, and sharks. The last must have been very
abundant, as their teeth occur everywhere in the Shell-sandstone,
and here and there in great quantities. These teeth are smooth,
shining, compressed, flat in front, slightly convex behind, pointed
at the apex, and with both edges sharp; and they have, on
account of their form, received the popular names of "stone-
tongues" and "birds' beaks." Fourteen species from the
Molasse have been distinguished, two of which have been already
referred to (vol. ii. p. 89), the *Cacharodon megalodon* and *Lamna
cuspidata*, the latter having been of most frequent occurrence.
To these genera six more species may be added, such as *Carcha-
rodon polygyrus*, *C. Escheri*, and *Lamna contortidens* and *dubia*;
and the Shell-sandstone has furnished the teeth of several species
of *Oxyrhina*, *Notidanus*, *Hemipristis*, and *Galeocerdo* (*Oxyrhina
leptodon*, *O. hastalis*, *O. Desorii*, *Notidanus primigenius*, *Hemipristis serra*, *Galeocerdo aduncus*, and *G. minor*). The family
of the Chimæroids possesses one species (*Ischyodon helveticus*,
Eg.), which has been discovered on the Bucheckberg; and of
the rays two forms (*Zygobates Studeri*, Ag., and *Ætobates arcu-
atus*, Ag.) occur in the Shell-sandstone of the Canton of Aargovia. The whole of these Molassic fishes are extinct; but,
with the exception of the *Hemipristis*, they belong to genera
which possess similar species now living in the European and
tropical seas.

The few osseous fishes which have as yet been furnished by
the marine Molasse belong to the Gymnodontes and the Labroi-
dei. A *Diodon* and a *Labrus* (*L. Ibbetsoni*, Ag.) have been found;
the former probably had the body closely set with spines, and
the latter was probably adorned with varied colours.

Three species of Cetacea visited or inhabited the Swiss Molassic
region. The bones of a manati (*Halitherium Studeri*, Myr.) have
been discovered on the Lindenbühl, on the Randen, and in the
Shell-sandstone of the Canton of Aargovia. It is so nearly allied
to the Tongrian species already mentioned (vol. ii. p. 89) that
the two ought perhaps to be regarded as united. In the Shell-
sandstone of Othmarsingen and Zofingen the long beak-like

jaws of a dolphin (*Delphinus canaliculatus*, Meyer) have been discovered ; this animal at that time was very widely distributed. A second species (*D. acutidens*, Meyer) has been discovered at Molière.

Side by side with the remains of these animals, which undoubtedly lived in the sea, shells and bones of land animals are found in the marine Molasse, having been carried down by floods into the sea, and thus accidentally associated with the true marine fauna.

Land Mollusca have been already mentioned, some of which (such as the *Auriculæ*) very probably lived on the sea-shore, whilst others (such as the freshwater species and many snails) may have been swept down to the sea from a great distance. Among the Mammalia the teeth of two mastodons (*Mastodon angustidens* and *tapiroides*) are found in the Shell-sandstone ; and the remains of the tapir, of two rhinoceroses (*R. incisivus* and *R. minutus*), of a *Hyotherium* (*H. Meissneri*), of a *Hipparion* (*H. gracile*), and of two deer (*Cervus Scheuchzeri*, Meyer, sp., and *C. minor*) have been collected from the marine Molasse, proving that at that time these animals inhabited Switzerland.

CHAPTER X.

Description of some Swiss Miocene Localities.

Lausanne; the Hohe-Rhonen; St. Gall; Locle; the Molasse of the Canton of Zurich; Œningèn.

IF we wish to have a picture of nature, either as it once existed or as it is now to be seen, we must confine our attention to particular localities. Let us therefore endeavour to sketch such a picture of separate parts of Switzerland as may be suitable to give a clear idea of the natural characters of the flora of the country in Miocene times.

1. *Lausanne in Miocene times.*

It has been already shown (vol. i. p. 300) that at the time of the lignite formation a lake stretched from the neighbourhood of Vevey to the Paudèze, in the vicinity of Lausanne. The marl of Monod near Chexbres and that of Rochette in the little valley of the Paudeze enclose the remains of an abundant flora which once clothed the shores of this lake. In the Plate of "Lausanne in Miocene times" an attempt is made to reproduce this flora, and to show the character of the plants of that locality and period. Let us therefore transport ourselves in imagination to the shore of this lake, and cast a glance upon the landscape, which, freed by the magic wand of science from the durance of hard rocks, may rise from the bosom of the earth to a new life.

In the foreground the magnificent fan-leaves of the sabal-palms and of the great *Flabellariæ* are seen, and near them the long plumes of the *Phœnicites* are visible. To the left rises a camphor-tree with its numerous branches, the shining foliage of which converts the dense ramification into dark masses ; while the

laurel bushes growing at its foot and under its shelter, although still small, serve to develop a dark green coppice. These are two representatives of the evergreen trees of the period, which constituted the greater part of the forests, and were associated with thick-leaved fig-trees, some peculiar oaks, Proteaceæ, and hollies living on the shores of the lake. On the right-hand side of the Plate an *Acacia* rises from the herbage, showing its pods and elegant pinnate leaves, which stand out beautifully from the smooth mirror of the lake, stretching away towards the right, and here concealed by long-leaved willows, on which are seen two twining ferns (*Lygodium Gaudini* and *L. Laharpii*). These ferns constitute a special form of climbing plants, with which shrubby *Berchemiæ* and spinous sarsaparillas were blended.

Only a few branches come into view of a maple rising further to the right from the dense forest, and exhibiting its indented foliage. Leaves of a water-lily (*Nymphæa Charpentieri*) float on the surface of the lake, associated with a handsome *Nelumbium* (*N. Buchii*), the shield-shaped leaves of which rise into the air; but the Charas (*Ch. Meriani* and *Ch. Escheri*), which filled the water with green masses and supplied a refuge for *Limneæ* and *Cyclades* creeping over their leaves, as well as for water-beetles (*Hydrophilus Gaudini*) swimming about among them, are immersed in the water and do not appear in the picture. Large-leaved sedges and sweetrushes (*Cyperi*) crowned with long tufts of leaves rise from the lake close to its shore, which is also here and there fringed with large reeds.

In the middle distance a group of palms is seen; the leaves of young fan- and feather-palms (*Sabal, Phœnicites,* and *Manicaria*) spread over the soil, and are reflected in the dark waters. From this luxuriant mass of leaves rises the column-like stem of the great fan-palm (*Flabellaria Ruminiana*) waving its proud leafy crown towards the azure of heaven; the feathery *Phœnicites* (*P. spectabilis*) shows its long and finely divided pinnate leaves at the summit of a tall cylindrical stem; and the large flat leaves of the *Manicaria* (*M. formosa*) are seen here and there torn by the wind.

The background of the Plate is occupied by a group of Weymouth pines (*Pinus palæostrobus*), and to the right of these by a walnut (*Juglans acuminata*), as well as by a plant allied to the pine-apple (*Puya Gaudini*), the spiny leaves of which, united into a crown, spring from a woody stem. A crocodile close by is about to leap into the water, from which some tapirs are emerging after their bath. In the distance a herd of rhinoceroses is approaching the marshy shore, whilst some *Anthracotheria* advance from the shadow of the forest towards the cool waters.

At the present day, to see similar forms of vegetation we must transport ourselves some 15 degrees further south; and even then we shall nowhere find them assembled together in the same way as in the Miocene period. The best comparison may be made by visiting the morasses which in the southern United States of America spread over an immense district. There the fan-palm (*Sabal Adansoni*, the swamp-palmetto) covers wide regions of marshy land; many large grasses form lofty reed-beds, sometimes united into almost impenetrable masses; the drier spots are covered with the magnificent foliage of Weymouth pines, evergreen oaks and hollies, lofty walnut- and maple-trees, and shining magnolias and tulip-trees, often entwined by vines, sarsaparillas, and shrubby *Berchemiæ*.

The swamp-cypress (*Taxodium distichum*) penetrates into the most marshy localities, spreading its mighty roots over the soil, and forming with its branches, covered with elegant feathery twigs, a wide-spread dome supported on a lofty trunk. Here and there in these morasses small lakes are formed. Lesquereux describes one of these in the interior of the Great Dismal Swamp of Virginia, which vividly resembles the Swiss Miocene marshy lakes. "It is," says Lesquereux, "only accessible in a boat; for when we approach the shore some of the trees descend into the lake, so that only their summits are visible, whilst others have their trunks half covered with water. When once we have got away from the trees and into the true lake, the view is wonderful. Not that it is exactly picturesque; but the perfect uniformity of its surroundings and colours harmonizes admirably with the absolute solitude and death-like stillness of the scene. I saw there no single creature except the Negro whom I met in the forest and who guided the canoe, which glided so gently over the black waters that, although I was entirely occupied with my investigations, a deep melancholy affected my heart, as if I had been alone upon a desert island or in a new world."

2. *The Hohe-Rhonen.*

We find a perfectly similar flora to that of the Canton de Vaud in the lower lignite formation on the shore of the great lake which took the place of the sea in the alpine zone. The marls which enclose the lignites of the Hohe-Rhonen contain a rich herbarium which gives us valuable information with regard to this flora; they have preserved to our time a fragment of the marshy shore of the lake. Several beds of pebbles and sand were spread over this locality; and these probably by degrees filled up the bed of the lake and converted it into a muddy shore. Gradually a peat-moss was produced; but its formation was from time to time interrupted by deposits of mud, which now lies between the lignites in the form of dark-coloured marl. Large reeds and reed-maces (*Typha latissima*), numerous *Cyperi*, sedges, and rushes, *Spargania*, and Irids leave no doubt as to the nature of the soil; nay, in Greith, we can even indicate certain spots at which small brooks traversed the marshy forest ground, marked by bands of brittle black marl filled with fruits carried down by water (especially those of the maple), fine confervoid filaments, and small bivalve shells (*Cyclas*). A *Grewia* (*G. crenata*), the trilobate maple (*Acer trilobatum*), and species of *Liquidambar*, willows, and *Myricæ* must have grown there in abundance, as great numbers of their remains are found in the mud; the *Widdringtoniæ*, *Glyptostrobi*, and *Taxodia* (swamp-cypresses) were plentiful; and the last probably pushed forward, like their existing relatives, into the soft ground, forming the extreme outpost of the forest. Of palms we meet with three fine species at Hohe-Rhonen (namely *Sabal hæringiana*, *Phœnicites spectabilis*, and *Manicaria formosa*), where, in conjunction with the numerous evergreen oaks and leathery-leaved Proteaceæ, laurels, and fig-trees, they clothed the shore of the lake with an evergreen fringe. The abundant ferns (*Lastræœ*, *Aspidia*, and species of *Pteris* with long feathery fronds) probably grew in the shady forest, and, together with the bilberries, hazels, jujubes, sumachs, and buckthorns, formed its undergrowth.

In this primæval wooded district dwelt a tapir and two species of rhinoceros, a deer, and the *Chalicotherium*. They had, in the dog-like carnivorous animal *Amphicyon intermedius,* an associate whose rapacity probably often disturbed the peaceful silence of the old forest.

The other parts of the shore of the Alpine lake with which we are acquainted present us with a very similar flora. They consist of some small patches at Rufii near Schännis, and more to the north at Wäggithal, at Rothenthurm, and the Rosenberg, in which are found the same species of plants, intermixed with some other peculiar forms.

3. *St. Gall.*

A very different picture is presented by the environs of St. Gall during the Helvetian stage. To form an idea of this scene we must imagine all the hills and mountains removed which now so charmingly environ the town of St. Gall, for the material of which these elevations consist was only accumulated in Miocene times. The country between St. Gall and the Cretaceous mountains of Appenzell consists of Lower Freshwater Molasse, and was clothed with plants, in the remains of which twenty-two species have been found in the sandstones of Teuffen and at the Ruppen. With about forty species known from the Lower Molasse of the neighbourhood of St. Gall, they form a small flora which gives us some information as to the Miocene vegetation of the district. It was wooded with evergreen camphor and laurel trees, as well as with walnut-trees, poplars, and *Robiniæ* and fine-leaved *Acaciæ.* Several species of Cyperaceæ and a reed-mace (*Massetta*) indicate a marshy soil. This flora probably maintained itself south of St. Gall during the whole period of the formation of the Molasse; but in the vicinity of St. Gall it was destroyed by the irruption of the sea which took place during the Helvetian period. At this epoch we find traces here of a sea-shore. The quarry in the immediate vicinity of St. Gall shows the spot where a brook, flowing from the south, emptied itself into the sea. Its banks were fringed with reeds and reed-maces, the remains of which we now find in the marls. Leaves are met with of the trilobate maple, of a species of bilberry, a holly, and some dogwoods and buckthorns, probably growing upon its banks; whilst two rigid-leaved *Banksiæ* (*B.*

helvetica and *Deikii*) and two oaks (*Quercus sclerophyllina* and *elæina*) flourished upon the drier and more distant land. If we trace the brook to the place where it falls into the Miocene sea, we come upon a brackish-water formation, which is recognizable at once by the softness of the rock and its bluish colour. It is about 15 feet thick, and must have originated from an extremely fine mud. Together with the leaves and a few land Mollusca (*Helices* and *Auricula oblonga*), which were swept down to the sea and buried in its mud, we find thousands of a small brackish-water animal (*Paludina* or *Bythinia acuta*), and in the uppermost portion numerous cockles (*Cardium hispidum*), whole families of clamshells (*Chama gryphina*, Lam.) and *Diplodontæ* (*D. rotundata*), and here and there a few scattered oysters (*Ostrea crassissima*). This brackish-water stratum overlies a deposit containing numerous shells of *Venus* and *Lutraria*, which no doubt hollowed out their dwelling-places in the mud; and still lower we meet with a layer of *Turritellæ* and *Pandoræ*. The soft marl found in the brackish water is covered by a pebble-bed about 1½ foot thick, which offers us the traces of a rich marine fauna that lived among the pebbles. Attached to and among these rounded stones are tubicolar Annelides, small corals, and numerous *Vermeti* (*V. intortus*); and within the fragments of limestone are many living bivalves (*Gastrochænæ, Saxicavæ, Spheniæ*, and *Pholades*) which there formed a dwelling, whilst others sheltered themselves in the tubes and passages formed by the boring Mollusca, such as the *Petricolæ, Gastranæ*, young *Limæ*, and *Mactræ*, which we now find in the interior of these stones. Among the pebbles we see whole colonies of *Turbos* (*T. muricatus*) and *Murices* (*M. trunculus* and *vaginatus*), and numerous species of *Pleurotoma, Fusus*, and *Buccinum*. Shining cowries (*Cypræa sanguinolenta*), curious *Xenophoræ* (*X. Deshayesi*), beautiful *Ancillariæ* and *Columbellæ*, and species of *Mitra, Oniscia*, and *Cassis* are also discovered if we carefully search this friable rock. Favourable conditions were here afforded for the development of Veneridæ (*Venus multilamella, Cytherea crassissima*, and *Lucinopsis Lajonkairei*), of *Pholadomyæ* (*P. arculata*), *Dosiniæ* (*D. Adansoni*), and *Diplodontæ*. For so rich a fauna there must have been at this spot a sheltered bay, into which at first a brook discharged itself, the direction of which subsequently perhaps became diverted by its bed being filled up with pebbles and rubbish; for the brook disappears in the pebble-bed of the brackish-water formation, which shows us a purely marine fauna such as lives within the littoral zone.

The brackish-water formation ceases at the distance of six minutes' walk to the east of the quarry (near the Tivoli), and it also disappears at the Steinach, a distance of fifteen minutes' walk to the west of the town, so that it was not of great extent. Hence only a small brook here fell into the sea, forming a narrow delta which now constitutes the marl of the quarry. In the sandstone rocks quarried in the deep ravine of the Sitter, near the Krätzernbrücke, at Stocken, and at Kobelmühle, as well as near the Martinsbrücke and in the wild ravine of the Goldach, we have a thin freshwater layer between the marine beds; but the strata enclosing it exhibit conditions varying from those of the quarry, and prove that even at this small distance the deposits were differently formed. On the Sitter we have repeated alternations of conglomerate, sandstone, and marl-beds, demonstrating that constant changes took place in the transportation of the materials of which these rocks consist, and that consequently diverse modifications of the fauna also occurred. We find, according to Carl Mayer, at the bottom, beds with oysters and cones, then strata with Veneridæ and species of *Tapes*, and still higher blue marls full of *Turritellæ*; but the brackish-water formation and the overlying pebble-bed (which is so rich in animal remains characterizing the quarry) are wanting. Everywhere in the environs of St. Gall we meet with a peculiarly constituted marine fauna, and with traces of the alternate action of marine and land conditions. This is also the case if we study the marine Molasse of Lucerne or of Bäch. On the great sandstone slabs of Bäch we not unfrequently see the most distinct ripple-marks. We meet with slabs the surface of which looks as if it had been swept in one direction, and with other slabs traversed by numerous interlacing undulated lines, in the depressions of which carbonaceous particles and indistinct plant-remains have accumulated, just as may be seen in the sandy mud of the sea-shore; sometimes roundish impressions may be observed which have been ascribed to the action of rain-drops, or long galleries resembling the tracks of marine animals. Cylindrical bodies, which in some parts of the sandstones of Bäch occur in great quantities, are probably due to the filling-up of the dwellings of bivalve Mollusca and wormstones, the work of marine worms. We have therefore everywhere before us sea-shore formations into the sand of which animals have either penetrated or have been driven by the force of the waves; and their fossil remains have thus been covered up and preserved to the present time.

4. Locle.

The white freshwater limestones of Locle offer us a portion of the later Miocene flora belonging to a period when the sea had disappeared from these regions. They were deposited during the Œningian stage at the bottom of the lake which then spread over the district. The innumerable carapaces of a small ostracod crustacean (*Cypris faba*, fig. 205, p. 6), the pond-mussels (*Anodonta Heerii*, May.), and the remains of water-beetles (*Dytiscus Nicoleti*) and of pondweeds and Charas furnish evidence of the existence of this lake; and the leaves of reed-maces (*Typha*) and reeds inform us that it had a marshy sedgy shore. The fan-palm (*Sabal Ziegleri*) and a large *Equisetum* also probably lived in the marsh. The flora which surrounded the lake must have been very rich in species; for the limestone encloses the remains of 140 species, 104 of which were trees or shrubs. The most abundant tree is a laurel (*Laurus princeps*); consequently a laurel-forest must have adorned the landscape. An *Andromeda* (*A. protogæa*) and a small-leaved maple (*Acer decipiens*) were also plentiful. The liquidambars, poplars, and willows, of which ten species occur, probably spread along the river-banks; whilst the small-leaved Proteaceæ, the evergreen oaks, and numerous Leguminosæ no doubt clothed the drier hills. One of the peculiarities of this flora is the great prominence of the Proteaceæ (nine species); the latter were spiny twining plants which climbed up the shrubs and trees and garlanded them with their heart-shaped leaves.

5. *The Molasse of the Canton of Zurich (Albis, Horgen, Elgg, Veltheim, Irchel).*

In Western Switzerland the only remains of the Œningian period are found in the flora of Locle, and in a certain number of trees (principally poplars and willows) which probably fringed the brook flowing from the Vosges mountains through the valley of Delsberg. After the retreat of the sea belonging to the Helvetian stage from Switzerland, the Cantons of Vaud, Friburg, and Berne were probably dry land; and they appear to have possessed no lakes in the muddy deposits of which the fragments of the flora of the country might have been preserved.

In Eastern Switzerland, however, a large freshwater lake spread over the Cantons of Zurich and Thurgau, in which were deposited masses of sand and pebbles, forming the Upper Swiss freshwater Miocene. This lake has been already noticed in vol. i. p. 302 of the present work; and the lignite-beds, and the remains of plants contained in various portions of them, show that in several localities the lake had been converted into peat-bogs and marshes.

From the Albis, from Irchel, Stettfurt, Berlingen, and Steckborn Prof. Heer has obtained a number of leaves belonging to sixty species of plants. The most abundant trees were the poplars (*Populus latior, P. balsamoides,* and *P. mutabilis*), camphor-trees (*Cinnamomum polymorphum*), and the beautiful *Podogoniæ*; and the forests also contained liquidambars, laurels, willows, maples, dogwoods, and buckthorns.

At Käpfnach a peat-moss has been found. The brownish yellow bituminous marl and marl-shale with compressed shells which underlie the bed of coal represent the white bottom; the black shales which here and there intersect the coal are the muddy deposits of the water which from time to time inundated the marshy ground. They only contain scanty remains of reed-like plants; and the lignites present here and there compressed palm-stems, probably belonging to the *Sabal* (see vol. i. p. 336). The complete absence of the leaves of trees would seem to prove that there were no forest trees in the neighbourhood. The bones and teeth are preserved of numerous mammals which strayed into the marsh and perished there.

At Elgg (two Swiss miles east of Winterthur) the teeth and bones of mammals are found in the lignites, and the blue marls overlying them contain many leaves lying densely packed together. Probably the water had poured down on the moss in the autumn, and had carried down with it the fallen leaves of the forest, which soon became imbedded in a deposit of mud. Most of the leaves were furnished by a fig-tree (*Ficus tiliæfolia*); there are also numerous twigs of a conifer (*Glyptostrobus europæus*), and less frequently the remains of a large-fruited maple (*Acer otopterix*) and of some beautiful ferns are met with. The fig-tree occurs also at Herdern and Œningen, so that it was probably diffused over the whole region. In the fig-tree forests lived the ape which has been already referred to; here also dwelt great mastodons and rhinoceroses, some peculiar species of pigs, deer, and equine *Anchitheria*; on the shores of the lake the little beaver (*Chalicomys minutus*) built its ingenious dwelling; whilst the otter concealed itself in holes of the ground, and the calling-hare (*Lagomys œningensis*) made its nest among the stones.

While the lignites of Elgg announce a slow and quiet formation of peat, the sandstones of Veltheim (twenty minutes' walk north of Winterthur) indicate a place where a brook probably flowed into the lake. They contain a good deal of rolled gravel and rounded fragments of marl; and in these beds are found teeth of large Mammalia (*Mastodon angustidens, Rhinoceros incisivus*, and *Hyænælurus Sulzeri*), which were swept together by the waters; and the remains of large tortoises are also found, which lived at the mouth of the river. This sandstone-formation may be traced as far as Irchel, and in many places contains the leaves of plants (especially willows, poplars, and camphor-trees) which were carried down into the shallow water.

The neighbourhood of Zurich probably at this time formed the bottom of a shallow lake, upon which here and there dwelt Charas, crustaceans, and aquatic Mollusca. Their remains are met with near Schwammendingen and at Faletschen. The entire absence of leaves of trees in the Zurich Miocene seems to show that no forests then clothed the dry land of that neighbourhood. The bones and teeth of a mastodon and of a rhinoceros found near the Weid and in the tunnel of Wipkingen

probably belonged to animals which were carried by water into
the lake.   At the Albis, in the south-west of the Canton
of Zurich, numerous leaves make their appearance in the
sandstone; they furnish indications of twenty-seven species of
plants, among which poplars and camphor-trees once more
predominate.   In all these places, however, the leaves are badly
preserved; they lie in a coarsely granular mass mixed together
in all directions, and are to be regarded as forest leaves dropped
from trees and swept together by the action of water.   Fortunately, in Œningen, on the frontier of Switzerland, we possess a
a locality at which the plants and animals of the surrounding
country accumulated for many years, and were preserved in a
remarkably beautiful manner for the study of a later age.
Œningen has been celebrated for the last 150 years, and has
become the most important place in the world for the investigation of the Miocene land-fauna and flora.   It merits now a
special description.

6. Œningen.

Wangen and Œningen are situated on the north or Baden side
of a narrow arm of the lake of Constance leading to the Rhine.
These localities stretch along the southern slope of a chain of
hills which projects into the lake of Constance and is partially
surrounded by its arms.   If we ascend from either Wangen or
Œningen, in about half an hour we reach the limestone-quarries
which contain the fossils.   The quarries really belong to the
domains of the communes of Wangen and Schienen; but as
their fossils were first made known through the monks of
Œningen, the name of that place has been conferred upon them.
Two quarries are worked.   The lower one is about 550 feet
above the lake of Constance; the upper quarry is about
150 feet higher.   The strata of the two quarries do not correspond with each other, and were probably formed in two separate small pools, or perhaps in two separate corners of the same
lake.   The bottom of the lake-basin is composed of soft Molasse; upon this there was, first of all, deposited a clayey marl
which prevented the water from draining away.   Over that bed
succeeded numerous strata of limestones and marls, which exhibit great differences in their constitution in the two quarries.

In the *Lower Quarry*, immediately upon the yellow marl, there is an extremely fine-grained limestone, which is only 1 inch in thickness, and splits into yellowish or grey layers as thin as paper. In these layers the plants and insects are imbedded, and often are so wonderfully well preserved that they look as if they had been painted. The *insect-bed* consists of about 250 lamellæ, or layers, the formation of which probably occupied a long series of years, during which plants and animals were deposited at all seasons of the year in this book of Nature. The layers that contain the flowers of the camphor-trees and poplars were probably produced in the spring, those which furnish winged ants and the fruits of elms, poplars, and willows in the summer, and those containing the fruits of the camphor-trees, the *Diospyros*, the *Clematis*, and the Synanthereæ in the autumn. The deposits must have been formed in quiet water and at a distance from the mouth of any river. Probably poisonous gases or vapours rose from this spot into the air and killed the insects flying over the water. The prodigious number of species of insects here met with shows us that not only the animals of the neighbouring shores, but those of a large area, must in the lapse of time have here found their graves.

Above the insect-bed, in the lower quarry, are several strata of a sandy calcareous marl and white, bluish, and reddish-grey limestones, here and there containing round pebbles, which show that they were produced under the influence of water flowing into the lake. But during the whole period of their formation no aquatic vegetation settled in this spot, perhaps because the gases emitted were unfavourable to the development of plants; and only the leafy trees and cypresses (*Glyptostrobus*) of the neighbouring forest furnished a certain number of remains of plants, to which were added small vegetable fragments carried by the wind from greater distances.

In the *Upper Quarry* the compact indigo-blue marl which covered the bottom of the lake is overlaid by a hard bituminous limestone, which has received the name of *Kettlestone*. It is the chief source of the fossil plants of Œningen. The leaves, the organic matter of which is preserved, are generally of a brown or brownish-yellow colour, and stand out in beautiful relief on the white stone. True aquatic plants are very rare, but the stems and rhizomes of reeds and reed-maces are tolerably abundant; so that there were evidently reed-beds in the neighbourhood, in which probably flourished the beautiful iris (*Iris Escheræ*), the marsh Umbelliferæ inhabited by the species of *Lixus*, and sedges and *Cyperi*.

The greater part of the leaves belong to leafy trees. Among these the three-lobed maple predominates; then follow poplars (*Populus latior* and *mutabilis*), soap-trees (*Sapindus falcifolius*), a walnut (*Juglans acuminata*), and a *Podogonia*; all these trees probably lived in the vicinity of the shore. The maple and the poplars no doubt grew upon swampy ground, as did also the alder, the *Myricæ*, and the sumachs. It is probable that the other plants did not grow in the marshes themselves, but in the more or less humid forest ground which immediately adjoined the swampy shore. Among the inhabitants of the forest were *Podogonia*, soap-trees, and walnuts, with which a number of other trees and shrubs were associated, including the camphor- and cinnamon-trees, the lime-leafed fig, the *Diospyros*, the oleander-leafed oak, a *Robinia* (*R. Regeli*), the bladder-senna (*Colutea*), and the *Cæsalpiniæ*.

Besides these plants, the "Kettlestone" contains many insects belonging to land and water and some crustaceans. There are but few species; but the number of individuals is very great, proving that they lived in the same neighbourhood. The Kettlestone has preserved a portion of the marshy shore of the lake. Plants and insects which lived on the spot are chiefly met with, and are intermingled with a few which were conveyed from greater distances by currents either of air or water.

A considerable time probably elapsed in the formation of the Kettlestone, as the different seasons of the year are represented in it: layers are found with the flowers of the *Podogonia*, maples, and poplars, which indicate the spring; others with ants' wings and summer insects and fruits of poplars and willows, which ripen in the summer; and others, again, with fruits of the maple, camphor-tree, and plane tree, and with twigs of poplar-bearing flower-buds like those of the existing species in the autumn.

Higher up the plants become more scarce, and in the thick white bed which covers the Kettlestone there are only a few isolated leaves of land-plants. But the upper bed contains large pikes, and has furnished gigantic frogs, a small tortoise, a fine large salamander, and the bones of calling-hares. In the bed called the "Dillstecken" the plants have entirely disappeared. Probably the shore part of the lake gradually became shallower, the mouth of the river no longer maintained its position, and by degrees the marshy ground was laid dry. Hence the bed of calcareous marl hardened, and a number of regular fissures were formed in it, dividing its entire surface into quadrangular clods. In this manner the origin of the singular sharp-edged blocks formed by the deposit may be explained. Volcanic action may have assisted in the drying-up of the stratum ; and afterwards the district was again laid under water, probably on account of the mouth of the river having been brought into its vicinity. First of all a number of pond-mussels (*Anodonta Lavateri*) established themselves in the locality ; their shells now cover the rock which overlies the "Dillstecken," and is coarse and sandy, showing that at the time of its formation the bottom of the lake was covered with sand. The ground was well fitted to receive the sand-loving *Isoëtes Braunii*, which has been found there in great abundance and formed a dense green tuft ; it also produced a pondweed (*Potamogeton geniculatus*), which appears in such quantities that the stone is permeated by it in all directions, and has received from it a dark colour. On the shore, reeds, willows, and poplars again appear. The number of species of plants, however, is small, and there are but few in the strata next above it, which have received the names of "cotton-bed," "black bed," "tortoise-bed," and "salamander-bed," the last two being the chief sources of large tortoises and salamanders. It would appear that the bottom of the lake had become deeper, or that it was removed further from the shore, so that the leaves which were floated into the lake no longer reached this point. The black bed alone contains many leaves, but almost exclusively those of a poplar and a willow (*Populus mutabilis* and *Salix angusta*), which shows that these two species must have grown in abundance upon the shore.

The salamander-bed is overlaid by about 4 feet of a hard limestone, known as the great and little "Mocken." The great quantity of reeds, reed-maces, and pondweeds that are met with in the "great Mocken" indicates that the spot was near the shore. The tenches which characterize this rock also demonstrate a shallow muddy bottom. But the plants gradually disappear, and the "little Mocken," which may have been in the middle of the mouth of the river, contains no plants.

A period of perfectly still water succeeded, in which a great quantity of larvæ of dragonflies swam about among Charas and Ulveæ (*Enteromorpha stagnalis*). These larvæ are found by hundreds in the dragonfly-bed; but few of them are well preserved. Other insects are very scarce; and of land-plants only a few small leaves of an elm, a *Weinmannia*, and an *Edwardsia* have been found. Large leaves are entirely wanting, as are also the shore-plants, such as reeds and reed-maces; the locality seems to have become a quiet bay, the shore of which was almost destitute of plants, and small leaves of a few plants which grew upon the shore were carried into the little bay by the wind.

From the fact already mentioned (vol. ii. p. 24) that dragonfly-larvæ of all ages lie intermixed in certain slabs, it would appear that these insects had been suddenly killed, and that they were subsequently enveloped by snow-white limestone. Had there been no violent action, it would be difficult to explain how such quantities of these larvæ could have been buried in the rock, some in a running, others in a resting position, with the mask extended or retracted. Dragonflies may have lived on the spot during the formation of both the higher beds and the "Kettle-stone"; but they were not disturbed in their development; when completely developed they rose into the air, and no traces remain of their larvæ. In the next higher bed, dragonflies entirely disappear; the pondweed again makes its appearance, and with it numerous white fish (*Leuciscus*). One bed higher, and both plants and fish entirely vanish; but in this bituminous rock, which is known as "Mollen"-stone, fine teeth of a mastodon (*M. tapiroides*) have been found. Sandy calcareous marls which follow the "Mollen"-stone show a destitution of plants. Both the Mollen-stone and the calcareous marl exhibit a great variation in thickness (from ½ foot to 5 feet) within a very small space, showing that the mouth of the river probably opened into this spot; whilst the higher calcareous beds, which form rubbish-beds, must have been deposited in rather quieter water, seeing that in them some leaves of poplars and camphor-trees again occur. These leaves show that the youngest and uppermost beds belong to the same period as those below them.

From this description it appears that in the course of time great changes took place in precisely the same spot in the lake of Œningen, probably occasioned chiefly by the river which opened into the lake, and aided perhaps by a rising and sinking of the ground, which might be due to volcanic agency. Prof. Arnold Escher de la Linth has ascertained that in the bed of the brook below the lower quarry at Œningen there occurs a very peculiar dark-coloured volcanic rock, which, by its pisolitic grains, its fragments of limestone, and its rounded and angular fragments of blackish fine-grained granite, often as big as a man's fist, resembles the phonolitic and basaltic tuffs of the neighbouring Höhgau. The same rock also occurs on the road between Solenhof and Langenmoos, above and below the level of the upper quarry; and the dark brown arable clay in the immediate vicinity of the upper quarry seems also to indicate a volcanic origin, and resembles the soil produced from the decomposition of the tuffs of Höhgau.

The occurrence of these volcanic rocks in the bowl-like environs of the quarries of Œningen renders it probable that during the Upper Miocene period volcanic eruptions here took place, and that, as in the Höhgau, volcanic rubbish accompanied by fragments of limestone and granite were brought to the surface. By the action of these causes the Molassic ground of the region acquired a bowl-like depression, in which water accumulated and a lake was formed. It is manifest that the volcanoes of the Höhgau were in activity at the same time with those of Œningen, as the plants contained in the tuffs of Hohenkrähen agree with those of Œningen. From the district of Ochsenwang (south of Kirchheim) in northern Wirtemberg Prof. Heer is acquainted with a dark basaltic tuff which is proved to be contemporaneous with the Œningian formation by the plants and insects which are contained in it.

A summary of the species of plants and animals belonging to Œningen is given in the following Tables :—

Number of Species of Plants discovered at Œningen up to 1865.*

Cryptogamia	43
Gymnospermia	12
Monocotyledones	57
Apetala	86
Polypetala	169
Gamopetala	66
Not classified	42

Number of Species of Animals discovered at Œningen up to 1865.

Mollusca	4
Crustacea	7
Spiders and Mites	29
Insects	826
Fishes	32
Reptiles	12
Birds	6 (?)
Mammals	6

Of the plants of Œningen, 143 species have been also found in the Swiss Miocene; but the majority are only known from Œningen itself. Most of them were no doubt at that time distributed over Switzerland, only they have not been preserved. It is obvious that the remains of delicately constructed insects and spiders must have had favourable circumstances for their preservation in this locality. A glimpse into the wonderful world of the Miocene period is afforded in the rich carpet of

---

* In the ' Tertiary Flora of Switzerland,' 465 species have been described from Œningen by Prof. Heer, who has since received 10 new species, namely *Smilax Targionii*, Gaud., *Sparganium alternans*, *Myrica Studeri*, Heer, *Cypselites Parlatorii* and *pulchellus*, *Bignonia Damaris*, Heer, *Myrsine gracilis*, *Rhus hydrophila*, Ung., sp., *Myrtus œningensis*, and *Crataegus Buchiana*, 9 of which are also new to the Swiss flora, so that the number of species in the latter is raised to 929.

plants which once adorned the district of Œningen, and in the varied fauna which filled the forests, the meadows, and the waters with life.

Very different is the picture if we now ascend from the quarries of Œningen to the summit of the Schienerberg. We may sit upon the ruins of the old Schrotzberg, and glance from our wooded height over the fertile hill-country of the Thurgau, where vineyards and orchards alternate with meadows and cornfields; and beyond them we may gaze on the blue mirror of the lake of Constance, environed towards the south by high mountains, whilst to the north is a gently undulating plain, from which rise the volcanic cones of the Höhgau.

CHAPTER XI.

CLIMATE OF THE MIOCENE DISTRICT.

PLANTS and animals were doubtless subjected to the same laws in former ages as in the present day. Every species now, as in geological times, requires for its development a definite amount of light and heat, of air and water, and its distribution over the surface of the earth is dependent upon these conditions. So much influence has particularly been exerted by heat and water, that, owing to these agencies, each species of the animal as well as the vegetable kingdom has been confined within definite limits. Important information is thus afforded by fossil plants and animals respecting the climate of bygone ages. When a collection of plants is laid before a botanist who is familiar with the geographical divisions of the vegetable world, he will be able to decide on the climate of the country from which the plants are derived. A climatal limitation of area applies also to animals, and particularly insects, which differ greatly in accordance with the conditions of climate. If correct inferences can be drawn from existing plants and animals as to the climate of the country to which they belong, accurate conclusions may also be possible with respect to extinct or fossil species; and our deductions will attain more certainty in proportion to the abundance of the materials at our command, and to the near alliance of the animals and plants to those now living.

A great number of species have been found in the fauna and flora of the Tertiary epoch which are nearly allied to existing forms. Among the inhabitants of the sea the relationship in many cases amounts to a perfect identity of species; and the approximation between moderns and ancients in many species of land plants and animals is so close that the Tertiary species may with great probability be regarded as the ancestors of the existing species.

In the Miocene a rich fauna and flora are spread before us, showing the development of a complete series of phenomena of plant and animal life both on land and in the water; and all agree in telling us that the Miocene country must have had a warm and, indeed, subtropical climate.

It has been already shown (vol. i. pp. 310, 311) that the flora of the Miocene was much richer in species than that of the present day, and that its numerical proportions are such as now occur in subtropical regions. The insects, reptiles, and Mammalia also present a surprising abundance of species, such as southern lands alone can now show, and such as is possible only where the earth is clothed by a luxuriant vegetation. That the flora of the Miocene period must have been greatly in excess of the existing Swiss flora is proved by the Swiss Miocene trees and shrubs far exceeding in number of species the united floras of Germany and Switzerland at the present day. The majority of the woody Miocene plants (between two thirds and three fifths of the whole Miocene flora) possessed evergreen foliage, as may be demonstrated by the leathery consistence of the leaves and the analogy of nearly connected living species. This state of vegetation characterizes warm zones (see vol. i. p. 311), and it could not be maintained in a country subject to cold snowy winters such as we now have in Central Europe. A single severe winter would have utterly destroyed evergreen forests similar to those of the Miocene.

Œningen and the marls of the Schrotzburg have furnished Prof. Heer with remarkable information as to the course of the seasons. Plants, as is well known, are dependent on the seasons and on climate for the constantly recurring cycle of their development. This influence, however, affects some plants in a greater degree, and other plants in a less degree; and therefore the intervals of the developmental epochs, such as the period of flowering of the same plants, are not the same in all latitudes. Such epochs in northern latitudes are generally more distant and more distinctly marked, and in the warmer zones they are brought closer together. Whenever we can ascertain what trees burst into leaf and flower in the Tertiary period at the same

time, we shall acquire important data as to the climate of the
Tertiary district.   Upon these points we obtain evidence by
submitting to a careful examination the plants and insects lying
together upon the same slab of stone.   If these are well preserved and lie exactly in the same plane of bedding, they must
have been simultaneously enveloped by the stony mass.   We
should, however, take into consideration that only such objects
have come down to us as were enclosed by the stone in a short
time, while those which lay longer in the water became decom-
posed and perished.   An exact comparison of many slabs from
Œningen and the Schrotzburg has proved that in Miocene
times the periodical phenomena of the vegetable world were of
the same nature as those now going on in the subtropical zones.
On a slab of stone from the Schrotzburg the flower of the camphor-tree lies quite close to the male flowers of a willow (*Salix
varians*), and very near to leaves of the plane, the liquidambar,
and the maple.   The willow and camphor-trees consequently
bloomed at the same time ; the planes already unfolded their
leaves, and were likewise in flower ; and it appears that at the
same time the poplars flowered, for upon another slab Prof.
Heer has seen associated with the male catkins of the poplar
(*Populus latior*) the leaves of planes, elms, liquidambars, and
willows.   This is a condition of things which no longer occurs
in Switzerland, or indeed anywhere in the temperate zone.   The
willow above referred to is most nearly allied to the crack-
willow (*Salix fragilis*), which flowers in Central Europe at the
end of April and the beginning of May; the development of
the leaves and flowers of the plane takes place later.   Until
towards the middle of May the plane remains perfectly bare;
then the buds begin to open, the leaves break forth very gradually, and simultaneously with them appear the globular catkins; but it is only towards the end of May that the plane
acquires its green mantle and comes into full bloom, and it is
some time longer before it arrives at its perfect foliage.   At the
time when the crack-willow begins to flower, the planes are
therefore quite bare in Switzerland, and three or four weeks
elapse before they bear fully developed leaves.   If we assume
that the flowering of the willow lasts fourteen days, there is still
an interval of one or two weeks between the fall of its flowers

and the leafing of the planes. If we turn to southern latitudes we find that, in Madeira, the planes are leafless in winter; from the middle to the end of March their buds begin to open; and at the beginning of April they have flowers and young leaves, which, however, are fully developed only at the middle of April. Thus the development of the leaves and flowers of the plane (at least in the neighbourhood of Funchal) commences from six weeks to two months earlier than at Zurich. The Swiss *Salix fragilis* does not occur in Madeira; but its place is taken by a species (the Canarian willow) which is most nearly related, on the one hand, to the Swiss crack-willow, and on the other to the species of the Miocene, both of which it represents in the Atlantic islands. This Canarian willow certainly begins to flower about a month earlier than the plane; but its flowering-time lasts much longer, and is continued until the end of April, so that in Madeira the willows and planes are seen at the same time in flower and with fully developed leaves. Here, therefore, these phases of development coincide with each other, because the period of flowering lasts longer, and is not so sharply defined as in more northern latitudes: many trees put forth flowers and fruit throughout the year; and in those which are limited to particular seasons the transitions are less perceptible and flow more into each other than in temperate climates. That this was the case also in the Miocene district is shown by two slabs with well-preserved willow-flowers and plane-leaves lying side by side, as also by a slab with a female catkin of a willow (*Salix Lavateri*) and the leaves of the liquidambar. If we may further infer from such facts that these trees bloomed and put forth their leaves at the same period as their existing near allies in Madeira, this period would be about the end of March. It is interesting also to notice the presence of a flower of the camphor-tree lying side by side with flowers of willow and leaves of the plane, *as in the gardens of Madeira the camphor-tree flowers exactly at the same time*—about the end of March.

We arrive at the same results if we extend our investigations to the flowers of the poplars. The Lombardy poplar begins to flower at Funchal in Madeira at the end of March, therefore at the same time as the plane, whilst in Switzerland and Germany it precedes that tree by more than a month. But we have already mentioned that, on a slab from the Schrotzburg, male flowers of the poplar lie besides plane-leaves, which never appear before the flowers. We learn also, by the comparison of the leaves lying on the same slab*, that the hornbeams were already in leaf at the flowering-time of the willows and poplars, and therefore at the end of March (whilst at the present day in Switzerland they only acquire their leaves in the middle of May) ; and from the evidence of the Miocene slabs the liquid-ambars, the elms, and the narrow-leaved maple also bore perfectly developed leaves at the same time with hornbeams and with the flowers of willows and poplars. Thus trees with deciduous foliage, in Miocene times, developed their leaves as they now do in warmer zones, about a month or six weeks earlier than in the modern Swiss climate. We know already that at the time of the Upper Miocene the evergreen trees and shrubs formed nearly half the total number; but at the same time the woody plants with deciduous foliage also retained their green mantle considerably longer than do their allies in the existing Swiss flora, and a much milder climate was indicated by the flowering and foliation of the deciduous trees at the same time.

The warmth of the climate is also proved from the occurrence of certain fruits. The fleshy fruits of the laurels are soon destroyed when they are exposed to the influence of the weather. We find, however, the fruit and leaves of a cinnamon-tree close beside catkins of the poplar ; they were therefore imbedded in the spring ; and the cinnamon consequently probably bore ripe

---

* These relations are discussed in more detail in Prof. Heer's work 'On the Flora and Climate of the Tertiary district' (pp. 59 *et seqq.*). In these investigations it must not be forgotten that the autumn-falling leaves of many trees (such as the beeches) remain well preserved for a long time on the ground, whilst others (such as those of the maple) soon decay. The former may consequently be easily swept down by water in the spring; and then it is often impossible to distinguish between the spring and autumn leaves. But if the leaves are still attached to the twigs, if they are not quite mature, or if, being divided into lobes and teeth, they are spread out and well preserved, we may assume that they were imbedded soon after their fall.

fruit at that time, just in the same way as the Canarian vinhatico (*Persea indica*, Linn., sp.). On another slab there is a similar fruit side by side with leaves and bud-scales of the camphor-tree; and such bud-scales are thrown off in the spring. Even if the Swiss cinnamon (*Cinnamomum Scheuchzeri*) had borne fruit during the winter, the climate in that season must have been very mild.

In the preceding description Prof. Heer has had under consideration plants which are very nearly allied to or homologous with living species, so that he could compare the phases of their development with those which are directly accessible to observation at the present time. But even with regard to the extinct types of plants some information may be obtained, as the insects here assist in the research. On a slab from Œningen side by side with the ripe delicately formed fruits of the *Podogonia*, winged ants are seen. The species (*Formica lignitum* and *pinguis*) are most nearly allied to the large wood-ant (*F. herculeana*). The winged individuals of the latter swarm between the beginning and the middle of the summer, when they quit their nests in immense bands and pair in the air. Hence, like all the winged ants, which often appear in incalculable numbers and not unfrequently perish by millions in Swiss lakes, this insect announces summer. The winged ants lying beside the fruits of the *Podogonia* therefore supply evidence that those trees ripened their fruit in the summer. If this be the case, the season of flowering must have occurred very early in the spring; and in favour of this view we have a leafless poplar-twig which lies beside an equally bare flowering twig of *Podogonium*. From this we learn further that in the *Podogonia* the flowers appeared before the leaves, in accordance with the well-known rule in very early-flowering trees and shrubs. At the end of March, however, they were in leaf; for we find a leaf with some willow-flowers on the same slab.

These are all inferences founded upon ascertained facts; and they form the starting-point from which we may endeavour to form the following general view of the course of the seasons in the Œningian period of the Miocene formation.

The *Podogonia* (fig. 196, vol. i. p. 367) were probably the first

K 2

trees in flower in the primæval forest; in March the willows and poplars followed, and soon afterwards the planes and camphor-trees, and undoubtedly also the maples, liquidambars, and walnut-trees, in which the leaves and flowers were simultaneously developed. In the same month the leafy trees which shed their leaves in the late autumn acquired a new green foliage. At this season storms and heavy rains were doubtless frequent; leaves, flowers, and twigs were torn away from the trees and shrubs, swept down into the lakes, and covered by the sinking mud; and hence we find many deposits of fossil plants belonging to the spring season. About the middle of May the poplars and willows ripened their fruits, which were carried off by the wind and scattered among the leaves, where they are now frequently found, especially at Œningen. At this time also the elms cast off their winged fruits, which would be carried far away by the wind, and may thus have been transported into the insect-bed of the lower quarry at Œningen. About midsummer the long-stalked fruits of the beautiful *Podogonia* arrived at maturity, and also those of the birches and *Poranæ*, which are enclosed in the same stone with them. Great swarms of winged ants appeared and performed their lively dances on the fine summer evenings on the shore of the lake, in company with numerous midges and large Termites, and while thus engaged were frequently driven over the water and drowned. *Cicadæ* raised their monotonous song on the ash trees; in the grass below numerous grasshoppers produced their peculiar chirp; and near them were many little froghoppers; whilst from the neighbouring marshes was heard the music of large frogs and toads. Beetles were engaged upon the shore in working up into new forms the excrements of the mammals which came from the neighbouring forests to drink in the lake. Many of these dung-beetles rose into the air and perished in the mud; they were added to the rich collection of insects which has been preserved for us at Œningen. A small *Hister* (*H. coprolithorum*, Heer) was even inserted with the fruit of a *Podogonium* and a winged ant in the same leaf of this wonderful book of nature; and the slab tells us that this insect once lived in the summer season by the Lake of Œningen.

We now come to the autumn, when the planes and liquid-ambars were hung with their spherical fruit-catkins, some of which probably, as in their existing relatives, remained on the trees until the following spring, and were buried in a soft marl at the same time with the flowers and other vernal organs. Most of the trees with deciduous leaves bore their foliage longer than those now growing in Switzerland; so that the forests, so far as they consisted of such trees, probably did not lose their leaves until quite the end of the year.

Whilst these trees had definite periods of repose in the course of their life, others retained their leafy covering throughout the winter; many of them probably put forth flowers and fruit all the year round; so that in this primæval forest life was constantly renewed in wonderful abundance, reminding us of those fortunate zones where nature never goes to rest.

If we bring together those species of the Miocene flora which can be compared with living species, we find those of the temperate zone * represented by 131 species, those of the warm zone by 266 species, and those of the torrid zone by 85. The majority, therefore, indicate the warm zone, comprising regions which have an average annual temperature of between 59° and 77° Fahr. (15° and 25° Centigrade), and are situated between 45° and 24° N. lat. This is a broad zone; but a careful comparison of the most important forms of plants does not allow us to reduce it within more restricted limits.

---

* To the tropics (or torrid zone) Prof. Heer refers the countries lying between the tropics; to the warm zones the southern part of the United States of America, the mountain-country of Mexico, the Mediterranean countries, Asia Minor, Southern Caucasus, Persia, Northern India, Japan, Chili, the Cape of Good Hope, and extra-tropical Australia; and to the temperate zone those countries in the northern hemisphere which lie between 45° and 58° N. lat. In America Prof. Heer reckons Virginia and Kentucky among the northern States. According to Asa Gray, the boundary-line thus drawn separates naturally the warm southern States from the colder northern ones. With regard to the numbers given in the text, it is to be observed that they are not obtained by the addition of the numbers given in vol. i. p. 370. Such an addition would not have led to a correct result, as the same species appears under several categories whenever its living analogue occurs in different parts of the world or in different zones.

If we next consider the tropical forms, we remark first some ferns (see vol. i. p. 322), the feather-palms, the *Poranæ* (fig. 176, vol. i. p. 354), fig-trees, Brazil-wood trees (*Cæsalpiniæ*), Cassias, and true Acacias. These trees could not have supported the winters of the temperate zone; but it is very likely that a climate such as that of Madeira may have sufficed for them; for at present the caoutchouc-tree (*Ficus elastica*), the *Eugeniæ*, the *Cæsalpiniæ, Cassiæ*, and true *Acaciæ* (such as *A. lophanta* and *dealbata*) flourish admirably in the gardens of Funchal, where the pisang, the Indian mango, the guava, and pine-apples also ripen their splendid fruit. Of the palms those with fan-shaped leaves extend into the warm zone; and the dwarf palm (*Chamærops humilis*) grows on the southern coasts of Spain, Sicily, and Naples, and has its northern limit near Nice (in latitude 43° 41′ N., with a mean temperature of 60°·2 Fahr. or 15°·6 C.). The Chinese dwarf palm (*Chamærops excelsa,* Thunb.) is still hardier, and supports the winter of the south of England. In America these dwarf palms are represented by the swamp-palm (*Sabal Adansoni*, Guerns.), which occurs very plentifully in the swamps of Florida, Georgia, and Carolina, and extends to 35° N. lat. This palm bears the winter at Montpellier. The umbrella-palm of the West Indies (*Sabal umbraculifera*, Jacq., sp.) is of larger size; but its distribution is restricted within narrower limits. The feather-palms of the Miocene differ greatly from all existing forms. Two of them constitute peculiar extinct types; two others may be arranged in existing tropical genera. But we are acquainted with no existing species homologous with or nearly related to them, and they may have been organized for a cooler climate than their living but remote congeners. Among the existing feather-palms, the American wax-palm seems to require the least warmth, since it ascends upon the Cordilleras to considerable elevations, where the summers are cool and the winters are not cold, the extremes of temperature being much softened down between the tropics. In the Old World the date-palm, of all feather-palms, extends furthest towards the north; but even in the hottest districts of Europe (with the sole exception of Elche in Spain) it rarely ripens its fruit. It requires an annual mean temperature of at least 68° F. (20° C.) to bring its fruit to perfect maturity.

Those Miocene plants which represent such as are now met with in the temperate zone, and do not extend into the tropics, demonstrate that Switzerland had not at that time a tropical climate. We find a considerable number of species in the Miocene district the nearest allies of which now live in the plains of Central Europe or in North America. Most of these, however, extend their range into the warm zone: thus the common bracken (*Pteris aquilina*) is as abundant in Madeira as in Switzerland, and it is also found in California and Japan; the relatives of the Swiss Miocene species of *Equisetum* extend to the south of the United States; the *Isoëtes* and the little pondweed occur even in Brazil; the common reed (*Phragmitis*) lives in Italy, on the Caucasus, in Japan, and in America; the reed-mace (*Typha latifolia*) grows in the Crimea and in South Carolina, the branched burr-reed (*Sparganium ramosum*) in Persia and Carolina, and rushes in Madeira and the Canary Islands; while the red maple extends down to the south of the United States: and these are all species representing Miocene forms which we have classed as belonging to the temperate zone.

With regard to other species, to which cultivation has given an artificial area of distribution, it is manifest that they can support higher temperatures: thus the planes and poplars and walnut-trees thrive well in Madeira; and in the south of Spain splendid elms and white poplars are seen side by side with southern *Meliæ* and *Phytolaccæ* in the public gardens of the towns. Hence the occurrence of the types of plants of the temperate zone in the Miocene flora may be easily explained, if we assume that at that period Switzerland had a climate similar to that of Madeira. It must be remembered that the plants of the temperate zone suffer much less from higher temperatures than those of warm countries do from cold. Too great heat does not so much limit the extension southwards of plants as the great dryness of the hot season.

The combination of types of plants of the tropical and temperate zones in the Swiss Miocene flora is by no means surprising, as we meet with the same conditions at the present day in Madeira and the Canary Islands, where the zones of distribution of many southern and European forms meet; they indicate a similar climate for the Swiss Tertiary district. A still stronger proof is furnished by the numerous forms of plants of the warm zone which constituted the principal portion of the flora of that epoch. The distribution of their homologous living species is of so much importance for the settlement of this question that we shall notice particularly a few of the trees to which we have already referred (see vol. i. pp. 325–331).

These plants may be divided into two classes—namely, those which can support the winters of the temperate zone, and those which cannot bear that climate and consequently cannot be planted in Switzerland in the open air. Of the first class the following species are nearly allied to widely distributed Miocene trees—the swamp-cypresses, the *Sequoiæ* and *Glyptostrobi*, the liquidambars, the Italian date-plum (*Diospyros*), and the tulip-tree. All these trees are natives of the warm zones; but yet they thrive in the plantations of Central Europe, although most of them do not ripen their fruit here, showing that in this region the extreme limit is attained of their artificial area of distribu-bution. They do not flourish in a temperature lower than $46°·4$ Fahr. (or $8°$ Cent.). Thus we find that the tulip-tree regularly blooms near Zurich, but rarely forms germinable seeds; in North Germany it seldom blooms, and in the north of Prussia (as near Stettin) it is killed by cold winters; on the coast of the Baltic (as near Dantzig) it can no longer bear the climate, any more than that of Kiev in Russia, where the mean January temperature is $6°·2$ Cent. (or $20°·8$ Fahr.). In Dublin it thrives well and flowers, but without forming seeds; in the south of England it sometimes produces ripe seeds; but north of Edinburgh it no longer blooms, and does not grow to any size. Hence the temperature of $9°$ Cent. (or $48°·2$ Fahr.) may be regarded as the northern boundary-line of this tree. It finds its most luxuriant development in the swamps of the southern United States; and the gigantic trees which we meet with in the gardens of Madeira prove that it is well suited to a subtropical climate.

In the second class, viz. plants which cannot support the win-ter of the temperate zone, the camphor-trees, the Japanese cinnamon-tree, the *Sapindi*, the Proteaceæ, *Celastreæ*, and jujube-trees are all included, and laurels with respect to Switzerland. The most important are the camphor- and cinnamon-trees, as the homologous Miocene species are common everywhere, and furnish us with the best standard for ascertaining the climate. Both species are inhabitants of Southern Japan; the camphor-tree also lives in China. In the gardens of Madeira the camphor-tree grows to a considerable size; it also thrives in Sicily (at Palermo) and at Pisa and Florence, where, however, it never ripens its fruit. At Padua it requires to be protected in winter by a glass roof. In the Botanic Garden at Montpellier it was frozen down to the ground in the winter of 1853–54, but threw up fresh shoots from the bottom. On the Isola Bella of the Lago Maggiore, which is celebrated for its mild climate, a fine camphor-tree stands in the open air; but it is protected from the north wind by a high wall, and can be partly covered in winter. In the winter of 1856 the branches were killed by a frost of 14° Fahr.; so that they had to be pruned back to the main stem, which, however, pushed forth again; and in the autumn of 1864 Prof. Heer saw the tree in full foliage. It is of the size of a large plum-tree. In the same neighbourhood, at Pallanza, there is also a camphor-tree in a sheltered situation in a garden; but it has to be wrapped up in straw in the winter; and even with this precaution the young shoots are frozen, and require to be cut back nearly every year. Like the tree of the Isola Bella, it flowers annually, but without ripening any fruit. The camphor-tree therefore requires for its development a warmer climate than that of Provence and North Italy. To thrive it needs a mean annual temperature of 18°–19° Cent. (or 64°·4–66°·2 Fahr.); and its northern limit cannot pass beyond the isotherm of 15° Cent. (or 59° Fahr.). This applies also to the Canarian laurel and the vinhatico; and even the European laurel will not stand the winter of Switzerland.

A careful comparison of the characters of the vegetation of the different stages of the Miocene shows that during that period some diminution of temperature took place. We have already seen (vol. i. pp. 316, 317) that the evergreen trees form about three fourths of the whole in the Aquitanian stage, and only about half in the Œningian stage, and that in the latter the

European and North-American types become more prominent. If the living species most like the Swiss Miocene plants are distributed into three zones, we obtain the following numerical proportions :—

Analogous species. (Vascular plants.)	Temperate Zone.		Warm Zone.		Torrid Zone.	
		Per cent.		Per cent.		Per cent.
In the Aquitanian stage (Lower Miocene)	47	15	114	36	47	15
In the Œningian stage (Upper Miocene)	94	18	174	33	38	7

In the Upper Miocene (of Œningen) the tropical types constitute only 7 per cent. of the total number of vascular plants; whilst in the lower Miocene (Aquitanian) the tropical types are 15 per cent. of the whole, which shows that a decrease of temperature must have taken place, although the frequent occurrence of the camphor- and cinnamon-trees, and the appearance of feather- and fan-palms, demonstrate that Œningen still enjoyed a warm climate.

If we sum up all the data furnished by the flora, we are led to the conclusion that the Swiss Lower Miocene district possessed a climate similar to that now prevailing in Louisiana, the Canaries, North Africa, and South China—namely, a climate with a mean annual temperature of 20°–21° Cent. (or 68°–69°·8 Fahr.); and that the Swiss Upper Miocene district had a climate resembling that of Madeira, Malaga, and the south of Sicily, Southern Japan, and New Georgia, with an annual temperature of 18°–19° Cent. (or 64°·4–66°·2 Fahr).

The following Table gives the mean temperatures of the above-mentioned regions :—

	Winter.		Spring.		Summer.		Autumn.		Annual Mean.	
	Cent.	Fahr.	Cent.	Fahr.	Cent.	Fahr.	Cent.	Fahr.	Cent.	Fahr.
I. Representing the Lower Miocene:—										
St. Cruz, Teneriffe....	18·1	64·58	21·3	70·34	24·9	76·64	23·4	83·12	21·9	71·42
Cairo	14·7	58·46	21·9	71·42	29·2	84·56	23·6	83·48	22·4	72·32
Tunis	13·2	55·76	18·3	64·94	28·3	82·94	21·9	71·42	20·3	68·54
Canton	12·7	54·86	21·0	69·80	27·8	82·04	20·7	69·26	21·0	69·80
New Orleans	13·3	55·94	20·4	68·72	27·5	81·50	21·0	69·80	20·5	68·90
II. Representing the Upper Miocene:—										
Funchal, Madeira	15·8	60·44	18·9	52·42	20·9	69·62	19·6	67·28	18·3	64·94
Malaga	12·4	58·12	17·5	63·50	26·0	78·80	20·7	69·26	19·1	66·38
Messina	12·8	55·84	16·4	61·52	25·1	77·00	20·7	69·26	18·8	65·84
Nangasaki	8·4	47·12	15·5	59·90	27·7	81·86	21·6	70·88	18·3	64·94
Savannah, in New Georgia	11·9	53·24	19·0	66·20	25·7	78·26	19·3	66·74	18·9	66·02

Of these stations there is not any one which exactly represents the climate of the Swiss Miocene district; but we approximate to it by ascertaining with what existing climatal conditions
it was probably most in accordance.   The mixture of tropical
plants with plants of the temperate zones indicates that the
winters were mild and the summers not very hot ; the climate was
that of a coast or an island.   The winter, however, was probably
rather colder and the summer a little warmer than is the case
at present in the Atlantic islands of Madeira &c.; so that the
best standard by which to judge of the conditions of temperature
for the Lower Miocene would be furnished by New Orleans,
and in the Old World by Tunis.   For the Upper Miocene,
Savannah and Messina would furnish the most suitable points
of comparison to determine the temperature of that portion of
the Swiss Tertiary district.

At the present time the very great difference of elevation of
the land and the influence of the snow-clad chain of the Alps
form, as it were, a barrier against the Miocene climate of Switzerland.   The following summary explains these conditions :—-

	True Mean Annual Temperature.		Calculated.			
			At 250 feet above the sea.		At the level of the sea.	
	Cent.	Fahr.	Cent.	Fahr.	Cent.	Fahr.
Zurich, 1360 feet above the sea-level	9·02	48·24	11·22	52·20	11·72	53·10
Basle, 830　,,　,,　,,	10·03	50·05	11·13	52·03	11·63	52·93
Geneva, 1263 ,,　,,　,,	9·25	48·65	11·25	52·25	11·75	53·15
Berne, 1684　,,　,,　,,	8·12	46·62	10·92	51·66	11·42	52·56
Means........	..	..	11·13	52·03	11·63	52·93

Estimating the refrigerant influence of the mountains at $\frac{1}{2}$°C.
(or nearly 1° Fahr.) we should probably have in Northern Swit-

zerland (supposing it brought down to the sea-level, and the
Alps reduced to a low hill-country) a mean annual temperature of 12°·13 Cent. (or 53°·83 Fahr.) at the sea-level, and of
11°·63 Cent. (or 52°·93 Fahr.) at an elevation of 230–250 feet
above the sea. Consequently, assuming that the mean annual
temperature of the Swiss Lower Miocene was 20°·5 Cent. (or
68°·9 Fahr.), that of the Swiss Upper Miocene 18°·5 Cent.
(or 65°·3 Fahr.), and the elevation above the sea 250 feet, the
temperature of the Lower Miocene will have been 8°·87 Cent.
(or 15°·96 Fahr.) higher, and the temperature of the Upper
Miocene 6°·87 Cent. (or 12°·36 Fahr.) higher than at present.
Thus in the Lower Miocene times the climate of Europe was
probably 9° Cent. (or 16°·2 Fahr.) hotter than at present; and
in the Upper Miocene period the climate had an elevation of
temperature of 7° Cent. (or 12°·6 Fahr.) above the European
climate of the present day.

Water exerts great influence upon the life and development
of plants. The great abundance of woody plants and evergreen
trees, the numerous marsh-plants, and the lignite-deposits, indicating extensive peat-mosses, leave no doubt that the climate was
humid, and the rainy days probably spread over the greater part
of the year. In this respect it will have differed considerably
from that now prevailing in the Canary Islands and Madeira,
and probably approached nearer to that of Louisiana and the
southern United States generally, in which extensive swamps
also occur such as must have existed in the Miocene district.

Among the animals of the Swiss Miocene the types of the
warm zones predominate; but with them are mixed others which
belong to temperate and tropical climates. Not only do the
large and striking animals, such as the crocodiles, the great
tortoises and gigantic frogs, the tapirs and rhinoceroses, opossums and apes, give to the Swiss Miocene fauna the character
of the warm subtropical zones, but similar proofs of a warm
climate are furnished by the wonderful multiplicity of forms in
the little population of insects which enlivened the primæval
forest and the quiet lakes and streams of Miocene land.

Marine animals were also influenced by conditions of temperature; and species of the same animals still living depend upon
similar conditions of life to those which characterized them in

the past. We have already shown (vol. ii. p. 92) that most of
the species of Mollusca of the Helvetian sea belong to the fauna
of the Mediterranean, and that many tropical but no exclusively
northern types occur among them ; and thus the Middle Miocene
fauna acquires a more southern aspect than that of the Mediterranean. Thus of the 147 Mollusca of the Helvetian stage
which are still found living, 20 (or about 14 per cent.) are at
present exclusively inhabitants of the tropics ; 38 species (or
26 per cent.) occur on the coasts of England, but almost all of
them are species which also live in the Lusitanian and Mediterranean zones, and therefore are not to be regarded as northern
forms ; 120 species (or about 82 per cent.) still inhabit the
Mediterranean. Of the extinct species the majority represent
Mediterranean types, but many are connected with tropical
forms. It is consequently not in the latitude of Switzerland,
but in that of the Mediterranean that we meet with most of the
species of Mollusca agreeing with the species of the Swiss
Miocene ; and indeed, owing to the intermixture of tropical
forms, the majority rather belong to the southern than to the
northern coast of the Mediterranean. The same temperature
which now prevails in the North-African or Madeiran sea must
therefore have characterized the fourth stage of the Swiss Miocene, immediately preceding the Œningian stage.

We see, therefore, that the inhabitants of the land and of the
sea concur in giving the Swiss Miocene country a subtropical
character. This is not deduced from a few plants or animals,
but from an abundant fauna and flora, which lays before us an
entire series of the most multifarious phenomena, such as can
only be explained by the occurrence of such a climate.

The same natural character is manifest in the Miocene flora
and fauna, not only of Switzerland, but of the whole of Central
Europe * ; the north of Europe, however, had a colder climate.
There was consequently even then a diminution of temperature
towards the north, but certainly in a much less degree than at
the present day. We see this even in the flora of the most
northern parts of Germany. In Samland (the old amber-

---

* Prof. Heer has demonstrated this in his ' Recherches sur le Climat et la
Végétation du pays Tertiaire.'   C. Gaudin's translation, pp. 66 et seqq.

country), as well as on the margins of the great bay of Dantzig, numerous fossil plants have been collected in the lignites and in the shales formed of mud and clay *. The palms are entirely wanting ; so far as we know, they did not pass the latitude of 51°·05 N. in Germany. But in the Bay of Dantzig we still find some fig-trees and laurels, two cinnamons (*Cinnamomum Scheuchzeri* and *C. lanceolatum*), besides evergreen oaks and species of *Andromeda* and *Myrica*. The swamp-cypresses (*Taxodium distichum*) were very abundant, as were also the *Sequoiæ*. In Samland a poplar (*Populus Zaddachi*) and a *Rhamnus* (*R. Gaudini*) are associated with the fruits and seeds of a *Gardenia*. At the present day Dantzig has a mean temperature of 7°·6 Cent. (or 45°·7 Fahr.). If we assume that in these northern regions, as in Switzerland, the temperature of the Lower Miocene was 9° Cent. (or 16°·2 Fahr.) higher than at the present day, we shall have for these localities a climate of 17° Cent. (or 62°·6 Fahr.), which would be quite suitable to the above-mentioned Miocene flora. Professor Göppert has discovered at Schossnitz, near Breslau, a rich flora of the Œningian epoch. In it tropical and subtropical forms are naturally wanting ; for if we calculate the temperature of the fifth or highest stage of the Miocene according to the existing ·temperatures, we obtain a climate of 15° Cent. (or 59° Fahr.), which explains the presence in Silesia of the swamp-cypress, of the liquidambars, and of some evergreen oaks ; but, on the other hand, excludes the palms, cinnamon-trees, and acacias from that part of Germany, although they adorned the Miocene forests of Switzerland and Northern Italy.

The hypothesis of a lowering of temperature in the north is confirmed by the Miocene flora recently discovered in the arctic zone †. Thus, in the fossil flora of Spitzbergen, between 78° and 79° N. lat., the Swedish naturalists Nordenskjöld and Malmgren have discovered more than 100 species of plants. In this num-

---

* Prof. Heer has described them in his 'Miocene Flora of the Baltic.' Königsberg, 1869.

† Prof. Heer has described these plants in his 'Flora Fossilis Arctica,' vol. i. 1868, vol. ii. 1871, with 108 plates.

ber the conifers predominate. Two species of cypress are among
the commonest plants of Spitzbergen, which is the more remarkable as one of these species, the swamp-cypress (*Taxodium
distichum*) still exists in the south of the United States, and
the other (*Libocedrus Sabiniana*), although extinct, is very
analogous to a species which is also living in America. The
Abietineæ furnish two species still living—namely, the red fir
(*Pinus Abies*, Linn.) and the mountain-pine (*Pinus montana*,
Mill.) : these have not yet been found elsewhere in Miocene deposits ; and their remains show us that Spitzbergen is probably
the original country of the swamp-cypress, as well as of the red
fir and the mountain-pine. Other species of pines and firs
are extinct, but have many relations with American forms. A
similar remark applies to two *Sequoiæ*, one of which (*S. Nordenskjöldi*, Heer) is peculiar to Spitzbergen and very common
there. Of the leafy trees the poplars are the most abundant.
Two species (*Populus arctica* and *P. Richardsoni*, Heer) were
spread over all the country between Bell Sound and King's Bay.
There are hardly any willows in the Spitzbergen Miocene.
Alders and birches are rare ; a hazel is rather more common.
Two oaks with large leaves (*Quercus grœnlandica* and *Q. pla-
tania*), a plane tree, a lime (*Tilia Malmgreni*), and a walnut
(*Juglans albula*, Heer) are of great interest. A water-lily
(*Nymphæa arctica*) and a pondweed (*Potamogeton Nordenskjöldi*)
indicate a freshwater formation, the neighbourhood of which
was probably occupied by turbaries, on which grew *Cyperi*,
Carices, Spargania, and irids (*Iris latifolia*).

Among these Miocene plants of Spitzbergen we do not find
any tree or shrub with evergreen foliage. The local Miocene
flora differs totally from the existing flora of Spitzbergen, and
has the character of that of the temperate zones, such as we
now observe in Northern Germany : it therefore indicates a
mean temperature of 8° Cent. (or 46°·4 Fahr.).

The Miocene flora of the western coast of North Greenland
(in 70° N. lat.), which is better known to Prof. Heer, has a
rather more southern character. Among 137 species discovered
there, Prof. Heer finds a *Magnolia* with persistent leaves (*M.
Ingelfieldi*), a chestnut (*Castanea Ungeri*, Heer), a *Salisburia*, a

Liquidambar, a *Diospyros,* and a *Sassafras.* *Sequoia Langs-dorfii* is very common, as are also the species of poplar which were met with in Spitzbergen. The oaks furnish seven species, the planes two, and the vines two, one of which (*Vitis Oriki*) is remarkable for the size of its handsome leaves. This flora therefore indicates a climate analogous to that now character-istic of the neighbourhood of the Lake of Geneva. Nor was it only in Spitzbergen and North Greenland that a warmer climate formerly prevailed; the fossil floras of Iceland, of the shores of the Mackenzie River in North America (65° N. lat.), and of Alaska exhibit remains of trees and shrubs of which the homo-logous species no longer occur in those latitudes, and which in-form us that the arctic zone possessed a much higher tempera-ture in the Miocene times than it does at present.

For Switzerland the climate of the Miocene fauna and flora was sufficiently explained by adding 9° Cent. (or 16°·2 Fahr.) to the present temperature; but this is not the case with the arctic zone. Spitzbergen, in 78° N. lat., has a mean temperature of −8°·6 Cent. (or 16°·7 Fahr.); and Greenland, in 70° N. lat., has −7° Cent. (or 19°·1 Fahr.) : if we add 9° Cent. (or 16°·2 Fahr.) we get for the latter country 2° Cent. (or 35°·6 Fahr.), and for Spitzbergen 0°·4 Cent. (or 32°·72 Fahr.), which would not be correct as the temperature of the known Miocene flora. We must estimate for these arctic countries, between the Ter-tiary epoch and the present day, a difference of temperature of 16°–17° Cent. (or 28°·8–30°·6 Fahr.). The difference of tempe-rature between the Miocene and the existing floras is therefore much more considerable in the arctic than in the temperate zone; and the change has been the greatest in the extreme north.

If we turn from Switzerland towards the south we notice, in the Lower Miocene flora of Upper Italy, splendid palms which have been found near Cadibona, at the Monte Vegrone, and at Chiavon. In Greece, near Pikermi in Attica, a great mass of bones is accumulated, which show that in Upper Miocene times giraffes, large gazelles, monkeys, and great mastodons inhabited the south-east of Europe. The Miocene marine fauna also had a somewhat different character in the south and in the north of Europe. In Piedmont (at Sassello) extensive coral-reefs are found composed of splendid madrepores, and reminding us of those in tropical seas; and the eastern sea which washed Styria in Lower Miocene times likewise presents extensive reef-formations, which may be traced up to 47° and 48° N. lat. The Swiss sea was destitute of these coral-formations, as was also the ocean which in the Lower Miocene period spread over Germany. With regard to the marine fauna that lived in the Helvetian period on the shores of Madeira and Porto Santo, Prof. Heer has had interesting information from M. Carl Mayer*. Although this fauna approaches the organic remains of the Middle Miocene of Europe, it contains more tropical forms; and in Porto Santo large stony corals occur. At present the islands of the Madeiran and Canarian groups are quite destitute of coral reefs, and the marine fauna has a less southern character than that of which the remains are imbedded in the Miocene tuffs. Out of the 169 species of Mollusca that Mayer has determined, 65 are still living, or 38 per cent. The majority of these species live in the Lusitanian and Mediterranean zones; but 19 of the species are now found only between the tropics. The tropical forms therefore in this case constitute 29 per cent. [of the living species], whilst among the Mollusca of the Helvetian stage in Switzerland the proportion is only 14 per cent., which shows that at that time the waters of those regions had a higher temperature than either those of the Swiss Miocene sea or those of the present seas in the same latitudes.

There is a formation in Java which, according to recent investigations, is to be regarded as Upper Miocene, but which may perhaps be younger; and the fossil plants in these strata approach nearly to those of the existing flora of Java; also the majority of the fossil marine animals found therein still possess their descendants in the Indian seas, or have their nearest relatives in those waters. Hence these plants and animals lived under similar climatic conditions, in the Miocene period, to those now prevalent; and if this formation really belongs to the Upper Miocene, it would follow that the temperature in the tropics was then the same as in our times.

---

* See M. C. Mayer's "Systematisches Verzeichniss der fossilen Reste von Madeira, Porto Santo, und Santa Maria," in Dr. G. Hartung's ' Geologische Beschreibung der Insel Madeira und Porto Santo,' Leipzig, 1864.

The principal results of this investigation may be shortly stated in the following numbers, expressing approximately the conditions of temperature of the Miocene districts :—

A. In the Lower Miocene Epoch.

		° Cent.	° Fahr.
1.	Upper Italy (at 250 feet above the sea) had a mean annual temperature of .	22	71·6
2.	Switzerland	20½	69
3.	The basin of the Lower Rhine . . .	18	64·4
4.	The vicinity of Dantzig	17	62·6
5.	Spitzbergen (78° N. lat.)	8	46·4

B. In the Upper Miocene Epoch.

1.	Sinigaglia	21	69·8
2.	Upper Italy	20	68
3.	Switzerland	18½	65·3
4.	Silesia (Schossnitz)	15	59

CHAPTER XII.

QUATERNARY PERIOD.

It is intended in the Plate opposite to sketch the district of Dürnten, on the southern frontier of the Canton of Zurich, at the time of the paper-coal or lignite formation. The Speer, the Schäniserberg, the peaked Mürtschenstock, and the chain of the Wäggithal mountains, with the snow-clad Glaris Alps, are in the background. These mountains have remained unchanged since the time of the formation of the paper-coals. But in the foreground of the picture the present green covering of the fields has been removed, and the world buried beneath the surface has been brought again to life. The plants are not different from those of our time. It is the *common Swiss reed* which fringes the pools, the *Swiss pine* that occupies the foreground, the *white birch* that spreads over the marshy flat, an *oak* that grows up into a vast tree on a dry spot, and the *common red fir* which to the left raises its stately form.

But the elephant, the rhinoceros, and the urus (*Bos primigenius*), which we see in the picture, are animals quite strange to modern Switzerland; they give the landscape an ancient character. And where, it may be asked, are the proofs that such strange animals lived in Switzerland contemporaneously with the plants of its existing flora? and what justified the assumption that at that time the Alps in their present form already made the background of the Swiss landscape? These questions are answered by the paper coals or *lignites*. These strata are consequently of great geological significance, and must here be described. In the commune of Dürnten (515 metres, or 563 yards, above the sea) the paper coals, the mode of formation of which has been already explained (see vol. i. pp. 30, 31), occur at a distance of only a few minutes' walk from the village, on the

Oberberg and Binzberg. On the Oberberg (between 1854, in which year the underground working was commenced, and June 1862) 8090 square fathoms of the carboniferous deposit were dug out, and 736,800 hundredweight of fresh lignite, furnishing about 482,000 hundredweight of dry coal, were obtained. This quantity represents approximately in heating-effect 14,030 cords of birch wood or 22,044 cords of fir wood (of 108 cubic feet to the cord). In the first three years the workings produced yearly more than 100,000 hundredweight; but in the year 1862 the produce fell to 29,185 hundredweight; and it may be foreseen that the supply will shortly be exhausted.

Mining was commenced in the deposits on the Binzberg in 1862; and 29,552 hundredweight of lignite were obtained in the first year from 770 square rods. In a north-westerly direction the deposit disappears for a short distance; but it is again found in the Schöneich near Unterwetzikon, about 1½ Swiss mile from Dürnten; and here it has also been worked since 1862. In 1865, 251 square fathoms had been removed, with a yield of 16,536 hundredweight of saleable coal. The thickness of the deposit containing marketable coal is here 2¾ feet; in some spots it increases to 5 feet, but in others decreases to 2 feet or even less. The carboniferous area here contains about 40,000 square feet. It was probably connected formerly with the coal-deposit of Dürnten, and was produced in the same manner and at the same time. At the Oberberg, however, its thickness was much greater. Here and there it was as much as 12 feet thick, whilst in other places it diminished to 5, 3, and 2½ feet thick. The mean thickness of saleable coal has been estimated at 3·75 feet. Between the lignites bands of loam occur, the number of which is determined by the thickness of the whole deposit: where this was 12 feet thick it was traversed by six bands; but where it was 2 feet thick there were only two bands.

The lignite-deposit of Dürnten rests upon a fine yellowish-brown clay. A shaft which was sunk through this to a depth of 30 feet below the lignite showed that at the bottom there is a mass of rolled stones imbedded in the clay; but the Miocene was not reached, as the influx of water prevented the shaft from being dug deeper. In one place there are many rolled pebbles in the clay immediately below the lignite-deposit; they are of

flint and sandstone, and may have originated from the conglomerate of the surrounding mountains. In one spot, where the
lignite was of great thickness, it was traversed in the middle by
a deposit of clay which thinned out in the form of a wedge. In
another place this clay-bed was divided into several bands, distinguished by their light colour and greater thickness from the
dark-coloured loam-bands of the coal already mentioned (which
the workmen call " silver"). The deposit here, probably after
its formation, had been ruptured by a slip and separated into
very irregular and variously bent layers by the intercalations of
clays. In one place a portion of the lignite-deposit is placed
almost perpendicularly, and only covered by a thin layer of
arable soil, while elsewhere the deposit is generally in a horizontal position and covered by a bed of stratified sand and
pebbles.

At the spot where the lignite-deposit was of great thickness
the following section (fig. 328) was to be seen. It contained in

Fig. 328.

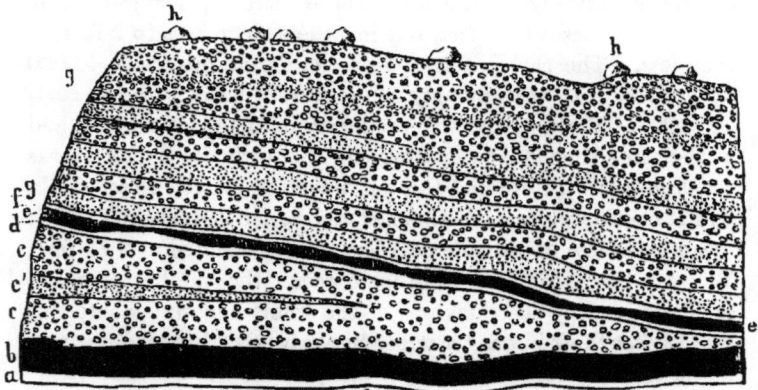

Section of the paper-coal or lignite deposit, and pebble-beds, at Dürnten:
a, loam (lake-chalk); b, lignite, or paper coal; c, pebbles and sand;
d. f, loam; e, upper thin band of paper coal or lignite; g, layers of
pebbles and sand; h, erratic blocks.

ascending order :—

1. A layer of fine yellowish sand and loam (*a*).

2. The lignite-deposit (*b*).

3. A layer of pebbles several feet thick (*c*), in the midst of which was a nest of pure sand (*c′*).

4. A layer, about 6 inches thick, of light-coloured loam, containing here and there nests of pebbles (*d*).

5. A thin coal-band (about 6 inches thick), composed of peat-plants with a few fragments of wood (*e*).

6. Loam, a thin layer (*f*).

7. Seven alternating layers of sand and pebbles (*g*).

8. On the top a few erratic blocks, originating from the Alps, and partly consisting of Alpine limestone and sernifite (*h*).

The thickness of the masses of pebbles and sand covering the lignites or paper coals varies at very short distances, and amounts here and there to 30 feet. The composition of the lignites shows clearly that they originated from peat, as has been already noticed (vol. i. pp. 29, 30) ; and their thickness proves that this formation of peat must have gone on for very many years. From time to time, no doubt, it was interrupted by inundations and the deposition of fine mud, which now forms loamy bands ; but it afterwards recommenced, and continued until an end was almost entirely put to it by the country being covered up with pebbles and sand, merely containing here and there some traces of peat formation, such as is seen in the thin band of lignite among beds of gravel (fig. 328, *e*).

The lignite, or paper coal, of Unterwetzikon presents the same conditions of deposition as that of Dürnten. It lies at a depth of from 13 to 30 feet, and is covered with masses of stratified sand and gravel. Below the lignite there is a light-coloured loam which contains small freshwater shells; and beneath the loam occurs a bed of gravel, in which striated fragments of limestone, a block of granite from Pontaigles, and a boulder about 6 feet in diameter have been found.

The lignite deposits of the Canton of St. Gall, especially that of Utznach (fig. 329), are of much greater extent than those of

Fig. 329.

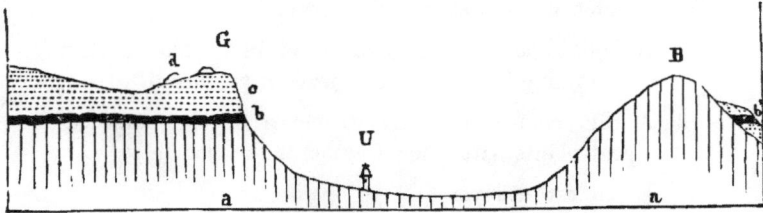

Ideal section of the valley of Utznach. (The vertical scale is to the horizontal as 8 : 1.) G, Gubel; U, Utznach; B, Lower Buchberg. *a*, upturned Miocene; *b*, lignites of Utznach; *b'*, lignites of Wangen; *c*, pebble-bed; *d*, erratic blocks.

the Canton of Zurich. The deposit of Utznach is situated 92 metres (or about 100 yards) above the bottom of the valley, and 512 metres (or about 560 yards) above the sea-level. As we ascend the road leading into the Toggenburg, we arrive, in about a quarter of an hour, at a number of shafts which have been sunk through the beds of sand and gravel. In the hill-chain of the Gubel these beds are exposed in a wall about 100 feet high, in which the edges of their strata are turned towards the valley. On the lignite there is, first, a gravel-bed; then follows a layer of reddish-grey sand, and upon this numerous beds of gravel, the pebbles in which consist of limestone, flint, sernifite, and sandstones; they are surrounded by sand, loosely held together, and of all sizes, from 1 inch to several inches in diameter. On the hill there are two enormous blocks of variegated conglomerate.

Three deposits of lignite lie one above the other in the Gubel hill : the highest deposit is 5 feet thick, the middle one only a few inches in thickness ; and the lower one is about 3 feet thick. Towards the north the thin middle bed disappears, and there remain only the upper and lower layers, which are separated by a light-coloured deposit of loam from 16 to 20 feet thick.

Whilst the stratified masses of gravel and sand vary much in thickness, and thereby cause considerable differences in the depth of the shafts, the lignite-deposit itself lies almost horizontal, showing that the ancient peat-deposit has preserved its original position; while the overlying masses of sand and gravel, which might have been originally deposited in various thicknesses, have subsequently also been here and there removed by denudation. Hence the surface of the soil is by no means parallel to the deposit of lignite, but presents small depressions and undulating elevations.

The precise extent of the lignite formation of Utznach cannot at present be ascertained. The longest galleries following the deposit extend into the neighbourhood of Gauen. They have been worked underground for about forty years, and have certainly furnished a great quantity of coal. But as there is no measurement, and the mining is carried on in a very primitive fashion, the annual product of these pits cannot be accurately stated. Some years ago it was estimated at 500,000 hundredweight; but only half that quantity is now raised.

Formerly the lignite-deposit of Utznach was in connexion with that of Dürnten, which is shown by a small deposit of lignite at Eschenbach (between Utznach and Dürnten). It lies almost exactly at the same height (515 metres, or 563·2 yards) above the sea-level. Near Wangen, on the Buchberg, opposite Utznach, and near Kaltbrunnen, traces of lignite are also found nearly at the same elevation. These render it probable that formerly the valley was occupied by a lake from 90 to 100 metres (or about 98 to 109 yards) in depth from the bottom of the valley, the shores of which to a great extent were swampy. As the Lower Buchberg rises from the bottom of the valley from Wangen to Grinau, another lake would have been produced if the two narrow gaps between Grinau and Utznach and between Wangen and Schübelbach had been filled up, which was probably the case at the period of the lignite formation. The lignite-deposits show the old swampy shores of this lake, which overflowed its banks at certain periods, and thus deposited mud, covering the peat, and forming what is now a band of loam, over which a fresh formation of lignite took place—a series of phenomena which may still be observed in many turbaries. Another change was effected by an accumulation of masses of gravel covering the lignites.

All the above-mentioned lignites belong to the basin of the Limmat and the Lake of Zurich; but the deposit of Mörschweil (564 metres, or nearly 617 yards, above the sea) between St. Gall and Rohrschach belongs to the basin of the Lake of Constance. Its average thickness is about 2 feet. It furnishes annually about 50,000 hundredweight of coal. Above and below it are beds of rolled erratic blocks. In the Hüttenweid, in the commune of Mörschweil, the following strata are distinguishable, in descending order, according to Prof. Deicke *:—

1. 10 feet of loam. -
2. 16 feet of erratic stones, not striated or polished. Among them are boulders weighing 10 hundredweight.
3. 8 feet of loam with lignite, in which the trunks of trees are upright.
4. 13 feet of erratic stones with small boulders, not exceeding 1 foot in diameter.
5. 6 feet of ash-grey loam, with scattered fragments of lignite.
6. 17 feet of small erratic pebbles, among which there are boulders about 1 foot in diameter.

Nearly the same succession of beds occurs in the Kröpfel; but the lignite-bed, which is 3 feet thick, lies 70 feet below the surface; and 15 feet lower down a second, thinner deposit makes its appearance.

In the Brunnenweis, which lies to the eastward, the shaft shows the following strata in descending order :—

1. 21 feet of sand, with large boulders.
2. 16 feet of ash-grey loam, with lignite, in which there are trunks of trees, 6 feet long and 3 feet broad, standing upright.
3. 3 feet of gravel, with small rolled pebbles.
4. Fine sand.

* See "Nachträge über die Quartärgebilde zwischen den Alpen und dem Jura," by Prof. J. C. Deicke, in ' Bericht der St.-Gallischen Gesellschaft,' 1861.

The upright trunks of trees always indicate the dying-out of the lignite-deposit; in other parts the trunks lie horizontally.

With regard to the plants which produced these lignites some information is derived from the remains found partly in the lignite itself and partly in the intercalated clay-beds. They are, for the most part, badly preserved, and it is difficult to determine them; but twenty-four species may be recognized. Among these we find eight trees and one shrub. The trees are as follows:—

1. The common fir (*Pinus Abies,* Linn.). Prof. Heer has obtained fine fir-cones from Dürnten, Wetzikon, Utznach, and Mörschweil. Most of them are smaller than the full-grown cones of the living tree; but there are among them specimens which attain a length of 120 millimetres (or 4·7 inches), and are therefore not inferior in size to the cones of Swiss firs. The smaller cones are probably not mature, and they have consequently only small seeds. The scales of the ripe cones agree in form and size with those of the living tree, as do also the two seeds which lie under each scale, as shown in. fig. 333, *a.* The scale is traversed by fine longitudinal striæ, and narrowed above into a short lobe, which is sometimes emarginate (fig. 333, *b*), sometimes obtusely rounded off (fig. 333, *a*). The scales are generally somewhat more rounded at the apex than in the Swiss firs; and in this they agree with the firs of Northern Russia. When fresh and moist the scales usually press against each other; but in drying they spring asunder, and thus acquire a ragged appearance, which is increased by the partial breaking of the scales as they become rigid. Besides the cones, Prof. Heer finds at Dürnten trunks, the wood of which agrees in its microscopic characters with that of the common fir; he can therefore hardly doubt that the fir of the lignites belongs to the same species as the common Swiss fir.

2. Pines, including the common pine (*Pinus sylvestris*) and the mountain-pine (*Pinus montana,* Mill.). At Dürnten and Utznach the trunks of pines constitute a considerable portion of the lignites. They must have sunk into the peat-bog; for they lie crossing each other in various directions. In the fresh and moist state the wood is soft, and may be easily cut with a knife;

Fig. 330.   Fig. 332.   Fig. 331.

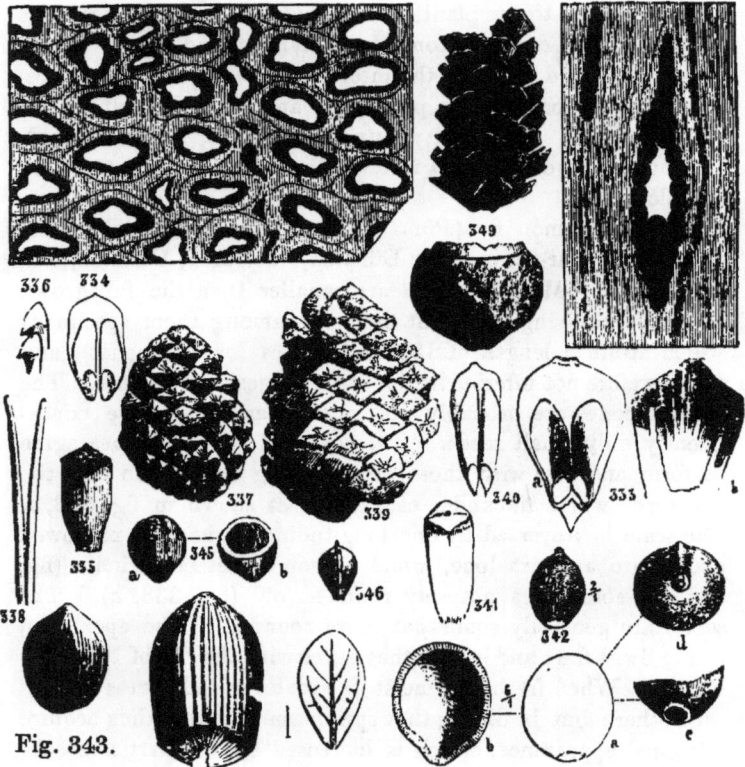

Fig. 343.

Fig. 344.   Fig. 347.   . Fig. 348.

Fig. 330. Specimen of pine wood from Utznach, a transverse section, enlarged 360 diameters.

Fig. 331. Pine wood from Utznach, enlarged 100 diam.

Fig. 332. Cone of *Pinus Abies*, the scales bitten off by squirrels, from Utznach.

Fig. 333. *Pinus Abies.* *a*, scale, from the inside, with the seeds, from Mörschweil; *b*, the upper half of a scale from Utznach.

Figs. 334–338. *Pinus montana*, Mill.

Fig. 334. Scale, from the inside, with the seeds, from Mörschweil.

Fig. 335. Scale, from the outside, from Mörschweil.

Fig. 336. Scales, side view.

Fig. 337. Entire cone, from Mörschweil.
Fig. 338. A pair of leaves, from Utznach.
Fig. 339. *Pinus sylvestris*, Linn., cone from Mörschweil.
Fig. 340. Ditto. Scale, from within, with the seeds, from Mörschweil.
Fig. 341. Ditto. Scale, from the outside.
Fig. 342. *Taxus baccata*, Linn., nut, twice nat. size, from Dürnten.
Fig. 343. *Corylus avellana*, Linn., *ovata*, from Dürnten.
Fig. 344. *Corylus avellana*, from Mörschweil.
Fig. 345. *Menyanthes trifoliata*, Linn., from Dürnten, three times nat. size. *a*, seed, lateral view; *b*, seed, section.
Fig. 346. *Scirpus lacustris*, Linn., fruit, from Dürnten, three times nat. size.
Fig. 347. *Vaccinium Vitis idæa*, Linn.?, four times nat. size.
Fig. 348. *Holopleura Victoria*, Casp., from Dürnten, six times nat. size. *a*, side view; *b*, longitudinal section; *c*, aperture left by the throwing-off of the operculum; *d*, upper surface with the operculum.
Fig. 349. *Quercus Robur*, Linn., cupule from Mörschweil.

in the air it dries and becomes brittle, and as hard as bone *. The trunks are often still clothed with the rough bark, and variously branched; but the branches cannot be followed out to the finer twigs. The wood has been examined microscopically by Prof. Heer's friend, Prof. Unger of Vienna, and found to be identical with that of the pine. Fig. 331 represents a longitudinal section cut parallel to the bark, which shows the medullary rays cut across. The medullary rays are sometimes simple, consisting only of one row of cells, but are sometimes composed of several rows, such as the pines possess. Transverse sections show that the annual rings of growth were of considerable thickness. In these transverse sections (fig. 330) we see that the cells are closely pressed together. It is impossible to decide whether this wood belongs to the common or the mountain-pine; but fortunately the lignites have also preserved twigs bearing the leaves and numerous cones, which demonstrate that both species † at that time inhabited Switzerland.

* It frequently has a dark brown colour, and then is regarded as walnut-wood by the workmen at the pits.
† The common pine (*Pinus sylvestris*, Linn.) forms lofty trees, becoming umbrella-like when old, with a reddish-yellow bark; the flat upper surface of the needles or leaves is powdered with blue, and their apex is pointed. The female catkins are stalked and bent down; the ripe cones are pendent,

In the lignites two kinds of pine-cones are found:—one in which the scales have flat shields (fig. 339), and the seed-wings are about 2½ times as long as the nucule, and are narrowed towards the apex (fig. 340); and another in which the shields of the scales project (fig. 337), being either convex or hooked, and the seed-wings are not more than twice as long as the nucules. The former belong to *Pinus sylvestris*, Linn., the latter to *P. montana*, Mill. As the scales of the cone in the mountain-pine never have flat shields, the former belong to the common pine. In general the cones are smaller and less acutely conical at the apex [than the cones of the common Swiss pines]; but this is chiefly due to the young condition of the cones, which is also shown by their seeds being not fully mature. Thus the seeds represented

---

of an ovo-conical form, and about 50 millimetres (or nearly 2 inches) long. The wings of the seeds are usually about three times as long as the nucules.

The mountain-pine (*Pinus montana*, Mill.) is sometimes an upright tree of variable height, with a pyramidal conical crown, but sometimes forms decumbent crooked wood with curved ascending branches. The bark is dark grey; the needles are green on both sides, and less pointed at the apex; the female catkins are at first erect, but afterwards incline a little, although they never become recurved; the cones are sessile; the scales have a prominent shield, frequently hooked; and the boss is surrounded by a black ring. The seed-wings are about twice as long as the nucule. According to its mode of growth and the structure of its cones, this species may be divided into several races, namely:—*a*, the hooked pine (*P. montana uncinata*), with a rather lofty erect trunk, unsymmetrical cones, and usually very strongly developed hooks; *b*, the bog-pine (*P. montana uliginosa*), forming small gnarled trees, the shining brown cones of which are furnished with very prominent hooks directed downwards; *c*, the decumbent pine (*P. montana humilis*), bushy, with decumbent branches, oval or ovo-conical unsymmetrical cones, with convex shields, on which, however, the hooks are but slightly developed; and, *d*, the dwarf pine (*P. montana pumilio*), of the same aspect as the last, but with nearly spherical or shortly oval, sessile cones, the convex shields of which are of the same size and structure all round the cone.

The mountain-pine is spread over all the Swiss mountain-country; and the forms *c* and *d* ascend in some places to 7000 feet above the sea; in the low ground it is rare, and appears only as the hooked pine; thus it is found on the Uetliberg, where it descends to Maneck. The common pine, as is well known, is spread through the whole plain, and occurs on the mountains only in small groups or associated with firs.

in fig. 340 were evidently not quite ripe, and they were enclosed in an ovo-conical cone 38 millimetres (or about $1\frac{1}{2}$ inch) in length. Most of the cones of the mountain-pine which have come under Prof. Heer's inspection are also not quite ripe, the seeds not being fully developed. But the scales represented in figs. 334, 335, and 336 were from a perfectly ripe cone. Fig. 335 shows a scale from the outside, with its convex shield and the boss in the middle of the latter. Fig. 334 shows a scale from the inside, with its two seeds, the wings of which are not quite twice as long as the nucule and are bluntly rounded at the apex. This cone is 40 millimetres (or 1·57 inch) in length, oval, somewhat unsymmetrical, the shields on one side being slightly developed, whilst on the other they project nearly in the form of hooks. In certain smaller cones the hooks project still more, are bent downwards, and have an excentric boss. In their short oval form and convex shields these cones most nearly resemble those of the decumbent pine (*P. montana humilis*) of the Swiss mountains, and differ from the hooked pine (*P. montana uncinata*) and the bog-pine (*P. montana uliginosa*) by the smaller development of their hooks. But as the length of these hooks is very variable, and it is impossible to ascertain whether this pine was a tree or a bush, it cannot be referred with certainty to any of the numerous subordinate forms of the mountain-pine. It belongs, however, to the *Pinus montana*, and under this head agrees most closely with the *Pinus montana humilis*. All the carbonized twigs densely covered with leaf-needles that Prof. Heer has hitherto seen from Utznach belong to the mountain-pine, as is proved by their stouter needles, less pointed at the end (fig. 338). The pine-trunks, as thick as the body of a man, which have been found in the lignites of Utznach Dürnten, and Wetzikon, on the contrary, belong in all probability to the common pine.

Hence it is manifest that at this early period the two species of Swiss pines were already in existence. Even if they do not perfectly agree with the living types, so that they cannot with absolute certainty be referred to any of the numerous forms into which these trees have been developed, yet the two species, which are so nearly related to one another, move within the same cycle of forms, which has been assigned to them during uncounted ages.

3. The larch (*Pinus Larix*, Linn.). From Mörschweil and Utznach Prof. Heer has procured some cones which may probably belong to the larch. They are small and oval, and have striated scales, not thickened at the apex and obtusely rounded like those of larch-cones. But as they are strongly compressed, their scales are injured, and no seeds are to be seen, they cannot be certainly determined.

4. Of the yew (*Taxus baccata*, Linn.) Prof. Heer found the nucule at Dürnten (fig. 342) : it agrees perfectly in form and configuration with that of the living yew, but is a little smaller. It has a roundish umbilicus, a very finely wrinkled shell, and a small projecting point at the apex.

5. The birch (*Betula alba*, Linn.). The trunks of this tree, of considerable thickness, with their white bark, are, next to the pines, everywhere the most abundant woody plants in the lignites. In the fresh state their layers may be peeled off from the bark, as in the common Swiss birch; and the same striate lenticels are shown. On the slender rod-like branches the white bark is wanting, and they are of a brown colour. The leaves, fruits, and seeds have not yet been found, and the species consequently cannot be determined with certainty; but the perfect resemblance of the wood and bark renders it very probable that they belong to the common Swiss birch.

6. The oak (*Quercus Robur*, Linn.). As yet only an acorn with its cup has been found at Mörschweil; it was forwarded to Prof. Heer by Prof. Deicke. The tips of the bracts which form the cup are in part preserved, and they agree with those of the Swiss oak; but the cup itself is rather larger, and somewhat contracted above. Whether the fruit was sessile or pedunculate cannot be decided; so that Prof. Heer cannot ascertain whether it belongs to *Quercus pedunculata* or *Q. sessiflora*; and these two forms have recently been again united under one species.

7. The sycamore (*Acer Pseudoplatanus*, Linn.). Of this tree Prof. Heer has discovered a few remains of leaves, 3 inches long, in the lignitiferous clays of Binzberg near Dürnten. In their strong secondary marginal veins and delicate venules issuing

nearly at right angles, they agree very well with those of the existing tree.

Of bushes, only a species of hazel has hitherto been discovered. Its fruits are traversed by deeper longitudinal furrows than the Swiss hazel-nuts; but this is caused solely by their having lain long in a damp locality; for the hazel-nuts of the pile-dwellings and of the English bone-caves present the same characters, so that this hazel cannot be separated as a distinct species. What is very remarkable is that the hazel-nuts of the lignites occur in precisely the same two forms as those of the existing species *. The most abundant nut of the lignite epoch is the short-fruited one (*Corylus avellana ovata*, W., fig. 343); it is of a short oval form, and but little longer than broad. Its length is 15 millimetres (or ·591 inch), and its breadth is 13 millimetres (or ·512 inch). Prof. Heer has obtained it from Dürnten and Mörschweil. In form and size it agrees perfectly with nuts from the pile-dwellings of Robenhausen and with those of the present day. In the second form (*Corylus avellana*, Linn., fig. 344) the nut is elongate-oval and considerably longer (24 millimetres, or ·945 inch). The length is much greater than the breadth. Prof. Heer has received two specimens from the lignitiferous clays of Mörschweil through Prof. Deicke; they are not distinguishable from those of the pile-dwellings or from those now growing.

· Of herbaceous plants the bog-bean (*Menyanthes trifoliata*, Linn.) and the common reed (*Phragmitis communis*, Tr.) are most abundant. Of the bog-bean, or marsh-trefoil, Prof. Heer knows only the seeds—small, shining, brownish-yellow, lenticular bodies (fig. 345), which are found here and there in great abundance in the lignite at Dürnten, Utznach, and Mörschweil.

---

* The nuts of the Swiss form are almost globular, scarcely compressed; those of the other are elongate-oval and slightly compressed. In the former the young twigs, the petioles, and the base of the cupule are richly clothed with glandular hairs (as in the *Corylus glandulosa*, Schoutlew., *Corylus avellana ovata*, W.); in the latter these glandular hairs do not occur or are very scanty, and the cupule is shorter than the fruit. But the short-fruited form is also found with a short cupule, and the hairs scarcely glandular (as at Schambelen), so that this character is not constant. The short-fruited form ripens its nuts earlier, and is therefore known as the " August nut."

They cannot be distinguished from the seeds of the living species, which occurs in the pile-dwellings of Robenhausen. The common reed is most abundant at Utznach and Dürnten in the earthy dark-coloured intercalated bands ("silver"); these are in places closely traversed by shining black bands, formed by the jointed rhizomes and leaves of the reed, the latter marked with numerous longitudinal lines. Sometimes the branches and fibrils issuing from the knots of the rhizomes have been preserved. Frequently these masses of reeds fill whole beds, to the exclusion of all other plants; hence they probably formed the whole of the sedgy growths where the peat was covered by a clayey layer.

Of the bulrush (*Scirpus lacustris*, Linn.), only the fruits (fig. 346) have been preserved; but these are not uncommon in the clay beds at Dürnten, and agree exactly with those of the living plant, which has also reached Prof. Heer from the pile-dwellings of Robenhausen. In the same clays at Dürnten Prof. Heer found a few seeds of the raspberry (*Rubus idæus*, Linn.), of the water-pepper (*Polygonum hydropiper*, Linn.?), and of the water-chestnut (*Trapa natans*, Linn.?). The determination of the two species last mentioned, however, is not quite certain. Of the *Trapa* Prof. Heer has found no entire fruit, but only spiny fragments, which, however, suit this plant very well.

Of the white bedstraw (*Galium palustre*, Linn.) the fruits are tolerably plentiful at Utznach and Dürnten; they occur as little spheres of the size of grains of powder, slightly wrinkled externally, and are scattered through the lignite-beds. A cranberry (*Vaccinium vitis idæa*, Linn.) is known only by a single coriaceous leaf (fig. 347) collected at Dürnten. It is well preserved; but its determination is still doubtful.

All these plants of the lignite still grow in Switzerland; those which occur in the lignites themselves grew on peat-bogs, whilst the species found in the intercalated clays (namely the yew, the hazel, the raspberry, and the water-nut) were swept down by water from the neighbourhood and deposited with the soil carried down at the same time. The only flowering plant which cannot be referred to any existing species is a water-lily, which, in the structure of its seeds, the only remains of it that have come down to the present time, differs so greatly from our water-lilies that Caspary, of Königsberg, has formed for it a distinct genus (*Holopleura*)*. These seeds are oval, brown, and 2½ to 3 millimetres (or ·098 to ·118 inch) in length; at one end (fig. 348,*a,c*) they are furnished with a little circular operculum, which bears a semilunar umbilicus and a small tubercle (fig. 348, *d*). The seed-coat is very thick (fig. 348, *b*); and its superficial layer of cells have sinuous walls. The seeds are of the size and form of those of the common white water-lily, but differ from them in the solidity of the seed-coat and the presence of the operculum; in these respects they rather approach the seeds of the *Victoria regia*, Lindl., in which, however, the cell-walls are much less thickened.

The Cryptogamia are chiefly represented in the lignites by the mosses†, which in some places occur in great quantities, and form dense felted masses. The bog-mosses (species of *Sphagnum*), which are now so plentiful in turbaries, have one species (*Sphagnum cymbifolium*) at Dürnten. Three species of feather-mosses have been found at Dürnten, the most abundant of which (*Hypnum lignitorum*, Schimp.) stands between *Hypnum palustre* and *H. ochraceum*, which grow in mountain-brooks upon stones and rotten wood. A second and abundant species (*H. priscum*, Schimp.) is very like the *Hypnum sarmentosum*, Wahlb., which grows in Lapland and on the loftiest summits of the Sudettes; and the third species represents *H. stramineum* and *H. trifarium*, which live in peat-bogs and forest-streams. From Mörschweil a species (*Thuidium antiquum*, Schimp.) has been obtained, very like one (*T. delicatulum*) which now lives in forests.

---

* Prof. Caspary, of Königsberg, has founded this genus upon seeds found in the lignites of Dornheim and Wölfersheim, in the Wetterau. Prof. Heer sent him specimens from Dürnten which he considered to agree with these. They are identical not only in external form, but also in the structure of their cells. These, when macerated, acquire a fine blue colour with sulphuric acid and iodine, showing that the cellulose has been well preserved notwithstanding the many thousands of years during which the seeds have lain in the earth.

† Prof. P. Schimper, of Strasburg, whose knowledge of mosses is most profound, had the kindness to examine and determine these specimens.

Of the Vascular Cryptogamia Prof. Heer only knows the jointed and striated stems of a species of horsetail (*Equisetum limosum*, Linn. ?).

Although the number of plants hitherto found in the lignites is not great, it is sufficient to enable us to form an idea of the appearance of the vegetation of the peat-bogs at the time of their formation; and Prof. Heer believes that the flora must actually have appeared very much as shown in the Plate of Dürnten.

Characteristic forms of animals, the elephant, the rhinoceros, and the *Urus*, are seen in the restored landscape; and they merit attention.

Of the elephant two very beautifully preserved molars were found at Dürnten, together with fragments of large bones at the bottom of the lignite. The grinding-surface in the back molar of the lower jaw (fig. 350) is 67 millim. (or 2·638 inches) in transverse diameter, and is traversed by twelve transverse laminæ, the enamelled edges of which are undulated, and here and there form projecting angles. This is the tooth-structure of *Elephas antiquus*, Falc., which appears to be most nearly related to the African elephant, and was very probably of the same size and form. In the mammoth (*Elephas primigenius*, Blum., fig. 351) the transverse plates run parallel, stand closer together, are much less crenulated, and have no projecting points.

Of the rhinoceros a nearly complete skeleton was found in the clay of the lignite-deposit of Dürnten; but, by an unfortunate accident, it was almost all lost. Nevertheless a number of bones and some of the teeth reached Prof. Heer; and these enable him to recognize it as *Rhinoceros etruscus*, Falc.*. It differs

---

* Hermann de Meyer regarded it as *Rhinoceros Merkii*. According to him (see 'Palæontographica,' vol. ix. 1864, p. 242) there were in Germany two quaternary species of *Rhinoceros*:—*R. Merkii*, in which the nostrils are separated by a bony septum only in the anterior part of their extent, and of which the molars are not surrounded by enamel; and *R. tichorhinus*, Cuv., with a complete nasal septum, and molars furnished with a thick layer of enamel. The existing and Tertiary species (as also the Pliocene species, *R. leptorhinus*, Cuv.) have no long nasal septum; and their incisor teeth are persistent. *R. tichorhinus* has been found frozen in the ground in Siberia, still retaining its skin and hair; and its teeth and bones have been noticed in many parts of

Fig. 350.

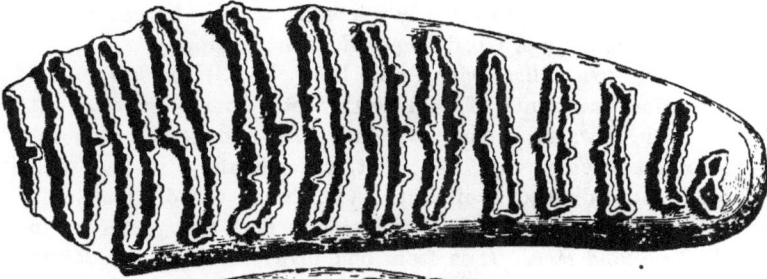

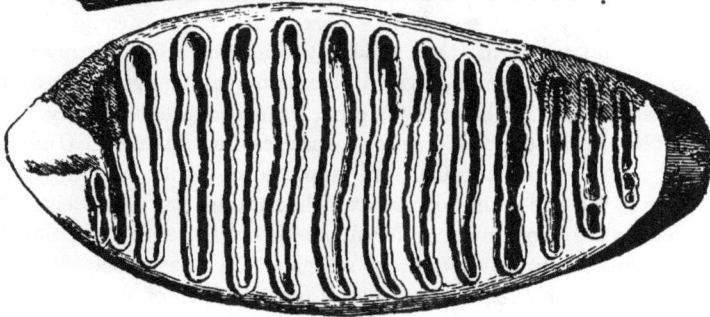

Fig. 351.

Fig. 350. *Elephas antiquus*, Falc. Back molar of lower jaw from Dürnten, half nat. size.

Fig. 351. *Elephas primigenius*, Blum. Ditto, half nat. size, from the
railway-cutting at Luttingen near Hauenstein, on the Rhine.

Europe. In the basin of the Rhine they are found in the Loess and in the
bone-caves. The remains of the *Rhinoceros Merkii* have been collected near
Mauer, in the valley of the Neckar, in a deposit of sand and gravel inferior to
the Loess; and at Mosbach, near Wiesbaden, it seems to occur in deposits
lower than those which contain *R. tichorhinus* in the neighbouring valley of
the Lahn. According to Hermann de Meyer, *R. Merkii* therefore made its
appearance before *R. tichorhinus*; it occupied the lower part of the Quaternary,
and the latter species the upper portion, although it is not proved that, in
some places, the two species did not live together. According to Lartet
(Ann. des Sci. Nat. 1867, vol. vii. p. 27), *R. Merkii*, De Meyer, is not the
species described by Jaeger and Kaup, but the same as *R. etruscus*, Falc.;
Prof. Heer therefore gives it the latter name.

considerably from all existing species, but seems, in its size, in the two horns with which the head was armed, and in the form of the teeth, to be most nearly related to the two-horned rhinoceros of the Cape of Good Hope (*R. bicornis,* Linn.).

Of the urus (*Bos primigenius,* Boj.), Prof. Heer has in his collection fragments of jaws with teeth from Dürnten. At Utznach, however, a complete skull with two great horns was discovered some years ago; but, unfortunately, it has been lost. According to Prof. Rütimeyer, this is the original stock of our domestic cattle, and its type has been best preserved in the Friesland race. It is from one fifth to one fourth larger than a very large cow. The horns first curve strongly backwards and outwards, then suddenly bend forwards and upwards, so that the points stand very high and perpendicularly above the forehead, and are bent slightly backwards at the extremity.

The elephant and rhinoceros became extinct during the Quaternary period; but the urus still appears as a wild animal at the time of the pile-dwellings (as at Robenhausen and Moosseedorf), and, as the progenitor of the domestic ox, it has become one of the most important species of animals. It was associated with the red deer (*Cervus elaphus,* Linn.), teeth of which found at Dürnten and Utznach are undistinguishable from those of the living animal. The bear, of which teeth and portions of the jaw have been met with in the lignite of Utznach, was, on the contrary, considerably larger than the existing bear of the Alps, and constitutes a distinct species, which occurred abundantly in the Quaternary period, especially in caves. From this last circumstance it has received the name of the "cave-bear" (*Ursus spelæus,* Blum.). Its forehead was more convex than that of the Swiss bear; and its teeth were much larger; there is a gap between the canine and the first true molars.

The existence of a squirrel in forests is indicated by the fir-cones, of which the scales are bitten away in exactly the same way as in cones from which squirrels have extracted the seeds * (see fig. 332, p. 156).

* Prof. Heer has seen, in the British Museum, cones treated in the same way from the forest-bed of the Norfolk coast (see Lyell, 'Antiquity of Man,' p. 215).

Of the lower animals Prof. Heer only knows a few species of Mollusca and insects. The former occur by thousands in the clays. Besides fragments of *Anodontæ*, only three species can be recognized, namely *Pisidium obliquum*, Lam., *Valvata obtusa*, Drap., and a variety of *V. depressa*, Pfeif. These are animals that still occur in the same district; the *Valvatæ* live in the brooks traversing the peat-bogs.

Insects are found partly in the lignite and partly in the clays. The former are almost exclusively species of *Donacia*; but these occur in such quantities that their elytra lie by hundreds in some parts of the lignite; they still retain their metallic blue and green colours, and form brilliant coloured specks on the black ground. The elytra are most frequently met with; the thorax and legs are less common, and the latter are generally separated from the body. No doubt these beetles lived on the aquatic and marsh plants of the turbaries. At their death they fell into the water and became broken up; and only the harder parts (especially the elytra) sank to the bottom with other organic matters, and thus got imbedded in the peat. When fresh from the pit they are admirably preserved; but as the lignite shrinks in drying, they are either destroyed by this process or so twisted and distorted that they are no longer fit for investigation. By the form and configuration of the elytra, two species may be distinguished at Dürnten and Utznach; these are identical with species now living about the Swiss lakes and marshes (*Donacia discolor*, Gyll., and *sericea*, Linn.). The most abundant species is *Donacia. discolor*, which was adorned with green and blue metallic tints, and agreed perfectly with the existing form in the configuration of the elytra, the fine transverse wrinkling, the punctate striæ and the mode of their union (fig. 353), and the uniformly and densely punctate prothorax (fig. 355). In the male (fig. 354) the posterior femora were also much thickened. The nearly allied *Donacia sericea*, Linn. (fig. 352) is less abundant; in this species the punctate striæ are less distinctly marked at the apex of the elytra, where they become confounded with the other punctures of that part. The larvæ of these two species, and their nourishment, are still unknown; in the adult state they are found all over Europe, even as far as Lapland, on reeds and sedges.

In the lignitiferous clays of Dürnten Prof. Heer has found

Fig. 352. Fig. 353. Fig. 354. Fig. 355. Fig. 356.

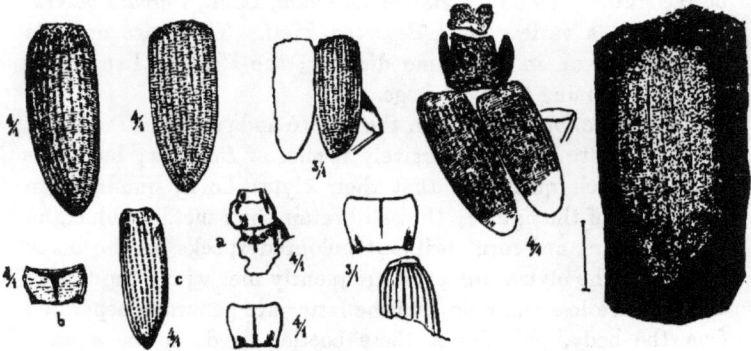

Fig. 357. Fig. 359. Fig. 358.

Fig. 352. *Donacia sericea*, Linn. Elytron, four times nat. size, from Dürnten.

Fig. 353. *Donacia discolor*, Gyll. Elytron, four times nat. size, from Dürnten.

Fig. 354. Ditto, male, from Utznach, three times nat. size.

Fig. 355. Ditto, four times nat. size, from Utznach.

Fig. 356. *Hylobius rugosus*, Heer, rather more than three times nat. size, from Dürnten.

Fig. 357. *Carabites* (*Harpalus?*) *diluvianus*, Heer, from Dürnten, four times nat. size. *a*, head and part of thorax; *b*, prothorax; *c*, elytron.

Fig. 358. *Pterostichus nigrita*, Fab., sp., three times nat. size, from Dürnten.

Fig. 359. *Carabites cordicollis*, Heer, four times nat. size, from Dürnten.

very beautifully preserved elytra of a weevil (*Hylobius rugosus*, Heer, fig. 356), an extinct species *, but very nearly allied

* Elytra coal-black in this species, twice as long as broad, traversed by rows of deep punctures, those in the sutural rows deeper and further apart than in the middle rows; interstices wrinkled. The punctures in the rows are very deep; the first and second rows were parallel to each other from the base to the apex; the third unites at the apex with the eighth, the fourth with the fifth, and the sixth with the seventh. These last two pairs stop within the space enclosed by the third and eighth rows. The interstices are coarsely punctured and transversely wrinkled. The punctures are deeper at the base than in the middle and at the apex of the elytra. The species differs

to *H. pineti,* which lives upon pines. In the light-grey clays, here and there are seen shining black scales, which on close examination prove to be the remains of the thorax and elytra of small beetles. They belong, for the most part, to the Carabidæ or predaceous ground-beetles. One species (fig. 358) agrees with a black beetle (*Pterostichus nigrita,* Fab., sp.) which is abundant all over Switzerland up to the subalpine region; while two other species (*Carabites diluvianus,* Heer, fig. 357, and *C. cordicollis,* Heer, fig. 359) cannot be referred to any living forms*. These predaceous beetles probably dwelt upon the banks of streams, and were drowned by the inundations which carried down the clays upon the peat-bogs.

A lignite formation like that of Utznach and Dürnten occurs at Chambéry and Sonnaz, in Savoy. Upon a bed of fine sand of unknown thickness lies a grey clay with a bed of lignite; this is followed by a layer of rolled pebbles, 8 metres (or 8·749 yards) thick, united in the upper part into a solid mass by a calcareous cement. This is covered in its turn by a thickness of 30 metres (or 32·809 yards) of unstratified but in part striated pebbles (erratics). This deposit consequently presents nearly the same conditions as those at Utznach and Dürnten. In the lignite are found fir-cones and birch wood; in the clay, leaves of willows (*Salix cinerea,* Linn., and *S. repens,* Linn.?), and the

---

from *H. pineti* by its smaller size and by having its elytra shorter with the same breadth, and somewhat different in configuration. In the first two striæ (near the suture) *H. rugosus* has only thirteen punctures, while *H. pineti* has from seventeen to twenty-four; the middle striæ or rows have the same number of punctures in both species. The interstices also are more coarsely wrinkled.

* *Carabites diluvianus* is distinguished by its broad short prothorax, with acute posterior angles (fig. 357, *b*). It has a smooth middle line, an impression on each side at the base, and a transverse row of punctures in front. The striæ of the elytra are punctured, and the interstices flat and smooth. The species is of the size of *Harpalus satyrus,* Kn., and has the thorax of the same form; but it is distinguished by the punctured striæ. Prof. Heer found several elytra, prothoraces, and a very well preserved head at Dürnten. It appears to belong to the genus *Harpalus. Carabites cordicollis* has a smooth cordate prothorax with its sides strongly incurved behind, a deep middle line, and a deep impression on each side at the base. It probably belongs to the genus *Pterostichus* (*Argutor*).

elytra of *Donaciæ* (*D. discolor*, Gyll., and *D. menyanthidis*, Fab.) and small Carabidæ *.   No mammals have as yet been met with here; the mammoth and cave-bear are always found, according to M. Pillet, in a later formation.   It is worthy of notice that this lignite formation has also been discovered in the south-west of France, near Biarritz, by Dr. C. Gaudin, a friend of Prof. Heer.   It contains the seeds of the extinct water-lily (*Holopleura Victoria*, Casp.) and of the bog-bean and a hazel-nut, and also coloured elytra of *Donaciæ*.

On a general review of the plants and animals of the lignites, it is manifest that they are completely different from those of the Miocene.   Œningen is the youngest member of the Miocene; but it has no single species in common with the lignites, and the general character of its fauna and flora is quite different. Between the Miocene and the lignite formation there has been consequently a vast interval, as may be seen by a comparison of the two landscapes of Lausanne and Dürnten.   In the former, near Lausanne, there is a subtropical group with trees which are now quite foreign to Switzerland; and in the Dürnten picture none but indigenous plants appear.   Thus a complete transformation of organic nature had taken place, and in the lignites the existing order of things had already commenced.   Although containing some extinct types, their fauna and flora were nevertheless much nearer to those now existing than to the Miocene; they announce a new period, and with it the dawn of the present creation.   But it is not only that organic nature appears in a new dress; even the form of the ground has become different, and, on the whole, assumed its present physiognomy.   Upon this point the conditions of deposition of the lignite furnish decisive data.   It has been already noticed (vol. i. pp. 286, 287) that the Miocene was upheaved along the Alps, whilst in the plain of Switzerland it retained a horizontal position.   At Utznach the sandstones are thrown into a perpendicular position (see fig. 329, p. 152) in consequence of this upheaval, as may be seen near the ruins of the old castle.   The lignite-deposit and the masses of

---

* Prof. Heer is indebted to M. Pillet, of Chambéry, for the communication of these specimens.

rolled pebbles rest horizontally upon this vertical Miocene. A traveller visiting the road which is being constructed to Gauen will see a section in which the horizontal strata of the lignite rest directly upon the tops of the perpendicular strata of the Miocene. It is therefore clear that the tilting-up of the Miocene must have taken place *before* the formation of the lignite. This upheaval of the Miocene, which may be traced all along the chain of the Alps, is directly connected with the change of form of the whole of the Swiss mountain region; and consequently the change in the external form of Switzerland occurred in the interval between the youngest Miocene of Œningen and the formation of the lignite, just like the transformation of organic nature; and it may be assumed that at the time of the formation of the lignite the Swiss mountains had essentially their present form.

Between the deposits of Œningen and the lignites there is no Swiss formation containing organic remains. Thus the lignites would appear to follow immediately after the uppermost Miocene beds; and hence the conclusion might be drawn that the above-mentioned transformation of inorganic and organic nature had taken place in a comparatively short time. To form a judgment upon this point, similar formations must be considered; and the most important data are to be obtained in England and Italy.

On the coast of Norfolk, in England, the shore for a great distance has been worn away by the waves. On that coast for about forty miles (from Cromer to Kessingland) the remains appear of an ancient forest. One may still see the erect trunks of many trees, the roots of which lose themselves in all directions in the underlying clay. These trees are covered by a clay-bed, which contains here and there thin layers of lignite. Between the trunks of the trees and these lignites are found cones of the fir and of the common and mountain pine*, the seeds of the yew, the fruits of the hornwort (*Ceratophyllum demersum*), and

---

* By the kindness of Sir Charles Lyell and Dr. Falconer, Prof. Heer was enabled, when in London, to make an examination of these remains of plants.

the seeds of the bog-bean, the short-fruited hazel (*Corylus avellana ovata*, W.), the oak, and the white and yellow water-lilies. With these plants are found the teeth of *Elephas antiquus*, Falc., and of two other elephants (*E. meridionalis* and *E. primigenius*, Blum., var.), and also remains of a rhinoceros (*R. etruscus*, Falc.), a hippopotamus (*H. major*), the ox, horse, stag, pig, musk-shrew (*Sorex moschatus*, Pall.), and the beaver. The bivalve and univalve shells found are identical with existing species; among them is *Pisidium obliquum*, Lam., as at Dürnten. The *Donaciæ* also are not wanting; and these, with the bog-bean and the water-lilies, indicate a swampy soil. This buried forest (the "forest-bed") of the Norfolk coast therefore probably represents the Swiss lignite formation. The fir and the mountain-pine have now disappeared from the English flora; but, like all other plants found in this locality, they are members of the existing flora of Europe, and with them, just as at Dürnten, a few extinct animals are associated, giving the fauna a foreign aspect.

On the Norfolk coast, immediately beneath the forest-bed, there is a marine deposit which, in some parts, contains numerous marine animals. It has been called the "Norwich Crag." Of the marine animals contained in it, 85 per cent. (69 out of 81) are still living; and among these there are no species of southern latitudes, but 12 of them are now only met with in northern regions. The Norwich Crag is followed, in descending, by another marine deposit, the "Red Crag;" and below this is another formation of the same origin, which has been called the "Coralline Crag." Of the Mollusca of the Red Crag the living species constitute 57 per cent.; and among these there are 8 northern and 16 southern forms. Of the Mollusca of the Coralline Crag the living species are 51 per cent.; and 27 of them are to be regarded as southern (26 Mediterranean and 1 West-Indian) and only 2 as northern forms. We see therefore that the temperature of the sea must have gradually diminished: the southern forms disappeared by degrees; and their places were taken by those of more northern latitudes.

England possesses no formation that can be compared with the Swiss Upper Miocene; so that Prof. Heer cannot ascertain the relation of this Crag formation to the Swiss Miocene by the examination of the conditions of stratification. But we have already seen (pp. 91, 92) that, among the marine shells of the Miocene in the Helvetian stage, the living species constitute 35 per cent. of the sea-shells, and, further, that in the uppermost or Œningian stage of the Miocene, no true elephants occur, although it possesses two mastodons, which are entirely wanting in the Crag. In the Crag there is another species of mastodon (*M. arvernensis*); and with this true elephants and *Hippopotami* occur. The English Crag formations are consequently younger than the Œningian stage, and occupy the interval between it and the lignites. The period of these Crag formations has been called *Pliocene*, and it is regarded as the third great division of the Tertiary epoch. In the Norfolk forest-bed, and in the Swiss lignites (which may be denominated the "Utznach formation"), an indication is afforded of a new period, which has been named the Quaternary or Diluvial period: it is distinguished from the Pliocene by the agreement of its flora and marine fauna with those of the present day.

A long interval of time manifestly elapsed between the formation of Œningen and that of Utznach; so that we need not be surprised to meet with a totally different flora in the Quaternary period. It would be very interesting to learn what was the character of the intervening period, and how the transition was brought about; and on this subject we may obtain some information from the fossil plants of Italy. The Upper Miocene flora of Northern and Central Italy, as exhibited in the gypsum-quarries of Stradella and Guarene in Piedmont, in the burnt and blue clays of the upper valley of the Arno in Tuscany, and near Senegaglia, presents the same characters as those of the Swiss Upper Miocene. There are found in the Italian Upper Miocene flora the same species of liquidambars, evergreen oaks, camphor-trees and laurels, *Taxodia, Glyptostrobi, Planeræ,* planes, hornbeams, *Sapindi,* and walnut-trees as in the Swiss flora.

Above the Upper Miocene formation in the valley of the Arno, in Tuscany, a yellowish-brown ferruginous sand occurs, which has received the name of "Sansino," and belongs to the Pliocene. It contains the same mastodon (*M. arvernensis*) that occurs in the Norwich Crag, and also an elephant (*E. meridionalis*), a hippopotamus (*H. major*), and a rhinoceros (*R. etruscus,* Falc.), which, in England, extend up into the forest-bed. Only five species of plants have as yet been observed in the Sansino. Three of them are peculiar to it; but two (*Glyptostrobus europæus* and *Cinnamomum Scheuchzeri*) are common to it and to the Miocene.

A greater number of plants have been discovered in Montajone, a lateral valley of the Val d'Arno. The sea formerly extended into this region; and the soft yellowish-grey sandstone consequently contains not only leaves but marine animals, of which about half, as in the Coralline Crag, belong to living species; hence this locality must be regarded as Pliocene. Among the plants many peculiar forms are met with; but half of them agree with species of the Œningian stage. Such are the planes, the hornbeams, the liquidambar, two or three poplars, the small-leaved elm, the *Planera,* one or two walnut-trees, a *Sapindus,* and the lime-leafed jujube-tree. But there are no tropical forms; and, from the analogy of the most nearly allied living species, nearly all of these plants would support the present climate of Tuscany.

Ascending one stage higher, we find in Tuscany compact tuffs (the travertines of Massa Marittima) which, in many places, contain impressions of plants. They show a remarkable mixture of extinct and living species. Among the former may be remarked, besides several Miocene trees (such as the liquidambar, the *Planera,* and *Betula prisca*), some peculiar forms, of which an arbor vitæ (*Thuja Saviana,* Gaud.) and a walnut (*Juglans paviæfolia,* Gaud.) are especially interesting. Of the existing species some are now confined to Southern Europe, namely the fig-tree, the manna-ash, the oriental hornbeam, the Judas tree (*Cercis siliquastrum,* Linn.), several South-Italian oaks, and the sarsaparilla (*Smilax aspera,* Linn.); but a portion of them also inhabit other regions, such as the beech, elm, white-beam tree (*Pyrus Aria*), the grey willow (*Salix cinerea,* Linn.), the maple and sycamore, and the ivy.

As yet no animal remains have been discovered in these tuffs, and there is only one species of plant common to them and the lignites; but the mixture of extinct forms of plants with others still existing renders it probable that the two deposits are of the same date. In favour of this view it may be noted that in the tuff of Aygalades, in the neighbourhood of Marseilles, a similar mixture occurs, comprising both extinct and living species of plants, among which are found the hazel, *Salix viminalis*, the lime-tree, the fig, *Cercis*, and laurel, and with them the remains of *Elephas antiquus*, Falc. Consequently, at the time when this elephant inhabited Europe, the flora on both sides of the Alps had the same character as at present, and consisted for the most part of the same species; whilst in the intervening Pliocene period the Italian flora differed materially from that now living in Switzerland. To this Pliocene period should be referred the lignites of Gandino, near Bergamo, and those of La Folla d'Indune, on the Lake of Varese, in Lombardy. In both localities are found a walnut (*Juglans tephrodes*, Ung.) which is remarkably like an American species (*J. cinerea*), and shows that some American forms continued into Pliocene times.

The same species of walnut occurs also in the Pliocene lignites of Wetterau, which are united by it and by a species of pine * (*Pinus Cortesii*, Brongn.) with the Pliocene formation of Italy. And, curiously enough, two of the Utznach plants also occur in it, namely the mountain-pine and the water-lily (*Holopleura Victoria*, Casp.) ; so that, owing to the species just mentioned, these lignites form the transition between the Pliocene and the Utznach formations. To the same period probably belong the lignites of Rippersrode, in Thuringia, from which Prof. Heer has seen some species known to occur in the uppermost lignites of Wetterau (*Corylus bulbifera*, Ludw., *C. ventrosa*, Ludw., *Magnolia cor*, Ludw., and *Cytisus reniculus*, Ludw.).

* Ludwig has described it as *Pinus resinosa* and *Schnittspani* (Palæontographica, Band v. Taf. xviii.) The *Pinus* represented in Taf. xix. fig. 4 is probably *P. Abies*, Linn. That shown in Taf. xix. fig. 1 Prof. Heer at first regarded as *P. sylvestris*, but the strongly marked and convex shields are in favour of its being *P. montana*.

While these lignites are rather older than the Utznach formation, and belong to the uppermost Pliocene, the masses of sand and pebbles which in the valley of the Rhine underlie the Loess were very probably deposited at the same time as the lignites. In them we find, besides the remains of elephants, hippopotamus, ox, beaver, horse, and stag, those of *Rhinoceros Merkii*; whilst in the loess itself another species of rhinoceros (*R. tichorhinus*) occurs with the mammoth.

CHAPTER XIII.

GLACIAL HISTORY.

THE section at Dürnten given in fig. 328 (p. 150) shows that the lignites at that place are covered by a great deposit of stratified gravel and sand, upon the surface of which isolated blocks are found. At Utznach the lignites (fig. 329, p. 152) are also covered by gravel and sand, and separate blocks occur on the surface of the deposits. Beds of stratified pebbles and sand are seen continually in the gravel-pits opened for mending the roads; they prove that these deposits are spread over the low grounds of Northern Switzerland, and that the formation exemplified at Dürnten and Utznach is distributed over a great portion of the lower district of the country. This formation has been described as *Stratified Diluvium* [and also as *Drift*]. It consists of more or less rolled fragments, which generally vary in size from that of a walnut to that of a man's fist, lying in more or less horizontal beds, sometimes alternating with bands of sand. The pebbles mostly have belonged to rocks which are not found in the Swiss plains, but which originally appertained to the neighbouring Alps. In the Canton of Zurich the gravel-pits contain a mass of red pebbles, composed of the sernifite of the Glaris Alps; with these are fragments of limestone, representing the various calcareous formations of the high Swiss mountains. In the vicinity of the Lake of Constance and the Rhine, as near Diessenhofen, Stein, &c., everywhere are found vast beds of rolled pebbles, the materials of which are derived from the valley of the Rhine. The plain between Thun and Thierachern and up to the shore of the Lake of Thun is covered with masses of sand and pebbles, the origin of which may be traced to the neighbouring Alps; and on the shores of the Lake of Geneva gravel

beds are met with of which the materials have come from the
Valais. The same phenomenon is presented by the southern
slope of the Alps, where great beds of sand and gravel extend
down into the plain of Italy, as, for instance, to the south of the
Lago Maggiore.

These stratified pebble-beds are so like the gravels deposited
by the Swiss mountain-streams, that, without doubt, they were
produced in the same manner.

We must, however, distinguish from them the *unstratified
gravels* which have been characterized as the Erratic formation,
and which consist of unstratified masses of sand and stones, and
of isolated blocks of all sizes. Where they lie together in great
masses, large and small fragments of rock are heaped together
without any order : some of them are rounded ; others still possess sharp edges and angles ; and their surfaces are not unfrequently traversed by straight striæ or scratches, sometimes
parallel to each other, sometimes crossing in various directions. The stratified drift is uniformly spread over the bottoms of the valleys, and is only cut through by brooks and
rivers, which wear it away and form steep cliffs, whilst the unstratified drift forms chains of hills standing out more or less
abruptly from the surrounding surface. These chains frequently
follow the slopes of valleys and run parallel with them, or they
cross the valleys in the form of crescent-like ramparts or
moraines.

The most remarkable of these moraines, for the investigation
of which we are chiefly indebted to M. A. Escher de la Linth,
are shown on the geological map at the end of this volume.
Two such moraines occur in the neighbourhood of Berne—one
near Muri, a Swiss mile south of the town, the other in the city
itself. Several moraines in the Cantons of Lucerne and Argovia
are still more distinctly marked : thus a curved chain of hills
from 100 to 200 feet high, and of about the same breadth, surrounds the northern end of the Lake of Sempach, resting at one
end against the boulder-deposits of the hill of Sempach, and
at the other extremity abutting on the masses of rocks of
Wartensee. A second mound, cut through by the Sur, traverses
the same valley lower down near Staffelbach, and runs towards
Mooslerau. The northern extremity of the Lake of Baldegg is

enclosed by a chain of hills like that of Sempach; and this is the case also with the Lake of Wauwyl, which has now been drained. The peat-bog of this lake, so celebrated for its pile-dwellings, is surrounded in a bold curve by a chain of mounds composed of erratic blocks.

In the basin of the Limmat we find five similar moraines. The first, which indeed is not strongly marked, is situated between Schübelbach and Tuggen; the second runs from Rapperschweil towards Hurden, and, by the formation of the peninsula of Hurden, separates the upper from the lower Lake of Zurich; whilst the little islands of Ufnau and Lützelau are the remains of an uptilted reef of conglomerate, the peninsula of Hurden (which is from 50 to 60 feet in height) consists only of sand, gravel, and erratic blocks of sernifite and limestone, which also lie in the lake for a distance of 3 kilometres (or nearly two British miles). These blocks, measuring from 4 to 12 feet long, may also be traced, in the form of a curved moraine, to the opposite bank near Rapperschweil. The third moraine, which is much larger, bounds the northern extremity of the Lake of Zurich. It commences near the Flühgasse, and is continued along the base of the Burghölzli, through the vineyards above Reisbach, as far as the Kreuzbühl and the high promenade. The rampart-like ridge of the Winkelwiese and the Upper Zäune, and the hill situated between the market-lane and the cattle-market, the Lindenhof, the mound in the Botanic Garden (known as the " Cat "), and the Brandschenke above Sellnau, are parts of this extensive moraine, which forms the subsoil of the city of Zurich, and probably had originally the shape of a connected rampart like a crescent. It is continued on the left bank of the Lake of Zurich over the Freudenberg and the Bürgli to the church of Wollishofen. The chain of hills which extends from the neighbourhood of Kirchberg towards Horgeregg, and, further, towards Hirzel and Schönenberg, consists also in its upper part of similar unstratified débris covering up the Miocene that forms the lower stratum of this district.

In the city of Zurich the boulder formation is found everywhere in digging cellars, wells, and foundations. It was easily recognized some years ago in the Canons' Platz near the Cathedral during the lowering of the street; and fig. 360 (p. 191) gives a view of a portion of this subsoil of the city copied from a daguerreotype. The large angular stones consisted of Alpine limestone, sernifite, and Miocene; one block of limestone was about 10 feet long and 4 feet high. The smaller, rounded and smoothed pebbles are composed of the same materials; they surround the large blocks, and are intermixed without order. Numerous large blocks lay in the ground near St. Anna and the Felsenhof; some also appeared in the mound of the Botanic Garden. At the Sellnau the construction of the road and the diggings for the foundations of houses opened up the interior of the hill, which consisted entirely of erratics *. The road-cutting executed in 1864 near the Brandschenke exposed a great quantity of Alpine rocks, among which were vast blocks of sernifite and Alpine limestone, confusedly mingled with large fragments of sandstone and conglomerate.

The fourth moraine of the basin of the Limmat may be traced from the monastery of Fahr, through Schönenwerd to Altstetten; and the fifth is to be seen at Spreitenbach, Kilwagen, and Oetweil.

In the valley of the Glatt similar hills, forming a sort of parapet, appear in the neighbourhood of Schwerzenbach, Ofen, and Dübendorf, rising some 50 feet above the bottom of the valley.

The hills here referred to are in general covered with vegetation, and it is only by accident that their internal structure becomes known. But in a great many places the blocks lie separately on the surface of the ground, either isolated or piled up into great heaps, and are called *Erratic blocks* or *boulders*. Many of them are of extraordinary size, and have received popular names. The *plough-stone*, which lies 140 metres (or about 153 yards) above the sea-level between Erlenbach and Wetzweil, stands out of the ground more than 60 feet; and, notwithstanding the diminution which it has already undergone, it contains (according to Prof. Escher de la Linth) about 72,000 cubic feet of stone, and weighs about 90,000 hundredweight. Another gigantic block stood near Höngg, and furnished the

---

* In the spring of 1870, in digging for the foundation of a maypole here, an enormous block was found; it has been placed in the Annex of the Palace of Justice as an evidence of the ancient moraines.

material for building a house, which has obtained from it the name of " Red Acrestone " ("zum rothen Ackerstein "). In the Steinhof, near Sceberg (in the Canton of Berne) there lie three enormous granite-blocks, the largest of which contains about 61,000 cubic feet. In the Canton of Neuchâtel a block of fine-grained granite, 50 feet long, 20 feet broad, and 40 feet high, has received the name of the "club-footed stone" (" Pierre à Bot"); another of 12,500 cubic feet, above the village of Mont-la-Ville at the foot of the Jura, is called the "Pierre de Milliet;" the block " du Trésor," near Orsière, has a cubic content of 100,000 feet; and the " Monster Block" on the hill of Montet near Devent, contains 161,000 cubic feet. These are only a few examples of such gigantic blocks; but they are found in many places over a great part of Switzerland *.

It is remarkable that in some places masses of blocks of the same kind are to be found lying together. Thus south of Fäl-landen a number of rock-fragments consisting of sernifite (red acrestone) are piled one upon another, so that the traveller might suppose himself in the midst of the ruins of a landslip. A still more remarkable accumulation of similar blocks, in this case consisting of granite, is to be seen above Monthey, to the west of the Rhone, in the lower part of the Canton of Valais. If we go up from Monthey for a walk of about a quarter of an hour, we see on the side of the mountain innumerable fragments of rock, the edges and angles of which are well preserved. Among them are blocks of 8000 or 10,000, and others of from 20,000 to 50,000 cubic feet in size; and one of them (*Pierre des Marmettes*) is estimated at 60,500 cubic feet, and forms a vast isolated rock. Another (*Pierre des Mourguets*) consists of two enormous blocks, the upper one of which in its settlement over the lower one has been split throughout its entire length, thus leaving a wide opening.

The mode of distribution of the erratic blocks in Switzerland is shown by the geological map at the end of this volume. The Miocene country between the Jura and Alps has been left white;

---

* J. de Charpentier has figured several of these erratic blocks in his ' Essai sur les Glaciers;' and Bachmann has represented some of the largest belonging to the Canton of Berne in ' Die erratischen Findlinge im Canton Bern,' 1870.

and the areas of distribution of the blocks are indicated upon it by means of shadings of longitudinal fine lines and dotted lines. But it must be borne in mind that the erratic blocks are very irregularly distributed, and that in the plain of Switzerland there are large spaces in which none of these blocks are found.   For instance, in many portions of the low ground there are no blocks, or they occur very sparingly; whilst they may be met with up to considerable elevations on the sides of the hills and mountains. In the lateral dales of the lower part of the Canton of Valais and about the Lake of Geneva they extend up to several thousand feet above the bottom of the valley.

In the Jura the boundary of the blocks forms a remarkable curve, the highest part of which may be found about opposite to the middle of the basin of the Lake of Geneva.   On the Chasseron, to the north-west of Yverdon, the curve of blocks is 3100 feet above the valley-bottom (1400 metres, or 1531 yards, above the sea); at the Chaumont it is 2400 feet above Neuchâtel, at the Chasseral 2000–2200 feet, and near Orvin 700 feet, sinking near Soleure into the low ground.   The western part of the curve reaches the bottom of the valley at Gex to the north-west of Geneva.

Similar phenomena are met with in Eastern Switzerland.   In the Canton of Zurich there are vast accumulations of blocks of Alpine limestone, sernifite, and granite near the Gyrenbad (2400 Paris feet above the sea), and almost up to the summit of the Bachtel ; they are found on the entire chain of the Albis to the Uetliberg, and also upon the chain of hills fringing the right bank of the Lake of Zurich from Pfannenstiel to the Zürichberg.   At the Lägern, in the Canton of Zurich, the blocks extend to within a few hundred feet of the ridge of the mountain. The hills surrounding the Lake of Constance are, in several places, dotted even to their summits with erratic blocks; and similar blocks are found on the hill of Hohentwiel in the Höhgau.

The rocks from which the whole of the materials of the Erratic formation have been derived are quite foreign to the localities in which these materials are found; for similar rocks do not occur in position anywhere in the Miocene district.   Whole mountain-masses and ranges consisting of exactly the same materials, how-

ever, are in the Alps ; and in many cases the path may be traced
that they have followed from there into the low grounds by
the blocks and débris belonging to the same mountains along its
course. Thus near Katzenrütihof, on the Katzensee, a block
is found consisting of a very peculiar variety of granite, such as
occurs nowhere in the whole Alpine region, except at Pontel-
jestobel, above Trons, in the Canton of the Grisons.

Blocks of the same granite are scattered over the range of
hills on the right bank of the Lake of Zurich, and in the district
lying further to the east, as, for instance, in the Gaster, in the
valley of Wallenstadt, and in innumerable quantities from
Sargans to Ragatz, and on the left side of the Rhine up to
Trons. The same granite blocks may be traced from Sargans
and through the lower Rhine valley as far as Rorschach. All
these blocks lie upon the left side of the Rhine; and it is remarkable that not a single fragment occurs on the right bank. The
innumerable blocks of sernifite (red acrestone) which are scattered
over the Canton of Zurich no doubt originated in the sernifite
mountains adjacent to the basins of the Linth and of the Wallensee. As several varieties of sernifite occur in that region, there
are many cases in which the mountain masses may be ascertained
from which the blocks probably took their origin. Thus the
rock of the enormous " ploughstone," above the parish of
Erlenbach in the Canton of Zurich, agrees perfectly with the
fine-grained porphyroid sernifite of the Gantstock in the middle
of the Canton of Glaris, and probably came thence; indeed
this mountain mass is still surrounded by innumerable vast
rocky fragments, and has received its name from this circumstance.

In the basin of the Reuss are found immense numbers of
blocks of gneiss and gneissic granites from the St. Gothard.
They may be observed on the west side of the range of the Albis
and Uetliberg; and near the Schnabelpass, in the gorge of the
Albis ridge, some granites have been transported to the eastern
side, while still more have traversed the hollow ravine of the
Mutschelle between the Uetliberg and Hasenberg, and penetrated into the valley of the Limmat. On the other hand a few
blocks of sernifite have been removed from the basin of the
Limmat into that of the Reuss.

In the river-basin of the Aar the blocks coming from the Bernese Oberland extend only into the neighbourhood of Berne; further to the north the Diluvial débris have had their origin from the basin of the Rhone. The whole of Western Switzerland is covered with materials from the mountains near the Rhone, as has been shown by Prof. Guyot, who has carefully investigated the kinds of rock and the distribution of erratic blocks all over this region, and has discovered that they may be traced to the Alps of the Valais*. He has shown that the mountains covered with mighty glaciers and immense fields of granular snow which separate Switzerland from Italy, between the St. Bernard and the Simplon, were the chief sources of the materials of the innumerable erratics of the basin of the Rhone. These Pennine Alps, and especially the mountain masses at the head of the valleys of Ering and Bagne (in the Canton of Valais), were the primæval home of the blocks of talcose granite (arkesine†) which are scattered over a great part of the Rhine basin, and have advanced as far as Seeberg. From Monte Rosa blocks of serpentine and of a peculiar variety of gabbro (euphotide) take their origin. A white granite comes from the south side of the Bernese Oberland Alps in the Upper Valais.

From the Val Ferret a fine-grained Alpine granite has been transported, which forms the vast blocks above Monthey, in the Valais, and is also met with at the foot of the Jura. A similar Alpine granite came from the mountain-mass of Mont Blanc, and reached the lower Valais through the vale of the Trient. The black-spotted grey sandstones of Val Orcine may have originated from this valley, or from the slopes of the Dent de Morcles; they occupy principally the right side of the basin of the Rhone, and are especially numerous in the neighbourhood of Vevey in the Canton of Vaud. They form a broad zone which bends at the outlet of the valley of the Rhone, and ex-

---

* See Prof. Guyot's important memoir "Sur la distribution des espèces de roches dans le bassin erratique du Rhône" (Bull. de la Soc. des Sci. Nat. de Neuchâtel, 1847). The question of the place of origin of the erratic blocks has been carefully treated by F. Mühlberg in his work on the Erratic formations of the Canton of Aargau.

† This is a greenish-yellow variety of granite, consisting of a mixture of quartz, felspar, steatite, amphibole, and chlorite.

tends along the Alps of Friburg into the neighbourhood of Friburg and Guggisberg. They are also found in the vicinity of Lausanne and on the plateaus near Yverdon.

It may naturally be asked, How have such enormous masses of rock come into these regions? what sort of force was it that transported such immense blocks to a distance of fifty or sixty Swiss miles? The solution of this problem for a long time occupied the attention of Swiss geologists; and various suggestions were made.

A satisfactory explanation of the mode of transport of these Alpine débris has been given by the careful investigation of the glaciers of Switzerland, and of the rock-masses which are deposited on their surface and are either borne along upon them or accumulated at their edges.

To understand the transport of débris on Swiss glaciers, let a person place himself on one of the gigantic Swiss mountains, where, even in the summer, he will be surrounded by boundless masses of snow, which fill up every hollow. On the sides of the mountain and in the ravines these great fields of granular snow descend and become converted into glaciers. The name of *névé* (or *firn*) is given to the frozen and more or less granular snow, and that of *glacier* to the snow which has been converted into ice by being thawed and then again frozen. When the mountain is high, and the fields of granular snow (or névé) are extensive, the glaciers usually descend low into the valley. Most of the Swiss glaciers terminate at elevations of between 1100 and 2300 metres (or from 1203 to 2515 yards). The lower Grindelwald glacier descends to 1039 metres (or 1136 yards) above the level of the sea. In many instances the lower extremity of a glacier comes down to the region of cornfields and orchard trees, where from spring to autumn it must decrease by the melting of its ice.

The glacier would therefore be constantly retiring, if its materials were not continually replaced by the advance downwards of the mass of the glacier. The enormous masses of snow accumulated in the fields of névé on the cold summits of Swiss mountains are constantly being carried down to lower regions and converted into water. Brooks take their source from the melted ice, and, flowing from the base of the glacier, hurry down the slope into the plain below. Numerous observations have proved that the advance of the glacier takes place during the whole year, although it is much greater in the spring and in the beginning of summer than during the winter, but that the volume of the ice and the inclination of the ground beneath it exert a great influence upon the progressive movement; and thus each glacier has a peculiar rate of progress. The Mer-de-Glace of Mont Blanc from 1788 to 1832 advanced * at the annual rate, on the average, of 114 metres (or nearly 125 yards); in the Unteraar glacier, according to Agassiz, the annual mean advance from 1841 to 1846 oscillated between 52 and 71 metres (or from nearly 57 to 77·648 yards); in the upper part of the glacier of the Aar an advance of 1428 metres (or about 156·1 yards) took place from 1827 to 1840, being at the annual rate of about 100 metres (or 109 yards).

Rigid and compact as the ice of a glacier appears, it is nevertheless very slowly and continuously moving downwards, and it may be compared to a stream which, in obedience to the laws of gravity, flows slowly towards the low ground. In this way the masses of snow which are produced during the greater part of the year upon the remote deserts of the granular snow-fields, gradually descend into warmer regions, where they melt, and with them are carried along any foreign bodies that may have been deposited upon the back of the glacier. The Swiss mountains are exposed to a slow but continuous wearing and destruction by atmospheric influences. Even from the most solid rocks certain materials are slowly dissolved by the action of air and water; small pores and fissures are formed, into which water penetrates, and this by its irresistible expansion, during the constantly recurring frosts, splits the rock. Violent storms and torrents of rain set in motion the loosened fragments, which rush down carrying other fragments with them. In the region of the granular snow-fields there is less of disintegration, since an unbroken mantle of snow covers the entire surface of the

---

* [The advance of the glacier is thus described by Lord Byron in his dramatic poem of Manfred:—

> " The glacier's cold and restless mass
> Moves onward day by day."

EDITOR.]

ground; but in the middle and lower Alpine regions, where water is frequently converted into ice and again melted, there is is a more active breaking-up of the surface of the mountains. Hence fragments of surrounding rocks fall frequently upon the glaciers traversing these regions, and, remaining on the surface of the glacier, are carried down by it towards the outlet of the valley.

Regular foci of destruction may be often observed, from which many blocks of rock fall down every year upon a glacier; and as the glacier advances, the disintegrated fragments will not collect into a heap of rubbish, but those of the previous year will perhaps have been pushed forward some 300 feet, those of two years before 600 feet, and so forth. They will consequently form at the side of the glacier a more or less continuous wall, which may be traced from their place of origin to its extremity, and which will be higher in proportion to the number of points from which it has received accessions. Every one who has visited Swiss glaciers must have been struck with these walls of débris, which are often several miles in length. In the Valais they are called *Moraines,* in the Bernese Oberland *Gandecken* and *Guffer,* and in the Canton of Glaris *Firnstöss.* Of these popular names, the first, which was adopted by Charpentier, has found general acceptance.

Moraines are first formed at the edges of the glacier, bounding its two sides, and are then called *lateral moraines.* They rest upon the glacier, and are pushed forward with it. But if the glacier melts at the sides and thus diminishes in volume, the masses of rubbish are left on the slope of the valley-side, and form walls upon the solid ground more or less distant from the glacier, according as its melting has taken place to a greater or less extent. The lateral moraines of the two sides of the glacier remain quite separate on wide glaciers advancing in broad and flat valleys; but when the valleys become narrower, the moraines approach nearer to each other, the central part of the glacier moves more rapidly on, and the lateral moraines approach the middle of the glacier. A similar effect is produced with timber floating down a river, when the pieces of wood leave the banks and collect in the central current. In the lower parts of the glacier the lateral moraines widen and spread over the whole of its surface; and it is not unusual to see a portion of a glacier quite covered with mud and stones.

Most glaciers also possess in the middle of their surface *central moraines,* which sometimes consist only of a single row of blocks, and at other times form a thick line of débris running down the whole length of the glacier, and following all its curves and bendings. Looked at from great elevations the central moraines appear like regular dark lines, which may often be traced for miles over the bluish-white ice. The central moraines are produced by the union of two or more glaciers. When two glaciers issuing from separate valleys unite, a central moraine, formed by two of the lateral moraines, is produced; and therefore, as a rule, every glacier will have as many central moraines as it has received tributary glaciers. On the Aar glacier a great central moraine commences where the Lauteraar glacier and the Finsteraar glacier unite; it attains a height of 42 metres (or nearly 46 yards), and increases in width to 200 metres (or 218·7 yards) at its extremity. To the left of this there are seven other moraines, and to the right of the central moraine there are eight others, each of which possesses its peculiar kinds of rock. The Gorner, the Rosetsch, the lower Bernina, and many other glaciers exhibit very fine central moraines. As the stones of the moraines protect the ice beneath them from the influence of the sun and of warm air, the ice under the moraines is not melted to so great an extent as that which is exposed to the open air. Thus valleys and ranges of heights are produced on the glacier; and as some of the stones lying on the elevated portions slide down into the hollows between them, the materials of different moraines in very long glaciers become gradually intermingled.

Great heaps of stones accumulate at the termination of the glacier, the stones having been carried down the valley in the lateral and central moraines. By the melting-away of the extremity of the glacier these masses of stones fall to the bottom, and form the *terminal moraine,* which usually surrounds the melting mass of ice in a crescent-shaped curve at the lower part of the valley. If the glacier remains unchanged for many years, all the débris that it has picked up in its course are carried to this point and heaped up into a vast moraine; if it diminishes, a second crescent-shaped curve will be formed near the glacier;

and if the glacier advances it will upset the old moraine and deposit another further down the valley. The two last-mentioned moraines indicate the greatest and the least extension that the glacier has ever attained.

Most of the rocky materials that fall on the surface of the glacier remain there; but wherever the glacier is traversed by fissures or *crevasses* the fragments of rocks drop down these openings and fall to the bottom of the glacier. Facilities for the dropping-down of débris especially occur at the sides of the glacier, where there is not unfrequently a fissure between the mass of ice and the adjoining mountain. The stones thus deposited and carried along under the glacier form *ground-moraines* (moraines du fond). In their onward movement the fragments of rock become rounded and polished by the friction to which they are exposed. The bed of the glacier is also smoothed when the ice is in immediate contact with the rock; and where stones and sand are frozen into the ice it is scratched by them. The same scratching and polishing takes place on the rocky walls which enclose the sides of the glacier, especially in places where the bed of the glacier is narrowed, and where, in consequence of greater inclination, the mass of ice moves more rapidly downwards. Here the rocks are often regularly polished, and traversed by sharp straight striæ, produced by the hard sand-grains and splinters of rock which, being imbedded in the ice, are carried forward with it. In fine-grained rocks these lines are often as sharp as if they had been cut with a diamond; and sometimes they may be traced for several yards. But where the bottom of the glacier is but little inclined, or the mass of ice can spread itself out, the glacier does not possess the power of scoring the underlying rock. Sometimes the glacier is separated from the ground below it, and the melting of the ice causes the formation of galleries and deep caverns.

The water flowing from the glacier carries off the mud produced by friction, and is rendered turbid by it; and as the glacier-stream must pierce through the terminal moraine, it will carry away some of the rocky material composing that mass of débris. Hence a glacier-stream will disperse the fragments brought down by the glacier, and in its action will round off angular stones, efface their glacial scratches, and redeposit them at a distance from the glacier proportionate to the volume of the water and to its motive power.

A stratified form will be characteristic of the beds thus brought into being; the stones will be more or less rounded, and often will appear as if they had been washed, while in the moraines themselves fragments of rocks of every form and size, scratched and polished, angular and rounded, will be found lying with no regularity, and mixed with sand, earth, and mud.

A careful comparison of the phenomena of the Erratic formation of Switzerland with the processes constantly going on in the Swiss glaciers, shows so perfect an agreement between them that they must be ascribed to the same causes; and thus the occurrence and general diffusion of Alpine rocks in the low grounds of Switzerland is fully explained.

The ramparts of stones that are found on the slopes of valleys are the lateral moraines of glaciers; and the crescent-like walls have been the terminal moraines, their unstratified masses of scratched and polished stones, mixed with fine débris and mud, agreeing exactly with terminal moraines of the present day. The representation given in fig. 360 of a portion of a moraine discovered in a public place of Zurich, near the cathedral of that city, shows the effect produced by existing glaciers. The stratified beds of stones are the débris dispersed by the glacier-streams, which filled up the depressions and were covered up by the further advance of the glacier. Over all the hollows of valleys and lakes the glaciers formed bridges, over which masses of mud and earth, as well as the largest rocks, were carried forward, and thus gradually reached great distances, and were borne onwards to the summits and ridges of hills rising high above the bottoms of the valleys.

In the north of Switzerland there were five great glaciers; in Italian Switzerland only two. Their distribution is indicated in the geological map *.

The largest glacier came from the Canton of Valais, as that

---

* This is based upon the map published in 1852 by Prof. A. Escher de la Linth; and for the southern slope of the Alps Prof. Heer has consulted the works of M. G. de Mortillet.

Fig. 360.

Moraine in the Canons' Platz in the city of Zurich between the first pastor's house and the Schoolhouse.

Road-section, drawn from a Daguerreotype taken in 1849.

great Alpine district furnished it with the greatest number of affluents. This glacier extended over the Lake of Geneva as far as the Jura, where it attained its greatest elevation at the Chasseron, in the direction of a prolongation of the valley of the lower Rhone; and the depression of the line of blocks produced by the moraine towards Bienne, and on the other side towards Gex, represents the thinning of the icy covering in these two directions. This line was formed at the time of the greatest extension of the glacier, which then filled the whole of the principal valley of the Canton of Valais and its numerous lateral vales, and reached several thousand feet above the valley-bottom, as is proved by the polishing of the rocky walls and the presence of accumulations of boulders.

The direction taken by the moraines over this enormous sea of ice has been ascertained by Prof. Guyot, who distinguishes two periods in the history of the glacier. In the first of these its area had its greatest extension, and its subordinate glaciers spread into the high valleys of the Jura belonging to the Cantons of Vaud and Neuchâtel. At this time the terminal moraine was pushed forward as far as Aarwangen and Zofingen. The *right lateral moraine* stretched along the mountains of Friburg, and was composed chiefly of grey sandstones derived from the sides of the Dent de Morcles (conglomerates of the Val Orcine) ; the *left lateral moraine* issued from the mountain-mass of Mont Blanc, and conveyed the Alpine granites through the valley of the Trient into the basin of the Rhone; it may be traced on the side of Savoy as far as Geneva. The *central moraines* came, in the first place, from the Upper Valais, from which they brought white granites; secondly, from the masses of Monte Rosa, which furnished the serpentines and euphotides ; thirdly, from the head of the valleys of Erinz and Bagne, which sent down enormous masses of talcose granite (*arkesine*); and, fourthly, from the Val Ferret, from which the immense erratics of Monthey are derived. Following the widening of the glacier at its issue from the valley of the Rhone, the intermediate moraines spread out in a radiating manner, and their materials were conveyed to the slopes of the Jura. In the *terminal moraines*, which extend from Aarwangen to Guggisberg, the rocks are seen in the same sequence : near Guggisberg there are the grey sandstones from the Dent de Morcles, between Schwarzenberg and Könitz the granites of the upper Valais, in the district west of Berne and Burgdorf the rocks of Monte Rosa, near Seebach the talcose granite of the Ering valley, and near Aarwangen the alpine granites of Mont Blanc. .

In the second period the glacier had become smaller. It filled the basin of the Lake of Geneva, but did not extend so far towards the north-east as in the first period. The left lateral moraine had the blocks from Mont Blanc which had passed through Martigny ; and the right lateral moraine was formed of the grey sandstones and the rock from the upper Valais. The latter moraine spread over the Jorat, and also deposited great masses of rock at Lausanne (on Montbenon), at Morges, at Aubonne, &c., and consequently had a different direction from that of the first period. The same deviation may be noticed in the central moraines, which extended over the present position of the lake of Geneva, and probably deposited great masses of débris and rocks in the bottom of the lake during the subsequent retreat of the glacier. The intermediate moraines running near the sides became afterwards lateral moraines. Thus at the time of the first glacial dispersion the blocks of the Val Ferret undoubtedly formed a central moraine which extended as far as the Jura. But as the glacier subsequently became smaller, and at the same time its level was lowered, this moraine came nearer to the edges, and was deposited at 400 feet above the bottom of the valley of Monthey for a distance of five miles in the form of a rampart from 500 to 800 feet thick, in which many blocks lay one upon the other in the most singular positions, such as are only seen among rocky débris at the lateral moraines of Swiss glaciers.

It is further worthy of notice that the moraines of the first period chiefly contain rocks from the highest mountain-masses, and that the moraines of the second period comprise fragments from lower regions—from which it has been inferred that in the former period the fields of granular snow-reached higher up the mountains, and that only the topmost peaks projected above them. This circumstance, as well as the direction which the moraines follow, show that in the first period there was a greater extension of the glaciers.

The glacier of the Aar filled up the valleys of the Bernese Oberland, and smoothed the walls of rock up to a height of 2000 feet above the present valley-bottom. It covered the basins of the lakes of Brienz and Thun, and stretched over the ground to the north of Thun. Its northern boundary was near Berthoud, where its further advance was prevented by the glacier of the Rhone.

The glacier of the Reuss united with glaciers from the valleys of the Canton of Uri, the Engelberg, and the Muottathal. The main glacier came from Uri ; at the Righi and the Hochfluh it must have been divided into two branches, of which the left made

an inroad into the basin of the Lake of the Four Cantons, and
thence gradually covered the Canton of Lucerne with a bed of
ice, whilst the right branch, after uniting with the glacier of the
Muottathal, advanced between the Righi and the Rossberg to the
Canton of Zug, and thence spread over the districts of Freiamt
and Affoltern.   The two branches probably united again to the
north of the Righi.   A great central moraine brought down innumerable blocks of the St.-Gothard (Geissberg) granite, which
cover the mountain-terraces above the lake of Uri (as, for instance, near Seelisberg and Morschach), and are scattered over
the Cantons of Lucerne and Argovia and the district of Affoltern.   A lateral moraine carried down immense masses of limestone, which extend high up on Mont Pilate, and which form
near Hergottswald an enormous rampart cut through by mountain-streams.   At the time of its greatest extension the glacier
of the Reuss reached to the chain of the Albis, and stretched its
branches through the Schnabel pass and the Mutschelle into the
region of the Limmat, carrying over the same St.-Gothard granite.   The fine terminal moraines of the Cantons of Argovia
and Lucerne, which have already been mentioned (p. 178), indicate a time when the glacier terminated in that region.

Between the glaciers of the Reuss and the Aar, and the terminal moraine of the Rhone basin, there was, at the period of
the greatest extension of the glaciers, a small island stretching
from the district of the Napf to the Aar, which remained un-
covered by ice, and possesses no trace of erratic boulders in any
part of its formation.

The glacier of the Linth received its principal supply from
the Canton of Glaris, although a vast glacier must have come
through the valley of the Wallensee to unite with the Linth
glacier near Wesen.   The whole then advanced through the
Gaster and March, towards the basin of the Lake of Zurich.   It
covered a great part of the Canton of Zurich with a thick icy
mantle, which, at the time of its greatest extension, reached the
Bachtel, and on the other side extended to the ridge of the
Uetliberg.   At that time its surface was loaded with several
moraines, one of which started from the Glämisch, the Rauti,
and the mountains bordering the Linth valley, and brought the
limestones of those high regions to the Canton of Zurich, where

they now form long chains of hills on the left bank of the lake (as well as near Hütten, at the foot of the Hohe-Rhonen). A second and very large moraine took its rise in the mountain-masses of the valley of the Sernft, and brought down innumerable blocks of sernifite ("red acrestone") to the environs of the Lake of Zurich; and here and there this moraine received large accessions from the Freiberg, as well as from the Gant-stock. A third moraine began at the Kurfirsten and the Speer, and conveyed from those mountains limestones and blocks of conglomerate to the eastern parts of the Canton of Zurich; additions to this moraine arrived on the glacier pushing down from the Grisons into the valley of the Lake of Wallenstadt, carrying the granites of Ponteljes to the other rocks; and so all these lines of débris concentrated into one district. Curved ramparts of hills indicate the retreat or diminution of the glacier. The terminal moraine of Wührenlos shows its greatest extension; and the vast terminal moraine which surrounds the north end of the Lake of Zurich demonstrates that at the time of its formation the retreat of the glacier had been stopped, and that for many years the masses of débris had accumulated in that district. As the great terminal moraines of the valley of the Glatt, of the Lakes of Baldegg and Sempach, and of Berne, lie nearly in the same line, they were probably formed at the same time, and represent a long period during which glaciers remained in that part of Switzerland. The moraines of Rapperschwyl and Tuggen show the further retreat of the glacier and its gradual melting.

The fifth great glacier is that of the Rhine, which drew its materials from the lofty mountain-country of the Grisons. At the Schollberg this glacier divided into two branches: that on the left formed the glacier of the Lake of Wallenstadt; whilst that on the right occupied the valley of the Rhine, buried the Lake of Constance and its environs under a thick covering of ice, and extended as far as the Höhgau, leaving stones commemorative of its presence on the summits of those hills. The valley of Ponteljes furnished materials to a large moraine, whose blocks of granite have been deposited on the left side of the valley; and near the Schollberg the moraine spread over a great part of the glacier, so that the blocks from Ponteljes

were carried down to the lower regions both upon the glacier
of the Lake of Wallenstadt and on that of the Rhine. The
moraines coming from the Prättigau and Montafun remained
upon the right side of the Rhine, where they formed a long
lateral moraine. The other valleys of the Grisons also furnished
abundant materials, which now form an important part of the
soil in the Cantons of Thurgovia and St. Gall, and furnish numerous round and flat pebbles below Constance.

On the southern slope of the Alps all the phenomena of glaciers observed on the northern side recur. A great glacier
descended from the Canton of Tessin into the plain of Lombardy,
and filled the basin of the Lago Maggiore. A second glacier
came from the Splügen and the valley of Bergell, and, uniting
with the glacier of the Valteline, formed a bridge over the lake
of Como, and pushed forward its terminal moraine into the
neighbourhood of Monza. The beautiful peninsula of Bellaggio
enclosed on both sides by the Lake of Como, is dotted over with
rocks which can only have been derived from the Alps. Even
the Lago di Garda, on the smiling shores of which now bloom
the orange and the citron, was once covered with an icy glacier,
upon which were borne along great masses of Alpine débris,
covering the country to beyond Peschiera. The glacier of
Monte Rosa advanced the furthest towards the south; breaking
forth from the narrow valley of Aosta, it spread over the plain
near Ivrea, and as far as Caluso covered the ground with Alpine
débris, which now form the chain of hills rising from the plain
to an elevation of as much as 1500 feet, and resting on the
marine Pliocene formation.

In the glacial period of the development of the earth a thick
icy crust spread over not only the Swiss mountain-country of
Central Europe, but extended itself to the northern part of the
continent, and advanced to the sea, where it pushed out and
formed innumerable floating icebergs. By these glaciers and
icebergs immense masses of rock were brought from Scandinavia
and the north of Russia into Northern Germany, where they
now rise here and there in the form of low ranges of hills above
the vast sandy plains of that empire. Scotland and a part of
England were likewise covered with glaciers, upon the extension

of which the English geologists have given important information. We have already (pp. 171, 172) mentioned the forest-bed
of Cromer on the Norfolk coast, and shown that it probably belongs to the same period as the Swiss lignites. This forest was
situated on the sea-coast; for the masses of fine sand and clay
which cover it contain animals of both fresh and brackish water
(*Cyclas*, *Valvata*, and *Mytilus*); above these strata is a deposit
consisting of unstratified masses, and containing angular polished
and scratched stones. Among the latter are found granite,
syenite, and porphyry, which, according to Lyell, have come on
icebergs from Scandinavia, and have been deposited there. It
is covered with masses of sand and rolled pebbles. They are
submarine glacial deposits, which here and there attain a thickness of 400 feet, thus giving a depth to which, at the least,
the land must have sunk : afterwards it was upheaved. At one
place (near Mundesley) there is a valley formed by denudation,
the bottom of which consists of a bed of rolled pebbles; and
upon this is a bed of peat overlain by a bed of yellow sand,
which has been deposited since the Glacial period. Hence it is
manifest that on the Norfolk coast, just as at Utznach and
Dürnten, there had been a formation produced by glaciers above
the deposit with *Elephas primigenius* and the Rhinoceros, but
that in England this glacial formation had been connected with
great changes in the level of the land.

Similar phenomena occurred in Scotland. According to
Lyell (Antiquity of Man, p. 241), three phases of development
may be distinguished. At the time of the formation of the
forest-bed of Cromer (contemporaneous with the Swiss lignite-
formation) a gradual elevation of the land took place, to the
height of 500 feet above the level of the sea. In Scotland large
glaciers were produced which have left records of their presence
in the polishing and scratching of the rocks, and in their moraines still to be found in the valleys; subsequently the land
sank, so that by degrees a great part of it became submerged,
and the only remains of Scotland, England, and Ireland consisted of several small islands, represented at the present day by
the mountains. Great quantities of ice came down from the
north, bringing with them large masses of rocks and débris,

which fell to the bottom of the sea, and in some portions of their accumulations buried marine animals which had been living there, and which belonged to a northern race. At a later period there occurred another elevation of the land, upheaving from the depths of the ocean the glacial débris which are now met with in some places at a height of 1400 feet above the sea. To this extent, at least, the land must have been elevated; and probably the upheaval was still more considerable. If the soil of Great Britain were to be now elevated about 600 feet, it would join the European continent, and become connected with Denmark, Holland, and France. And this result appears to have taken place at that time.

During the second continental ice-period the mountains of Scotland and Wales were covered with glaciers, which have left behind them traces of their action. But a gradual depression of the land again occurred; and this by degrees produced the present configuration of land and sea. On the Norwegian coast at the present time the land is observed to be gradually rising; its upheaval is estimated at the rate of 2½ feet in a century. If this standard be assumed as a basis for the calculation of movements of the land, its depression to the extent of 1400 feet would require 50,000 years, and its re-elevation to the same height would occupy the same amount of time. Such numbers are arbitrary, yet they suffice to demonstrate that the Glacial epoch must have lasted very long, and that a continued succession of ages allowed sufficient time for the slow dispersion of the erratic blocks.

Scandinavia, like England and Scotland, affords evidence of two glacial epochs. Lofty stratified masses of débris (Osars) lie, in Northern Europe, on the smoothed surfaces of rocks; these had very probably been produced under the sea; and upon them are found erratic blocks which, like the smoothed rocks, indicate a time when glaciers spread over all the country.

Local causes do not explain glacial phenomena, as the traces of glaciers are seen in North America in the same way as in Europe. After the close of the Tertiary epoch such a diminution of temperature must have occurred over the whole of the Northern hemisphere that the glaciers of the Alps descended into the plains, and at the same time the northern masses of ice advanced southwards. The process must have been very gradual; and hence the Glacial epoch must have continued for many thousand years. If we assume, in accordance with previous statements (p. 186), that a glacier advances about one league in 50 years, it will have taken one thousand years for the block (*Pierre-à-Bot*) to be transported from the chain of Mont Blanc through the Trient valley to its present position, and the granite blocks of Seeberg will have passed two thousand years on the glacier in traversing the country from the head of the valley of Ering to the locality where they now are; the "plough-stone" above Erlenbach will have advanced in the first hundred years to the neighbourhood of Glaris, in the second century it will have approached Urnen, in the third it will have got on as far as Utznach, in the fourth it will have been near Rapperschwyl, and in the sixth century it will have reached its present home.

Probably the glacier-movement took place much more rapidly, as the speed of advance is in proportion to the size of the glacier; but these numbers may give an approximate notion of the length of time required for the extension of the glaciers and the transport of the masses of rock carried down by them. Additional evidence of the very slow movement of the glaciers in their invasion of the highlands is given by the stratified drift. This chiefly consists of Alpine rocks, and must therefore have been dispersed during the Glacial epoch. The immense pebble-beds which overlie the lignites of Utznach were very probably deposited at a time when the glacier occupied the valley between Utznach and the Buchberg, bringing with it, in its lateral moraines, a mass of material which was swept away by the streams flowing from the glacier, and was spread over the area of the lignites. Let it also be remembered that the water flowing from the right mountain-side must have been dammed up by the glacier that filled the valley, and no doubt here and there formed small pools, whilst in other parts the stream ran along the side of the glacier, and thus probably assisted in the dispersion and deposition of the rubbish of the glacier. When the glacier afterwards rose, it covered this stratified drift, and in its subsequent retreat deposited erratic blocks on the surface.   In the same manner were effected the dispersion of the stratified masses of rolled gravel in the Sihlfeld near Zurich, in the lower parts of the basin of the Lake of Constance, and in the basins of the Lago Maggiore and the Lake of Como south of the Alps.   Glaciers must have passed over the lakes upon bridges formed by ice, and have been dispersed by the streams flowing from the glaciers.   The conglomerate formation of the Schienerberg near Œningen, the Uetliberg, and the Au, already mentioned (vol. i. p. 289), probably dates from this epoch.   As it was deposited on the Uetliberg, the glacier must have extended as far as the ridge of the Albis.

It is manifest that the lignites of Dürnten and Utznach were formed before the stratified drift, as they lie below it.   To judge from the plants that they contain, the climate was like that of the present day.   At any rate it was not warmer, as is shown by the occurrence of the mountain-pine, which now only descends at a few places into the temperate zone of the Swiss hill-region (as on the Maneck).   The climate may, however, have been rather colder, as the known species still thrive in the mountain region at a mean annual temperature of from 6° to 7° C. (42°·8–44°·6 F.), as well as in corresponding northern latitudes.   Most of the mountain-pines extend up to the limit of trees; but the occurrence of the ash and yew, and of the thick trunks of the pines with broad annual rings, show that at the time when these trees grew in the lignite district no Alpine or Arctic climate can have prevailed.   The known facts lead to the assumption of an annual temperature of 6°–9° C. (42°·8–48°·2 F.).   This condition of things must have lasted some thousands of years, in order to produce the thick deposit of peat from which the lignite originated.   But gradually the climate became colder, the glaciers advanced from the Alps and changed the whole aspect of the country.   Again the temperature became warmer; the glaciers slowly melted, and retreated, after many oscillations, to their present limits.

The transition from the warmth of the Miocene epoch to the temperate climate of the lignite formation and the cold of the Glacial epoch was probably effected very slowly, and with numerous alternations of temperature. No regularly continued transition appears to have occurred; but a cold period separated the lignite formation from the Miocene.

Two glacial epochs are indicated by the mode of dispersion of the boulders in the basin of the Rhone. The second of these epochs corresponds with the later condition of the Rhone glacier, when it had been melted back as far as the basin of the lake of Geneva. Prof. Morlot * has shown it to be very probable that formerly the Rhone glacier retreated not only into the region of the Lake of Geneva, but also to the main valley of the Canton of the Valais (he supposes, to an elevation of from 3000–4000 feet above the sea), and that again the glacier advanced, but in the second period merely spread itself over the basin of the Lake of Geneva. According to this view there were two glacial epochs, separated by a period during which the glaciers disappeared from all the plains of Switzerland. In the second Glacial epoch the streams flowing from the hills near the Lake of Geneva mingled their débris with those of the lateral moraines; and thus the deposits were formed which produce a line of terraces along the lake, and which here and there show stratification and contain numerous scratched and angular erratics, thus resembling the deposits sometimes found on the existing glaciers at points where lateral brooks flow towards them and form small lakes and pools, which are gradually filled up by the moraines.

Prof. Morlot found the principal evidence in favour of these two glacial periods in the ravine of the Dranse, near Thonon. At the bottom of the gorge there is (1) a deposit of débris 12 feet thick with striated fragments of Alpine limestone; and above this is (2) a bed of rolled and stratified pebbles (drift), 150 feet thick; and, again, above this bed are (3) striated erratic blocks. Between the formation of the first and third of these deposits, which were produced by a moraine, intervened

* "Note sur la subdivision du Terrain Quaternaire en Suisse," par A. Morlot (Bibl. Univ. 1855). According to Scipio Gras, two glacial deposits are to be distinguished in the Lower-Rhone basin. See his memoir "Sur la période Quaternaire dans la vallée du Rhône, et sa division en cinq époques distinctes" (Bull. Soc. Géol. France, xix., Nov., Dec.).

the deposition of the stratified mass which shows by its great thickness that the glacier had disappeared from this spot for a long time. In Eastern Switzerland, until recently, the upper erratic formation only was known, which overlies the stratified pebble-beds. At Utznach, in a section on the road to Gauen, now again covered up, Prof. A. Escher de la Linth saw quite distinctly the direct superposition of the lignite formation upon the Miocene; so that, at least at this point, there was no trace of erratic blocks to be seen between the Miocene and the lignites (see fig. 329, p. 152). At Dürnten, also, the clays under the lignite deposit only contain such stones as may have been derived from the conglomerate of the surrounding hills. The hypothesis of two glacial periods does not, therefore, seem to be supported by the facts observed in Eastern Switzerland. Nevertheless, at Wetzikon, Alpine rocks showing all the signs of glacial transport (see p. 151) are found under the lignites. This deposit of lignite, however, is only of small extent; but it lies horizontally, and presents the same sequence of clay and coal as at Dürnten; so that it cannot be supposed that these erratics have got under the lignite deposit by displacement of the soil. In Mörschweil also, according to the investigations of Prof. Deicke (p. 154), erratics are overlain by the lignites.

Fortified by these facts, the conclusion may be adopted that at two different periods glaciers invaded Switzerland, and that the lignite formation occurred in the interval between them, thus representing an episode of several thousand years in the long Glacial epoch, the intercalated period having been sufficiently long to diffuse over the low country a new vegetable covering. The stratified deposits of rolled pebbles must have taken place at the following periods:—1. After the epoch of the lignites, which may be called *interglacial*. 2. During the great extension of the glaciers, *glacial drift*. 3. After the second glacial epoch, *postglacial drift*.

For the Quaternary period the chronological order shown in the following Table may be regarded as established:—

Chronological Table of the Quaternary Period.

Switzerland.	Countries Foreign to Switzerland.
5. *Postglacial deposit of rolled pebbles.* Gravel-beds in the Canton of Basle, with Mammoth (?).	Tuff of Cannstatt. Gravel-beds of the Somme, with Mammoth and stone implements. Rolled-pebble beds of Mundesley; bone-caves, Hoxne. Appearance of man. England still united with the continent. Retreat of the glaciers. America: period of *Mastodon ohioticum* and Mammoth.
4. *Second glacial epoch.* Erratic blocks. Moraines. Heaps of débris at Aubonne and Morges, with Mammoth. Alpine flora in the plain.	Loess-formation of the basin of the Rhine, with Mammoth. Second continental period of England. Glaciers on the mountains of Scotland. Scandinavia elevated. Dispersion of erratic blocks.
3. *Interglacial deposit of rolled pebbles.* Stratified drift at Utznach and Dürnten; Strätlingen on the Lake of Thun. First appearance of *Elephas primigenius* (?).	British Islands chiefly under the sea. Dispersion of northern erratics. Scandinavia in great part submerged. Formation of the Osars. North America in part submerged. Laurentian formation of Desor.
2. *Lignite formation.* Lignites of Utznach, Dürnten, Wetzikon, Mörschweil, Annecy. *Elephas antiquus* and *Rhinoceros etruscus*, Fal. Flora of the plain predominant.	Calcareous tuff near Marseilles, with the *Elephas antiquus*. Buried forests of Norfolk. Beds of *Mytilus* at Spitzbergen (?)
1. *First glacial formation.* Striated stones and erratics below the lignites of Wetzikon. Lower deposit of Thonon. Arctic Alpine flora in the plains.	First British continental period. Scotland covered with glaciers. Period of the polishing of Scandinavian rocks. Scandinavia, land covered with glaciers. America: smoothing of the rocks.
Pliocene.	Norwich Crag of England.

Organic nature will be found to confirm the inferences derived from the rocks as to the aspect of Switzerland during the drift period. If the same phenomena which are now witnessed in high northern latitudes, as well as in the Alps, formerly occurred in Switzerland, the traces of them will remain in the flora and fauna of that country.

At the time of the greatest extension of the glaciers, when an icy mantle some thousands of feet in thickness was spread over the low Swiss grounds, organic life must have been almost entirely banished.   Yet even then some islets stood out of the sea of ice, such as the land between the Napf and the Aar ; and in the highest regions rocky peaks projected above the ice—which is proved by the numerous erratic blocks which constituted a part of the moraine.

Organic life in plants * and insects is met with at the present day on the highest summits of the Alps, and on the remotest islets and moraines of the granular snow, to an elevation of 11,000 feet; and, in like manner, during the Glacial epoch some life was preserved.   In connexion with this question it must be remembered that Prof. Heer is acquainted with 111 species of Phanerogamous plants from Spitzbergen, and with more than 320 from Greenland, although boundless glaciers cover these countries and descend even to the sea.   When, in Switzerland, the glaciers melted and left the plains no longer covered with ice, vegetation pushed its way over the low grounds and clothed afresh the desert country.   The plants of the lignite beds inform us that the flora which then penetrated into Switzerland was the same as the vegetable kingdom now flourishing there, as well as in other parts of Central Europe and of the temperate portions of Asia, but that to the modern flora one or two mountain-plants (*Pinus montana* and *Acer pseudoplatanus*) should be added.

When the glaciers again advanced from the Alps and extended into the plain, the change of climate essentially altered the flora. At the time when the numerous terminal moraines were deposited, Alpine plants were no doubt conveyed by them, and by

---

* In the Grisons Prof. Heer has collected 106 species of flowering plants in the highest region, between 8500 and 11,000 feet above the sea-level.

the streams flowing from the glaciers, into the low country, where they established themselves in the vicinity of the glaciers and moraines. The Albis, the Uetliberg, the Zürichberg, and indeed all the chains of hills lying above the glaciers were probably covered with forests, as are now the slopes surrounding the Bernina glacier, and many other districts into which great glaciers descend.

From the time of the greatest extension of the glacier in the Canton of Zurich to the epoch of its retreat from the district, all degrees of transition occurred; and, on the hypothesis of two glacial periods, these intermediate stages were repeated more than once. A similar alternation is implied in the conditions of temperature. At the time of the greatest extension of the glaciers the temperature must have been at its lowest point; it must then have risen again; and the vegetation must have followed these changes. It is to be supposed that in the coldest period of glacial action the spots free from ice and snow were covered with a vegetation like that which is now seen on the Swiss Alps; and as the glaciers afterwards retreated these plants also retired up into the mountains, and other vegetable forms occupied the vacant places in the plain. Just as the Swiss Alpine plants now fringe the fields of granular snow, and live on moraines and glacier-islets, adorning them with the most charming colours, so they formerly accompanied the glaciers down into the lower country, presenting the same phenomenon that may still be witnessed in Iceland and Greenland, where the Alpine flora descends with the glaciers even to the sea-coast.

Unfortunately organic remains of the Glacial period have reached modern times in very scanty measure, which is probably due chiefly to the unfavourable nature of the deposits of this epoch for their preservation.

Of plants, only a few fir-cones (*Pinus Abies*, Linn.) are known, which Prof. Morlot has found in the glacial débris of Thonon and in a lignite-like formation near the Signal of Bougy, with a species of moss (*Hypnum diluvii*, Schimp.). The fir-cones teach us that at the time when the glacier extended down as far as the Lake of Geneva there must have been forests of firs in that vicinity; and the moss is most nearly allied to a species from Lapland and of the Sudetes (*H. sarmentosum*).

Very scanty information is given in other countries foreign to Switzerland respecting the flora of the drift period. The tuffs of Cannstatt, near Stuttgart, constitute the most important locality for such remains. They have as yet furnished twenty-nine species, three of which are extinct, namely:—the mammoth oak, with its obtusely and widely lobate leaves, 6 inches broad, and oval acorns nearly twice as large as those of the *Quercus pedunculata*; a poplar (*Populus Fraasii*, Heer) with large cordate leaves, the edges of which are only faintly undulated; and a walnut-tree which resembles the American species *Juglans nigra* and *cinerea* in the toothed pinnæ of its leaves.

Among the species which still inhabit the same region as the lignites Prof. Heer remarks the red fir, the white birch, the hazel, and the sycamore; and the formation of the forest was also assisted by the white fir, the aspen, and the silver poplar, the pedunculated oak, the hornbeam, the elm, the lime-tree, and the spindle-tree; whilst the undergrowth consisted of several willows (*Salix monandra, fragilis, aurita, viminalis*, and especially *Salix cinerea*), the cornel (*Cornus sanguinea*), two dogwoods (*Rhamnus frangula* and *catharticus*, Linn.), the box, and the black whortleberry (*Vaccinium uliginosum*, Linn.), which have left their impressions in the tuffs. The herbaceous plants are very scarce; they are the great manna-grass (*Glyceria spectabilis*, M. & K.), the reed, and the hart's-tongue fern (*Scolopendrium officinale*). With the exception of extinct species and of the box, these are all plants which now occur in Wirtemberg. Yet the sycamore and the whortleberry are not found in the neighbourhood of Cannstatt; the sycamore grows on the mountains, and the whortleberry in peat-bogs. On the whole, climatal conditions are implied in the flora of Cannstatt similar to those now prevalent in the same locality. Probably the tuffs of the Cannstatt basin which there covered the Loess, were deposited in the latter part of the Quaternary epoch at a time (after the retreat of the glacier) when the climate again approximated to that which is now existing.

Of plants indicating a colder climate than we have at present, only two have been discovered. In old turbaries of Ivrea, and in drift débris near Mur in Styria, trunks of the Siberian pine (*Pinus cembra*) have been found; and at Bovey Tracey, in Devonshire, a white clay covering a great Miocene deposit of lignite contains willow leaves and well-preserved leaves of the dwarf birch (*Betula nana*, Linn.*). The latter is not now found in England; but it grows upon the mountains of Scotland. It is widely distributed in the Arctic zone, and occurs also in Switzerland, but only in the peat-bogs of the Jura and of Einsiedeln.

The two last-mentioned plants, the dwarf birch and the Siberian pine, at least furnish an indication that Alpine and northern plants have lived in lower and more southerly situations. In 1872, near Schwerzenbach in the Canton of Zurich, an Alpine flora was found, in drift loam, comprising the *Betula nana*, *Salix retusa*, *S. reticulata*, *S. polaris*, *Polygonum viviparum*, and *Dryas octopetala*. A remarkable phenomenon is noticed in the existing Swiss flora, which can only be satisfactorily explained on the supposition that the Alpine flora once extended down into the plains. This is *the occurrence of colonies of Alpine plants on the hills and in the peat-mosses of the plains of Switzerland*. It is not surprising that the glaciers and rivulets going down into the valleys should have been accompanied by many Alpine plants which remain isolated on their borders; but colonies of the vegetable inhabitants of the mountains are met with on the hills of the low country, far from the mountain-streams and from the Alps. They appear then like lost children of the Alps, surrounded only by plants belonging to the plain. Leaving out of account the species accidentally floated down, the Canton of Zurich comprises 123 mountain-plants, 55 of which have their home in the Alps, and may therefore be characterized as Alpine plants; and yet the highest point in the Canton scarcely attains an elevation of 4000 feet above the sea. It is true that the chain of the Hörnli is not far from the high mountains, yet is it separated from them by the broad valley of the Toggenburg. Nor are the Albis range and the Hohe-Rhonen directly connected with the Alpine system; and the Uetliberg, the Irchel, and the Lägern are very remote from it.

---

* Prof. Heer has figured this in his memoir "On the Fossil Flora of Bovey-Tracey," in the Phil. Trans. 1862, pl. lxxi.

The largest colony of Alpine forms occurs in the upper Tössthal, where 74 mountain-plants are found with 40 alpine species. Prof. Heer has there seen Alpine roses (*Rhododendron*) and yellow auriculas, gentian, and mountain buttercups, the odoriferous *Nigritella*, and the Alpine forget-me-not; nay, on the Schnebelhorn, the Professor was surprised to find the *Soldanella alpina*, the dwarf willow (*Salix retusa*, Linn.), and the rock-speedwell, which he had been accustomed to see only in the higher Alps. The same phenomena are presented also at the Hohe-Rhonen, which possesses 36 mountain-species, of which 18 are Alpine plants. But even the low Albis range (which nowhere exceeds 2800 feet above the sea) and the Uetliberg comprise 7 Alpine plants*. And it is still more remarkable that even the Lägern and the Irchel, notwithstanding their greater distance from the high mountains, have yet received some Alpine colonists.

In the low country the peat-bogs furnish plants which belong particularly to the Alps or to high northern latitudes †; and, what is still more remarkable, this is the case also in the peat-bogs of Bavaria.

As the Alpine vegetable colonies do not lie in the domain of the rivers flowing from the Alps, these streams have not brought down the plants into the lower portion of Switzerland. Nor can their seeds have been conveyed by the wind; for in two thirds of the Alpine colonists comprised in the flora of Zurich neither the fruits nor the seeds possess wings or any other arrangements which might have fitted them for transport

---

* On the Albis Prof. Heer has found the *Alnus viridis*, Linn.; on the Uto, *Epilobium Fleischeri*, Koch, *Linaria alpina*, Linn., *Saxifraga aizoides*, Linn., *Campanula pusilla*, *Pinguicula alpina*, and *Pinus montana*, Mill.; on the Lägern, *Draba azoïdes*, *Arabis alpina*, *Ribes alpinum*, *Saxifraga aizoon*, and *Adenostylis albifrons*; on the Irchel, *Alnus viridis*, *Arctostaphylus Uva Ursi*, *Aira montana*, *Veronica urticæfolia*, *Sambucus racemosa*, *Trifolium alpestre*, and *Thesium alpinum*; and on the ridge between Rorbach and Bulach the *Alnus viridis*.

† Prof. Heer mentions as Alpine plants the chive (*Allium schœnoprasum*), the bogberry (*Vaccinium uliginosum*), the Alpine cotton-grass (*Eriophorum alpinum*), and the *Sedum villosum*; and as northern plants, *Carex chordorrhiza* and *Scheuchzeria*. *Saxifraga oppositifolia*, Linn., which grows in large masses near Strad, not far from Constance, is also a plant of the Arctic flora which has become acclimatized in the Swiss Alps.

through the air*. Besides, there is a relation between the distribution of these Alpine plants and the dispersion of the Alpine erratic rocks. On the Uetliberg the Alpine toad-flax (*Linaria alpina*) and the willow herb (*Epilobium Fleischeri*) are found associated exactly as on the terminal moraines and in the localities deserted by Alpine glaciers. These arctic plants occur on the Albis, the Bachtel, and the Lägern, at the same elevation with rock-masses coming from high mountains. In this respect the localization of the two Swiss Alpine roses (*Rhododendron*) is very instructive. The species with fringed leaves (*R. hirsutum*, Linn.) keeps chiefly to the limestone mountains, and occupies a lower zone than the rusty-leaved species (*R. ferrugineum*, Linn.). We should therefore expect to find the former and not the latter in the Jura †. Yet it is only the rusty-leaved Alpine rose that occurs in the Jura, and this is precisely the species that grows everywhere in the mountains between the Simplon and St. Bernard (which, as has been already seen, furnished the erratic blocks on the Jura), whilst the fringe-leaved species is wanting there ‡. As the rusty-leaved Alpine rose has the same

* On the erratic blocks of the plain a good many Alpine Cryptogamia are found, and especially Lichens (for instance, according to Dr. Hepp, *Lecidia badio-atra, spuria, discolor, micropsis, dispora, atro-alba, saxatilis*, and *Lecanora badia*). It may be remarked that on the plough-stone (Pflugstein) of Erlenbach an Alpine and northern fern (*Asplenium septentrionale*) is found which occurs nowhere else in the whole Canton of Zurich.

† In the Bernese Alps opposite the Jura (the Stockhorn chain) *Rhododendron hirsutum* is abundant.

‡ The fringe-leaved Alpine rose occurs in the mountains of Savoy, for example at the Môle, and the Brezon, near Bonneville; but as it is wanting in the intermediate localities (between Bonneville and the Jura), for instance at the Salève, it is probable that it reached the Jura with the erratics of the glaciers coming from the Alps. Of the 198 species of Alpine plants diffused over the Jura, 179 also occur in the Alps of the Canton of Valais, so that the great majority of these plants might come from that Canton. It is, however, very probable that the Alpine plants have reached the Jura by another course, since a certain number of Arcto-Alpine plants are found in the Jura. There has also evidently been an immigration coming from the south-west, by which the flora of the Jura has been enriched with Mediterranean elements. But as the Jura sinks to the south of the Cluses de Nantua, and nearly all the Alpine plants there disappear to flourish again near the Grande-Chartreuse, where the mountains rise again to the Alpine region, we must not seek in that district for the origin of the Alpine flora of the Jura. In this

home with the erratic blocks and masses of débris which have been dispersed from the Valais over the Jura, it has probably issued originally from the same region, and was transported at the same time *.

These phenomena lead Prof. Heer to believe that the date of these colonies of Alpine plants belongs to the Glacial epoch. At that time probably an Alpine flora was spread over the plain, clothing the moraines and those spots that were not covered by ice with the same flowers which now so charmingly adorn the solitudes of the great Swiss glaciers. When afterwards the glaciers retreated and the formation of the lignites began, the flora of the plain advanced into this region, while the Alpine flora took refuge in the mountains. When the country was again covered with glaciers, the Alpine flora descended to the plain, and a second time abandoned the low country as the glaciers retreated to a higher region. Hence in the existing vegetation the Alpine flora forms the most ancient element, and it was probably dispersed at two different periods over the whole country wherever the land was free from snow and ice. With a change of climate the flora of the plain gradually advanced, and became so completely dominant that at last only a

---

flora are found *Campanula pusilla, Saxifraga aizoides, Linaria alpina, Gypsophila repens,* and *Polygonum viviparum,* which are met with everywhere in the glacial soils and on the ancient Alpine moraines. Besides these species, Prof. Heer also met with *Saxifraga oppositifolia, S. muscoides, Ranunculus alpestris, Asplenium septentrionale, Silene rupestris* (at the Passwang), *Helianthemum alpestre, Primula auricula, Erigeron alpinus,* and *Aster alpinus,* which grow in the fissures of Alpine rocks. Hence these plants of Alpine origin may have reached the Jura by the immense moraines and monstrous blocks which no doubt formed real islands on the sea of ice.

* The rusty-leaved Alpine rose (*Rhododendron ferrugineum*) also occurs on a great block of St.-Gothard granite at the Axenstein, above Brunnen. It is probable that it descended from the St. Gothard with the immense blocks of granite which are dispersed over the whole terrace of Morschach. In the Canton of Aargau erratic plants are also met with on ancient moraines; thus *Alnus viridis* grows upon a thick bed of loess, which rests upon the White Jura of Waltersburg. In the same way, near Schönenwerth, in the valley of Jonen, Prof. Heer has seen *Viola biflora* upon an Alpine block; and *Asplenium septentrionale* occurs upon a block of granite near Künten. (See Mühlberg, die erratischen Bildungen im Aargau, p. 184.)

few vestiges of the Alpine flora remained in mountain-ravines, on hill-ranges, and in cold damp moory grounds. Of these remains of the former Alpine flora of the plain, individual species have disappeared century by century, as is proved by the fact that in the pile-dwellings of Robenhausen are found the cones of *Pinus montana* and the seeds of a small mountain water-lily (*Nuphar pumilum*). It may also be observed that the sycamore (*Acer pseudoplatanus*) was, in remote times, spread everywhere over the plains, as appears from its frequent occurrence in all the ancient tuffs.

The dispersion of the Alpine flora in the plain took place at the period of the greatest extension of glaciers, which comes between the Pliocene period and the time of the formation of the lignites. At that period Alpine plants were probably diffused not only over the plain of Switzerland, but also over Germany. This is indicated by the remarkable fact that nearly half of the Swiss Alpine flora reappears in Scandinavia, and generally in high northern latitudes. The northern flora shows a great uniformity, consisting principally of the same species, forming, as it were, a girdle round the earth. Of these northern species many appear on the North-German mountains, on the Hartz and the Sudetes (in Silesia), where they constitute the Alpine flora. The Sudetes possess no peculiar plants ; all the species which do not occur in the plain have been obtained from Scandinavia. Some few species stop there (*Rubus chamæmorus, Saxifraga nivalis*, and *Pedicularis sudetica**) ; but most of them are met with further south, and reappear upon the high mountains of Switzerland. The same facts are observed in America and Asia. On the Rocky Mountains, and even on the mountains of North Carolina, plants are found which are identical with those of the northern flora. Similarly on the Altai†, and even on the Hima-

---

* In the Snow-cavity of the Giant Mountains (north-west of the Sudetes) *Pupa arctica*, Wahlbg., has been found. This is a native of Lapland, and of the localities where *Saxifraga nivalis* is met with.

† In Ledebour's 'Flora Altaica' there are 80 Phanerogamous plants of the Swiss Alps, 54 of which belong to the Arctic and Laplandic flora. The flora of Ajan, in the north-east of Siberia, on the sea of Ochotsk, includes 62 plants of the Swiss Alps, among which 45 are Arctic-Laplandic species. Lapland possesses 115 flowering plants in common with the Swiss mountain-flora.

layas (although these are situated so far south), plants are found belonging to the northern flora. These are, for the most part, species which also occur in the Alps ; so that the Swiss mountains have a number of plants in common with American and Asiatic ranges, and these plants have issued from the north as from a common source. It is therefore very probable that, during the Glacial epoch, the Scandinavian flora was spread over a great part of Germany and also dispersed in Switzerland. As only the principal glacier of Eastern Switzerland (the Rhine glacier) extended as far as Germany, while the other Swiss glaciers were bounded by the chain of the Jura, greater opportunities for the immigration of the northern flora were presented at the eastern side, which may explain the remarkable fact *that Eastern Switzerland, and especially the Canton of the Grisons, has a number of rare plants and animals* in common with high northern latitudes, which are wanting to the rest of Switzerland.* Hence a considerable portion of the Swiss Alpine flora probably came from the north, and reached Switzerland during the Glacial epoch. Afterwards, as the climate became warmer and drier, they found in the Alps suitable places for their development, where they have maintained their position, as in the north, down to the present day, whilst they have disappeared from the plain, except in the colonies of northern plants, and are now almost entirely wanting in the whole of that wide region that lies between the Alps and Scandinavia.

[Sir Charles Lyell mentions, in his ' Student's Elements of Geology,' p. 144, that the boulder formation had been termed " Diluvium," but that geologists observed it to be characteristic of high latitudes, and that the great development of the boulder formation with large erratics so far south as the Alps, favoured the hypothesis that there was some intimate connexion between it and accumulations of snow and ice†.]

Remains of Mollusca and Mammalia have been found in the deposits of the drift. It has been noticed (p. 189) that the glacier-streams contain much mud and sand produced

---

* *Carex Vahlii, Juncus castaneus, J. stygius, Trientalis europæa, Thalictrum alpinum; Leiochiton arcticum, Cymindis angularis, Attalus Cardiacæ,* Linn., sp., *Biston lapponarius,* Boisd., *Chelonia Quesnelii.*

† Editor.

by the friction of stones and rocks ; this drift is carried away by the streams, and often deposited at a considerable distance from the glaciers. Masses of yellowish sand and mud produced in this way are to be found in the whole basin of the Rhine, from the Schollberg (Canton of St. Gall) to Hesse and Nassau. In the neighbourhood of Mayence they occur of great thickness. This formation [is termed " fluviatile loam " by Sir Charles Lyell, and] is known under the name of Loess. Here and there it contains great quantities of snail-shells, almost all belonging to living species. In Switzerland such shells were found by Professor A. Escher de la Linth in a Loess formation at the Schollberg (between the Hochwand and Trübbach) and in the bay of Murris, which opens towards the south (below the ruins of the Wartau) in the St.-Gall portion of the Rhine valley. The 21 species * determined by Professor Mousson still, without exception, occur in Eastern Switzerland, most of them in the valley of the Rhine or at the foot of the nearest mountain-slopes. One of the most abundant species (*Helix ruderata*, Stud.), however, is now wanting in the plain, and is a characteristic form of the high mountain-region, occurring in the mountains of Glaris, the Prättigau, and the Sentis chain. *Helix sericea glabella*, Stud., and *H. arbustorum subalpina* also belong to the mountain-regions. All the other species are either forest-snails from the region of leafy trees, or species which prefer shady moist places. Inhabitants of dry sunny localities are wanting. These shells probably remain from a time when the glacier had retreated into the neighbourhood of Sargans or Ragatz, and the fine sand and mud were deposited upon the old bed of the glacier. The intermixture of some mountain forms which are no longer to be found in the low country, shows that the glacier

---

* See Mousson, " Ueber den Loess des St.-Gallischen Rheinthales " (in Mittheil. der Zürcher naturf. Gesellsch.1856. The species found are:—*Succinea oblonga*, Drap.; *Helix nitidula*, Drap., var. *vitrina*, Hoch.; *H. nitidosa*, Fér.; *H. nitens*, Mich.; *H. crystallina*, Müll.; *H. fulva*, Drap.; *H. ruderata*, Stud.; *H. rotundata*, Müll.; *H. sericea*, Müll., *glabella* and *hybrida*; *H. villosa*, Drap.; *H. strigella late umbilicata*; *H. pulchella costata, obvoluta*, Müll.; *H. arbustorum subalpina*; *H. hortensis*; *Bulimus montanus*, Drap.; *Achatina lubrica*, Müll., with var. *pulchella*; *Pupa dolium, P. bigranata, P. secale, Clausilia dubia*, Drap. It is very remarkable that the variety of *Helix strigella* with a wide umbilicus still occurs near Sargans, and is peculiar to that district.

was still in the vicinity. Whilst this deposit belongs to the period of the retreat of the glacier, the loess of the lower part of the Rhine valley probably originated at an earlier period, when it had a greater extension. Of the numerous snails which have been collected in it, the species of shady moist localities certainly predominate; and with them are mixed several forms (such as *Helix hispida*, Müll., *H. ruderata*, and *H. arbustorum subalpina*), which at present are met with only in high mountains, whilst no species occur which belong to warm sunny localities.

The Mollusca of the drift agree with those now living in Switzerland; but the Mammalia present six peculiar extinct types. Seventeen species of mammals have at present been discovered in Switzerland. Three of these have been already noticed in the lignite formation, namely :—the cave-bear, the teeth of which have been found in the Wildkirchli cavern, under a bed of calcareous tufa; the red deer, which is widely spread in the Quaternary formation; and the urus (*Bos primigenius*), remains of which have been collected in the drift-formation of the Isteinerklotz. Besides the urus, a second species, the aurochs (*Bos bison priscus*), has been found in Switzerland. Its great horn-cores and a portion of the skull were found in a railway-cutting at Bollingen, near Rapperschwyl. Hence the two wild oxen mentioned by Seneca and Pliny were in existence in the period of the drift-formation. The aurochs or bison is a large fierce animal, with a long mane like the American buffalo. Both the urus and the aurochs are found in the Swiss pile-dwellings; and even in the middle ages the aurochs was widely spread in the European forests, but is now preserved only in the great forest of Bialowicza. The giant stag (or Irish elk, *Cervus eurycerus*, Ald.), of which remains have been found at the Isteinerklotz, was an animal of nearly equal size. Of the elk (*Cervus alces*, Linn.) an entire skeleton was brought to light in the Val Travers.

In the Wildkirchli the bones of the foot of a chamois (*Antilope rupicapra*, Linn.) were found in the same place as the teeth of the cave-bear, so that this animal was already in existence in the Quaternary period. This is confirmed by remains found in the valley of the Rhine, which demonstrate that at that time the chamois, as well as the ibex and the marmot, inhabited the low country. Of the former the horn-cores have been found in a gravel-bed of the Rhine valley; of the marmot the cranium and bones occur near Zimmerwald and in the drift-formation of Niederwangen near Berne, as well as in the moraine which stretches from the Bois de Vaux to the Perandette, and forms the promenade of the Montbenon near Lausanne, celebrated for the splendid view which is enjoyed from it. Near Benken, in the Canton of Zurich, antlers have been obtained so like those of the reindeer that they probably belonged to this northern animal, some traces of which are also preserved in the deposits of the drift formation of the valley of the Rhine.

The badger and wild cat have left their remains in the drift formation near Zimmerwald in the Canton of Berne, and the cave-hyæna (*Hyæna spelæa*, Goldf.) near the Isteinerklotz. The hyæna is most nearly allied to the spotted hyæna (*H. crocuta*, Linn.) of the Cape of Good Hope; it was, however, larger and stronger, and is now extinct. Teeth of horses have been collected here and there in gravel-pits. According to Professor Rütimeyer most of them belong to the common horse (*Equus caballus*, Linn.), such as the teeth from the gravel-pit of Bülach and from the Rhine valley; hence this animal inhabited Switzerland at a very early period. But with it occurs a second extinct species (*Equus fossilis*, Cuv., Owen), which differs in some peculiarities of the structure of the teeth from the existing horse, and approaches the Miocene *Hipparion*. According to Rütimeyer, this species has hitherto been found in the western parts of Switzerland only (in a gravel-pit of Riez at Cully).

Most of these animals still inhabit the European continent; and the extinct species are nearly allied to existing ones; but two pachyderms constitute quite peculiar types now strange to the Swiss fauna, namely the woolly rhinoceros and the mammoth elephant. Each of them was covered with a thick hairy coat, and therefore adapted to a more rigorous climate.

The rhinoceros (*R. tichorhinus*, Cuv.) was most nearly related to the South-African *Rhinoceros bicornis*, but had a longer and narrower head, a stouter body, and shorter and thicker legs. It bore two strong horns on its nose. Its remains have been found in the gravel of the Rhine valley, and near the Isteinerklotz. The mammoth (*Elephas primigenius*, Blum., fig. 351) was much more abundant. It was rather larger than the Indian elephant, to which it is more nearly related than to the African. Its tusks were from 8 to 15 feet long, and more strongly curved than those of the Indian elephant; and the molars have more numerous and narrower transverse plates with parallel margins, by which they are also distinguished from those of *Elephas antiquus* (compare figs. 350 & 351). If we imagine a very large Indian elephant, clothe it with long blackish-brown hairs forming a mane on the neck, give it large ears fringed with hairs, long strongly curved tusks, and thick massive legs, we obtain a picture of this remarkable animal. It has been found in many Swiss localities; but it is unfortunately difficult to say at what period in the Quaternary epoch it first made its appearance in Switzerland. Its remains are generally discovered in gravel-pits; but as masses of sand and pebbles were deposited during the whole of the Quaternary period, we cannot in most cases decide to what section of that period they are to be referred. In the beds of rolled pebbles which immediately cover the lignites at Dürnten, Wetzikon, and Utznach (see section, p. 150, fig. 328, *c–g*, and p. 152) no remains of animals have as yet been found; but they occur in the gravel-pit of Irgenhausen, near Wetzikon, which very probably belongs to the same division. Here M. Messikomer discovered large bones no doubt belonging to an elephant; but it is still doubtful whether this was the mammoth or the *Elephas antiquus*. Undoubted molars of the mammoth, however, have been found in the gravel-pit of the Holzerweid (near Bussenhausen, above Pfäffikon) and in those of Huntwangen and Maschwanden, as also in those of the Cantons of Berne, Basle, and Neuchâtel, and near Morges. Near Neuchâtel a tooth was found in stratified gravel, resting upon polished rocks. But this smoothing of the rocks, was probably effected during the first Glacial period, as it was only at that time that the great Rhone glacier reached so far; hence this fact only proves that the mammoth came into the Neuchâtel district after the first Glacial period. The locality near Morges is more important. Here, in a section formed by the Boiron rivulet, half a mile west of the town, a fine molar and a tusk were found lying at a depth of about 12 feet in stratified gravel. The gravel belongs to a terrace situated about

80 feet above the lake, and consisting entirely of Alpine material, which was probably deposited there during the second Glacial period. As the teeth lay in its upper stratified portion, they probably arrived there at a time when a rivulet flowed towards the basin of the lake then occupied by the glacier, and formed the gravel-bed probably after the ice-masses had disappeared from the district. In the Canton of Berne teeth and fragments of bones have been found at Neubruck and Rapperschwyl (near Affoltern), and in the city of Berne, not far from the Federal Palace. In the latter locality a tooth was obtained in a deposit of glacial gravel derived from the great terminal moraine, the formation of which probably dates from the close of the Glacial epoch*. In the Canton of Basle, where the gravel-beds have furnished remains of the mammoth at various places (as near Liestal, Diegten, Dornach, Gröllingen, and Münchenstein), they may have been deposited in the interglacial or the postglacial period; and a similar observation applies to the remains of animals collected at the Isteinerklotz below Basle. At this point the rock of the Jura projects into the Rhine, and objects floating down the Rhine are frequently cast upon the bank. This was the case even in the drift epoch; for remains of the mammoth, urus, horse, giant stag, hyæna, and cave-bear have been found here; so that the river must then have had its present course. But whether these animals were stranded during or after the Glacial period cannot now be ascertained. The mammoth-remains discovered in the Canton of Soleure (near the city and near Trimbach), the great tusk found in the bed of the Aar near Aarau, and the fine molars exhumed near Luttingen in the neighbourhood of Hauenstein, throw no light upon the matter. The teeth of the mammoth at Luttingen (p. 165, fig. 351) lay among remains of bones of the urus (*Bos primigenius*) in a marshy soil which was covered with a bed of loam, and occupied a basin enclosed by primitive rocks of the locality. From the facts hitherto ascertained we learn that the mammoth appeared in Switzerland at the end of the second Glacial epoch.

* See Isidor Bachmann, ' Ueber die in Bern vorkommenden versteinerten Thierreste:' Bern, 1867.

During the interglacial period, at the time of the formation of the lignites, the *Elephas antiquus* probably came into Switzerland in the summer time from Italy, where it was abundant, and the mammoth (*Elephas primigenius*) immigrated into the Swiss region from more northern localities. The remains of the mammoth are everywhere found in Central and Northern Europe, in Northern Asia *, and in North America; its area of distribution was more extended than is usual for animals of such vast size. In Germany the valley of Cannstatt and Stuttgard was an especially favourite resort of the mammoth and woolly rhinoceros; and in that basin great quantities of the bones and teeth of these animals have been found in a sandy loam (the Loess), which in many places is covered with tuffs. In the plain of the Rhine the Loess contains bones of the same two pachyderms.

Small as is the number of animals found in the Swiss drift (Diluvium), the remains are very remarkable on account of the singular mixture of species. Side by side with forms which may be regarded as belonging to the temperate zone, such as the horse, the urus (*Bos primigenius*), the stag, the badger, the bear, and the wild cat, there are true Alpine animals, such as the chamois, the ibex, and the marmot, and inhabitants of the northern regions, such as the elk and the reindeer; and with these are associated a rhinoceros and an elephant, the nearest relatives of which now live only in the torrid and warm zones; but, at the same time, they differ from their living representatives by their hairy covering, and thus demonstrate that they were organized for a cold climate.

The drift-fauna presents the same character in all parts of

---

* It is probable that the mammoth was originally a native of Eastern Siberia, and that it lived there as early as the epoch of the Swiss lignites; it is also likely that, the temperature decreasing more and more during the second Glacial period, it emigrated and arrived in Central Europe. This hypothesis is supported by the fact that in Siberia the mammoth passed the Arctic circle and reached even the 80th degree, while in Europe it has never attained the Arctic circle (see Prof. Heer's 'Flora Fossilis Arctica,' i. p. 43). In Siberia several perfect specimens of this animal with the skin and hair have been found buried in the frozen soil; and the teeth are there so abundant that fossil ivory constitutes in that country an important article of commerce.

Europe : chamois and marmots have been found even in the plain of the Rhine; and there the elk and the reindeer were associated with the musk-ox, which is now met with only in the extreme north of America and in Eastern Greenland, and with two species of lemming, one of which (*Myodes lemmus*, Linn.) now inhabits Sweden and Norway, whilst the other (*M. torquatus*, Pall., sp.) lives in still higher latitudes. This occurrence of Arctic and Alpine animals in the plains of Switzerland and Europe in general very probably coincides in point of time with the diffusion of an Alpine flora over the low country, and constitutes an important confirmation of the hypothesis of a glacial epoch.

At a later period none of the higher animals of the Alps and of Northern Europe could maintain their position on the numerous hills in the low country, as they had not sufficient ground in those localities; and as the human race advanced into that region, large animals would be obliged to give up to man their share of the land; but the smaller animals, such as the insects, and the plants remained. In the upper part of the valley of the Töss are seen on the same mountain-plants the *Petasites*, the *Adenostyla*, and the blue and golden *Chrysomelæ* (*C. gloriosa* and *tristis*), as in Central Switzerland. In the brooks are found small water-beetles (*Hydroporus septentrionalis*, Gyll., and *H. griseo-striatus*, Deg.) pertaining to the north and to the Alps; and on the Tösstock a beetle (*Nebia Gyllenhalii*) has settled which is wanting in the northern mountains, but is found everywhere in the Alps of the Grisons and of Uri, and involuntarily reminded Prof. Heer of the Pouteljes granite which had been formerly carried into this locality. On the Zürichberg, the Uetliberg, and the Randen, also, some vestiges are met with of the distant Glacial epoch *.

In another characteristic the Swiss insect-fauna shows an analogy with the flora of the drift-period. Switzerland in its drift possesses a considerable number of entomological species which are also common to high northern latitudes, although they are absent from all the intervening countries. Prof. Heer

---

* As such souvenirs may be indicated *Carabus auronitens*, Fab., *C. irregularis* Fab., *Cychrus rostratus, Pterostichus ovalis* and *metallicus, Leptura virens, Callichroma alpina, Pachyta quatuormaculata*, and *Lathrobium alpestre.*

was most agreeably surprised when, for the first time, he found
on the Bernina a minute insect (*Leiochiton arcticum*) which is
widely diffused in Finland and Lapland; and at Fetau he met
with an elegant beetle (*Cymindis angularis*) which at the present
time is only known in Lapland.   Lastly, in 1849, near Samaden
and Bevers, Prof. Heer discovered a splendid moth (*Euprepia
flava*, Amstein) which also occurs in Siberia.   Such instances
form a few novel links in a complete chain of phenomena, the
explanation of which is to be sought in the Glacial epoch.

All these facts leave no room to doubt that a great diminution
of temperature occurred in the drift-period, and consequently
that the glaciers moved from the Alpine zone, and invaded the
plain.   At present only a few Alpine and northern animals and
plants have been found fossil in the drift; but the constitution
of the flora and fauna of Switzerland, and of the northern zone,
confirm the conclusions founded upon the dispersion of the
Alpine rocks.   In connexion with the facts already noticed,
they furnish the means of forming a distinct conception of the
landscape of the period.   The plate at the commencement of the
present volume, "Zurich in the Glacial Epoch," is intended to
show the appearance of the immediate vicinity of Zurich at the
close of the second Glacial period.   The glacier is in retreat.
The chains of hills formerly covered with ice are once more free
and clothed with forests of conifers : the surface of the lake is
still occupied by the glacier, upon which run two long lateral
moraines.   The northern end of the glacier is torn and split by
crevasses; and numerous fragments of ice have broken loose and
float towards the land.   The foreground is formed by the terminal moraine, vast blocks of which have been brought by the
glacier to their present position.   They are scantily clothed
with dwarf pines and Alpine alders.   A family of marmots is
sporting about among the blocks; on the right appear some
mammoths, and further on·a troop of reindeer are going to
drink.   In the background the snow-white Alps are visible,
from the Glärnisch to the Windgelle; these mountains supply
the sources of the glacier which moves down from them into the
plain.

If a Glacial epoch of this kind passed over the hemisphere in
which Europe is situated, it must have left traces of its occur-

rence in the inhabitants of the sea; and accordingly a more northern character has been observed in the marine fauna of the drift-deposits of Sweden, Scotland, and England. A northern character has also been manifested in the drift-fauna of the Mediterranean as far as Sicily. Forms of animal life belonging to the extreme north descended towards the south, and were afterwards driven back to the north. Hence most of them are only found in the fossil state in the drift-deposits of the above-mentioned countries, although some still exist at great oceanic depths, or at places where cold springs burst through the sea-bottom; and thus the same phenomenon is reproduced by the sea with which we have become acquainted in the case of land plants and animals. Thus colonies of Norwegian Crustacea occur in the gulf of Quarnero, in the Adriatic, and also colonies of Arctic animals in the lakes of the Norwegian coast, which were formerly united with the sea, and have been separated from it by the upheaval of the land.

On glancing over the numerous facts furnished by both organic and inorganic nature, Prof. Heer is compelled to conclude that the warm Tertiary epoch was followed by a period in which the climate was much colder than at present. Even during the Tertiary epoch a gradual diminution of temperature took place, as is proved by a comparison of the Œningian flora with that of the Lower Miocene; and in Pliocene times the climate approximated to that of the present day (see p. 174). In the subsequent drift-period the temperature fell at the time of the greatest development of the glaciers several degrees below the present mean. If the temperature were now to fall about 4° or 5° C. (or 7°·2 or 9° Fahr.), the glaciers would again make their way irresistibly down into the low country and spread over the plains, and this would take place the more rapidly in proportion to the moisture of the climate and the amount of aqueous precipitation. Only a slight diminution of temperature, therefore, is requisite in order to explain the phenomena of the Glacial epoch; at the same time it is certainly remarkable that at the very commencement of the Glacial-drift period the glaciers spread over the plain of Switzerland and then again retreated, and during thousands of years a quiet formation of peat took place in the same country where the glaciers had formerly been,

the lignite district being in its turn invaded by a fresh advance
of the masses of ice. This solves the apparent contradictions
presented by the animals and plants of the drift deposits, species
both of the temperate and cold zones which they have preserved
for us being explained by the changes of climate which took
place during this long period. The remarkable fact that the
Swiss flora has retained so few Miocene types of plants is also
thus accounted for. It may easily be understood that all the
forms of the torrid and warm zones could not be introduced
into the present flora of Switzerland, as these would have disappeared even in Pliocene times; but the Swiss Miocene flora
contained a number of species representing those of a temperate
climate, which would very probably have remained under altered
circumstances in the existing flora if a great interval had not
separated the flora of our time from the Miocene. This interval
was caused by the Glacial epoch, to which it is owing that the
planes, the red maple, the balsam-poplar, the walnut, the tulip-
trees, the liquidambars, &c. have so little part in the constitution of the existing Swiss flora, whilst they reappear in America
in very nearly allied forms. These species support the Swiss
climate admirably, and are seen here as foreign cultivated trees,
while their ancestors in Miocene times were among the most
abundant Swiss plants. In the uppermost Pliocene deposits
some Miocene types are still met with which are now exclusively
American, and which were exterminated in Switzerland during
the first Glacial period; so that even at the time of the formation
of the lignites all traces of them had disappeared, and the flora
had acquired its present Asiatico-European character.

Prof. Heer is of opinion that with the drift or diluvium a
period was reached when man appeared on the stage of life.
Only some obscure traces of human beings have been hitherto
found in the Swiss drift-deposits.

The lake-dwellings of Switzerland belong to a much later
time, as is shown in the section of the Wetzikon district near
the Lake of Zurich (vol. i. p. 27), where the remains of lacustrine
habitations are found over a series of lake-chalk, drift-débris,
lignites or paper-coals, and gravel-beds.

Facts have been ascertained in France, Belgium, and England
which give great probability to the existence of Man contempo-

rancously with the mammoth and the woolly rhinoceros; and rude implements manufactured from flint have been found associated with remains of these animals in caves and gravel-beds; and drawings have been observed on the bones of animals found in the drift which were probably scratched by the hand of Man.

From the investigations of Sir Charles Lyell, who has given a clear and admirable summary of the results obtained in his time, it appears that the most ancient remains of Man * were

---

* Sir Charles Lyell, ' Geological Evidences of the Antiquity of Man,' London, 1863. The Vertebrata of the Tertiary epoch, and even those of its uppermost Pliocene division, are quite different from those of the present day. Prof. Heer therefore regards it as extremely improbable and contrary to all analogy that Man should have, at that time, existed upon the earth. Moreover no single fact can be adduced in favour of this opinion. It is quite otherwise with the Drift-period. This offers us plants and animals identical with those now living; and even among the most highly organized animals, the Mammalia, we find living species coexisting with types now extinct. The occurrence of Man at this period, therefore, cannot surprise us; and his first appearance may have taken place at its very beginning. This, however, is not yet proved; and a careful examination of the facts hitherto ascertained shows that the first traces of Man in Europe coincide with the Postglacial period. From striæ and furrows observed upon bones of *Elephas meridionalis* in an anteglacial deposit of gravel at St. Prest, near Chartres, Desnoyers regarded these marks as due to the hand of Man, and concluded that Man existed before the Glacial epoch. But these striæ and furrows might just as well have been produced by predaceous animals in gnawing the bones, as has been pointed out by Lyell (Appendix to the third edition of the ' Antiquity of Man,' p. 1 *et seq.*); and as no other indications of the presence of Man occur in the locality, this opinion of Sir Charles Lyell seems much more probable.

In the interglacial lignites there seems to be a nearer approach to certainty of real traces of man. M. Rütimeyer has received, from Wetzikon, lignites in which are found four pointed rods; and he is of opinion that these rods received their points from the hands of human beings. This circumstance, according to Professor Heer, only forms a feeble and doubtful evidence of the existence of Man in the interglacial epoch, especially as previous researches, conducted during fifty years, had not led to any other traces of Man in Swiss lignites. E. Collomb (Bibliothèque Universelle, July 1860) has endeavoured to prove that the drift of the Somme (which contains the flint implements of which so much has been said) was deposited before the Glacial epoch. He has compared it with the gravel-beds of the Vosges, which are covered by moraines, and founds his inference upon this comparison; but Prof. Desor

discovered in the deposits immediately following those of the Glacial epoch, forming the fifth stage of Prof. Heer's Table (p. 203). At this period the mammoth and the woolly rhinoceros were still living, and were widely distributed. Most of the localities where these animals were found seem to belong to the Postglacial period, which long preceded the age of the pile-dwellings.

In the period of the Swiss lake-dwellings the urus and the elk are met with, but there are no traces of the mammoth and rhinoceros, and the stone implements differ in form from the most ancient examples. The remains found by Lartet in the caverns of Périgord and of the Pyrenees probably belong to the intermediate epoch, as well as the instruments in bone which have been collected near Schussenried and at the Salève. Remains of reindeer are seen, with sculptures on the palmate portions of the antlers, which must have been worked by human agency.

During the drift-period Europe was perhaps united by continental land with the Atlantic islands, as the Azores, Madeira, and the Canaries have a great number of plants and of lower animals in common with Europe, thus demonstrating that these islands are more connected with Europe than with Africa. In more northern latitudes the European continent seems to have been united with America; for the mammoth, as well as the horse and the musk-sheep (*Ovibos moschatus*) lived in North America as well as in Europe. Subsequently the musk-sheep became extinct in Europe, the horse disappeared in America, and the mammoth no longer lived in either country. An explanation of many remarkable phenomena will be afforded if we

---

has proved (Les Phases de la Période Diluvienne) that this assimilation is inadmissible. He regards the Drift of the Somme as Postglacial; and the researches of Lyell (Antiquity of Man, p. 228) are in agreement with this determination. Lyell has shown that all the occurrences of human remains in England are in deposits which date from the Postglacial period, and that the gravel-beds of the Somme probably belong to the same time. D'Archiac also adopts this latter opinion (Du Terrain quaternaire et de l'ancienneté de l'homme dans le nord de France, 1863, p. 47); only he erroneously places the English localities which have furnished the clue to the determination of the horizon of the French deposits in the middle of the Quaternary epoch and *before* the second Glacial period.

suppose that during the Miocene epoch there was an extension of an Atlantic continent from the Arctic zone far towards the south, so as to unite America and Europe, from Iceland to the United States of North America *. Such an Atlantic continent would account for the fact that, of 56 species of Miocene plants that Prof. Heer knows from Alaska †, 17 occur in the Swiss Miocene flora. In this number there are 3 species of poplar, 3 willows, the liquidambar, a walnut, &c. Under these circumstances it may be understood how the planes and the sabal palm established themselves everywhere in Europe, how the tulip-tree migrated into Iceland and Switzerland, and how Swiss fossil remains comprise gigantic frogs, long-necked tortoises, *Belastomata,* and *Gyrini,* such as are now only to be met with in American waters.

The hypothesis of an Atlantic continent would explain in a

---

* The objection urged, that this Atlantic continent would have occupied exactly the deepest parts of the ocean, is not well founded; for the greatest depth of the ocean occurs much further south, namely between Southern Africa and South America. The greatest breadth of this continent would correspond to the line of the transatlantic telegraph, which lies at a mean depth of 0·439 of a geographical mile. The identity of the Miocene corals of the south-west of Europe with those of the Antilles is a proof of the existence of shallow shores running from one continent to the other, as the corals will not build in a deep sea. If the southern shores of the supposed Atlantis were fringed with coral-reefs, such as are now met with in the Miocene of Porto-Santo, the identity between the coral fauna of Miocene Europe and that of America is easily explained, whilst if the two continents were separated by a vast and deep sea this explanation would be very difficult (see the 'Flore Fossile des pays arctiques,' by Prof. Heer, i. p. 52).

† Dr. Newberry has just discovered several species which belong in common to the Miocene of Fort Union, Dacotah, and to that of Europe, e. g. *Onoclea sensibilis,* Linn. (*Filicites hebridicus,* Forbes, from the island of Mull), *Glyptostrobus europæus,* and a fan-palm very nearly allied to the *Sabal major.* The Arctic zone having been, in Miocene times, a very important vegetable focus from which plants could spread in all directions, many species probably had from thence their origin, such as the *Taxodium, Sequoia Langsdorfii, Glyptostrobus,* and others. It is not unimportant to observe that the species common to the Swiss Miocene flora and to that of North America are especially species of the temperate zone; these species probably originated in the North. Nevertheless tropical forms are not wanting; but such plants as the sabal palm could not come from Arctic countries.

general way how it happened that Europe, in the Miocene epoch, possessed a whole series of plants and animals the nearest allies * of which now belong exclusively to North America, and that some types of animals and plants of the Tertiary epoch (vol. i. pp. 348 & 370), as well as some American types, have maintained themselves to the present day in the Atlantic islands. Probably the depression of the great Miocene continent, which has here been designated under the name of Atlantis, was contemporaneous with the elevation of the Alps, and the sinking of the land continued until the close of the drift epoch. By this depression the continuity of Europe and America became broken; and whilst during the Miocene period the organic world of Europe possessed numerous American types, these disappeared during the drift period. Their place was taken by species of plants and animals coming from the east, which constitute the greater part of the flora and fauna of the Swiss plains; and the Alps received numerous immigrants of Scandinavian origin, which now form an integral part of the Swiss Alpine flora.

Organic nature does not seem to have undergone in America so strongly marked a change as in Europe. The existing American flora much more closely resembles the Miocene flora both of America and of Europe. Tertiary types may be more easily preserved, owing to the form of the American continent, which stretches through both hemispheres, and consists of immense territories not for a long period invaded by the sea; whilst the contour of Europe is indented, and its area is of smaller extent, so that the Tertiary types have been in great measure destroyed. A certain number of these types, however, have maintained their ground in the Mediterranean zone, and have become the parent plants which bind the flora of that zone to the Tertiary flora.

Is the Atlantic continent, the existence of which we have just assumed in accordance with the facts stated, the same as the

* In this question, the analogy of the species has quite a different bearing from that of the genera; which Prof. Oliver seems to have forgotten in his treatise, "The Atlantis hypothesis in its Botanical aspect," Nat.-Hist. Rev. 1862.

legendary Atlantis of the Greeks? It may have happened that man inhabited the Atlantis as well as France and England; and in that case the remarkable statement of Plato in the 'Timæus' and 'Critias' acquires a new interest. History related, according to the tradition of the Egyptian priests, that in ancient times there existed, beyond the Pillars of Heracles (the Straits of Gibraltar), an island larger than Asia and Libya united, clothed with a rich vegetation, and inhabited by a very powerful people; but, subsequently, earthquakes and enormous waves swallowed up the island. Plato has poetically embellished this obscure and ancient legend, for which probably there was a foundation in great geological events* terminating at the close of the drift epoch.

The present boundaries of the Mediterranean sea were only settled during the drift-epoch. All the borders of the northern coast of Africa have a Southern-European character, which indicates that the separation of Europe from Africa did not take place until the same types of organic nature had been established in the borders of both countries.

During the Miocene epoch Greece was united on the east with Asia Minor (vol. i. p. 297). Then occurred a considerable depression which separated Europe from Asia: the numerous Greek islands are only the remains of this vast intermediate country. Probably this depression took place at a period when Man was in existence, and afterwards gave rise among ancient nations to legends respecting the deluge.

The preceding statements lead us to regard the drift-period as stormy and changeful. During its course many modifications of climate occurred, and exercised a great influence on the constitution of the flora and fauna. Although the principal mountain-heights of Switzerland were fixed, and the sea

---

* [The poet Beattie adopts the Platonic tradition in the following line :—

" Where the Atlantic rolls, wide continents have bloomed."

Plato described the island of Atlantis as " the way to other islands, and from the islands you might pass to the whole of the opposite continent " (see Dr. Jowett's translation of Plato's Dialogues, vol. iii. p. 609).—EDITOR.]

no longer invaded the heart of Europe, a peculiar character belonged to the epoch from the enormous masses of water which
were produced by active condensation, originating mighty glaciers, and from the elevations and depressions still frequently
modifying the limits of this part of the world.   It has been well
defined as "the period of inundations."

If traces of Man belong to the drift-period of the earth's
history, human beings were contemporaneous with those troubled
times, and would be affected by them.   Hence narratives
of the Deluge would be current among all ancient peoples—
among the savages of America as well as among the civilized
nations of antiquity.   These are obscure memories of ancient
races relating to magnificent and real events, but poetically embellished and adapted to certain definite localities.   Phenomena
which may have lasted thousands of years are summed up in a
short space of time ; in fact, when the poet wishes to call up a
general image before our minds, it is his custom to bring distant
events together and combine them within a narrow frame.   It
is when he succeeds in melting these grains of gold into an
harmonious stream that he contributes to the well-being of
humanity.

With the presence of man commences a new world, the world
of the intellect, which does not lie within the domain of this
work, the scope of which is limited to primæval formations anterior to man.

Homage is here due to the memory of those distinguished
persons who, by raising the veil that concealed the Glacial epoch,
laid open to the world one of the most wonderful episodes in
geological history.

J. Venetz was the first to demonstrate the analogy of erratic
blocks scattered over the plain with the débris on the moraines
of glaciers.   He first put forward this idea in a treatise dated
1821, and afterwards addressed the Swiss Society of Natural
History on the subject when it met at St.-Bernard in 1829.   A
scientific basis was given to the theory by John de Charpentier,
in a series of conscientious researches, and by a careful combination of known facts.   His views formed the starting-point of
researches subsequently carried on by Agassiz, Desor, Escher,

Guyot, Forbes, and many other observers, and now forming an established part of the general domain of science*.

---

* The first paper by Charpentier on glaciers appeared in the 'Annales des Mines,' vol. viii., and in the 'Mittheilungen aus dem Gebiete der theoretischen Erdkunde,' von Julius Fröbel und Osw. Heer, Zurich, 1836, pp. 482 *et seqq.*, under the following title: "Anzeige eines der wichtigsten Ergebnisse der Untersuchungen des Herrn Venetz über den gegenwärtigen und früheren Zustand der Wallisergletscher," read at Lucerne before the Swiss Society of Natural Sciences in 1834. Since that time the question of glaciers has given rise to an abundant literature. Among the principal works we may cite :—J. de Charpentier, ' Essai sur les Glaciers et sur le terrain erratique du Bassin du Rhône,' Lausanne, 1841; and L. Agassiz, ' Etudes sur les Glaciers,' Neuchâtel, 1840. Prof. Mousson has published a most learned work which sums up the investigations made upon existing glaciers, ' Die Gletscher der Jetztzeit, eine Zusammenstellung und Prüfung ihrer Erscheinungen und Gesetze,' Zurich, 1854.

CHAPTER XIV.

GRADUAL changes taking place in the crust of our earth are admirably illustrated in the Swiss Alps. Whether the traveller crosses the Alpine chain by the Julier and the Bernina, by the Splugen or the St. Bernard, by the St. Gothard or by the mountains of Berne or the Valais, he will everywhere find enormous masses of fallen rocks and débris, which here and there cover the slopes and bottoms of the valleys, and afford evidence of the constant weathering of mountains and of the impossibility of vegetation advancing so rapidly as to cover all the rocky fragments with its green mantle.

Deep ravines have in various places been formed by the action of running water; and torrents forcing their way through these gorges have carried down heaps of stones and earth into the valleys, and have thus occasioned the formation of tall cones. By the continual process of lowering heights and filling up valleys, lofty peaks gradually diminish in elevation, and lake-basins are filled up. Thus the northern part of the Lake of Wallenstadt will in turn be converted into dry land. Already, within the last fifty years, since the river Linth was conducted into the lake, a considerable delta has been formed, which is continually increasing, and now fills the north-western portion of the lake, so that the mouth of the river Linth is constantly advancing into the former lake-basin, and the bed of the river has to be constantly elongated and deepened.

At present, as the Swiss mountains become disintegrated, all the masses of rock remain in the vicinity where they fall; but in the drift-epoch the broken pieces were carried away to great distances, covering the soil of the plain of Switzerland, and in some parts raising it considerably. If we imagine all these gravel-beds and moraines put back again on the mountains from which they were removed, there were would be a great increase of height to the Alpine range.

Traces of Man and of his works are found in Switzerland in the higher stratum of the country, in peat-bogs and tufas which are continually increasing. Prof. Heer does not consider that there are any such traces in the drift gravel-beds lying beneath the soil which contains the remains of the inhabitants of pile-dwellings. The plants of this epoch almost exactly resemble those of the present day, and the fauna only offers us a few exotic types; if, however, the Miocene rocks are examined which lie immediately below these drift gravel-beds in Switzerland, another world of life meets the view. As the glaciers and granulated-snow fields which encircle the Alpine chain with a white girdle constitute a boundary-line for animal and vegetable life, the glaciers of the first drift-period form a far more important barrier between the drift and the Tertiary fauna and flora.

Even the rocks which contain their remains are very different. The drift deposits consist chiefly of pebbles and sand, here and there, indeed, united into solid masses, but not forming true rocks; whilst the Tertiary deposits have largely assisted in the formation of mountains. Descending still lower, we meet with a long series not only of different rock-formations, but also of different animals and plants, succeeding one another step by step; so that when a general survey is made, a world is revealed to us rich in organized beings which formerly lived upon the earth, and we ascertain that Switzerland contains memorials of all periods from the drift to the coal-formation. Below the anthracite rocks which represent the Carboniferous period, crystalline rock-masses are found, which have been essential to the construction of the Alps, and which consist of numerous varieties of granite and gneiss, micaceous, chloritic, and talcose schists, and amphibole*. Quartz, felspar, and mica are the constituents of granite and gneiss, the latter being distinguished from granite by its stratification. In the mica-schist mica pre-

---

* [*Amphibole* comprises hornblende, actinolite, tremolite, &c. (Lyell's ' Elements of Geology,' chapter 28).—EDITOR.]

dominates, and felspar is entirely or almost entirely absent; the
allied chloritic and talcose schists are characterized by a general
green colour and a softer consistency.   In some places the talcose schists are worked for making pots and stoves.   The am-
phibolic masses, which occur chiefly on the southern slope of the
Alps, are distinguished by the presence of the black variety of
amphibole.   In some places serpentine and gabbro* also occur,
which have formed a part of the mountains of the Valais, of Uri,
and of the Grisons.   These rocks contain no traces of fossils;
so that they are destitute of any indications of organic life; and
hence they have not improperly been denominated *Primary
Rocks*.   They have prepared the ground on which living creatures were in after times to appear.

Crystalline rocks form the highest Swiss mountains, and constitute the nucleus of the central Alps, on which are grouped to
the north and south the deposits of the Jurassic, Cretaceous,
Eocene, and Miocene periods.   Even in the Miocene basin of
Switzerland, if we could penetrate to great depths, these older
rocks would be reached.   In northern Switzerland they reappear
near Laufenbourg.   The gneiss of Laufenbourg is connected
with the crystalline rock-masses of the Black Forest, which are
surrounded by a zone of Triassic and Jurassic rocks, consisting
in some places on their edges of a conglomerate manifestly produced by the weathering of gneiss.

In Switzerland the anthracite-shales are found lying over the
crystalline rocks, and must therefore be regarded as the most
ancient fossiliferous formations which have yet been discovered
in that country.   But from the geological constitution of other
countries it is known that a long period elapsed before the formation of the Carboniferous rocks; and the earlier strata have
been principally observed in Germany, Bohemia, Russia, Sweden,
England, and North America; and they are divided into four
sections, namely the Laurentian †, Cambrian, Silurian, and De-

---

* [Saussurite (tough Jade) constitutes gabbro rocks (Greg and Lettsom's
Mineralogy, p. 114).—EDITOR.]

† [An account of the Laurentian system is given in Sir Willian Logan's
' Report of the Canadian Geological survey,' 1863 (chapter iii.), in which the
Laurentian strata are described as " altered to a highly crystalline condition,

vonian formations. In some places these formations are of great thickness; and they consist chiefly of clay-slate, of breccia (Grauwacke), and limestone. The Cambrian and Silurian formations contain only marine organisms. About twenty species of plants are known, all of which seem to belong to the Algæ. The precise nature of *Oldhamia* and *Murchisonites* cannot yet be regarded as settled. Of animals, small Brachiopods and Trilobites appear in the upper strata of the Cambrian series. In the Silurian they are developed in a multiplicity of forms; but the same species in part occur in high northern and more southern latitudes in North America and Europe, and even in China. The Trilobites, which are the earliest known Articulate animals, and belong to the Crustacea, disappear entirely in the mountain-limestone of the Carboniferous formation, whilst the Brachiopods have continued in existence to the present day; indeed one genus (*Lingula*), a species of which now burrows into the sand of tropical coasts, was represented even in the seas of the Cambrian epoch, showing us that certain types of animals are continued through all the ages of the world's history. Most of the Brachiopods of the early Palæozoic rocks belong to genera which do not now exist. Besides the Brachiopods, the Cephalopods are the Mollusca that occur most frequently in these ancient seas. We find them with straight and twisted shells, the septa of which are simple like those of the Nautilus. In the Silurian strata they offer a wonderful multiplicity of species. In these deposits corals also make their appearance, even at such an early period taking part in the formation of the crust of the earth, and forming reefs in which numerous crinoids, very simply constructed Sea-urchins, and Sponges found a dwelling-place. Fishes first appear in the uppermost Silurian stratum; in the upper Devonian deposits their species are tolerably numerous. All the forms, however, differ greatly from those now existing, and they in part form

---

and as composed of felspathic rocks interstratified with important masses of limestone and quartzite." The area in Canada occupied by the Laurentian series is supposed to be about 200,000 square miles.—EDITOR.]

peculiar families belonging exclusively to the early Palæozoic period—such as the *Cephalaspides*, which possessed great bony plates, some like a helmet covering the head, and others like a shield protecting the body.

Hitherto land-animals have not been found in the early Palæozoic rocks; and land-plants make their first appearance in the Devonian formation. But few species, however, are known; and these are most nearly allied to plants of the Carboniferous period. Monocotyledons and Dicotyledons are entirely wanting; and there are only a few Gymnosperms, which differ so widely from all existing forms that there is great doubt respecting their place in the botanical system.

Most of the plants of the early Palæozoic rocks belonged to the vascular cryptogams; and, as in the Carboniferous period, Ferns, Lycopodiaceæ, and Calamariæ constituted the vegetation which covered the green islands of the primæval sea. Among the Ferns, species of the genera *Sphenopteris*, *Cyclopteris*, and *Odontopteris* are met with; the Lycopods are represented by a *Lepidodendron*, and the Calamariæ by a number of peculiar types of which Unger has made genera and even distinct families; but as this determination is founded only upon a few remains of stems, Prof. Heer can form no distinct conception of their aspect.

As the early Palæozoic strata do not occur in Switzerland, or at least as no certain demonstration can be given of their existence in that country *, an intermediate place will be given to them between the Primary rocks and those of the Carboniferous period in the following Table (p. 235) of the chief periods in the history of the earth's crust.

If the deposition of the rock-strata had taken place from the commencement quietly and without disturbance, the evidences of these different periods would be found one above the other in

---

* Prof. Studer (Geologie der Schweiz, i. p. 346) thinks that the grey schists which surround the eastern central mountain-masses of the Vorarlberg, and traverse the Grisons as far as Ortles, may belong to the Silurian and Devonian formations, as rocks containing Silurian and Devonian animal-remains are found under similar conditions in Styria.

GENERAL TABLE.

PRINCIPAL EPOCHS.	PERIODS.	STAGES.		
Recent.				
Quaternary or Drift.	Quaternary.	Postglacial. Second Glacial. Interglacial 2. Rolled pebbles. / 1. Lignites. First Glacial.		
Tertiary.	Tertiary.	Pliocene (wanting in Switzerland).	Norwich Crag. Red Crag. Coralline Crag.	
		Miocene or Molasse.	Upper Miocene... Œningian. Middle Miocene .. Helvetian. Lower Miocene... 3. Grey Molasse. / 2. Lower Lignites. / 1. Tongrian.	
		Eocene.	Upper Eocene. Middle Eocene. Lower Eocene.	
Secondary.	Cretaceous.	Upper.	Danian. Senonian. Turonian. Cenomanian.	
		Middle.	Gault.	
		Lower.	Aptian. Urgonian. Neocomian. Valangian.	
	Jurassic.	White Jura.	Upper ... Portland, Kimmeridge (Purbeck). Middle... Coralline. Lower ... Oxford.	
		Brown Jura.	Upper ... Callovian. Middle... Bathonian. Lower ... Bajocian.	
		Black Lias.	Upper ... Toarcian. Middle... Liassic. Lower ... Sinemurian.	
	Triassic.	Keuper. Mussel-limestone. Bunter sandstone.		
Palæozoic.	Carboniferous.	Permian or Dyas. Middle Carboniferous. Lower Carboniferous.		
	Early Palæozoic rocks (not yet discovered in Switzerland).	Devonian. Silurian. Cambrian. Laurentian.		
Primitive rocks.				

the order here indicated. But all these stages are not found anywhere in a regular and unbroken succession. In nature, only some series of rocks have retained their position, as the original stratification has at different times been so modified and revolutionized that the natural sequence of the various formations has only been established by the labour of geologists continued for many years. The whole appearance of the country has been changed by these revolutions and by the phenomena connected with them, and the present form has been given to it. Prof. Heer has already repeatedly referred to these revolutions; and now all of them must be considered together, so far as is necessary to understand the present configuration of Switzerland.

CHAPTER XV.

GENERALIZATIONS ON THE DEVELOPMENT AND TRANSFORMATIONS OF NATURE IN SWITZERLAND.

Part I. Inorganic Nature.

Section 1. *Upheaval and Depression of Land.*

> " Vidi ego, quod fuerat quondam solidissima tellus,
> Esse fretum : vidi factas ex æquore terras ;
> Et procul a pelago conchæ jacuere marinæ."
> > Ovid, *Metam.* xv. 262.

> [" Straits have I seen that cover now
> What erst was solid earth ; have trodden land
> Where once was sea ; and gathered inland far
> Dry ocean shells " *.]

Marine shells are found in Switzerland, not only in low grounds but on the highest Alps ; and for the attainment of such a position either the sea may at some period have reached up to the lofty elevations where these animal-remains are met with, or the mountains may have been upheaved to their present height. At first the former supposition was generally received, and people imagined a primæval ocean covering all the land up to the summits of the highest mountains. But this notion is contradicted by the circumstance that in that case the earth must have had a larger diameter, which is certainly very improbable, and, fur-

* [See translation of Ovid's Metamorphoses, by H. King, M.A., p. 508, 1871.—Editor.]

ther, that we do not know whence the enormous mass of water
which it requires could have come. It is far more likely that
the level of the sea was never much further from the centre of
the earth than it is at present, and that thus it represents a surface stretched over the globe, to which the risings and sinkings
of the terrestrial crust can be referred. That such risings and
sinkings are constantly taking place is a fact ascertained by observation, and justifying the deduction of inferences as to former
conditions. In the present volume (p. 198) Prof. Heer has
noticed the rising of the Norwegian coast. The shores of
Devonshire have been upheaved in comparatively recent times ;
for near Torbay, considerably above the sea-level, a zone may
be seen containing animals all of which still live in the sea at
that place. A similar upheaval, but on a much greater scale, is
taking place on the coasts of Chili in South America, where
marine animals of the present epoch are found several hundred
feet above the level of the sea.

These upheavals may extend uniformly over whole continents,
and are then called *continental* ; or they may affect only particular regions, or exert themselves only in particular directions,
when they are denominated *partial*. A close relation has existed between the upheavals and the depressions of the surface ;
and the lowering of the ground forms part of a general system,
as when whole continents sank down and sometimes were again
covered by the sea, or they are only partial, when limited to
particular regions of the land and inducing wide-spread sinkings
by falls in the interior of the earth.

As to the *causes* of these upheavals and depressions, which have
been the chief agents in giving the crust of the earth its present
form, science has hitherto come to no conclusion. The hypotheses which have been invented to explain this grand natural
phenomenon are connected with opinions as to the formation
and earliest states of the earth; and the dispute is not yet
settled, which has been carried on for the last 2000 years, as to
whether fire or water has had most to do with the formation of
our planet.

As the spherical form of the earth, its flattening at the poles,
and its bulging-out in the equatorial regions compel us to
assume that during its formation it has been in a fluid, or at

least in a soft state, these circumstances also lead us to conclude that at one time the earth was in an igneous and fluid state. This hypothesis has been more readily admitted, as the temperature of the earth increases below the surface. At a depth of from 60–80 feet the sun's heat has no influence, the same temperature prevails throughout the year, and it corresponds to the mean annual temperature of the place. But if we go down still deeper into the earth, the temperature increases about 1° Cent. (or 1°·8 Fahr.) for every 100 feet. The observations of this increase have hitherto been made only to a depth of about 2000 feet, so that we have only suppositions as to the conditions of temperature at greater depths; but springs of water are known whose temperature reaches the boiling-point, and volcanoes cast forth masses of burning lava; so that the subterranean locality from which they proceed must have an extremely high temperature. If the heat increases in the same proportion below 2000 feet, we should find at 9000 feet the temperature of boiling water; at 100,000 feet a heat of 1000° Cent. (or 1800° Fahr.), which would melt many rocks; and at 200,000 feet every thing would be in fusion. Hence the Plutonists, or adherents of the igneous theory, consider the interior of the earth to be a mass of fluid lava, and regard hot springs and volcanic phenomena as connected with that state of internal heat. Thus it was easy to suppose that the whole earth was originally in a state of igneous fusion, and that a firm crust had gradually been formed by its cooling down in space, during which process the minerals became solidified in a definite sequence, according to the degree of heat required for the fusion of each kind.

When the temperature had become so far lowered that water could rest on the globe, thus producing the primæval ocean, stratified rocks began to be formed, a mass of materials being accumulated at the bottom, and deposited in beds and strata. From time to time fissures occurred in the crust of the earth, from which issued the fused siliceous rocks, breaking through, compressing, and even overturning the stratified masses, and so forming the immense mountains which traverse the centre of Switzerland. By the action of these protruded rock-masses the surrounding strata were materially altered, and became metamorphic. Here and there those rocks which had been originally

deposited in water might sink to great depths, and, having been
altered by the high temperatures, might be again thrown out in
a metamorphic form. Most geologists of our time are of opinion
that in this manner the mountains have been formed.

But the *Neptunists* advance a different theory. They deny
the existence of the fiery fluid nucleus, and derive the higher
temperature of the interior of the earth from chemical processes
which there take place and produce heat. They assert that
changes are constantly going on in the rocks, and that the
materials never rest, entering into one combination and modifying it, so that other forms are produced. The rocks may
lose substances (as by erosion), and will then crumble and
become fissured; or they may become associated with new substances conveyed to them by water; or they may pass into the
crystalline state and thus enlarge considerably in volume; and
when this takes place the masses will increase in magnitude,
burst out of the depths, and break through the crust above
them. The cause of upheaval must therefore be sought in slow
and gradual changes of the rock-masses, which in augmenting
their volume produce mountains.

Such processes do take place in nature, and may therefore
have had a share in the formation of the Swiss mountains; but
these changes do not suffice to explain a whole series of phenomena, such as the spherical form of the earth, the increase of
heat towards its centre, the eruption of volcanoes, or the higher
and more uniform temperature of the early periods of the earth's
history.

Changes have been wrought in the configuration of the ground
by upheavals, which have given a great variety to the forms of
mountains and valleys, and which merit consideration.

When pressure is exerted from beneath upon a horizontal
stratum, the latter will arch upwards so long as such a movement is permitted by the flexibility of the bed. The effect of
this pressure will be manifested at the surface by an undulating
line, that is to say by arched portions alternating with depressions, the slopes of which are more or less gentle. An idea of
the pressure may be given by a piece of paper or cloth submitted
to a similar movement. If the pressure be exerted upon several
superimposed beds of rocks, and the strata submit to elevation

without fracture, there will be a *complete arch* or *saddle* (fig. 361, A). But very often the upper beds are broken through at one or more places in consequence of the violent pressure, and an *open arch* is produced, forming a fissure-valley (fig. 361, D), the side walls of which rise into *ridges* (fig. 361, C); but the cor-

Fig. 361.

Fig. 362.

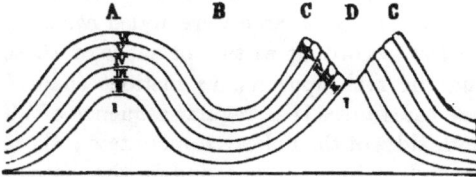
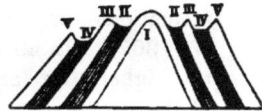

Fig. 363.

Fig. 364.

Fig. 365.

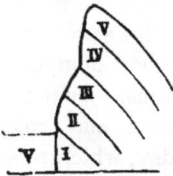
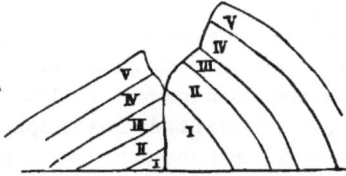
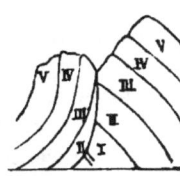

Sections of Mountains.

Fig. 361. A. Complete arch. B. Basin-valley. CC. Ridges. D. Open arch, fissure-valley. I. Primitive rocks. II. Carboniferous. III. Trias. IV. Jurassic. V. Cretaceous. VI. Tertiary.

Fig. 362. Denuded arch. I. Trias (arch). II. Lias (Liassic Combe-valley). III. Brown Jura (ridge). IV. Lower White Jura (Oxfordian Combe-valley). V. Upper White Jura (chain of the third order).

Fig. 363. Chain of a single series.

Fig. 364. Chain of two ridges.

Fig. 365. Chain with margins turned over.

respondence of the strata, although broken, will still be clearly shown. This fissure-valley is afterwards often enlarged by erosion and by dislocations; and the removal of the superior beds by these means may bring to light the unbroken inferior beds belonging to the same arch (fig. 362, I.). When the arch rises (as at the Weissenstein and the Blauenberg) into a lofty dome, it is surrounded by a valley, in the same manner as a fortress is girt round with a ditch and a wall.

Mountain-chains may thus be classified into different orders. Those chains formed by saddle-shaped mountains (with the arch complete) were called by Thurmann *chains of the first order*; those produced by the ridges on the opened arch were named *chains of the second order*; and those originating from the different rock-formations of the denuded arch were styled *chains of the third and fourth orders*, according as two or more of these formations surrounding the arch appeared as distinct chains* (fig. 362). In all these cases there is a regular sequence of all the higher strata on both sides of the upheaved mountain; those of the same age correspond to one another, and in the interior of the chain are directly connected.

In a second class of the phenomena of elevation an interruption is produced throughout the whole thickness of the stratified rocks, and the correspondence of the beds of the same age in the two chains is entirely destroyed. This mode of upheaval has been subject also to numerous modifications. Sometimes only one margin of the stratified mass is upheaved, and projects often several thousand feet above the other edge, which retains its original position or nearly so (fig. 363), so that its oldest bed comes into contact with the newest; sometimes both edges are thrown up, but very unequally (fig. 364), so that the strata in the two no longer coincide; or the edges are upraised (fig. 365), or inverted, and turned one over the other, so that newer rock-beds come to lie beneath the older ones.

The fissures running deep into the earth which are produced by these fractures of the rocks allow water to come to the surface, here and there, from great depths, and in these cases afford evidence of internal high temperature. Prof. Mousson has as-

---

* Thurmann subdivided the Jura into 162 chains. Of these he referred 30 to the first order (such as the Salève and Dôle), 80 to the second order (Chasseron, Blauenberg), 40 to the third order (Geissfluh, Lägern), and 12 to the fourth order (Passwang, Geissfluh). He reckons 100 basin-valleys, and 90 transverse clefts through mountain-chains. (See his " Résumé des lois orographiques générales du système des Monts Jura," in the 'Mémoires de la Société Helvétique des Sciences' for 1863.)

certained that the hot springs of Baden and Schinznach are situated upon the line of such a rocky fissure; and this is also the case with the baths of Aix in Savoy*.

With the stratified structure of the Swiss mountains the formation of the valleys stands in the closest connexion. The undulations of the mountains produced by upheaval are termed *longitudinal valleys*; they are described as *basin-valleys* (fig. 361, B) when they spread between the saddle-mountains, as *fissure-valleys* (fig. 361, D) when they are formed by the bursting of the arch, and as *combes* (fig. 362, II, IV) when they lie between ridges running in the same direction. They also have the form of clefts passing transversely through the mountain-chains.

When the outlet of a valley is closed by a transverse bar formed either by a rock in position or by masses of débris, water collects in it and a lake is produced. These accumulations of water may be formed in basin-valleys, combes, and clefts; and. to this is owing the varied character of the Swiss lakes †. Thus the Lac de Joux is a basin-valley lake, whilst the lakes of Wallenstadt and Brienz are regarded by Prof. Desor as combe-lakes, and those of Thun and Lowerz as cleft-lakes. Others are of a mixed nature: thus the arm of the Lake of the Four Cantons which runs towards Fluelen, is a cleft-lake, and that extending towards Unterwalden a combe-lake; and the Italian lakes present similar peculiarities. As in the cleft-lakes the rocky walls ascend steeply, often nearly perpendicularly from the water, and in many cases approach each other very closely (as on the Lac de Brenêts), they have a remarkably picturesque character; the combe-lakes are sometimes surrounded by boldly rising rocky masses; and on the basin-lakes the slopes rise in gentle undulations.

As these lakes belong to a period of upheaval, and owe their origin to fissures determined by the stratification of the moun-

* Mousson, "Ueber die natürlichen Verhältnisse der Thermen von Aix" (Denkschriften, 1847), and 'Geologische Skizze der Umgebungen von Baden,' 1840.

† This is demonstrated by Prof. Desor in his memoir "De la Physiognomie des Lacs Suisses" (Revue Suisse, 1860), and "Quelques Considérations sur la Classification des Lacs" (Atti Soc. di Lugano, 1861).

tains, they have been designated *orographic* lakes, in contra-distinction to those lakes which have been produced by erosion.

In order to explain the stratification of the Swiss moun-tains, some sections may here be noticed which Prof. Heer has borrowed from Studer's 'Geology of Switzerland' (vol. ii. p. 324) :—

Fig. 366.

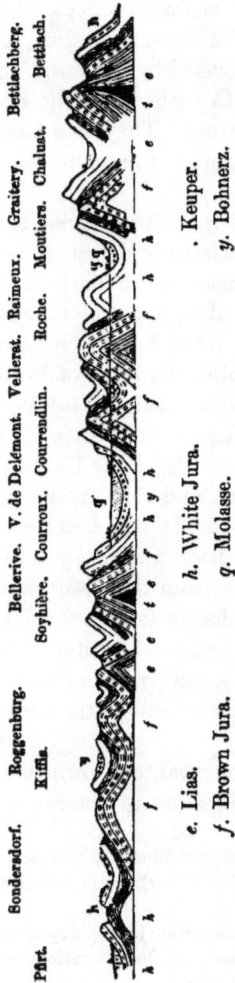

I. A section through the Jura in the direction from Soleure to Pfirt. The examination of this section shows the numerous undulations of the moun-tains, the open and denuded arches, and the basin- and combe-valleys which environ them. Here and there (as, especially, between Moutiers and Soy-hière) the mountain-chains are broken through by clefts which have revealed their internal structure. They show that here the Keuper forms the nucleus of the mountains, and that it is followed by the Lias, and then by the Brown and White Jura. In the broad valley of Delsberg the beds of the White Jura are covered by the Eocene deposit of the pea-ore; and over this is the Mio-cene, which also occupies the bottom of the valley of Moutiers.

II. A second very instructive ex-ample is furnished by the section from the Lake of Wallenstadt towards Ap-penzell (Studer, Geol. der Schweiz. ii. p. 193). Even in the Kurfirsten the Jurassic and Cretaceous beds are un-settled; and in the Appenzell Alps they are thrown together in so confused a manner that it was only by untiring investigations, continued for years, that Prof. Escher de la Linth succeeded in disentangling this Gordian knot. The section (fig. 367) shows six compressed arches, some of which

Fig. 367.

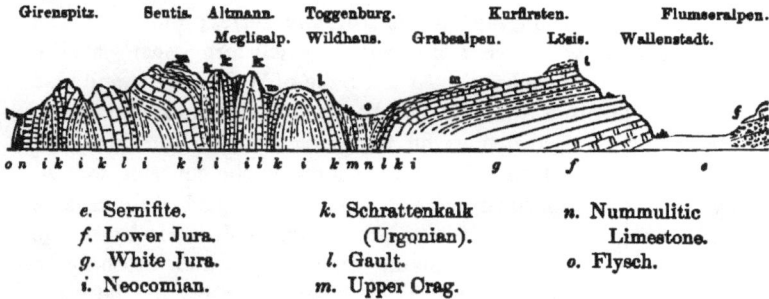

e. Sernifite.
f. Lower Jura.
g. White Jura.
i. Neocomian.

k. Schrattenkalk
   (Urgonian).
l. Gault.
m. Upper Orag.

n. Nummulitic
   Limestone.
o. Flysch.

rise so abruptly that their sides appear parallel nearly to the summit. At the top they are generally cleft down to the Lower Cretaceous or Neocomian deposits; but the highest point (the Sentis, 2504 metres) is formed by the Upper Cretaceous or Seewen Limestone. The newest formations represented in this mountain-system are the Nummulite Limestone and the Flysch.

III. The complication of the beds in the Canton of Glaris is still more decided, as may be seen by a glance at the section

Fig. 368.

a. Granite.
a'. Gneiss.
x. Diorite and iron-
   stone.

c. Sernifite.
c'. Quartzite Talc.
e. Jura.
g. Lias.

i. Neocomian.
o. Nummulitic Limestone
   and Flysch.

from Flums to Trons (fig. 368—from Studer's Geol. der Schweiz, vol. i. p. 423).

Here, in the valley of the Sernf, are seen the Flysch rocks, which have been already described (vol. i. p. 255), rising from the bottom of the valley to a height of several thousand feet. Upon these rocks there lies (as at Gantstock and Kärpf) a band of limestome belonging to the Jurassic series; and over the limestone are vast masses of sernifite, which forms nearly all the summits of the Freiberg. At the Lake of Wallenstadt, and also on the Glärnisch, the sernifite lies below the oldest limestone strata. Although it may be imagined that the sernifite had forced its way up from below, had penetrated the covering formed by the Flysch and calcareous deposits, and had pushed them aside and covered them up, still the occurrence of Jurassic limestone beds above the Flysch remains unexplained, and can only be accounted for by assuming that a large portion of the older masses slid over the newer rocks. A similar explanation is needed for the stratification of the Glärnisch, the foot of which consists of Nummulite limestone, over which are Jurassic and Cretaceous formations in a regular and partly in a horizontal position.

These upheavals and depressions have exerted the greatest influence not only upon the prominent features of Switzerland, but also upon the distribution of the Swiss waters. This is so much the case that even the direction of the flow of water and its collection in lakes is due to upheavals and depressions; and on these causes depends the distribution of Swiss land and water. As soon as the land becomes raised above the level of the sea, the water must run off; and it returns again when the land has sunk below its level. Prof. Heer has already repeatedly discussed this distribution of sea and land in various geological periods, and has endeavoured to illustrate it pictorially for the Middle Jurassic period (vol. i. p. 168, fig. 97), for the Cretaceous period (vol. i. p. 175, fig. 98), and for the middle stage of the Miocene period (vol. i. p. 296, fig. 154). A comparison of what has been said will give us an idea how these changes have gradually been brought about, and how Switzerland has slowly risen from the sea. In connexion with this subject Prof. Heer mentions that, probably at a very early period, a decided depression of the country took place between the island of the

Black Forest and that of the anthracite schists (the Carboniferous island), and that the lowering of the ground increased in the direction from the Jura towards the existing Alps, so that it attained its maximum on the southern side. Hence, when the land was upheaved, shallow water and firm land were produced along the Jura earlier than along the Alps. A marine lagoon remained along the Alps during the period of transition from the Jurassic to the Cretaceous epoch, and even to the Eocene period, the Jura being all the while dry. It is very remarkable that the Helvetic Miocene sea never invaded the region of the Alps, although it left deposits in the district of the Jura, as for instance at La Chaux de Fonds and at Locle. Therefore the land in the Alps must have been more elevated than in the Jura after the formation of the Flysch, and this upheaval continued to the time when the Helvetic sea covered the low grounds, and the Eocene Alpine formations rose above the sea, and the Jurassic Eocene was under water; and yet the Alpine Eocene strata had been produced in the sea and the Jurassic Eocene owed its origin to fresh water. These circumstances show us at the same time that as the Jura and the Alps present such different characteristics, the upheaval of the land mest furnish the best explanation of the phenomena under consideration.

To ascertain the *periods during which upheavals or depressions took place in Swiss mountain-masses*, we must consult the relative positions of the strata. Near Utznach the lignites, or paper-coals, lie horizontally upon the perpendicularly raised sandstone rocks (see p. 152, fig. 329); so that it is clear that the upheaval of the Miocene took place before the deposition of the lignites. Where we meet with a deposit of this kind unconformable with the strata below it, we may always conclude that in the interval between the two formations a great change had taken place. When strata of different ages follow one another uniformly no partial or local upheaval can have occurred, although there may have been a general upheaval. When of two superimposed strata, the lower contains freshwater animals, and the upper marine animals, we may conclude that at the time of the formation of the freshwater bed the land stood above the level of the sea, and that during the formation of the marine stratum the land had sunk down beneath the sea, even though a uniform and regular appearance may be presented by the rocks.

The alternation of freshwater and marine deposits, like unconformity of stratification, shows us that changes of level took place at various times, and must have exerted the greatest influence upon the configuration of the land.

The anthracite-schists with their land plants are covered in many cases (as near Petitcœur) by marine Liassic strata, and must therefore have been under the sea during the Lias period. Hence in the Liassic district a *depression* took place after the Carboniferous period. From the period of the Trias, however, a *rising* of the land is to be recognized in Northern Switzerland, since the Keuper follows upon the marine Mussel-Limestone (vol. i. p. 47). This rising continued up to the middle Schambelen beds of the Lower Lias, which represent the maximum of elevation (vol. i. p. 67) ; and then commenced a *sinking* of the land, which must have taken place pretty rapidly, seeing that the land formation of Schambelen is overlain by marine strata, which contain the same species of animals as the lower marine deposits.

This sinking of the land continued till the time of the Brown Jura. During the deposition of the White Jura a gradual upheaval again took place, and this attained its maximum at the close of the Jurassic period. The whole chain of the Swiss Jura rose from east to west out of the sea, and became dry land. We have, however, already shown (vol. i. pp. 171, 172) that during this long period many oscillations occurred, so that within its limits secondary upheavals and depressions may be recognized. The final result was an upheaval, the effects of which are displayed in France, Germany, and England, and must therefore be described as a continental movement. It attained its maximum at the time of the formation of the Wealden. Then a depression of the ground again occurred; as early as the Valangian stage the sea penetrated once more into the south-west of Switzerland, and, gradually spreading further and further, no doubt in consequence of a continued sinking of the ground, attained its maximum in the

middle of the Cretaceous period. At the period of the Upper
Cretaceous formation the land again began to rise; the sea disappeared from the region of the Jura, which, during the whole
Eocene period was converted into dry land (see vol. i. p. 271 *et
seqq.*); and this upheaval was continued until the end of the
Aquitanian stage of the Miocene period, the sea disappearing
also from the region of the Alps, and leaving only a few lagoons,
which then became converted into freshwater lakes, so that when
the upheaval had attained its maximum the sea for the first time
retired from Switzerland. During this long period of elevation
a partial upheaval must also have taken place in the direction
of the Alps after the deposition of the Nummulitic Limestone
and the Flysch, by which the whole region of the Alps was
finally removed from the influence of the sea. On the other
hand, during the Tongrian period, a depression must have
occurred in the north-west of Switzerland, permitting the
Tongrian sea to penetrate as far as Basle, Porrentruy, and
Delsberg.

A continental depression commenced, however, at the time of
the formation of the Grey Miocene, and attained its maximum
during the Helvetian stage, by which the Swiss low grounds
were once more covered by the sea. This was followed again by
a continental upheaval, so that at the time of the Upper Brown-
coal formation (in the Œningian stage) all the land was above
the level of the sea, and even the masses of sand and stone which
had been washed into the sea were elevated. The last upheaval
took place at a later period, after the whole of the stages of the
Swiss Miocene had been deposited; and this upheaval is the most
important of all, as it caused the present configuration of Switzerland. The Miocene is deposited horizontally in the Swiss
low grounds, and is upraised in the vicinity of the Alps, and
along the whole Alpine chain is not only thrown up in the shape
of a roof * (vol. i. p. 287), but is for a great extent even covered

---

* On the geological map the direction of this anticlinal line is indicated,
which may be traced from the valley of the Rhine to Geneva. In Eastern
Switzerland two folds may be recognized in it; so that two arches have been
formed, which, however, have been pressed close to one another.

by older strata which have been pushed over it, so that without doubt the upheaval of the chain of the Alps did not occur until after the deposition of the Miocene; and, as the Alpine upheaval was completed at the time of the formation of the paper-coal or lignite, it must belong to the intermediate or Pliocene period. During the Pliocene, therefore, the grandest changes in the orographic formation of Switzerland took place. At this time the crystalline rocks, which probably formed an island even in the Carboniferous period (vol. i. p. 3), were thrown up into stupendous mountains by an enormous pressure acting upon them from the interior of the earth. By them the stratified rocks, which in the lapse of ages had surrounded them like a mantle, were broken through and driven up by lateral pressure into lofty saddles, or cleft into ridges, or even tilted over, and their fragments, like the slabs of ice produced on the breaking-up of the ice in a river, were pushed one over the other; and in this way have been produced the infinitely varied mountain-forms which lend such a charm to Swiss scenery. "Just as a crater with an abrupt inner precipice surrounds a central volcanic focus," says Studer, in his 'Geology of Switzerland' (vol. i. p. 165), "so may one, two, or three limestone ranges lean towards the steep rocky walls of the granite mountains, often reaching up into the region of perpetual snow, and their strata may dip away from the central range." The origin of the most magnificent landscapes of Switzerland is therefore to be traced to the crystalline rocks traversing the centre of the country and forming its highest mountains. The central Alps follow generally a direction from west-south-west to east-north-east, by no means forming a connected mass, but capable of division into a number of sections, the massive rocks of which are separated by stratified (Neptunian) strata. Studer distinguishes eleven such central masses, apparently due to distinct foci of elevation, which, however, were probably all at the same time in activity.

The mass of which these central rocks consists belongs to the primæval formation of the earth; but it is only in comparatively late times that these ancient rocks have risen into vast mountains. No doubt the region of the Swiss Alps was a mountainous country in the Tertiary period (vol. i. p. 284); but the mountains probably were not high; for at the time of the formation of the Nummulitic limestone of the Flysch the sea extended into the middle of the region now occupied by the Alps. The Flysch, formed in the sea, was already elevated at the close of the Eocene period; but it was not until the Pliocene that it was thrown up to a height of 8000 feet above the sea; and the Tertiary shell-beds of the Dent du Midi occur at an elevation of 10,940 feet. This upheaval must consequently have been on a remarkably magnificent scale.

Contemporaneously with the upheaval of the Alps, the Jura mountains were elevated. A great part of the Jura had been raised above the sea-level in the Upper Cretaceous period; and a great alteration took place in Pliocene times, as in many places the margin of the Jurassic system has been thrown over the Miocene. The freshwater limestones of Locle, which belong to the Œningian stage, demonstrate that this Jurassic upheaval took place after the Œningian epoch. These limestones have not only been elevated, but thrown over, and they fall towards the north-west; and thus the newer formations have the appearance of being more deeply seated than the older ones. Hence, like the last upheaval of the Alps, the final elevation of the Jura belongs to the Pliocene period, and the movement of the two mountain-ranges was connected. But it is not ascertained whether a lateral pressure took place from the Alps, as supposed by Studer, and more recently by Thurmann, or whether the focus of the movement is to be sought in the Jura itself. A lateral pressure of such power from the Alps would have affected the horizontal stratification of the Miocene beds which spread between the Jura and the Alps; and their level position renders this theory doubtful. Under any circumstances the upheaval of the Jura will have been influenced by the crystalline rock-mass of the Black Forest*; and therefore, as regards the phenomena of elevation, the Jura near the Black Forest, and in the Cantons of Basle, Argovia, and Schaffhausen, differs much from the western Jura.

* See vol. i. pp. 48 & 168.

The following Table exhibits the various periods of elevation and depression of the ground in Switzerland :—

UPHEAVAL OF THE GROUND.	DEPRESSION OF THE GROUND.
	1. At the close of the Carboniferous period.
1. From the Trias to the Lower Lias.	
	2. From the Lias to the Brown Jura.
2. From the White Jura to the close of the Wealden (Lower Cretaceous formation).	
	3. From the Valangian stage (Lower Cretaceous) to the Middle Cretaceous).
3. From the Upper Cretaceous to the Aquitanian stage of the Miocene. A partial upheaval along the Alps at the close of the Eocene period.	At the Tongrian epoch (Lower Miocene) in North-western Switzerland.
	4. From the Grey Miocene to the Helvetian stage (Middle Miocene).
4. From the Helvetian stage (Middle Miocene) to the close of the Œningian stage (Upper Miocene).	
5. Upheaval of the Alps and Jura in Pliocene times.	

These changes of level did not occur suddenly, but in all probability very gradually. But when people assert that the last Pliocene upheaval of the Alps also took place so gradually and imperceptibly that, if the district had been inhabited by men, they would not have suspected what was going on, it must be borne in mind that the dislocations were colossal, that the tilting-over piled rock-masses several thousand feet in height one upon another, that deep fissures tore asunder whole mountains, and that enormous masses of débris accumulated which were thrown into valleys, and formed there complete mountains.

It is very improbable that the rocky wall of the Glärnisch, 6000 feet in height, could have quite imperceptibly slid over the newer Nummulitic deposits which underlie it, or that the tearing away of the Galanda from the chain of the Kurfirsten-Alvier, with which it forms so remarkable a semicircle round the Sernifite mountains of the Canton of Glaris, could have silently taken place, or that the descent from the Glärnisch of the hills which rise from the bottom of the valley of Glaris (the Bergli and Bürgli) could have noiselessly occurred. Formerly these great overturnings of hills were supposed to have taken place too suddenly and too rapidly; but now the opposite extreme is in vogue, and periods of millions of years are required, over which gigantic changes are continued, so as to adapt the movements of nature to what man has experienced and witnessed.

Let it be remembered how minute a portion of geological annals is embraced in the historic period, and how little man has seen of the prodigious revolutions which the earth has gone through. The notion that these processes have always gone on uniformly and without interruption can hardly be correct; and we rather find that after long periods of repose the grandest changes take place. Thus, after the long time of quiet development which characterized the Carboniferous period, came the stormy Permian epoch, which, in a comparatively short time, brought about a complete transformation of the character of nature; so also we have seen that the grandest transformation in the whole external features of Switzerland was effected in the comparatively short Pliocene period.

During Miocene times, in consequence of continental depressions and elevations, the Swiss low lands were overflowed sometimes by the sea and sometimes by fresh water; but these changes were far more superficial than the movement of the Pliocene period, when, by the elevation of the colossal rock-masses, not only was produced the marvellous structure of the Swiss Alps, but such a lateral pressure was exerted even upon the neighbouring Miocene that along its whole margin from the Lake of Constance to Geneva it was piled up, in a zone several miles broad, into hills and mountains which attained an elevation

of 1956 metres (or 2139 yards) in the Speer, and of 1800 metres
(or 1968·5 yards) in the Rigi.   And yet it is extremely probable
that the time between the formation of the first or Tongrian
stage of the Miocene and the fifth or Œningian stage of the
Miocene was much longer than the Pliocene period.   The stratification of the Swiss Alps shows that, in the history of their
development, periods of comparative repose have alternated with
times of deep-seated transformations.

   It may now be asked, In what relation do geological periods
stand to the eras of human history? and can the duration of the
various geological periods and the intervals up to the present
time be expressed in definite numbers?   Before answering these
questions let us try to ascertain what measure can be applied to
the examination of these relations.   Man employs, as a measure
of time, the length of his own life between his birth and his
death; and the influence that this exerts upon all his ideas of
nature has been shown by the academician Charles de Baer, in
the following ingenious manner, easy to be understood.   De
Baer takes for his basis that the duration of man's life may be
reckoned at eighty years (or about 29,000 days) : he supposes
that this number is reduced to the thousandth part, or 29 days,
and that simultaneously the pulse becomes proportionably more
frequent, and the conception of external impressions * more

---

   * The conception of an external impression is determined by the time that
elapses between the sensation of the impression and its reception by the mind.
Thus, as has been ascertained by direct experiment, the impression produced
upon the retina of the eye in Man requires $\frac{1}{15}-\frac{1}{8}$ of a second to make its way
to the brain, and to be there transmitted to the mind.   The duration of this
movement must exert much influence upon the general conception of the external world; and there would be a different conception if these external impressions were only transmitted to the mind in a minute, or in ten minutes,
&c.—and especially as there would also be a change with respect to the trans-
mission of impressions due to the constant phenomena of the undulations of
sound and of light.

   [Some consideration may also be given to the power of the human mind
over space and time.   Cowper beautifully alludes to the rapidity of man's
thought in his verses, supposed to have been written by Alexander Selkirk
during his solitary abode in the island of Juan Fernandez :—

rapid. Such a man would, in the whole course of his life, only witness *one* revolution of the moon ; the change of the seasons he would be acquainted with only by tradition ; and many generations might have passed away since that period of great cold which we call *winter*. Reduced once more to one thousandth part, that is to say to a lifetime of forty to forty-two minutes (such as that of many Ephemeræ), to such a being the alternation of day and night would be unknown ; and if he were sufficiently intelligent to notice that during his life the sun had approached a little towards the western horizon, he would have no ground for supposing that that luminary would ever again rise in the east. If we follow the line of argument as to increased duration, we may imagine the life of man a thousand times as long, and his sensorial power of receiving impressions a thousand times as slow as it actually is, in fact so slow that day and night would disappear for him, and the sun would no longer appear as a ball, but as a fiery ring ; for it is well known that a ball when swung round on a string appears like a ring as soon as it attains such a velocity as to exceed our perceptive faculty."

A rational creature whose lifetime should embrace merely a period of a single day, would therefore acquire quite a different conception of the world from one who might live for a hundred or a thousand years, and by this means the measure which the long-lived individual would apply to the universe must become quite different from that of the ephemeral creature. But the lifetime of Man, the innate human measure of time, is excessively minute when compared with the duration of the universe. We

---

"How fleet is a glance of the mind !
  Compar'd with the speed of its flight,
The tempest itself lags behind
  And the swift-winged arrows of light.
When I think of my own native land
  In a moment I seem to be there."

It is difficult to set bounds to the development of the human mind, even under imaginary cases of a great reduction or an extraordinary extension of the term of human life.—EDITOR.]

become aware of this immediately when we compare the relations of time and those of space, and when we examine the means which Man is obliged to employ in order to obtain an idea, or at least a presentiment, of their overpowering grandeur.

We should remember that, although the earth, when compared and measured with our bodies, is certainly very large, it is almost infinitely small in comparison with the universe. The distance of China from Switzerland seems to us to be very great; but what are several thousand miles to the 91,430,000 English miles which separate the earth from the sun, or the twenty billions * of miles between the solar system and the nearest fixed star? We know of stars which are distant from us from three to six of such star-distances, and innumerable stars which the instruments of astronomers are not able to reach, and for some of which we may assume distances of 10,000 star-distances. A glance at the starry heavens therefore shows us stars beyond stars to infinite and inconceivable distances. And our solar system comprises the planet which is assigned to us as a habitation. Its developmental periods must be measured by a similar standard to the conditions of space in the universe; and whilst mathematical astronomy has found the means of expressing these by numbers, at least for the stars nearest to the earth, these powers of numerical expression are still wanting to geology; and easy as it is now to determine the sequence of the formations, and to say what is newer or what is older, it is just as difficult or, rather, impossible, to express the measure of time even approximately in absolute numbers. All attempts that have hitherto been made to obtain absolute numbers from aqueous deposits and erosions, from the formation of coral-reefs, and from the oscillations of the ground have led to no satisfactory results, because in early times the conditions which now exist may not have prevailed, and thus the standard which we bring with us may be erroneous. Nevertheless there can be no doubt that in this inquiry we have to deal with very high numbers. Even if the . grounds should be uncertain on which the supposition of Morlot

* [Of this distance some idea may be obtained by remembering that light could not travel so far in less than three years (Ferguson's 'Astronomy,' edited by Sir David Brewster, vol. ii. chap. xi.).—EDITOR.]

is based, that since the deposition of the rubbish-cones of Clarens, near the Lake of Geneva, which belong to the end of the drift period, at least 100,000 years have elapsed, yet numerous phenomena indicate the lapse of many thousands of years.

It has been already noticed (p. 199) that the drift period must have continued for an enormous time, which is shown by the increase and retirement of the glaciers, the dispersion of erratic blocks over the lowlands, the formation of beds of rivers, and the distribution of plants and animals. These varied and remarkable phenomena certainly required an excessively long lapse of time; and going back to their commencement we arrive at the Tertiary period. Through the stormy epoch which gave to the Swiss Alps their present external configuration, we reach the Miocene period. Let us consider all that took place during the Middle Tertiary epoch, from the marine Miocene of Basle to the Œningian formation— all the oscillations in the level of the ground, and all the changes in the nature of the land—and we shall be obliged to admit that such transformations could be effected only in the course of many thousands of years. And yet we are still upon soil on which the world of waters in general had nearly the same character as at present. But if we look further back to the Flysch and Nummulitic formations, to the Cretaceous period and the Jurassic sea, to the Trias and the Carboniferous deposits, and the older Palæozoic rocks, and to those primæval periods when the earth was still desert and void, one strange picture succeeds another, somewhat as in the heavens star starts forth beyond star in immeasurable distances, until we give up the task of calculating the number of years which may express those periods of time. But although time and space may be compared to a shoreless ocean, the spheres of the universe which move in that ethereal sea are nevertheless *finite* magnitudes; and as the distances of the nearest stars can be measured, the human intellect will perhaps some day discover the means of determining the distances of time which separate the different phases of the development of our planet. At present, however, the duration of these vast periods is not known; and when we speak of a thousand millions and of ten thousand millions of years as required for one among many geological formations, we do not consider

that these numbers, by their immensity, are just as little com-
prehended by the human mind as are the natural phenomena
which they should lay open before us.

Section 2. *Action of Water.*

Movements proceeding from the interior of the earth, and
modified by the character of the terrestrial crust, have produced
those wrinkles of the surface which we call mountains and valleys.   But in their further development water has been a very
important agent.   When, in summer, we walk over a large
glacier, we see not unfrequently on the surface a regular system
of little hills and valleys formed by the water flowing over the
ice.   This gives us a good idea of the process that must take
place when a river makes its way down an inclined plane.   Its
action is defined by the degree of inclination of the surface and
the mass of the water.   Wherever firm land exists, this action
of water will commence, and during all geological periods
water has assisted in determining the configuration of Switzerland.   In the earlier ages of the world, when the sea
threw its waves upon the shore, this action influenced the
formation of the coast; but the present form of Switzerland is
especially due to the waters of the Pliocene and Quaternary
periods.

A glance at the Swiss map shows that the mountain-chains
and longitudinal valleys produced by the upheaval of the Alps
follow a direction from south-west to north-east.   The flow of
the waters in this region was determined by the valleys which
owe their origin to the upheaval; and the main rivers, the Rhone
and Rhine, have the same direction from Coire to Martigny.
From Martigny to the Lake of Geneva transverse valleys cut
through the mountains; and the Rhone, following these gorges,
bends nearly at a right angle and flows towards the north-west.
The same direction is taken by the Rhine from Coire to Sargans;
but there, instead of passing through the great valley-lake
of Wallenstadt, the river follows the fissure (*cluse*) of the
Schollberg and flows into the Lake of Constance.   Although the
direction of these rivers and brooks of the Alpine region is determined by the stratification of the Swiss mountains, the

streams themselves have for thousands of years been at work to
deepen their own beds. It could occur only to the boldest
Neptunist that the Rhine may have hollowed out the deep
ravines of the Roflen and the Via Mala, or that the Linth alone
formed the rocky cleft running from the Pantenbrück to the
Thierwehd, the depth of which may render a person giddy who
looks down it; but undoubtedly these mountain-streams, following natural fissures and gorges, have gradually widened and
deepened them.

A different result of aqueous action is seen in the region of
the Miocene. In Central and Eastern Switzerland the Miocene
formation is traversed by numerous brooks and rivers, the beds
of which have a direction nearly at right angles with the line of
the Alpine chain. Here we may observe that the Miocene lies
horizontally, and is only upraised at its edges, so that, at least
in the horizontal portion, neither hills nor valleys have been
produced by foldings. In this district hills and valleys could
only originate by erosions, which may have commenced in the
period of the Miocene, although their chief activity belongs to
the Pliocene period; for we see in many places that the strata
of the newest Miocene rocks on the two sides of a valley exactly
correspond, and therefore, no doubt, were once connected, whilst
they are now separated by a deep valley. We have already
(vol. i. pp. 301, 302, and vol. ii. p. 116) attempted to describe
the appearance of the land in the later period of the Miocene;
and the localities there described should be considered with
reference to the subsequent changes of the Pliocene epoch. It
would appear that these changes were connected with the large
freshwater lake spreading over the Cantons of Zurich and Thurgovia in Eastern Switzerland, along the Alps (p. 116). Precisely in this region the Miocene was much upheaved, and in
the place of the bed of the lake high mountains (such as the
Speer and the Righi) rose aloft. Great masses of water were
poured over the horizontal Miocene, and flowed off in a direction
almost perpendicular to the line of upheaval, causing, with the
waters coming from the ascending region of the Alps, those
enormous erosions which so greatly exceed any thing that we
now witness. All the gorges and valleys which traverse the
region of the Miocene have been eroded by rivers and brooks;

s 2

the chains of hills are merely the remains of the former surface of the Miocene; and in a similar manner the smaller lake-basins of that district may have originated *.

In the north of Switzerland the waters met the hard and lofty masses of the Jura, and flowed on at their feet until they arrived at places where transverse valleys had cut through chain of the Jura; through these openings the streams rolled from the country. That this grand furrowing was, for the most part, effected at the Drift epoch is shown by the fact that the distribution of the glaciers and of their moraines and boulders is governed by the present formation of the valleys, so that these must have been at that time in existence, as has been already shown (p. 184). The Rhine, also, then flowed in its present bed (pp. 217, 218); whilst during the Miocene period the waters took a different direction (vol. i. pp. 303, 304), and the outflow through Alsace was closed. Consequently the erosions of the Miocene coincide in time with the upheaval of the Alps, which took place gradually; and the rivers must have by degrees acquired a greater fall, and their erosive power must have increased. A new system of water-movement then prevailed, deriving its impulse and character from the upheaval of the Alps and the waters flowing down from them. The valleys produced by the upheaval of the mountain district were continued into the region of the Miocene; and even the river-valleys and lake-basins

---

* Professor Desor regards erosion as the cause of the formation of all lakes of the Miocene district, not merely the small ones (such as the lakes of Greifen and of Pfäffikon), but also the Lakes of Zurich, Constance, and Geneva. He therefore calls them " erosion-lakes." Such erosion, however, could take place only when the water had a fall; and it must therefore be assumed in the case of these lakes that the bed of their outflow was formerly much deeper, and has been filled up. But this is by no means the case to such a degree as the depth of these lakes would require. Thus the lake of Zurich is in one place 266 metres (or 291 yards) in depth, and its bottom is therefore only 142 metres (or 155 yards) above the sea-level, and 123 metres (or 134·5 yards) below the level of the Rhine at Basle. Between Zurich and Basle the river passes in many places over rocks in position, as at the Betznau, 323 metres (or 353·2 yards) above the sea-level; and therefore the bed cannot then have been deeper. This renders it improbable that the Lake of Zurich originated only by erosion, and leads rather to the assumption of a local sinking. This applies also to the lakes of Constance and Geneva. (See Studer, " De l'Origine des Lacs Suisses," Bibl. Univ. 1864.)

belonging to the plains and produced by erosion are connected with the depressions in the Alps.

After the hills and valleys were formed, the lowlands of Switzerland were strewed over with pebbles. This work was performed by the glaciers, as has been already shown in detail (pp. 177, 178). When the glaciers descended from the region of the Alps into the low grounds at the commencement of the drift-period, they first filled up the valleys and lake-basins. Thus they formed a bridge, over which the masses of stone which they brought from the mountains could be carried forward to great distances. If the lake-basins had not been covered by glaciers, the masses of rubbish must undoubtedly have filled them up, and we should therefore now find them, not in the neighbourhood of the lakes, but in their beds. When the glaciers afterwards retired, the waters of the lakes again became limpid. Obligation is therefore due to the glaciers for the preservation of the lakes, which are among the chief ornaments of Switzerland *. In those mountain-regions which are not covered by glaciers, lakes are consequently wanting, as in the Himalayas, because, as Falconer has shown, no glaciers have protected the clefts of the mountains from being filled up with rubbish.

Moraines have here and there been left by Swiss glaciers at the outlets of lakes, so as to impede the outflow of water, and to cause an elevation of the surface of the lakes. Thus, near Zu-

---

* Professor Escher de la Linth has demonstrated this fact in his memoir 'Ueber die Gegend von Zürich in der letzten Periode der Vorwelt,' 1852. The occurrence of stratified drift under erratic blocks has led M. G. de Mortillet to the opinion that the lake-basins were filled up with rubbish, but afterwards hollowed out by the glaciers (see his 'Carte des anciens Glaciers du versant Italien des Alps,' and Gastaldi and Mortillet 'Sur la Théorie de l'Affouillement Glaciaire'), so that the present lake-basins were produced by the glaciers deepening and eroding their beds. Professors Ramsay and Tyndall have gone still further, and suppose even the valleys of the Alps to have been furrowed out by glaciers. These hypotheses are contradicted by the fact that a glacier does not attack the ground beneath it very deeply (see p. 189), as is shown by the termination of the Rosenlaui glacier, where the water flowing off has hollowed out a deeper bed than the glacier above it. And what powerful action must we assume for glaciers, as the depth of the Lago Maggiore is 400 metres (or 437 yards), and the depth of the Lake of Como is 400 metres (or 447 yards)! Professors Studer and Desor have, with great justice, stated their opinion against any such view of the case.

rich the Limmat breaks through a moraine, and the lakes of Iseo and Garda are kept up by a barrier of ancient glacier-rubbish. Examples of moraine-lakes are shown at Sempach and Baldegg, as well as in the small lakes of Pusiano, Annone, and Alserio in the Brianza, since their outflow.is hemmed in by great masses of glacier-rubbish, which probably reach down to the old river-bed and have stopped it up.

Drift-glaciers have aided in the preservation of Swiss lakes; and they have also materially assisted in doing away with the inequalities of the land, since innumerable depressions have been filled up by the enormous masses of rubbish which they carried with them. By the melting-away of the glaciers vast quantities of water must have been produced, which have borne down sand and stones to a distance and have deepened the beds of rivers and brooks, and thus have taken an important part in changing the configuration of the land. During the drift-period a much greater amount of aqueous precipitation probably took place, and the climate was not only colder, but also more moist than at present; and thus an explanation may be given of the immense accumulation of ice at that epoch. Swiss mountains in those ages must have been worn and weathered on a grand scale, the evidence of which remains in the enormous mass of stones which have fallen down from them and been distributed all over the lowlands.

During the drift-period, as in our own days, the congelation of water was one of the principal agents in the disintegration of rocks. Water being absorbed by all the fissures of the rocks, and expanding by frost, the rocks split up or the fissures become enlarged; and the effect will be the greater the more frequently this succession of freezing and thawing takes place. Prof. Heer is convinced that in the High Alps of Switzerland, as well as in the extreme north, this phenomenon has a much more decided action than erosion.

Section 3. *The Climates of the various Geological periods.*

The plants and animals have shown us that the climate of the primæval world was very different from that in which we live, and that it was subjected to numerous changes. Thus, with re-

gard to all the older geological periods from the Carboniferous
to the Tertiary, their plants and animals, so far as they can be
compared with those now living, approach nearest to those of
warm and torrid zones ; and Prof. Heer cannot conclude with
any certainty as to there having been any rising or falling
of the temperature during this immensely long time. In the
Tertiary period, and especially during the Miocene epoch,
abundant materials illustrative of temperature are found; and
Prof. Heer has therefore entered into detail on this subject
(p. 126 &c.). He has found that, in the time of the Lower
Miocene, the climate of Europe was about 9° C. (or 16°·2 F.)
warmer than at present, and in that of the Upper Miocene the
European climate was about 7° C (or 12°·6 F.) warmer than in
our time, and that even then a distribution occurred of heat in
zones, of which no traces are found in the most ancient periods.
This higher temperature of Swiss Miocene land may be in part
explained by the form of Europe at that time. A different distribution of land and water is seen in the map of Central Europe
(fig. 154, vol. i. p. 296) at the Middle Miocene period. The
eastern sea, which extended into Switzerland, must have exerted
a warming influence, as it was connected with the Indian Ocean
through the Red Sea, and perhaps also through the Persian
Gulf. From this tropical sea a current of warm water, like the
existing Gulf-stream in the Atlantic Ocean, must have flowed
towards the northern seas and warmed their waters, exerting a
powerful influence upon the conditions of temperature of the
surrounding lands by means of the broad arms of the sea which
penetrated into the heart of Europe. The winter temperature
must have been elevated, and the climate must have been more
insular and uniform. The sea surrounding the land must have
produced a moist climate ; and the mountains, which, although
low, were nevertheless in existence, must have contributed to
the condensation of vapours rising from the sea, and to their
conversion into rain. The Gulf-stream, after being warmed in
Central America, moves across the Atlantic to Western Europe,
and raises the mean annual temperature of Western France (in
the latitude of Rochelle) by about 4° C. (or 7°·2 F.). If a
similar influence be assumed for Central Europe from the Miocene Indian Gulf-stream, we obtain the same elevation of 4° C.,

and there still remains a temperature of 5° C. (or 9° F.) to be accounted for.

As the action of an Asiatic gulf-stream could not extend to Iceland, Greenland, and North America, the high temperature of those regions in Miocene times requires explanation. It appears probable that a general source of heat existed in the Miocene period, influencing the whole northern hemisphere. In an earlier part of this volume the opinion has been expressed (p. 225) that, in the Tertiary epoch, a great continent united Europe with North America; and if this was the case, that extent of land must be taken into account.

A considerable influence must have been exerted by such an Atlantic continent on the climate of Europe, but not sufficient to explain the difference of 5° C. (or 9° F.), already mentioned. If the continent of Atlantis had extended across from Europe to America, the refrigerating influence of an icy sea could not have sent its icebergs into the Atlantic Ocean; and if the Atlantis had extended southwards to the tropical zone, the warm Gulf-stream would only have reached the south-west coast of France. The Atlantic continent should have raised the summer temperature of the northern hemisphere, and especially that of Iceland, comprised within its limits; and it ought to have lowered the temperature of the winter; but the hypothesis of this Atlantic continent leaves unexplained the elevated temperature of Greenland, Spitzbergen, and the north of America.

It is impossible, in the present state of science, to determine satisfactorily the circumstances from which the increase of heat in the Arctic zone at the Miocene period was derived, especially with reference to the Miocene flora. Nothing but hypotheses can be presented on this subject, among the most plausible of which are the following :—1. Change of climate arising from the diminution of heat belonging to the earth; 2. Modification of the sun itself; 3. Change of position of the earth with regard to to the sun; and, 4. Irregularity of temperature in ethereal space.

Before entering upon an examination of these different hypotheses, Prof. Heer reminds the reader that, from the Palæozoic period to that of the Cretaceous formation, the organic world of the different geological ages, so far as it is at present known, does not afford any evidence of changes of climate, and that the climate of the Arctic zone, at least during the Carboniferous and Lower Cretaceous periods, did not differ from that prevailing in the latitudes of Switzerland. In the Tertiary epoch a distribution of heat is observable in zones; but the decrease of temperature towards the poles was much less marked than at present. Whilst the tropical zone was probably scarcely warmer than in our time, Central Europe, during the Lower Miocene period, had a climate nearly equivalent to that of the southern United States (p. 140) and to the climate of the north of Africa. Under the Arctic zone in 78° N. lat., the island of Spitzbergen was covered with forests of swamp-cypress (*Taxodium distichum*), *Sequoia*, numerous species of pines, plane-trees, walnuts, oaks, and lime-trees—a fact which justifies the belief that forest vegetation extended to the pole itself, if this central locality was surrounded by solid ground. The difference between the fauna and flora of the Miocene epoch and that of the present day must have increased in passing from the equator towards the poles.

A decrease of temperature took place during the Miocene period (pp. 137, 138); and the diminution of heat continued during the Pliocene epoch, as appears incontestably from the change brought about in the marine fauna (p. 172). At the close of the Pliocene epoch the temperature may have been similar to that of the present day. During the drift-period it sank several degrees below the present mean temperature, and remained at this low point for thousands of years, thus constituting the first Glacial period. The formation of the Lignites, which followed this period, indicates a reelevation of temperature in Switzerland; and thus the temperature reached the point at which it now stands. In the south of France and in England the temperature seems to have been a little higher; in the forest-bed of the Norfolk coast the same species of plants have been found as in the Swiss lignite-beds, as well as the same species of rhinoceros (*R. etruscus*) and the same elephant (*E. antiquus*); to these animals must be added *Elephas meridionalis* and *Hippopotamus*. Together with these Pachyderms, there have been discovered at Grays Thurrock, in the county of Essex, a bivalve shell (*Cyrena fluminalis*) which no longer exists in

Europe, but still inhabits the Nile and the rivers of Asia Minor. In the calcareous tufas of Aygalades, near Marseilles, teeth of *Elephas antiquus* have been found with leaves of the European and Canarian laurels. From the island of Spitzbergen Prof. Heer has met with traces of a similar interglacial period which was a little warmer *.

The interglacial period was succeeded by a fresh increase of the glaciers, constituting a second Glacial period. It was followed by another elevation of temperature, which, taken as a whole, has continued to the present day, at least so far as we can ascertain by reference to human history †.

---

* See the 'Flora and Fauna of Spitzbergen' (p. 84), by Prof. Heer. As the phenomena of the Interglacial period have often been confounded with those of the Glacial period, several errors have been committed.

† It is probable that at the first appearance of Man in Switzerland the climate was considerably colder than at present. This hypothesis is founded upon the area ranged over by the reindeer in Europe at this period, which has been also called the "Reindeer period." In a station of reindeer near Veyrier, at the foot of the Salève, there have been found, besides bones, teeth, and fragments of the antlers of the reindeer, the bones of about thirty individuals of *Tetrao lagopus*, remains of the Alpine hare, the marmot, the chamois, the ibex, the bear, the lynx, &c. At Schussenried, near Ravensburg, the jaw of an Arctic fox and some mosses of the Arctic zone have been discovered with the reindeer. Advancing to the next stage in the history of Man, we arrive at the lake-dwellings. During the first part of that epoch which has been denominated the *Stone age*, the climate must have been the same as at the present day. This similarity of climate is demonstrated by well-preserved remains of plants. The lake-dwellers cultivated several kinds of grain, as, for example, barley, various species of wheat, among which are found the Egyptian wheat (*Triticum turgidum*), and two kinds of millet (*Panicum miliaceum* and *Setaria italica*). Among the weeds Prof. Heer has found the corn-cockle (*Agrostemma githago*) and the common centaury (*Centaurea cyanus*), which doubtless inhabited the cornfields, whilst the *Silene cretica* grew among the flax. Recently Prof. Heer has found several fruits of the *Silene cretica*, filled with well-preserved seeds, in bundles of flax-stalks buried in the lake-dwelling of Robenhausen; it now grows only in Mediterranean countries, where it is frequent in the fields of flax; and it thus indicates that the inhabitants of the Swiss lacustrine habitations imported their flax-seeds from the south of Europe, and that as the flax seed ripened at Robenhausen the climate of that locality was not colder than at the present day. This fact is confirmed by the spontaneously growing plants, among which Prof. Heer cites the yew (*Taxus*), hornbeam (*Carpinus*), holly (*Ilex*), and the water-chestnut (*Trapa*). The Arctic animals, such as the reindeer,

The first attempt at explaining these striking changes of climate was by the hypothesis of a decrease in the heat belonging to the earth. It was supposed that at its origin the earth had been a fused mass, which gradually became refrigerated in the cold medium that surrounded it. It is very probable that during the early Palæozoic and Carboniferous epochs the heat appertaining to the earth exerted a great influence upon climate. From the Carboniferous period down to the present day a slow and uniform decrease of temperature ought to have taken place : there are, however, no facts in confirmation of this hypothesis ; for the flora and fauna of the Jurassic period and of the Cretaceous period bear no traces of any such diminution of temperature. It is only in the Miocene epoch that the modification became strongly marked ; and at that geological period the temperate zone, and still more the Arctic zone, required so great an amount of heat that it was impossible to borrow it from the internal heat of the earth, seeing that the Miocene epoch, in point of time, is much nearer to the present time than to the Jurassic period, and it is still more distant from the Carboniferous epoch. Between the Miocene epoch and the present time a Glacial period occurred, indicating that during this intermediate epoch the temperature was considerably lower than that of the present day, at least in the northern hemisphere. If this phenomenon had been restricted to certain countries, it might have been in some degree explained by a different distribution of land and sea, and by changes of level. Very probably during the drift-epoch the land in the north of Russia was lower by some hundreds of feet, and, in consequence of this, the Arctic

---

have disappeared ; and their disappearance cannot be attributed to man, as the game which then inhabited the virgin forests of Switzerland is still abundant. The temperature of Switzerland was probably not higher than at the present day, as is shown by the presence of the mountain-pine (*Pinus montana*), the lowest region of which now in Switzerland is near the town of Zurich. Since the period of the lake-dwellings, the climate seems in general to have remained the same until the present time. Colder years alternate with warmer years ; and this alternation is observable for a series of years, so as to produce an advance or retreat of the glaciers in the Alps ; but these are merely inconstant variations, which do not enable us to infer profound and secular modifications of the climate of Europe.

sea was in connexion with the Baltic—a circumstance which must have lowered the temperature of the Baltic as well as of surrounding countries.

Professor Escher de la Linth first called attention to a second cause. Every inhabitant of the Swiss mountain-regions is aware that the warm south wind (known under the name of the "Föhn") exerts a great influence on the melting of the snow. It probably owes its existence, at least in part, to currents of hot air produced by the sands of the African deserts, and directed towards the north. But at the drift-epoch part of the desert of Sahara was submerged by the sea, as is proved by the marine animals that it contains; and this circumstance must have had an influence on the climate of Europe.

Charpentier and Lyell have expressed the opinion that the invasion of Switzerland by the glaciers might have been due to the greater altitude of the mountains, and to the general level of the country having been some thousands of feet higher than at present. If the whole mass of the Alpine rocks which now cover the plains of Switzerland could be replaced upon the mountains, the sides of the peaks and ridges would be considerably enlarged, and ravines and valleys would be filled up, but the absolute heights of the mountains would not be much increased. No evidence exists of a sinking of the whole of Switzerland since the Glacial epoch. At the level of the sea the temperature was lower in the drift-period than at the present day. This is proved by the discovery of species belonging to the Arctic fauna in the marine deposits of the drift-epoch in England, in Scandinavia, and even in Sicily. In whatever manner we regard the phenomena connected with glaciers, we find their traces not only in Europe, but also in the Caucasus, the Himalayas, in the Lebanon, the north of America, and even in New Zealand.

Dr. Blandet has maintained the hypothesis of a change produced in the sun itself to account for the changes of temperature in geological formations. He bases his theory on the ground advanced by Kant and Laplace, that at its origin the system consisted of an immense gaseous [revolving] mass, in which the planets were successively detached by the movement which had been impressed upon it. According to this hypothesis, the sun had at first a much greater volume, and by degrees became condensed in course of time to a smaller size. At the epoch when Mercury, the planet nearest to the sun, had not yet separated from the solar mass, and when the sun extended as far as the orbit of Mercury, the gigantic central luminary must have exerted upon the earth a very different influence from that of the present day, as the solar mass occupied about one fourth of the horizon. As the central body was then much less condensed than it is at present, a certain part of the sun would emit fewer rays, whether luminous or calorific, than it now does, and these rays would be more uniformly distributed over the earth.

The torrid zone, all the parts of which, at a given season, receive the solar rays perpendicularly, must have had a wider extent than at present. From this circumstance it follows that light and heat were more uniformly diffused over the earth, and that there could not be a night of six months about the poles. By degrees the mass of the sun, being more and more contracted by a continuous condensation, would be reduced gradually to its present volume. This hypothesis would explain more than one phenomenon of early geological ages, and especially the existence in high northern latitudes of arborescent evergreen plants ; but, in order to admit it, we must believe that a slow and uniformly continuous contraction took place in the mass of the sun, and that in consequence there was a slow and corresponding change in all the phenomena connected with the solar orb. It is very possible that during the earliest geological phases the sun was larger, and composed of a less dense mass than at present; but we must not lose sight of the fact that the Miocene epoch was comparatively near to our own time, at least if we appreciate the interval since the Miocene formation by a geological standard. At so late a period as the Miocene epoch it is improbable that the sun had remained in so imperfect a phase, while the crust of the earth and the plants and animals inhabiting it had attained to such a high degree of development. Besides, it has been already noticed that from the Carboniferous to the Cretaceous period no climatal changes can be proved to have taken place, whilst from the Miocene to the beginning of the Quaternary period, during a comparatively short time, a complete alteration took place, and the temperature of the Glacial epoch sank below the present level.   The hypothesis of Dr. Blandet does not explain these circumstances.

A change in the relative position of the earth and the sun has been suggested by Mr. James Croll in a series of memoirs, dwelling principally on the periodic changes in the excentricity of the earth's orbit.   This orbit, as is well known, is an ellipse, produced by the attractive influence of the great planets upon the movement of the earth ; and this ellipse moves within determinate limits in a cycle embracing thousands of years.   At present the orbit is constantly approaching the circular form, and in 23,900 years its excentricity will attain its minimum, and the orbit its maximum tendency towards a circle.   From that time it will gradually depart from the circular form.   The mean distance of the earth from the sun is 91,430,000 English miles. The greatest excentricity amounts to $\frac{1}{15}$ of this distance ; its smallest excentricity is only $\frac{1}{300}$.   At the period of the greatest excentricity the earth would be distant from the sun about 14,500,000 English miles more than at the period when the orbit most nearly approaches to the circular form ; this difference is at present 3,000,000 miles.

It must be borne in mind that in our time the earth is in perihelion during the winter of the northern hemisphere, and that in summer it is in aphelion.   This condition is also subject to a periodical change the cycle of which embraces about 21,000 years.   In about 10,000 years the summer of the northern hemisphere will coincide with the time when the earth is in perihelion, and the winter when it is in aphelion, whilst in the southern hemisphere these conditions will of course be reversed. It has, accordingly, been assumed that at periods when the orbit of the earth attained the maximum of its excentricity, and was at the same time in perihelion, one of the hemispheres had a shorter and warmer winter, and on the other hand a longer and cooler summer, whilst the reverse was the case in the other hemisphere—namely, a long and cold winter and a short and hot summer, because the greatest distance from the sun would then coincide with the winter.   From this Mr. Croll concludes that, during this long and cold winter there was formed so large a quantity of ice that the short summer, although hot, did not suffice to melt it entirely, that this ice, increasing and extending by degrees, would produce a decrease of temperature, and that the glacial epoch would be the result. Thus, while one hemisphere would pass through a glacial period, the other, on the contrary, would enjoy a warmer and more uniform climate, more especially as the marine currents which convey to high latitudes much heat proceeding from the torrid zone would take a different direction in consequence of the change of excentricity. Mr. Croll has determined the excentricity of the orbit for the last 3,000,000 years, and has thus found three periods of greatest excentricity. The first of these commenced 2,630,000 years ago, and terminated 2,460,000 years ago; the second commenced 980,000 years ago, and lasted 260,000 years; the third dates back 240,000 years, and would close 80,000 years ago. During these three periods of greatest excentricity the northern hemisphere would always be in one of its glacial periods when it had the longest winters (in its aphelion). During these periods the southern hemisphere would enjoy a milder climate. This state of things would change every 10,000 years. At each of these changes a warm period would succeed a colder one. According to this hypothesis, we should have not only a whole series of glacial periods interrupted by warmer periods, but also long periods in the most distant ages during which the climate would have been nearly like that of the present day. We might even say that these periods, taken on the whole, ought to be regarded as normal, whilst the others, corresponding to the great excentricities, would form the exceptions.

It may be objected to all these speculations that we do not sufficiently know the influence exerted upon the intensity or efficacy of the solar rays by the length of the course these rays have to traverse in order to arrive at the earth. Lyell has justly called attention to the fact that, according to Dove's calculations, the earth is warmer in the month of June (that is to say, in the season during which it is most distant from the sun) than in the month of December (when it approaches the sun most closely). This phenomenon is due to the distribution of land and sea, which is not the same in the northern and southern hemispheres, and hence the northern half of the globe has warmer summers than the southern hemisphere. This proves that the distribution of land and water is far more important in reference to climate than the greater or less excentricity of the earth's orbit, and that so predominant an influence ought not to be attributed to the variations of the orbit.

The plants and animals that the rocks have preserved for us by no means confirm Mr. Croll's theory. It is only for the Quaternary period that the Swiss can admit a glacial epoch, interrupted by the lignite formation of Utznach. As regards the geological ages anterior to the Quaternary period, no facts sufficiently well ascertained exist to enable Prof. Heer to draw the same conclusions as Mr. Croll*.

---

* Mr. Croll places the Quaternary (drift) glacial epoch between the years 240,000 and 80,000 before A.D. 1800; and he supposes that the period of the greatest excentricity of the earth's orbit which falls between the years 980,000 and 720,000 would correspond to a Miocene glacial epoch. But there is nothing to support this hypothesis, unless, indeed, it be the remarkable existence of blocks foreign to the locality which occur in the Miocene deposits of Superga, near Turin. Sir Charles Lyell is inclined to believe that these blocks were transported by glaciers (see 'Principles of Geology, vol. i. p. 207). These foreign blocks would have some analogy with the movement of the immense icebergs which still advance southwards as far as Newfoundland. But the presence of the blocks in the deposits of Superga is so isolated a fact that it is hazardous to base upon these blocks the theory of a Miocene glacial epoch, especially as the rocks which enclose them contain marine animals and land plants possessing the same subtropical character as those of other Miocene deposits. If at the Miocene epoch the country near Superga had had a colder climate, its effects would have made themselves felt by the flora and fauna, as is the case in the Quaternary glacial epoch. Mr. Croll places the third period of great excentricity between the years 2,630,000 and 2,400,000, which would correspond to the upper part of the Eocene. He supposes that this epoch had a glacial period.

In the Flysch rocks of this epoch large granite blocks occur in several parts of Switzerland, belonging to a granite foreign to the Swiss Alps. They have been considered in vol. i. pp. 256-270. The presence in the Flysch, at numerous localities, of foreign blocks combined with great poverty in organic remains is favourable to the hypothesis of Mr. Croll; but his theory does not rest upon data which have been scientifically investigated, and the facts are capable of other explanations. Mr. Croll accounts for the absence of traces of glacial periods in the older formations by modifications of the glacial soil due to erosions, which destroyed the ancient soil of the continents, carrying away with it all the débris of the glacial periods. Denudation has doubtless produced considerable modifications; but their importance is not so great as Mr. Croll imagines. Land deposits retain the masses of plants and animals

Perhaps the position of our planetary system in the heavens merits regard in the question under consideration. Besides the sun, there are in the heavens millions of starry bodies which transmit their luminous and calorific rays to the earth *. It is therefore possible that different regions of infinite space may possess different temperatures. This has been demonstrated by the celebrated mathematician Poisson, who noticed that the number of stars is so great that they form, as it were, a dome around us. We know also that the sun and the planets are constantly changing their position in space, and that probably the sun with the planets revolves round a centre of a higher order—that is to say, round a fixed star of much larger size, and vastly more distant. If, therefore, we may assume that the same temperature does not prevail throughout all space in the heavens, we shall obtain a simple explanation of the above-mentioned phenomena. Suppose the sun with its planets, during the Miocene epoch, to have traversed a portion of space warmer than that in which it now moves, all the regions of the earth must have participated equally in this increase of heat; the temperate, as well as the arctic zone, must have felt its influence. Hence at that time the distribution of heat on the surface of the globe would be more equable. In the epoch which may be termed a year of the planetary system, colder periods alternated with warmer ones: thus the Miocene period may be compared to the summer, the Glacial period to the winter, and the existing geological age to the spring, of the planetary system.

A good selection was made in the choice of the name Eocene to indicate the commencement of the Tertiary period: it may

---

of all geological ages, which formerly lived there. The soil of the ancient land is preserved in vast deposits of coal, as well as in those of lignite, which abound in so many localities, and also in the original sites of innumerable lacustrine formations of Europe filled with organic remains. For example, in the case of the Swiss Miocene, Prof. Heer finds in them the uninterrupted history of the flora and fauna of Switzerland without the intercalation of any glacial period.

* According to the investigations of Mr. Huggins, the heat produced by the radiation of the fixed stars is not unfelt on the earth, and may even be measured. With a calorimeter constructed by himself he has obtained manifest proofs of the heat furnished by Sirius, Pollux, and Arcturus.

be regarded as the dawn of the existing creation. It is announced by an abundant development of leafy trees (generally Dicotyledons) and of Mammalia. With the Eocene formation also began the distribution in zones of heat and life. The earth, and probably the whole solar system, in that epoch passed through a higher phase of their development. The conditions of terrestrial temperature were determined by the position of the globe with regard to the sun, and by the state of temperature in the regions of space. During earlier geological periods influences acted which had been connected either with the wide expansion of the solar mass or with the heat belonging to the earth itself. Temperature was, at all times, modified on the globe partly by the distribution of land and sea, and partly by the powerful agency of marine currents, which depended on the relative position of sea and land.

Part II. Organic Nature.

Looking back at the succession both of plants and animals in the various ages of the earth's history, we learn from numerous recent investigations that, at the limits of the geological periods, the species of animals and plants are as it were interlaced; and there is an analogy between these periods and the zones into which mountains are divided, to represent their characteristics at different elevations. Thus the higher boundary of the zone of trees indicates the spots where the forest ceases; but in favourable positions some trees may still be met with at a greater height. The zone of snow is at first represented by a few specks, and on going up the mountain we arrive at the fields of granular snow spreading far and wide. In like manner, geological periods have no sharp line of demarcation; they indicate the principal divisions of a *continuous development*, the limits of which are placed at those periods in which the greatest transformations were effected.

Organisms of different epochs are intimately connected. Species are found common to two consecutive periods; and the whole of organic nature, from its primæval commencement to the present day, has been altogether in perfect harmony.

A gradual approximation is manifest, in the organized world, of different geological periods towards the plants and animals which are living at the present day. On examining organisms belonging to the earlier ages of the earth's history, forms are found peculiar to those times, and foreign to the existing creation. But peculiar and strange as many of the ancient types appear to us, they all possess manifold relations to existing forms. They are constructed upon the same general plan. Hence the circle of living nature embraces the plants and animals of former ages. Even the most ancient plants and animals may find their place in systems of Natural History which are founded upon existing forms; nay, some genera of the present time actually range back to the earliest geological periods. We have already mentioned a genus of bivalves (*Lingula*, p. 233), which makes its appearance as early as the Cambrian stage of the Palæozoic strata; and in the Carboniferous formation and the Lias Prof. Heer is acquainted with a whole series of genera which agree with genera of the present day. As meteorites are in a manner messengers from distant spheres, which tell us that bodies moving in space consist of the same materials as the earth, so these genera of fossil animals are messengers from the most ancient times, declaring that from remote antiquity the same laws have prevailed, and the same types have been manifested down to our own time.

The number of *genera* common to recent and to preceding periods diminishes the higher we go in the series of animated nature : common *species* first make their appearance in the Cretaceous and Eocene periods. They are then few in number, and confined to the lowest forms ; but they become more numerous in the Middle Tertiary period, in which the genera were already for the most part identical with those now in existence. This approximation to living nature at the present day by no means occurs equally in all classes. It is manifested earlier in the simpler and older types of animals than in more recent and more highly organized forms. In the very ancient class of the Rhizopods some species identical with recent ones occur in the Cretaceous strata, according to Ehrenberg ; but this does not happen with the greater number of the species. Recent Mollusca cannot be traced beyond the Tertiary epoch ; and Mammalia are not only represented by different species in Tertiary times, but some of their genera in Tertiary strata are now extinct. With reference to another class of animals, the insect fauna of the Tertiary epoch differs more than the molluscan fauna from the living races of the present day; but among Miocene insects the cockroaches, grasshoppers, and Termites, which must be regarded as most ancient types, in some cases approach very nearly to existing forms.

The flora and fauna of the present day represent the most highly organized forms. Consequently in approaching a more perfect state of the vegetable and animal kingdoms, an advance in the organization of living creatures took place, and a definite progress may be traced in their development. In the most ancient periods we know only cellular Cryptogams (p. 233); in the Carboniferous epoch the vascular Cryptogams predominate, and from the Trias to the Chalk the Gymnosperms * (Conifers and Cycads). The Dicotyledonous flowering plants (leafy trees and shrubs) make their first appearance in the Cretaceous epoch, and only acquire their full development in the Tertiary period; and from that time they constitute the great mass of the flora. But in Tertiary periods the apetalous and lowest forms take the first rank, and the monopetalous types, which occupy the highest grades in the vegetable kingdom, only attain their fullest development in the existing creation. There is therefore unmistakably, on the whole, a progressive development from the more simply constructed towards the more complicated and consequently more highly organized types. And the same phenomenon is met with in the animal world. Palæozoic rocks offer us Zoophytes, Mollusca, Annulosa, and Vertebrata, or representatives of the four great main divisions of animals; but of the last there is only the lowest class, Fishes, and these are represented by peculiar forms indicative of a very inferior grade of

---

* Formerly Conifers and Cycads were united with Dicotyledons, but they are most nearly related to the vascular Cryptogams, and form the transition from the flowerless to the flowering plants, as is proved by the admirable investigations of Hoffmeister on the structure of their flowers and ovules. Their woody structure, also, is simpler than that of the Dicotyledons, as it consists of uniform cellls; and their pits, which were formerly regarded by some as of a glandular nature, cannot be taken as indications of higher organization.

organization. Reptiles first appear in the Carboniferous strata, and arrive at their full development in the Triassic and Jurassic formations. The Mammalia announce themselves, as it were, by a few prophetic species in the Upper Trias and the Jura; but these species belong to the Marsupials, which present the lowest grade of organization in the class, and the Mammalia only attain their great importance in Tertiary times (see vol. i. p. 275). The Palæozoic period may therefore be characterized as that of Cryptogams and Fishes, the Secondary as that of Gymnosperms and Reptiles, and the Tertiary as that of Dicotyledons and Mammals. Lastly, as the crowning achievement of the whole creation, appears *Man*, who, by his intellectual faculties, raises himself above all other animals, and is enabled not only to understand the laws of nature, and in some degree to subjugate Nature to his will, but also to find his God in the works of nature, and to become himself conscious of his own eternal destiny.

In the appearance of plants and animals in different geological ages a progressive development according to natural laws is manifested, beginning with the lower and more simply constructed forms and continued on to more highly organized creatures; and since this course of development has found its term in Man, no new species has been produced.

It must not, however, be imagined that in this gradual advance of organic nature link has followed link in a consecutive series; for instead of the highest plants approaching the lowest animals, it is found that the simplest unicellular animals are so nearly allied to the simplest plants that between them a line of demarkation can hardly be drawn. Consequently there is a common starting-point for the two kingdoms of nature as regards their simplest organisms; but on quitting this point each kingdom takes a special direction in its development, and their respective advances might very well be compared to a tree, which, branching in all directions, puts forth innumerable leaves and flowers, representing the existing fauna and flora.

The fundamdntal cause of this progressive development of the organic world in accordance with a definite plan must be innate; for the material elements were always the same, whilst the living creatures into which they enter are in a state of continual change, and present an infinite variety of forms and modes of organization.   Although, therefore, the typical distinctions of plants and animals are not produced by external conditions, such as climate and food, yet these two elements are of great importance both to animals and vegetables, which must adapt themselves to the world surrounding them in order that they may live in it.   In the most distant ages, when the sea still covered the whole earth, only aquatic plants and marine animals could have lived.   But aquatic life is less perfect than terrestrial life.   Aquatic plants and animals now generally possess a lower grade of organization than those of the land; and, indeed, both the vegetable and the animal kingdoms have their lowest and most primitive forms in the water.   That the inferior aquatic forms first appear upon the globe is therefore in accordance with the state of the surface of the earth.   As dry land was produced, new conditions of exist-ence were offered; and these must have prevailed more and more as the dry land increased in extent and in variety of structure, the climatic conditions being at the same time altered by the gradual cooling of the earth's crust and the frequent changes in the distribution of sea and land.   Hence, as the development of the solid crust of the earth advanced, its physical constitution became more and more complicated, and the fundamental condi-tions of the development of living organisms became more mul-tifarious.   But although, in consequence of these modifications of the crust of the earth a suitable place was furnished for the development of more and more highly organized creatures, the lower ones did not therefore disappear.   They are still repre-sented in the existing creation, and have still, as in the earliest periods of the earth's history, a definite purpose to fulfil.   The notion that the earlier creations were only the first essays, and " have served merely as preliminary studies for the highest pro-duction, namely Man," is consequently childish; for they also were perfect in their kind, inasmuch as they suited the conditions then prevailing on the earth.   But why our earth should have had to pass through such a course of development, and could not have come from the hands of the Creator fitted for the reception of the highest and noblest forms of life, is a question that could only be answered if we knew why we do not find here below any stability either for an isolated individual or for the ever moving and advancing intellectual and physical world.

There can be no doubt that in the course of ages the species of animals and plants have changed; but how this alteration has been effected, and why the older species have died out, and how the new ones have been produced, is still a mystery. Nothing but hypotheses are presented to elucidate the problem.

A withdrawal of the conditions of life brings about the extinction of ancient species. For instance, when there has been an upheaval of a district above the sea-level, the whole animal population of the water in the localities so raised up must have died off; and in like manner land animals must have perished in places which had sunk beneath the water. Species with a small area of distribution have thus, without doubt, become extinct, and, under similar circumstances, may still die out *. But these changes apparently have never affected the whole earth, and never thus produced a complete destruction of all living creatures. If we picture to ourselves the multifarious transformations which Switzerland has experienced in the lapse of ages, we shall always find, from the Trias to the Drift-period, firm land upon which terrestrial life could thrive, and also, up to the beginning of the Miocene period, sea in which marine animals could live. It may therefore be imagined that there has been no external cause for the important changes which have taken place in the organized world of Swiss regions.

We may conceive that to every species, as to every individual, a determinate age is assigned, and that a species must disappear

* Thus at the present day a beautiful large snail (*Helix subplicata*, Sow.) occurs only upon a small rock in the sea near Porto Santo. Formerly it was abundant upon that island, and occurs in its drift sand. If this rock should fall into the sea, this species would be extinct. The Seychelles palm (*Lodoicea sechellarum*) now only occurs rarely on the Seychelles Islands; and merely a few examples of the dragon-tree live in Madeira and the Canary islands: these remarkable trees are therefore approaching extinction.

[Dr. Le Maout and M. Decaisne, in their 'General system of Botany,' translated by Mrs. Hooker (p. 851), remark of the *Dracæna draco* that "the dragon-tree of Orotava is visited by all travellers in the Canary Islands. Its trunk below the lowest branches is 80 feet in height; and ten men holding hands can scarcely encircle it. When Teneriffe was discovered, in 1402, tradition affirms that it was already as large as it is now, a tradition confirmed by the slow growth of the young dragon-tree of the Canaries, of which the age is exactly known; whence it has been calculated that the dragon-tree of Orotava is the oldest plant now existing on the globe."—EDITOR.]

when its time has elapsed; but so long as we are unable to indicate a cause in the nature of the species for the limitation of time, there must be uncertainty in forming such limits of duration.

Darwin, in his celebrated book ' On the Origin of Species by Means of Natural Selection,' has endeavoured, in a most ingenious manner, to explain and combine the extinction of species and the origin of new ones. He starts from the ascertained fact that the number of individuals of plants and animals increases in geometrical ratio, which is not the case with their nutritive materials. A great number of plants and animals are therefore deprived of the space and nutriment which they require for life, and many must annually be destroyed. Thus a constant struggle for existence takes place, and is even produced between individuals of the same species, of which only a few attain maturity. If one of these individuals possesses any advantage over the others, it will more easily survive, whilst the weaker ones will languish and die. The former can bequeath its advantages to its posterity, and, when they increase in a definite direction, individuals may gradually be produced differing considerably from the first, and forming a new race.

This new race Darwin regards as a young species in course of formation; for if the development continues in the same direction, the difference by the continual accumulation during thousands of generations of deviations so small as to be scarcely perceptible, may become so great as to form what we call a species. The old species, however, would have disappeared because it could not sustain the competition with its younger and stronger descendants. Consequently old species would have been extinguished, and new ones produced in all cases where some of the younger individuals had acquired properties specially favourable to their continued development, and had transmitted these properties to their progeny, and, in consequence, displaced their unchanged relations. But the individuals of a species may also in course of time become developed in various directions, so that a whole group of species may originate from the divergent forms, and this is regarded as a *genus*. All the species of a genus would therefore have a species as their starting-point. But if we go still further back, the genera also coalesce; and then the species of an existing family would have had at their commencement a parent species from which they proceeded. In this way, Darwin arrives at the first beginnings of things, and assumes that there were only a few primitive fundamental types, from which all the species now living have been developed during an immeasurably long period of time.

To carry out this hypothesis consistently, we should have to admit that all species had a common origin, and that, becoming modified in the course of ages, they were developed in all directions. They would melt imperceptibly one into the other, so that if we could look over all that had ever been produced, no limit between one species and the species which follows would anywhere be found. What we call a species would be only the form manifested at a certain time, which can be distinguished from the allied species only because all intermediate forms have been lost, and have remained unknown to us ; and if we could discover these intermediate forms which once existed, all distinction of species would disappear. But everywhere in nature we see well-defined species, so that Darwin had to assume that we know only a very small portion of the plants and animals that have existed, and as it would be very remarkable if, in so extremely incomplete a series, any harmonious gradation had been displayed, the adherents of Darwin as much as possible explain away this gradation or deny it altogether.

As the Darwinian hypothesis seems to solve the great enigma of the origin and extinction of species in the simplest manner, Prof. Heer now inquires whether the natural phenomena of Switzerland admit of such an interpretation.

It has been observed that certain species pass from one geological period into the following one, and that of the Swiss Miocene marine Mollusca, even thirty-five per cent. are still in existence (pp. 91, 92). The descent of living individuals from those of the Tertiary period cannot be regarded as doubtful. Other species certainly differ in more or less essential points from those of the preceding period, but yet approach them so closely that we must assume the ancient species to have co-operated in their production ; and we cannot well imagine this cooperation to have taken place otherwise than by descent from the older species, the existing differences having been produced in the course of time. Many other plants and animals, however, completely differ from the earlier ones; they represent sharply defined types standing far away from all species known to Prof. Heer; and the bridge of transition is even wanting in the case of whole classes (*e. g.* the birds). Difficult as it may be to account for the origin of those types in which entirely new plans of structure are expressed, it seems more natural to derive them from the organic than from the inorganic world. Prof. Heer would have to assume that the great gaps have been produced by the extinction of species which have been lost. Prof. Heer therefore maintains that a genetic connexion exists through the whole organic world, because it is only by this supposition that he can form an idea of the origin of species, which can be brought into accordance with known and intelligible natural processes.

Here, however, arises the second important question—namely, *whether a perfectly gradual and imperceptible transformation of species, always going on without cessation,* really takes place, as Darwin and his adherents suppose, and which, of course, implies the constant production of new forms, even at the present time. This view is most decidedly contradicted by the facts which Prof. Heer has already communicated; for not only has no new species originated, so far as he knows, during the period of human history, but even the paper coals, which go back to a much earlier time, exhibit the existing flora.

Prof. Heer even meets with the same two varieties of the hazel which now clothe the Swiss hills, and a species of snail (p. 213, note) presents the same slight abnormal characteristic in the structure of its shell as its descendants now living near Sargans. Plants of the Swiss Alps also agree in part with those of the high northern latitudes; and these have probably issued from the same centre of origin. Even in the drift period such plants were moulded in exactly the same forms which they now exhibit in the high mountains of Switzerland as well as in the distant polar zone.

It has been already noticed that Mr. Darwin regards the mutual influence and selection of individuals as the principal agents in the variations of organic nature and in the origin of species; but it is manifest that the Swiss species on the Alps live under very different conditions from the Alpine species here and there found in the lowlands of Switzerland, and that these Alpine inhabitants of the plain exist under different conditions from their fellows of the same species in the polar zone.

The Swiss alpine species may be surrounded by species widely different from those of the original mountain-abode of the plants. They may be living under different physical conditions; yet they preserve their specific characteristics for thousands of years and during a succession of innumerable generations; and it is impossible to distinguish the descendants of the Alpine drift-flora now living in the Swiss Alps from plants of the drift-flora in Iceland and Greenland.

Marine animals justify similar observations. The "struggle for existence" was carried on under different conditions by the Norwegian lobsters inhabiting the depths of the Gulf of Quarnero, in the Adriatic, near Dalmatia, and by their fellows of the north of Europe; and yet they have preserved their forms and specific characters. Hence, it may be affirmed that no new species has had its origin since the drift-period. A certain number of species have disappeared, and great changes have taken place in the intermixture of forms. Under the influence of climate and of diverse localities, innumerable varieties have produced among themselves* fertile individuals; but so far as Prof. Heer knows, no new type has appeared.

A great geological division ended with the Tertiary period, which generally had its own species of plants and animals. The transformation of these organisms of nature occurred either at the end of the Pliocene epoch, or at the beginning of the drift-period; and there was no slow transition from the ancient to the modern species, but a transformation.

In the flora and fauna of preceding periods the same facts are observed. The same species maintain their existence through long periods of time, and often in all parts of the globe present

* Professor Heer agrees with Professor A. De Candolle and Dr. J. D. Hooker that a great number of the so-called species in our recent "Floras" are only varieties, which owe the specific ranks assigned to them only to the constantly increasing tendency to unnecessary subdivision. These varieties and races preserve their characters and prosper, especially where they are distant from their original stocks.

characteristics which are precisely the same*. If we examine the formation immediately following any early period which belongs to a new epoch, that formation may contain some species inherited from the preceding period, but the greater part of the species show us a new type, and present distinct characteristics.

Some common species may be found in the beds which separate two geological periods; but Prof. Heer has not noticed any form which would indicate a fusion of the species. The new forms contrast with the old ones as new money looks different from worn coins. Under the influence of altered climate and a change of locality, the new species may present numerous modifications, called "varieties," or they may have more decided variations, and give rise to "races;" but in their intermixture the species always produce fertile individuals, while the true hybrids are generally barren. Although a species may deviate into various forms, it nevertheless moves within a definitely appointed circle, and preserves its character with wonderful tenacity during thousands of years and innumerable generations, and under the most varied external conditions.

Prof. Heer maintains that in nature there is exhibited much less of a tendency towards the fusion of species than of a force manifested to preserve specific characteristics. Hence cultivated plants and domesticated animals show an inclination to return to their original wild forms, and between species there is usually

---

* The 'Bear-Island Flora' (French edition, p. 20) is instructive on this point. Almost all its species are identical with those of the lower formations of the Carboniferous period in Europe. The most important species occur also in the Greywackes of the Hartz and of Silesia, although these Graywackes belong to the upper stage of the Lower Carboniferous, whilst the strata of Bear Island form part of the lowest stage, and the whole formation of the Carboniferous limestone lies between them. Here, therefore, we have species which have remained the same during an immense lapse of time, and under very different external conditions. The Miocene flora of Spitzbergen presents analogous facts. Its bald cypress is identical with the species which now inhabits the Southern United States (*Taxodium distichum*), although it must have lived at Spitzbergen among quite different associates, and under different external conditions. Professor Heer has made the same observations with regard to the mountain-pine and the common fir (*Pinus Abies*, Linn.).

an infertility of hybrids *. Animals manifest a stability not only in their physical constitution, but also in their instincts, which Prof. Heer regards as decisive with reference to the continuance of specific characteristics.

Prof. Heer considers that this immutability demonstrates that the instincts of animals are not the result of imitation, but are innate, and have been given to them by the Creator †.

* Professor M. Wagner, in combating Darwin's theory, has, with justice, insisted that in the wild state of plants and animals the continual crossing of varieties which the species may present must always tend to efface deviations. Untrammelled mixture of the sexes of all the individuals of the same species will always produce uniformity, and bring back the type from those varieties whose characters have not become fixed during a whole series of generations; this is proved by wild horses, oxen, and dogs (Wagner, 'Die Darwinische Theorie und das Migrationsgesetz der Organismen,' p. 26). Under domestication or artificial cultivation the tendency to return to the original state is prevented by the influence of man; but in the natural state, natural selection cannot by any means replace that influence, the selection being purely accidental, and rendered ineffective by continual crossing. (Prof. Heer would also refer to the conscientious work of Prof. J. Huber, 'La Théorie de Darwin.') Professor Wagner ascribes great importance to the separation of individuals from the place of origin of their parent species; and consequently to the formation of isolated colonies. He regards such a formation of colonies as the principal cause of the creation of new species; and thus he opposes his theory of separation to Darwin's theory of selection. It is very probable that various modifications of the type forms have become constant in this manner, and that what are called local forms have been produced; but modifications so deep-seated as to explain all the richness of created forms cannot be attributed merely to changes of locality. The colonies of Alpine plants and animals upon the heights of the Swiss plateaux, the presence of the same species under Arctic latitudes and in the Alps, the immense areas occupied by the Miocene plants and those of the Carboniferous period, and the progress in the constitution of organic nature, are, in the opinion of Prof. Heer, opposed to the application of the Darwinian theory.

† The instincts of animals, as Prof. Heer terms the uniform innate animal impulses, are incomprehensible, and therefore marvellous. The Professor cannot explain how gnats and mayflies come to lay their eggs in water, an element which would quickly kill the mature animals if they were to fall into it, whilst their progeny are developed in it, and only quit it after their metamorphosis—how every butterfly finds the kind of plant on which its caterpillar should live, and on this lays its eggs, seeing that the butterfly draws its nourishment from quite a different source, the honey of flowers, and that since it lived upon the plant in its larval form, it has undergone a complete metamorphosis—or why land-crabs should suddenly quit the

If, as Darwin endeavours to demonstrate, instinct be the result of education, it would at the same time be capable of at-
taining perfection, and in the case of insects gifted with the

---

forests, and journey for days together towards the sea to deposit their
eggs there—or why birds migrate to the south in the autumn, often at a
time when they would still have abundance of food in Switzerland; and
in like manner there are thousands of similar natural phenomena which
seem marvellous to us, because we do not know their connexion. Whether the
animals of geological times possessed the same instincts as the homologous
species now living, it is of course impossible to ascertain; but it is very probable. On the other hand, it may certainly be shown that very likely the
instincts of the species still living have been as constantly persistent as their
external specific characters. The insects of England, no doubt, have the
same centre of origin as those of Switzerland; for they agree in species with
Swiss insects. The sea now prevents the passage of species from the Continent to England; so that it is generally supposed that at the drift-period
there was a communication by land, and that this explains the agreement of
the fauna and flora of England with those of the opposite coast. The immigration in question occurred in the earliest division of the drift-period; for
the plants and animals of the coast of Norfolk agree with those of the Continent (p. 172). If we assume that England has been separated from the
Continent by the sea ·for a hundred thousand years, this number would
according to Lyell and Darwin be regarded as rather too low than too high.
For so long, therefore, the animals of England have had a development in-·
dependent of those of the Continent; but nevertheless they exhibit exactly the
same instincts as their continental fellows. The wasps and hornets, which construct cells and combs as ingenious as those of bees, although of a different
material, make these in England precisely as in Switzerland; and the same
remark applies to the humble-bees, bees, ants, and a thousand other insects.
Darwin thinks that he has ascertained with regard to *Formica sanguinea* (the
sanguinary ant) that in England it keeps fewer slaves than in Switzerland, and
therefore occupies itself more with work; but these are insignificant differences which vary with the seasons and with the individual colonies; for
Darwin himself relates that he observed a nest which had more slaves, and
that these worked even outside the nest. In general, the species in England
presents exactly the same phenomena as in Switzerland. The workers carry
away the slaves in their mandibles when they migrate; they work with the
slaves in constructing the nest, and visit the aphides to get honey from them;
they milk these aphides in the same way by stroking them with the antennæ
on the abdomen to induce the emission of the sweet fluid from the honey-
tubes; they make the slaves aid them in the feeding of the young, &c. &c.
All this they have done now for at least a hundred thousand years in the
same way; for if the common ancestors of the English and Swiss ants had
not the same mode of life as their living descendants, it would be inconceiv-

most wonderful instinct, changes might be expected more rapid
in consequence of the very limited period of individual existence of each insect, and of the recurrence of animal transformations.

In the historical development both of the animal and vegetable
kingdoms in the present work an onward march is evident,
setting off with simple living organisms and moving on to highly
organized forms. This progressive advance does not agree with
the theory of selection; for, according to that hypothesis, characters most favourable to existence would prevail in the struggle
for life. Professor Nægeli has convincingly shown that the
principles of utility which form the living centre of the Darwinian
theory are not connected with progress in organization. It would
be difficult to understand how in this manner, and without any
determinate direction in the way of progress, the unicellular
plants and animals which are regarded as the parent stocks,
could have developed into highly organized forms. The same
difficulties arise in connexion with the question why, both in
the vegetable and animal kingdoms, Nature has not been contented merely to endow these beings with what is strictly necessary for the preservation of life, instead of ornamenting them
in such a varied manner *.

---

able that the species in England should exhibit the same mode of life as in
Switzerland, and that the species in both places should have been developed
in precisely the same manner during so long a period of time, when we see
that a few centuries have sufficed to convert Englishmen into a people peculiar in speech, manners, domestic architecture, &c., notwithstanding their
uninterrupted intercourse with other populations. What a gap separates
the Englishman of the present day from the first inhabitants of that island
with their stone implements; whilst the ants, which immigrated even at an
earlier period, still move in the same groove! This applies also to the insects
of Sweden. All that the admirable De Geer tells us of the economy of the
Swedish insects applies also to Swiss insects.

* A simple uniform and green calyx would have been a sufficient protec-
tion for the fecundation and formation of the seeds of plants; but instead of
this, Prof. Heer observes in flowers a marvellous diversity in the corolla, in
form, colour, and size. Darwin has endeavoured to explain this fact by the
supposition that the colour and size of flowers attract insects which favour
fertilization by the transportation of pollen. Plants with brilliant colours
would thus produce more seed, and would, consequently, by degrees supplant

All these facts afford arguments against a slow and uniformly progressive transformation of species, and lead to the conclusion that the transformation of organic nature took place in a period of comparatively limited duration.   For thousands of years the

---

the others. A botanist whose sagacity in other respects is generally admitted, having adopted these notions, has even maintained that all the beautiful ornaments of flowers would gradually disappear, and that all plants would have none but small green flowers, if the class of insects should be lost. The erroneous nature of any such proposition is demonstrated by what takes place in the Arctic zone, and in the high chains of the Swiss Alps; flower-loving insects are altogether wanting (as at Spitzbergen), or occur in such small numbers that their influence upon flowers must be very restricted. The flowers there ought consequently to have no colours; for there is no doubt that in Spitzbergen, where there are no insects frequenting the flowers, the present state of things has existed since the drift-epoch. Facts prove, with respect to colour and size, that the plants of the high Alps are distinguished from those of the plain by the brighter colours and larger dimensions of their flowers. Spitzbergen also possesses a considerable number of plants with fine flowers; and the same remark applies to Nova Zembla. Insects are not much attracted by the form, colour, and size of flowers, but almost entirely by the honey that they contain; for it is principally the sense of smell, and not the eyes, that guides them towards flowers. The plants with the smallest and least-striking flowers, such as the willow, the maple, and the lime-tree, are those most sought by bees, whilst plants with brilliant flowers, such as the tulip, are not visited by them. There are a great number of species of willows; but, notwithstanding the assiduity with which they are visited by insects, not one of these species has succeeded in surrounding its flowers even with a green calyx. The limes also are obliged to content themselves with a small whitish corolla. Every bee-keeper knows that it is the sweet odour of honey alone that attracts these insects; and hence they make their way in masses towards sugar-refineries, even at great distances, and often perish there in great numbers. They scent the honey even where they cannot see it, and seek by every means to get at it. Within the last few years a new species of larkspur (*Delphinium macranthum*) has been introduced into the Swiss gardens. The spur of this plant is so long that the proboscis of the humble-bees cannot reach the honey at the bottom of it. The humble-bees merely cut a hole in the spur, and pass the proboscis through it; by this means they attain their object. For the last two years Prof. Heer has observed, in the Zurich Botanic Garden, that all the humble-bees procure the honey of this species of larkspur by holes made as he has just described, whilst other insects with a longer trunk, such as the *Macroglossa stellatarum*, push their proboscis in by the ordinary course from the corolla.

new species preserved their characteristics unchanged. Hence the period during which the species persistently maintained their determinate forms has been longer than the time of their transformation.

Professor Heer employs for this occurrence the expression of *remoulding of species**, which does not imply an insensible fusion of species (for that would be opposed to the results of scientific research), nor does it trench on the privilege of geologists, who claim to have at their disposal tens of thousands of millions of years.

Professor Heer considers that we are still in the dark with regard to the *fundamental conditions of this transformation of types*; and yet the transformations through which many species of animals pass may give us some indications as to how we must conceive of this process. It is well known that most insects only attain their perfect form after they have undergone a metamorphosis. From the egg comes the caterpillar, from this the pupa, and it is from the latter that the butterfly rises. The caterpillar is quite different from the butterfly in the form and structure of its body, as is the maggot from the fly and the grub from the beetle; and if we did not know that these earlier forms of life are only young stages, we should undoubtedly place them in a different class of animals. Now these earlier forms of life are in many cases like the lower animals, of which the young, corresponding to the larva or caterpillar, propagate by division, so that a number of individuals proceed from a single larva; and these earlier animals differ from the individuals which occur at the final stage of the development nearly as the caterpillar differs from the butterfly; the species is therefore split up into several forms, which have been produced, not by a gradual transition, but by a sudden transformation.

This process, which has been termed "alternation of generations," resembles, at least in the subdivision of a species into

---

* See ' La Flore Tertiaire de la Suisse,' vol. iii. p. 256, and ' Recherches sur le Climat et la Végétation du Pays Tertiaire,' p. 56. Professor Suess ("Sur la différence et la succession de la faune Tertiaire dans les environs de Vienne," Sitzungs. der Akad. in Wien, May 1863) and Professor Kölliker (' Ueber die Darwin'sche Schöpfungs-Theorie,' Leipzig, 1864) have expressed themselves in the same way.

several forms, that change which Prof. Heer has termed "the remoulding of species." It may be admitted that several species of our epoch were invested, in earlier periods, with forms which bore a somewhat similar relation to the present form which the larva bears to the fully developed animal. Indeed many species of ancient periods may be compared to the larvæ or embryos * of those now living.

Under another point of view the remoulding of species differs materially from the alternation of generations (of the metamorphosis); for in that regenerative change all the individuals at their last stage of development acquire the form belonging to the mature insect, and only in the last form † attain to sexual maturity. The whole series of forms in this metamorphosis finally returns to the same point; and consequently the species always moves in the same circle, whilst the creation of new species advances in a spiral to reach new points of development.

Even when these new species owe their origin to species resembling them, they will not resume the characters of the species from which they proceeded, but for thousands and hundreds of thousands of years they will preserve their determinate typical characteristics which they obtained by their regeneration. To Prof. Heer the origin of forms is a secret, an enigma, in the explanation of which may be exercised the talents of divination, but which has not been fully and entirely solved either in the known phenomena of nature, or by the application of established physical laws.

* The featherstars (*Comatulæ*) are mounted on stalks when young, and resemble in that state the Encrinites of ancient epochs. Many fishes of those early periods agree in some characteristics with the embryos of existing fishes. Rütimeyer has recently shown that some Tertiary mammals exhibit a great resemblance in their dental system to the arrangement of the milk-teeth of several living species.

† [Sir John Lubbock, F.R.S., mentions that recently Prof. Wagner (Zeit. für Wiss. Zool. 1863) has discovered that among certain small gnats the larvæ do not directly produce in all cases perfect insects, but give birth to other larvæ, which undergo metamorphoses of the usual character, and eventually become gnats. His observations have been confirmed, as regards this main fact, by other naturalists; and Grimm has met with a species of *Chironomus* in which the pupæ (or chrysalises) lay eggs (Mém. de l'Acad. Imp. de St. Pétersbourg, vol. xv. 1870). 'On the Origin and Metamorphoses of Insects,' by Sir John Lubbock, p. 76.—EDITOR.]

Already, in the work, it has been seen that the transformation of the crust of the earth did not proceed in a uniform manner, but that long periods of comparative repose were followed by great revolutions (*suprà*, p. 250). In the process of development of organic nature the same phenomenon is met with, so that there is a correlation between the transformation of the crust of the earth and the evolution of organic nature.

Switzerland in the Pliocene epoch obtained its present configuration, and in the same period the chain of the Caucasus and the range of the Himalayas were upheaved. A large portion of the globe must, consequently, have been affected by this revolution immediately after the Pliocene in the Quaternary period, and the transformation also occurred of organic nature which has ever since retained the same characteristics.

Phenomena of the same kind are recognized in the Flysch formation, which is almost destitute of animals, in the upheaval of land at the close of the Jurassic period increasing the size of continents (vol. i. p. 174), and in the stormy Permian period which terminated the Carboniferous epoch. Hence there were times during which these transformations took place over vast districts; they were carried on with sufficient rapidity, and they gave rise to more general and more decided changes.

Times of creation occurred during which was accomplished a remoulding of organic types, and there was a primæval epoch during which the first species were brought into being. Even if the first species were extremely simple, for them an act of creation must be admitted, an act without example in modern times; for in our days plants and animals of decidedly low forms proceed from species already in existence.

Such periods of creation may be termed a geological spring-time, thus alluding to the succession of the seasons and recalling the law of periodicity, which may have been exerted in the renewal of organic nature. But the circle influenced by this law is so vast that human intellect cannot appreciate either its height or its extent. No means are afforded to determine with certainty these epochs of creation.

Great creative renewals are indicated within the limits of the principal geological periods; and during those periods important transformations also took place, the significance of which cannot at present be satisfactorily estimated. For instance, did new creations occasion the changes undergone by the faunas in the different stages of the Jurassic and Cretaceous epochs? or were those changes the results of immigration from different centres of life? As the knowledge of fossil organic nature increases, we shall be better able to appreciate how much of the influence of organic transformation is to be attributed to local and how much to periodical causes.

A magnificent series of phenomena opens out in the vista of the floras and faunas of different ages of the world. Progressive steps have been taken towards the existing creation, there has been a gradual advance in the organization of living creatures, and a wonderful correlation between the transformations of the earth's crust and the development of organic nature, as well as a succession at long intervals of the birth and extinction of species.

As yet we only know the rows of the building-stones of the immense edifice of creation; but as the wonders of the primæval world are revealed, the grander and richer will the edifice become, the gaps of the existing creation will be filled up, and the different parts will be grouped together in a harmonious whole.

Those intelligent beings who are ready to comprehend the subject, can alone appreciate the splendour of the edifice of creation. Let us take an example from the science of music. A musician alone will understand the meaning of one of Beethoven's symphonies: for him each note will have its significance, and from the different notes taken together an incomparable harmony will be produced.

Nature occupies a similar position. Individual phenomena, like separate notes, can only be understood when a person knows how to combine them and to appreciate the whole of them together. An idea of the grandeur of creation can only be formed by the collection of isolated facts.

Nature's harmony is felt in the soul by this grouping of known phenomena, a harmony resembling that of its sister in the domain of music, which raises us above the physical world, and produces in the mind a presentiment of a Divine intelligence, directing all that is, as it has directed every thing in past times.

An advanced knowledge of Nature leads to a profound conviction that the enigmas of the natural world and of human life can only be solved by a belief in an Almighty Creator, and in the creation of the heaven and the earth by Divine wisdom according to an eternal and preconceived plan.

Nature, as well as the heart of man, bears witness to the existence of God; and it is only when seen from this point of view that the marvellous geological history of Switzerland, with its plants and animals, appears in its true light, and affords the highest gratification.

APPENDIX I.

ADDED BY THE EDITOR.

Traces of Man in the Interglacial Deposit near Wetzikon, in the Canton of Zurich, Switzerland.

By Professor L. RÜTIMEYER, *of Basle*.*

SWISS pits have recently afforded abundant proofs of the pre-historic presence of Man associated with a fauna indicating very different conditions from those of the present time, and establishing a far higher antiquity for the human race than has been shown in the remains belonging to lake-dwellings in Switzerland.

France, Belgium, and England have contributed important data to illustrate remote prehistoric epochs; cosmopolitan characteristics have been noticed in the discoveries which have been made; and the larger proportion of extinct species of the fauna contemporaneous with traces of Man in those countries, as well as in Switzerland, gives a very distant period for the first appearance of the human race.

A standard of time may possibly be arrived at from the facts to be here narrated.

Prof. Arnold Escher de la Linth demonstrated that a vast glacial deposit had overlain the lignites worked in some parts of Eastern Switzerland, especially on the eastern shore of the Lake of Zurich from Wetzikon to Utznach, as well as in the neighbourhood of the Lake of Constance, between St. Gall and Arbon,

---

* From the Archives of Anthropology ('Archiv für Anthropologie'), a periodical of Natural History and of Primæval Human History, vol. viii., second quarterly number, August 1875, p. 133. Brunswick, 1875.

and that the bed underlying the lignites in some places (Wetzikon and Dürnten) also partook of an erratic nature and therefore owed its origin to glacial action.

Two glacial periods in Switzerland, according to the hypothesis
of Morlot, are considered to have been proved; and between the
two glacial deposits lignite-coal beds are found with abundant
remains of plants and animals, the existence of which appears to
prove that at that time a warmer climate had prevailed.

This fact acquired additional interest when Falconer and H.
de Meyer recognized, among the animal remains contained in
this lignite, an elephant (*Elephas antiquus*) and a species of
rhinoceros (*R. Merkii*), which were elsewhere referred to the
lowest strata of the Quaternary formation. With these were
associated animals of later type, such as the cave-bear and urus
(*Bos primigenius*), and of existing species, such as the common
stag. Prof. Heer has shown that the plants of the lignites in
that locality, as well as two insects found with them, belonged
to species now indigenous to Switzerland. For all details, both
as regards the deposition and the contents of these lignites, the
admirable descriptions may be consulted which Prof. Heer has
given of them in the 12th chapter of his 'Primæval World of
Switzerland' (vol. ii. p. 118 of the present work).

In the section of the strata in the pits at Wetzikon the presence of an erratic deposit under the lignite has lately been confirmed by Prof. Renevier of Lausanne and A. Heim of Zurich.
Prof. Rütimeyer has repeatedly examined the animal remains
from these lignites, and he has arrived at the same results as
before. Only the remains of elephant and rhinoceros (of which
the latter have unfortunately for the most part been lost) were
not included in his investigation, as Falconer and H. de Meyer
offered him a better security for their correct determination than
his own examination. To the previously known remains of
Ursus spelæus (a single impression of a series of mandibular teeth
at Utznach), *Bos primigenius* (a few mandibular teeth at Utznach), and *Cervus elephas* (abundant at Wetzikon and Dürnten)
there was added unmistakable evidence of the presence of the
elk in the lignite at Dürnten.

Recently in the Dürnten lignite proofs have been furnished
that, contemporaneously with the flora and fauna of which it

represents the remains, Man also inhabited these regions. These proofs are derived from the locality of Wetzikon, where the deposition of the lignite between two glacial deposits is most completely ascertained.

The lignite coals from Wetzikon are much employed as fuel in Basle, where the discovery was accidentally made. A legal gentleman, Dr. Scheuermann, had taken an interest in the multifarious impressions of plants contained in the lignite, and had therefore prepared with his own hands the pieces of that coal for his stoves, when he noticed (while he was thus employed) a number of pointed rods, which, although not differing from the surrounding coal, lay imbedded side by side in a large block of the coal; and he had the kindness to forward the block to Prof. Rütimeyer. He further assisted the Professor in proving with legal certainty, from the books of the commercial house from which he obtained the coals, that the coals were obtained from the " Schöneich " pit, near Wetzikon.

Four of the rods were taken out, which had been firmly imbedded side by side in the black lignite, and to a certain extent had amalgamated with it. The best-preserved rod is represented of the natural size in fig. 1 (p. 298)—a, the broken end; a'', the artificially cut point; a', a part where the rod is disintegrated, so that the interior is seen, which differs from the surrounding coal, c, only by the preserved woody texture, but not in colour.

Except for its artificial preparation, the rod does not differ from the remains of wood composing the principal mass of this lignite, which are beautifully preserved. As in these and other [fossil] contents (e. g. the jaws of deer, already mentioned), the original cylindrical form of the rod has been flattened by pressure, thus affording a sufficient proof that the rod had undergone carbonization along with the other constituents of the lignite.

For a short space, b b', the rod shows traces of having been tied, such as might have been produced by cords; and these marks have affected both the coal-black bark, which is still preserved (b), and the somewhat lighter-coloured wood (b' b').

There is a very similar second piece (fig. 2), which, like the preceding, lies imbedded in the surrounding crumbly coal (c), and to a certain extent forms one mass with it. At a the lon-

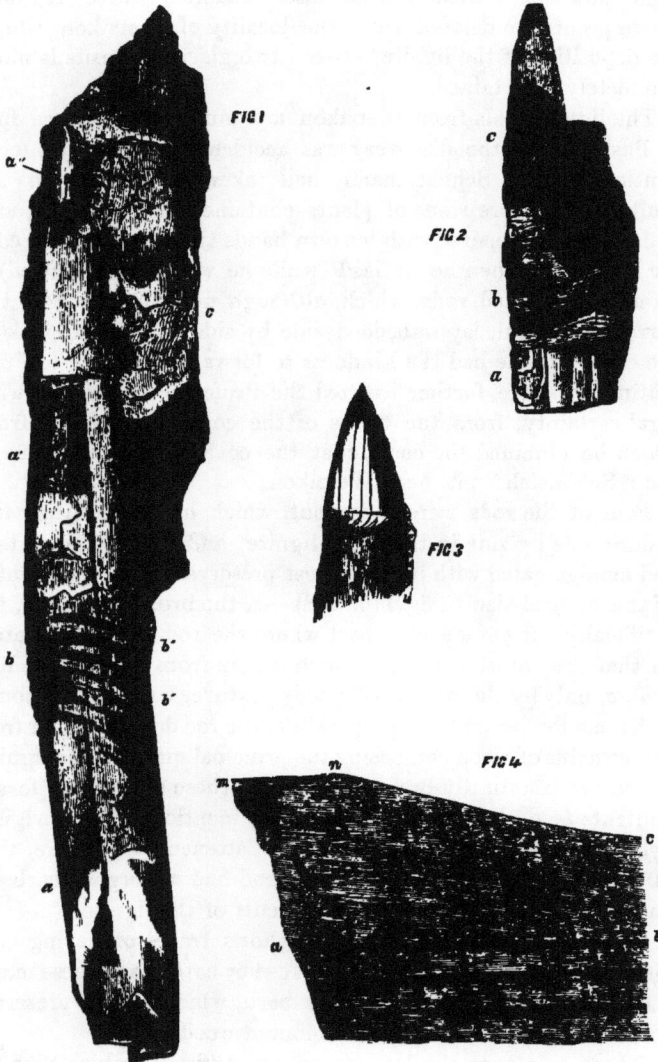

Fig. 1. Pointed rod of fir wood, from the Wetzikon lignite.
Fig. 2. Upper end of a second pointed rod of fir wood, from the Wetzikon lignite.

gitudinally fibrous woody body appears; at *b* it is transversely bound with a different bark.

The manner in which this rod has been pointed is shown in fig. 3, in which, by a section at the point of the rod, the annual rings are displayed. The interior of the wood in this, as in other hard woody fragments of which the coal to a great extent consists, appears light in colour and solid, so that a clear sharp section could be effected, showing that the annual rings one after another were removed. Consequently the section was easily prepared for microscopic examination, which confirms with all requisite exactness the employment of art in the pointing of the rod.

Prof. Schwendauer, the respected colleague of Prof. Rütimeyer, had the kindness to undertake the microscopic examination, which is thus described:—

" The fragments of wood from the Brown Coal or Lignite of Wetzikon handed to Prof. Schwendauer for examination are really more or less sharply pointed, and in such a manner as evidently to indicate the action of Man. From the microscopic examination the Professor concludes:—1. That the structure of the wood undoubtedly corresponds with the Coniferous type; 2. That the occurrence of resin-ducts in the wood, and the absence of the large oval pores and of the tooth-like thickening in the cells of the medullary rays, not only excludes the white fir (*Abies pectinata*), but also the species of the genus *Pinus* which occur in Switzerland (*Pinus sylvestris, montana*, Mill., and *cembra*). The spiral thickenings of the woody cells of the yew (*Taxus*), and the absence of resin-ducts in cypresses (*Cupressineæ*), exclude these trees from consideration; and there remains only, of the indigenous Coniferæ, the larch and the red fir (*Abies excelsa*), which cannot be distinguished from each other by

---

Fig. 3. Section at the point of rod, fig. 2, showing the annual rings in the wood.

Fig. 4. Microscopic section of the surface represented in fig. 3: *c*, pointing of the rod; *a b*, boundary of an annual ring.

The transverse spots and streaks indicate medullary rays which have been cut obliquely, as the section of the surface was not exactly radial. The shading is parallel to the direction of the fibres.

the character of the wood alone. The bark might be subject
to investigation; but unfortunately on the specimens placed at
the disposal of Prof. Schwendauer the bark is only here and
there preserved, and generally in such an imperfect condition
that it is difficult to distinguish foreign constituents from the
layers of tissue genetically related. However, the Professor
gives his opinion with tolerable certainty *that the fragments
of wood under consideration are derived from the red fir (Abies
excelsa)*. In this conclusion Professor Schwendauer depends,
in the first place, upon the fact that such cells as are porously
thick-walled and peridermic, characterizing the red fir, often
occur in the peripheral parts of the carbonized crusts, and that
in those crusts he has not observed the interlocking, undulating
and peridermic elements of the bark of the larch, with its elongated prosenchyma-cells *, although even these latter might
have been expected to occur in stem-organs of corresponding
age. Moreover no difference is perceptible between the brown
cellular tissue which follows immediately on the above-mentioned
porously thick-walled cells and zones of bark, as to the genetic
connexion of which with the wood there is no doubt. With this
evidence an error in the determination seems to the Professor
to be scarcely possible.

" Judging from the dimensions, and the repeated occurrence
of the rods, branches and not stems furnished the materials of
these pointed pieces of wood. The number of annual rings
varies between five and seven, and their average thickness often
does not reach even half a millimetre (·019 inch). At the same
time they consist almost entirely of thick-walled cells, or what
may be termed autumn wood; the thin-walled elements are reduced to about from one to three rows of cells. How far these
peculiarities are connected with the climate of the locality, Prof.
Schwendauer does not venture to decide, as the extant observations upon the changes of the annual rings in higher latitudes

* ["The tissue is termed 'prosenchyma' if the cells are pointed at the
ends and much longer than they are broad, and if at the same time their
ends penetrate between one another so that no intercellular spaces occur."
('Textbook of Botany,' p. 78, by Prof. Sachs, of the University of Würzburg;
translated by A. W. Bennett, M.A., B.Sc., F.L.S., assisted by W. T. Thisel-
ton Dyer, M.A., B.Sc., F.L.S. Oxford, 1875.)—EDITOR.]

only relate to stems, and their application to the case of branches is not directly admissible.

"The large scales of bark with a lighter-coloured surface which occur, especially upon one of the specimens examined, do not belong anatomically to the Coniferous wood of Switzerland, although externally they appear to have grown over with it. These scales are the remains of some bast-bearing dicotyledonous bark which was perhaps employed for uniting the individual rods; at least the scales in question lie in such a manner upon the wood that their longitudinal direction stands at right angles to the direction of the woody cells."

Prof. Rütimeyer regards speculation as superfluous relating to the mode of employment of these rods. It seems most probable that the remains of some rough basket-like structures are here preserved.

A past period of time is geologically exactly defined by the interglacial coal-bed, which contains the remains of the species of animals, chiefly extinct, already mentioned; and from the manner in which the wooden rods have been imbedded in the surrounding material, from the nature of the mechanical and chemical alterations which have taken place since the imbedding, and from the still perceptible mode of the rods having been prepared, certain proofs of human action are exhibited belonging to an immensely remote epoch.

The Professor does not discuss the epoch, to be estimated by geological time, in which these manufactured articles became associated with the process of the metamorphosis of their surroundings. For Switzerland, and probably also for a wider region, the rods may for the present be regarded as the oldest trace of Man. If, indeed, it is probable that discoveries such as those in the pits of Veyrier and Thayingen and at Schussenried demonstrate the existence of Man in close relation to the glacial period, even in the neighbourhood of so vast a source of glaciers as the Alps, we have here not only the evidence of the covering of a human dwelling-place by a deposit which was formerly considered to have been the work of the whole glacial period, but two additional new standards are offered for the calculation of the indigenous presence of Man—the transformation of human workmanship into lignite, and the contemporaneity of the remains with an elephant and rhinoceros hitherto believed to be foreign to the glacial period.

To assign a place in Swiss history to these newly found relics, we shall have to look back to the interglacial epochs as they have recently been made known, especially by Geikie on the authority of observations in Great Britain, and to refer to deposits containing similar fossil remains hitherto considered to be of what is called the Pliocene age in Northern Italy.

If recent and varied observations should assign to the Pliocene of Europe a position merely connected with the coast, the nearest neighbourhood to a district powerful as the source of glaciers would for the present be allowed, with respect to continental Pliocene times, as a dwelling-place for Man.

APPENDIX II.

ADDED BY THE EDITOR.

~ ~~~~~~~~~~~~~~~~~~~~~~~~~~~~~~~~~

Continental and British Measures, Weights, Degrees of Temperature, and Postage.

IN 1864 an Act of Parliament under the care of Mr. William Ewart, M.P., was passed for legalizing the use of the metric system of weights and measures in Great Britain and Ireland.

On the continent, and especially in scientific continental publications, the metric system is almost universally adopted. Its complete decimal character and its extreme simplicity recommend it to universal use ; and a series of metric tables has been compiled by Mr. C. H. Dowling, Civil Engineer, in which the British standard measures and weights are compared with those of the metric system *, and a tabular comparison is given of the scales of Fahrenheit's, the Centigrade, and Réaumur's thermometers. Mr. Dowling's tables have been frequently employed in converting Swiss measures and weights and degrees of temperature to British equivalents with reference to practical subjects alluded to in the present volumes.

Messrs. Macmillan and Co. have published a small treatise, by the Rev. Barnard Smith, M.A., on the metric system of arithmetic, containing the metric tables, with questions for students ; and a comparison of continental and English measures by Mr. Warren De la Rue, F.R.S., was published in Gutch's Almanack for 1864.

---

* Published by Lockwood and Co., Stationers' Hall Court, London.

A metre is the fundamental unit of measure and weight in the continental system.

1 metre	=	1·094 yard.
,,	=	3 feet 3·371 inches.
11 metres	=	12·033 yards.
1 decimetre	±	3·937 inches.
1 centimetre	=	0·394 inch.
1 millimetre	=	0·039 inch.
1 decametre	=	10·936 yards.
1 hectometre	=	109·363 yards.
1 kilometre	=	1093·633 yards.
,,	=	0·621 mile.
100 kilometres	=	62·10 miles.

---

1 inch	=	2·539 centimetres.
1 foot	=	3·047 decimetres.
1 yard	=	0·914 metre.
1 mile	=	1·609 kilometre.
100 miles	=	161·02 kilometres.

A gramme = 15·432 grains, and is equal to the weight of a cubic centimetre of distilled water at its greatest density, weighed in a vacuum.

1 kilogramme	=	1000 grammes.
,,	=	2·204 lbs. avoirdupois.
1 lb. avoirdupois	=	0·453 kilogramme.

The kilo, or kilogramme, is the usual weight employed on the continent in weighing goods.

1 cwt. (112 lbs.)	=	50·802 kilos.

Calculations are requisite, either in foreign sea-ports or in the British isles, for the conversion of kilos into hundredweights and pounds avoirdupois.

With respect to temperature, thermometers are graduated so that the range of temperature between the freezing- and the boiling-points of water is divided by Fahrenheit's scale into 180 (from 32° to 212°), and by the Centigrade into 100 (from 0° to 100°). Zero in Fahrenheit's thermometer is 32° below the freezing-point of water, and in the Centigrade thermometer the freezing-point of water is called zero.

A degree Centigrade is larger than a degree Fahrenheit in the proportion of 180 to 100, or 9 to 5; and to convert degrees of Fahrenheit into the Centigrade the rule is to subtract 32 and multiply the remainder by $\frac{5}{9}$; and the rule to convert degrees of the Centigrade into Fahrenheit's is to multiply the Centigrade by $\frac{9}{5}$, and add 32 to the product.

In scientific experiments the Centigrade thermometer is almost invariably employed, and is generally quoted in scientific books. New works on chemistry in the British Islands usually adopt metric weights and measures, as more convenient, and as better suited to the international communication of knowledge.

A commencement of improved international relations has recently come into operation under British postal authority, in the 1¼d. foreign postal card. Parliamentary sanction is still requisite in this country to render Mr. Ewart's Act of 1864 thoroughly efficient by empowering a dealer to recover debts in British commercial transactions where the goods have been sold by metric weights or measures.

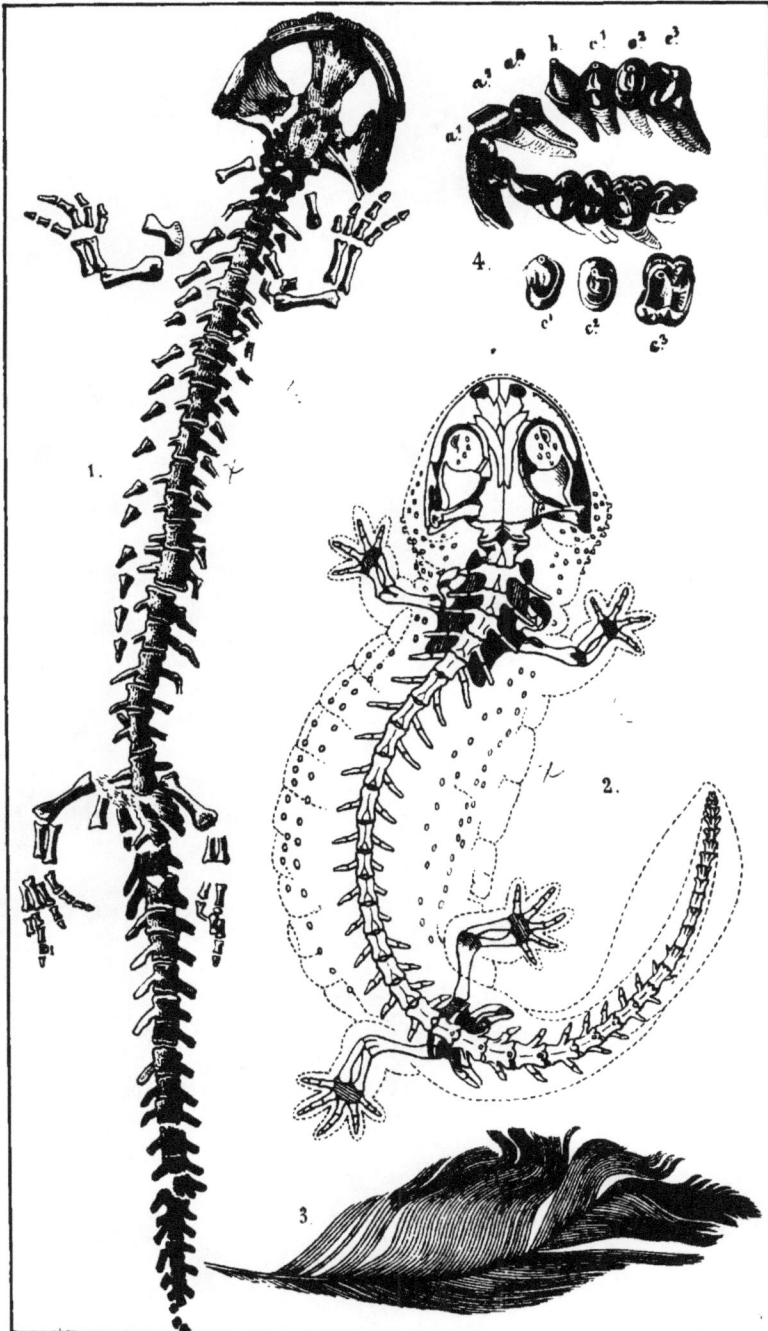

1. Andrias Scheuchzeri. 2. Andrias japonicus. 3. Feder. 4. Hylobates antiquus.

INDEX.

x 2

THE END.

PRINTED BY TAYLOR AND FRANCIS, RED LION COURT, FLEET STREET.